Windows Presentation Foundation 4.5 Cookbook

Over 80 recipes to effectively and efficiently develop rich Windows client applications on the Windows platform

Pavel Yosifovich

BIRMINGHAM - MUMBAI

Windows Presentation Foundation 4.5 Cookbook

First published: September 2012

Production Reference: 1150912

Published by Packt Publishing Ltd.
Livery Place
35 Livery Street
Birmingham B3 2PB, UK.

ISBN 978-1-84968-622-8

www.packtpub.com

Cover Image by Mark Holland (m.j.g.holland@bham.ac.uk)

Credits

Author
Pavel Yosifovich

Reviewers
Alon Fliess
Ariel Ben Horesh
Stas Shteinbook
Dan Vestergaard

Acquisition Editor
Rukshana Khambatta

Lead Technical Editor
Kedar Bhat

Technical Editor
Madhuri Das

Project Coordinator
Yashodhan Dere

Proofreaders
Aaron Nash
Maria Gould

Indexer
Rekha Nair

Graphics
Aditi Gajjar

Production Coordinator
Shantanu Zagade

Cover Work
Shantanu Zagade

About the Author

Pavel Yosifovich is the CTO of CodeValue (`http://www.codevalue.net`), a software development, consulting, and training company, based in Israel. He writes, consults, and trains developers on various software development topics, from Windows internals, to .NET enterprise systems, and almost everything in between. He's a Microsoft MVP and a frequent speaker at national events, such as Tech-Ed and DevAcademy.

In the past, he co-founded the startup company Quiksee that was acquired by Google in September 2010.

Writing a book is a tremendous effort, even if you know what you want to write (and I didn't some of the time). It wasn't possible without the support of my family: my wife Idit, and my kids, Daniel and Amit, and the latest recruit, Yoav. Thank you for the making the time and more than that – thank you for the support and encouragement along the way. It's certainly easy to give up, but you wouldn't let me – so thank you again!

About the Reviewers

Alon Fliess is the chief architect and founder of CodeValue. CodeValue is the home of software experts. CodeValue builds software tools, foundations, and products for the software industry and offers mentoring, consulting, and project development services.

Alon got his BSc degree in Electrical and Computer Engineering from the Technion, the Israel Institute of Technology. He is an expert on many Microsoft technologies, be it Windows client and server programming using C#/C++/.NET, Windows Azure Cloud Computing, or Windows internals. Microsoft has recognized his expertise and community activities and granted him two awards: Microsoft Regional Director (MRD) and a VC++ MVP.

Alon has deep knowledge and understanding of Windows and Windows Internals. He is a co-author of *Windows 7 Microsoft Training Program* as well as a co-author of the *Introducing Windows 7 for Developers* book (ISBN-10: 0735626820)

Alon delivers courses and lectures in many seminars and conferences around the world, such as TechEd Europe, TechEd USA, NDC, and in Israel. Alon is a senior Software Architect; he deals with vast and complex projects. Alon architected and designed the software for the revolutionary new line of industrial printing machine of Landa Labs. He is also the architect of one of the largest software project of the Israeli Air Force. Alon is responsible for several open-source projects.

Many thanks to Pavel and Yashodhan, who gave me the opportunity to take part in the creation of this book.

Ariel Ben Horesh is a well-known .NET expert, team leader, and community leader.

With more than 10 years of experience in the software industry, Ariel now works at CodeValue, a company he co-founded, where he creates products for developers, and consults and conducts courses around the world on UI development: WPF/SL, Web, Mobile, and UI architecture.

You can visit his blog at: `http://arielbh.com`

Stas Shteinbook is a senior development leader and solution architect who works at CodeValue. He has a long history in developing large enterprise applications, guiding their architecture and developing process, and creating end-to-end solutions involving rich user experience interfaces using WPF technology.

I would like to thank my family, my mother Ludmila and my father Zinoviy, for all the help and support.

Dan Vestergaard is currently working as a software engineer, with primary focus on .NET, and in particular, developing user interfaces using WPF.

He has worked in the consultant business and for several years in financial and industrial businesses. He is now a software engineer in a large world-wide industrial company, writing WPF applications for factory quality control systems.

He started working with WPF in the early beta days, back in 2006, and has loved it ever since.

www.PacktPub.com

Support files, eBooks, discount offers and more

You might want to visit www.PacktPub.com for support files and downloads related to your book.

Did you know that Packt offers eBook versions of every book published, with PDF and ePub files available? You can upgrade to the eBook version at www.PacktPub.com and as a print book customer, you are entitled to a discount on the eBook copy. Get in touch with us at service@packtpub.com for more details.

At www.PacktPub.com, you can also read a collection of free technical articles, sign up for a range of free newsletters and receive exclusive discounts and offers on Packt books and eBooks.

http://PacktLib.PacktPub.com

Do you need instant solutions to your IT questions? PacktLib is Packt's online digital book library. Here, you can access, read and search across Packt's entire library of books.

Why Subscribe?

- Fully searchable across every book published by Packt
- Copy and paste, print and bookmark content
- On demand and accessible via web browser

Free Access for Packt account holders

If you have an account with Packt at www.PacktPub.com, you can use this to access PacktLib today and view nine entirely free books. Simply use your login credentials for immediate access.

Instant Updates on New Packt Books

Get notified! Find out when new books are published by following @PacktEnterprise on Twitter, or the *Packt Enterprise* Facebook page.

Table of Contents

Preface

Windows Presentation Foundation has been in release since late 2006, as a part of the then .NET 3.0 Framework, also preinstalled on Windows Vista at the time. It promised to change the way rich client applications are written, and eventually replace the old, Win32-based Windows Forms.

WPF gained traction slowly because of its enormous breadth and the different kind of thinking that was required—using XAML, data binding, templates, and styles was very different from the classic WinForms way of working. The power of WPF was evident, but it was difficult to master, and had a steep learning curve.

Over the years things changed; developers started to get used to and appreciate the new way of doing things. XAML began to look convenient and powerful and not just an extra thing to learn with little benefit. Still, for the newcomer, with or without WinForms experience, WPF looks daunting and uncontrollable.

Patterns have emerged, most notably the Model-View-View Model (MVVM), a variant of other existing view-data separation patterns (MVC and MVP), that made life easier (most of the time) but more importantly set a standard way of interaction of view and data; and although many implementations are possible (this is just a pattern, after all), it does let an application be built in more confidence, piece by piece.

This book holds a set of recipes that show how to do common tasks. But don't just look at the recipes; instead, look at the other sections to deepen your understanding of WPF. No matter the number of recipes, there will always be other things an application needs that no book can cover; by understanding the foundations well, it's possible to tackle any problem. This is why I have tried to emphasise the why, and not just the how.

WPF led to a bunch of other technologies being built on similar principles, namely Silverlight (cross browser web client development in .NET), Windows Phone 7.x (Microsoft's Phone OS that uses a Silverlight variant), and lately Windows 8 and Windows Phone 8—all built around similar concepts such as XAML, dependency properties, templates, styles, and bindings—this shows the power and impact of WPF.

What this book covers

Chapter 1, Foundations, introduces the most important concepts in WPF. From the XAML language, to dependency properties, to attached events.

Chapter 2, Resources, discusses WPF's unique resource system that allows any object to be placed as a resource and consequently shared in an efficient and flexible way.

Chapter 3, Layout and Panels, discusses how WPF manages layout of elements, including looking at the standard layout panels, how they work, and how they can be combined to produce complex and flexible interfaces.

Chapter 4, Using Standard Controls, looks at the major controls in WPF and how they are typically used. The content model is also discussed, along with other control families.

Chapter 5, Application and Windows, takes a look at a WPF application from a higher perspective, including application level resources and the way windows are used and managed.

Chapter 6, Data Binding, discusses the powerful and important concept of data binding and the way it's used in WPF, including leveraging data templates, converters, and other ideas that make WPF so powerful.

Chapter 7, Commands and MVVM, looks at the way a moderately complex application might be built, by leveraging higher level abstractions known as commands (as opposed to raw events). The MVVM pattern is introduced with some implementation to show how commands, data binding and some extra ingredients can produce a complex, yet manageable, application.

Chapter 8, Styles, Triggers, and Control Templates, shows some of the ways controls can be customized in XAML only, without the need to derive new types for the sake of appearance only.

Chapter 9, Graphics and Animation, provides a tour of the major graphic and animation capabilities of WPF and how they integrate with other mechanisms such as styles and triggers.

Chapter 10, Custom Elements, shows what is required to create custom elements with the considerations that lead to a particular implementation path.

Chapter 11, Threading, discusses WPF's support for asynchronous operations, so that the UI is responsive at all times, including the support provided in C# 5.0 for performing asynchronous operations more easily.

What you need for this book

The books assumes the reader is a .NET developer working with C# (at least version 2.0, but 3.0 is preferred), and is comfortable working with generics, virtual methods, delegates, and lambdas (C# 3.0). Some WPF exposure is assumed. Visual Studio 2010 as well as Visual Studio 2012 for some features of .NET 4.5.

Who this book is for

The book is intended for developers who are relatively new to WPF, or those who have been working with WPF for a while, but want to a get a deeper understanding of its mechanisms and concepts.

Conventions

In this book, you will find a number of styles of text that distinguish between different kinds of information. Here are some examples of these styles, and an explanation of their meaning.

Code words in text are shown as follows: "the typical `Window` class is declared as `partial`, meaning there may be more source files describing the same class".

A block of code is set as follows:

```
class Book {
   public string Name { get; set; }
   public string Author { get; set; }
   public decimal Price { get; set; }
   public int YearPublished { get; set; }
 }
```

When we wish to draw your attention to a particular part of a code block, the relevant lines or items are set in bold:

```
<Window x:Class="CH01.CustomTypes.MainWindow"
   xmlns="http://schemas.microsoft.com/winfx/2006/xaml/presentation"
   xmlns:x="http://schemas.microsoft.com/winfx/2006/xaml"
   xmlns:local="clr-namespace:CH01.CustomTypes"
```

New terms and **important words** are shown in bold. Words that you see on the screen, in menus or dialog boxes for example, appear in the text like this: "right-click on the project node and select **Add** and then **Class...**".

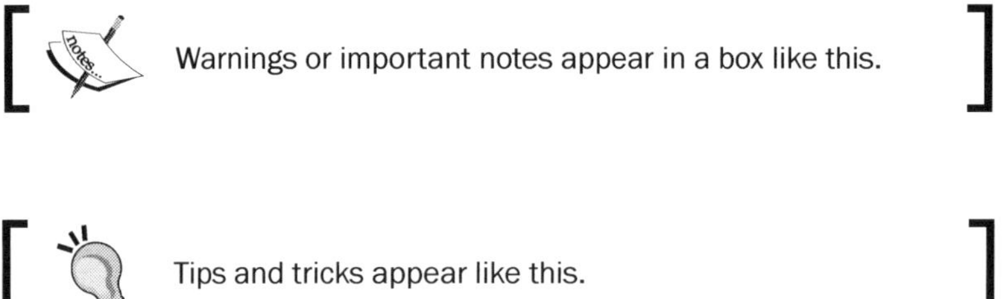
Warnings or important notes appear in a box like this.

Tips and tricks appear like this.

Reader feedback

Feedback from our readers is always welcome. Let us know what you think about this book—what you liked or may have disliked. Reader feedback is important for us to develop titles that you really get the most out of.

To send us general feedback, simply send an e-mail to `feedback@packtpub.com`, and mention the book title through the subject of your message.

If there is a topic that you have expertise in and you are interested in either writing or contributing to a book, see our author guide on `www.packtpub.com/authors`.

Customer support

Now that you are the proud owner of a Packt book, we have a number of things to help you to get the most from your purchase.

Downloading the example code

You can download the example code files for all Packt books you have purchased from your account at `http://www.packtpub.com`. If you purchased this book elsewhere, you can visit `http://www.packtpub.com/support` and register to have the files e-mailed directly to you.

Errata

Although we have taken every care to ensure the accuracy of our content, mistakes do happen. If you find a mistake in one of our books—maybe a mistake in the text or the code—we would be grateful if you would report this to us. By doing so, you can save other readers from frustration and help us improve subsequent versions of this book. If you find any errata, please report them by visiting `http://www.packtpub.com/support`, selecting your book, clicking on the **errata submission form** link, and entering the details of your errata. Once your errata are verified, your submission will be accepted and the errata will be uploaded to our website, or added to any list of existing errata, under the Errata section of that title.

Piracy

Piracy of copyright material on the Internet is an ongoing problem across all media. At Packt, we take the protection of our copyright and licenses very seriously. If you come across any illegal copies of our works, in any form, on the Internet, please provide us with the location address or website name immediately so that we can pursue a remedy.

Please contact us at `copyright@packtpub.com` with a link to the suspected pirated material.

We appreciate your help in protecting our authors, and our ability to bring you valuable content.

Questions

You can contact us at `questions@packtpub.com` if you are having a problem with any aspect of the book, and we will do our best to address it.

1
Foundations

In this chapter we will cover the following:

- Creating custom type instances in XAML
- Creating a dependency property
- Using an attached property
- Creating an attached property
- Accessing a static property in XAML
- Creating a custom markup extension
- Handling routed events

Introduction

Any attempt at mastering a technology, any technology, requires a good understanding of its foundations. This understanding makes it possible to grasp the more complex aspects of that technology; **Windows Presentation Foundation** (**WPF**) is no different.

In this first chapter, we'll discuss recipes concerning the very foundations of WPF – what makes it tick—and also along the way, what makes it unique.

XAML

The first noticeable facet of WPF is **XAML** (**eXtensible Markup Language**). XAML is an XML based language used in WPF to declaratively create user interfaces. Actually, XAML has nothing to do with UI. It's merely a declarative way of constructing objects and setting their properties. In fact, it's leveraged in other technologies, such as the Windows Workflow Foundation (WF), where it's used as a way of constructing workflows. To create objects in XAML, they must be "XAML friendly" - meaning they must have the following:

- A public default constructor
- Settable public properties

The second item is not strictly a requirement, but the lack of settable properties would make the object a bit dull. Note that starting with .NET 4, XAML is in fact capable of handling parameterized constructors, but WPF's XAML parser currently does not leverage that capability.

XAML is not an absolute requirement. In fact, you can create an entire application using C# or VB (or whichever .NET language you fancy) without a single XAML tag. However, that would be much more difficult and error prone with high maintenance costs, not to mention the difficulty of integration with your fellow designers.

XAML is about the what, not the how. This declarative style makes things easier (granted, after some getting used to), and is a paradigm shift in software development in general (the classic example in .NET being the LINQ-based technologies). XAML is neutral—it's not C# or anything like that—so other, non-developer tools can create or manipulate it. Microsoft provides the Expression Blend tool, which at its core, is a glorified XAML producer/consumer.

XAML and compilation

What happens to a XAML file? How is it tied to the code behind file created by Visual Studio? A XAML file is compiled by a XAML compiler that produces a binary version of the XAML, known as BAML. This BAML is stored as a resource inside the assembly and is parsed at runtime in the `InitializeComponent` call to create the actual objects. The result is bundled with the code behind file (the typical `Window` class is declared as `partial`, meaning there may be more source files describing the same class) to produce the final code for that class.

Browsing a typical WPF application, we won't find the canonical `Main` method, because it's generated by WPF. It constructs the singleton Application object instance and creates the first window specified by the `Application.StartupUri` property (if not null). We can find that code in the file `App.g.cs` (`g` stands for generated) inside the `Obj\x86\Debug` sub-folder.

Dependency properties

.NET properties are nothing more than syntactic sugar over set and get methods. What those methods do is up to the property's developer. More often than not, a property is a thin wrapper over a private field, perhaps adding some validation logic in its setter.

WPF requires more out of its properties. Specifically, WPF's dependency properties provide the following:

- Change notifications when the property's value is changed.
- Validation handler called as part of a set operation.
- Coercion handler that is able to "coerce" the provided value to an acceptable value.
- Various providers can attempt to set the property's value, but only one such provider wins at a time. Nevertheless, all values are retained. If the winning provider goes away, the property's value is set to the next *winner in line*.
- Property value inheritance down the visual tree (if so desired).
- No memory is allocated for a property's value if that value is never changed from its default.

These features provide the basis of some of WPF's strong features, such as data binding and animation.

On the surface, these properties look the same as any other property—a getter and a setter. But no private fields are involved, as we'll see in the following recipes.

Creating custom type instances in XAML

Sometimes there's a need to create instances of your own types, or other .NET Framework, non-WPF types within XAML. A classic example is a data binding value converter (which we'll explore in *Chapter 6, Data Binding*, but other scenarios might call for it).

Getting ready

Make sure you have Visual Studio 2010 up and running.

How to do it...

We'll create a simple application that creates an instance of a custom type in XAML to demonstrate the entire procedure:

1. Create a new WPF Application project named **CH01.CustomTypes.**
2. Let's create a custom type named `Book`. In the **Solution Explorer** window, right-click on the project node and select **Add** and then **Class...**:

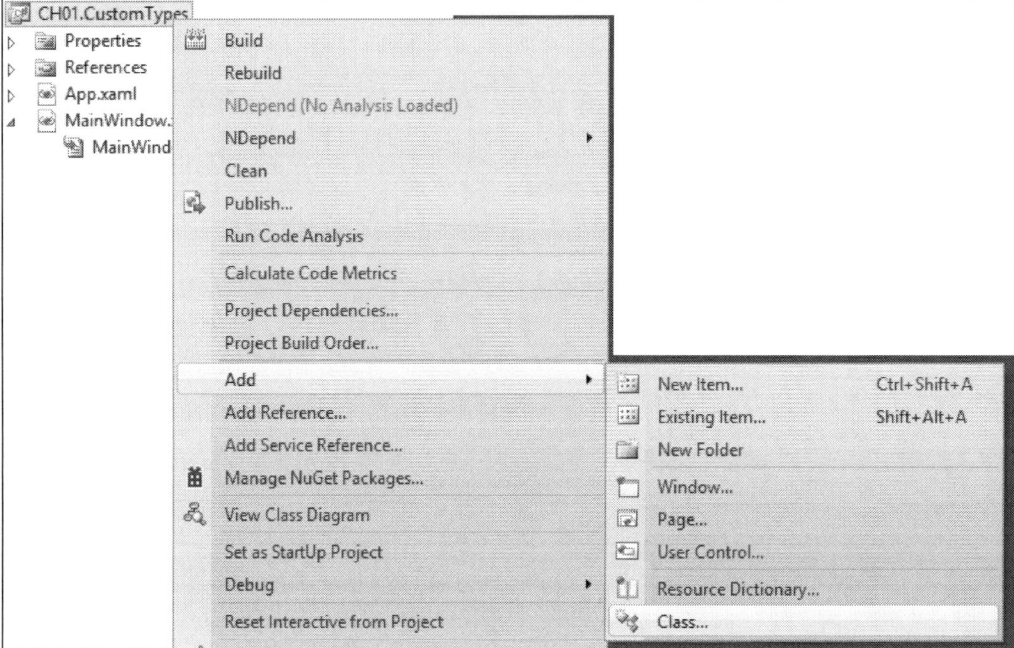

3. Type `Book` in the **Name** box and click on **Add**:

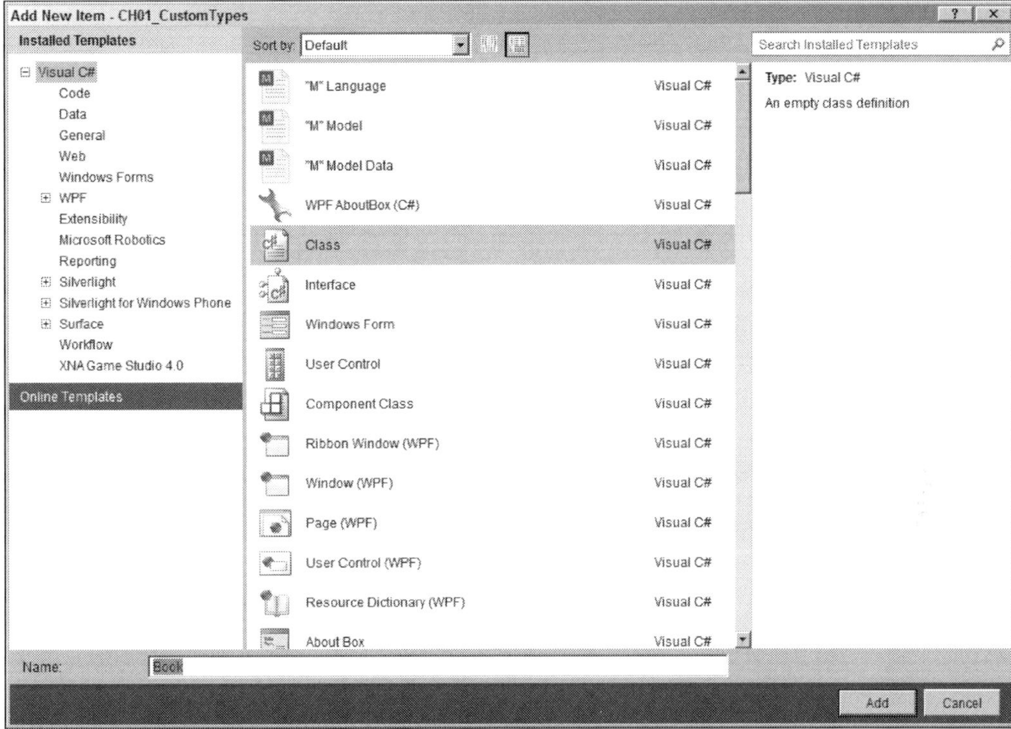

4. Add four simple properties to the resulting class:

```
class Book {
   public string Name { get; set; }
   public string Author { get; set; }
   public decimal Price { get; set; }
   public int YearPublished { get; set; }
 }
```

Downloading the example code

You can download the example code files for all Packt books you have purchased from your account at `http://www.PacktPub.com`. If you purchased this book elsewhere, you can visit `http://www.PacktPub.com/support` and register to have the files e-mailed directly to you.

5. Open the `MainWindow.xaml` file (using the **Solution Explorer**), which was created automatically by the project wizard. We would like to create an instance of the `Book` class. As a `Book` is not an element (does not derive from `UIElement`), we cannot simply create it inside our `Grid`. But, we can make it the `Content` property (that can be anything, as its type is `Object`) of a `ContentControl`-derived type, such as `Button`. Add a button control to the existing grid, as follows:

```
<Grid>
    <Button FontSize="20">
    </Button>
</Grid>
```

6. To create an instance of `Book`, we first need to map the .NET namespace (and assembly) where `Book` is defined to an XML namespace that can be used by the XAML compiler. Let's add a mapping at the top of the XAML near the default mappings added by the application wizard:

```
<Window x:Class="CH01.CustomTypes.MainWindow"
   xmlns="http://schemas.microsoft.com/winfx/2006/xaml/
presentation"
   xmlns:x="http://schemas.microsoft.com/winfx/2006/xaml"
   xmlns:local="clr-namespace:CH01.CustomTypes"
```

7. This says that anything prefixed by the string `local` (we can select anything here), should be looked up in the `CH01.CustomTypes` namespace (in the current assembly).

8. Now, we can finally create a `Book` instance. Add the following inside the `Button` tag:

```
<Button FontSize="20">
   <local:Book Name="Windows Internals"
   Author="Mark Russinovich" Price="40"
   YearPublished="2009" />
</Button>
```

9. That's it. We can verify this by adding a suitable `ToString` implementation to the `Book` type, and running the application:

```
public override string ToString() {
return string.Format("{0} by {1}\nPublished {2}", Name,
      Author, YearPublished);

}
```

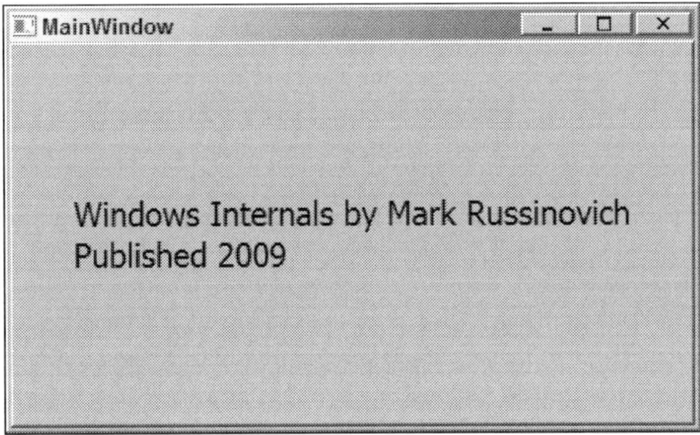

How it works...

The XAML compiler needs to be able to resolve type names such as `Button` or `Book`. A simple name like `Button` is not necessarily unique, not in the XML sense and certainly not in the .NET sense (there are at least four `Button` types in .NET, naturally in different namespaces) .

A mapping is required between an XML namespace and a .NET namespace, so that the XAML compiler can reference the correct type. By default, two XML namespaces are declared by a typical XAML file: the first, which is the default XML namespace, is mapped to the *normal* WPF namespaces (`System.Windows`, `System.Windows.Controls`, and so on). The other, typically with the `x` prefix, is mapped to the XAML namespace (`System.Windows.Markup`).

For our own types, we need to do similar mapping (but with a different syntax) means map the XML namespace prefix `local` to the .NET namespace `CH01.CustomTypes`. The following line:

```
xmlns:local="clr-namespace:CH01.CustomTypes"
```

This allows our `Book` class to be recognized and used within the XAML.

If the type was defined in a referenced assembly (not our own assembly), then the mapping would continue to something like the following:

```
xmlns:local="clr-namespace:CH01.CustomTypes;assembly=MyAssembly"
```

For example, suppose we want the ability to create instances of the `System.Random` type. Here's how we'd map an XML namespace to the .NET namespace and assembly where `System.Random` resides:

```
xmlns:sys="clr-namespace:System;assembly=mscorlib"
```

Now, we could create an instance of anything in the `System` namespace (that is XAML friendly) and the `mscorlib` assembly (such as `Random`):

```
<sys:Random x:Key="rnd" />
```

In this case, it's hosted in a `ResourceDictionary` (which is a kind of dictionary, meaning every value requires a key; we'll discuss these in more detail in the next chapter).

There's more...

It's possible to map a single XML namespace to multiple .NET namespaces. This is the same technique used by the WPF assemblies itself: a single XML namespace maps to multiple WPF namespaces, such as `System.Windows`, `System.Windows.Controls`, and `System.Windows.Media`.

The trick is to use the `XmlnsDefinition` attribute within the assembly where the exported types reside. This only works for referenced assemblies; that is, it's typically used in class library assemblies.

For example, suppose we create a `MyClassLibrary` class library assembly, with a type like the `Book` introduced earlier:

```
namespace MyClassLibrary {
   public class Book {
      public string Name { get; set; }
      public string Author { get; set; }
      public decimal Price { get; set; }
      public int YearPublished { get; set; }
   }
}
```

We can make all types within this assembly and the `MyClassLibrary` namespace part of an XML namespace by adding the following attribute:

```
[assembly: XmlnsDefinition("http://mylibrary.com",
"MyClassLibrary")]
```

The first argument to the attribute is the XML namespace name. This can be anything, but is typically some form of fictitious URL (usually a variation on the company's URL), so as to lower chances of collisions (this is exactly the same idea used by WPF). The second string is the .NET namespace mapped by this XML namespace.

Now, suppose we have another .NET namespace within that same assembly with some types declared within it:

```
namespace MyClassLibrary.MyOtherTypes {
   public class MyType1 {
      //...
   }

   public class MyType2 {
      //...
   }
}
```

We can add another attribute to map the same XML namespace to the new .NET namespace:

```
[assembly: XmlnsDefinition("http://mylibrary.com",
"MyClassLibrary.MyOtherTypes")]
```

This means that a single XML prefix (in some client application) can now map to multiple .NET namespaces:

```
xmlns:mylib="http://mylibrary.com"
```

This scheme can save multiple distinct XML prefix declarations. One consequence of this idea is that all public type names must be unique across the mapped .NET namespaces (as they are indeed within WPF itself).

Creating a dependency property

Dependency properties are the workhorse of WPF. This infrastructure provides for many of WPF's features, such as data binding, animations, and visual inheritance. In fact, most of the various element properties are Dependency Properties. Sometimes we need to create such properties for our own controls or windows.

Getting ready

Make sure you have Visual Studio up and running.

How to do it...

We'll create a simple user control with one new dependency property to illustrate the entire procedure:

1. Within Visual Studio 2010, create a new WPF Application named **CH01.DependencyProperties**.
2. We'll add a simple **User Control**, to which we'll add a dependency property. Don't worry if you don't understand exactly what a user control is; we'll discuss those in a later chapter. For now, just concentrate on the dependency properties we'll create and use. To create the **User Control**, right-click on the **Project** node in the **Solution Explorer** and select **Add** and then **User Control...**.

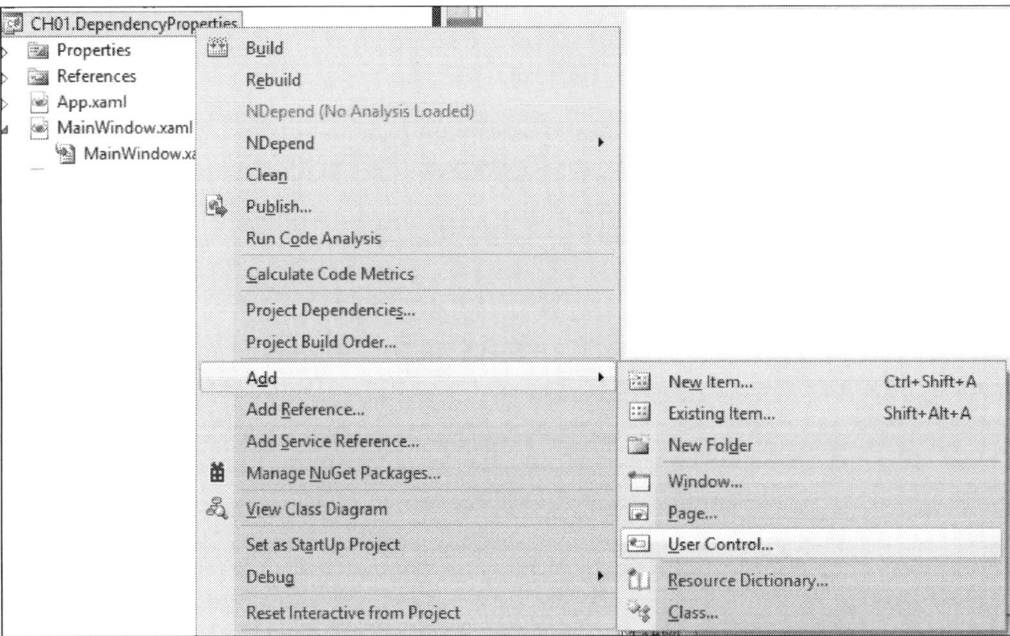

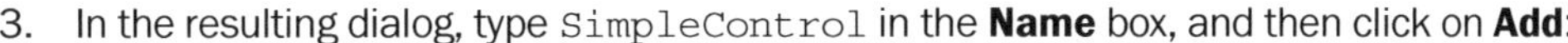

3. In the resulting dialog, type `SimpleControl` in the **Name** box, and then click on **Add**:

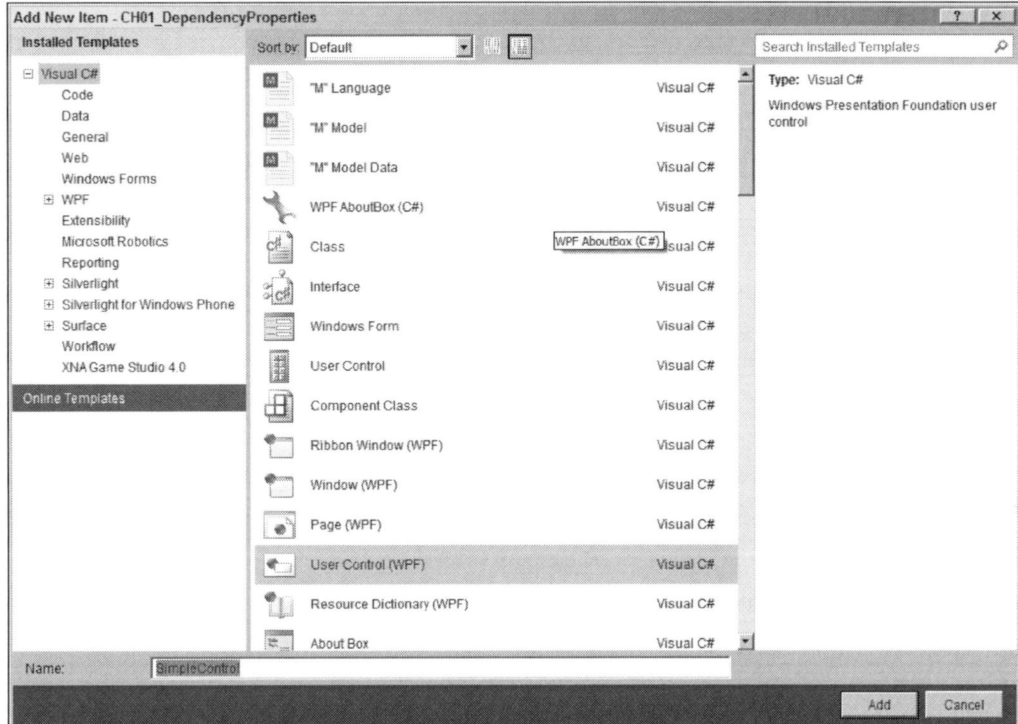

4. We'll add a dependency property to the `SimpleControl` class. A dependency property needs to be "registered" with the property system. Open the `SimpleControl.xaml.cs` file and type `propdp` just after the closing brace of the constructor. This is how it would look in the Visual Studio editor:

```
public partial class SimpleControl : UserControl {
   public SimpleControl() {
      InitializeComponent();
   }

   propdp
}  propdp    Define a DependencyProperty
            Code snippet for a property using DependencyProperty as the backing store
```

5 This is a code snippet that helps with the (somewhat unpleasant) details of properly registering the property. Press *Tab*; the code snippet is expanded to something like the following:

```
public int MyProperty {
   get { return (int)GetValue(MyPropertyProperty); }
   set { SetValue(MyPropertyProperty, value); }
}

// Using a DependencyProperty as the backing store for MyProperty.  This enables animation, styling, binding, etc...
public static readonly DependencyProperty MyPropertyProperty =
    DependencyProperty.Register("MyProperty", typeof(int), typeof(ownerclass), new UIPropertyMetadata(0));
```

The first part looks like a normal getter/setter of a property (although the implementation is anything but "normal"). The second part actually registers the property with some information (more on that in the *How it works...* section). Let's create a property named `YearPublished` of type `int`.

6. Press *Tab* to skip the `int` part (as that's what we want here). The focus should jump to `MyProperty`. Type `YearPublished` as the property name.
7. Press *Tab* again. Note that this changes the property name in the lower `Register` call to `YearPublished`. The focus should jump to the `ownerclass` part. Type `SimpleControl`.
8. Press *Tab* again. The focus should jump to the `0`. This should be the default value of the property, if not altered. Change the `0` into `2000`. After removing the (unhelpful) comment from the snippet provided, the code should look as follows:

```
public int YearPublished {
   get { return (int)GetValue(YearPublishedProperty); }
   set { SetValue(YearPublishedProperty, value); }
}

public static readonly DependencyProperty
   YearPublishedProperty = DependencyProperty.Register(
      "YearPublished", typeof(int), typeof(SimpleControl),
      new UIPropertyMetadata(2000));
```

9. Now let's test it. If that's indeed a dependency property, then there are a few things it can do, such as data bind. We'll add an instance of the `SimpleControl` class to our main window and bind the property we defined to some other control.
10. Open the `MainWindow.xaml` file. Replace the existing `Grid` with a `StackPanel`, and add an instance of our `SimpleControl`. The entire markup should look like as follows:

```
<Window x:Class="CH01.DependencyProperties.MainWindow"
        xmlns="http://schemas.microsoft.com/winfx/2006/xaml/
presentation"
```

```
        xmlns:x="http://schemas.microsoft.com/winfx/2006/xaml"
        xmlns:local="clr-namespace:CH01.DependencyProperties"
        Title="MainWindow" Height="350" Width="525">
    <StackPanel>
        <local:SimpleControl x:Name="_simple" />
    </StackPanel>
</Window>
```

11. Note the `local` prefix pointing to our .NET namespace (as explained in an earlier recipe of this chapter). Now let's add a `TextBlock` and a `Button` inside the `StackPanel`. The `Text` property of `TextBlock` should bind to the `YearPublished` property of the `SimpleControl` instance:

    ```
    <TextBlock Text="{Binding YearPublished, ElementName=_simple}"
    FontSize="30" />
    <Button Content="Change Value" FontSize="20"/>
    ```

12. When the button is clicked, we'll increment the `YearPublished` property and see if that changes the displayed text in the `TextBlock`. First, add a `Click` event handler; within the `Button` element type `Click=`. Visual Studio writes a pair of quotes and suggests adding a handler. You can press *Tab* to accept the default handler name, or type yourself an appropriate name, such as `OnChangeValue`:

    ```
    <Button Content="Change Value" FontSize="20"
    Click="OnChangeValue"/>
    ```

13. Right-click on the handler name (`OnChangeValue` in this case), and select **Navigate to Event Handler**:

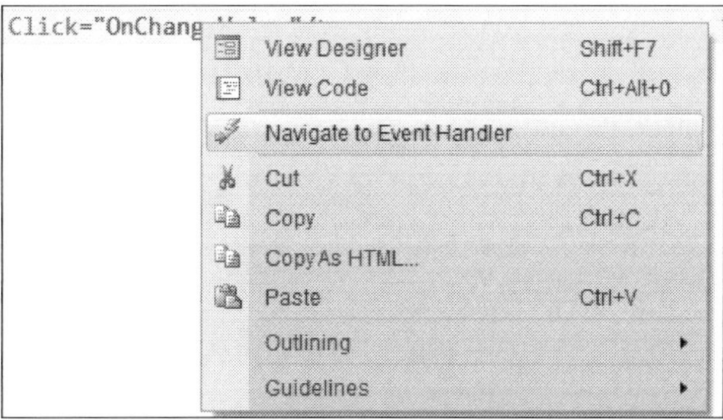

14. Visual Studio switches to the `MainWindow.xaml.cs` file inside the event handler. Add a simple increment of the `YearPublished` property of `SimpleControl` named `_simple`. The entire method should look as follows:

    ```
    private void OnChangeValue(object sender, RoutedEventArgs e) {
       _simple.YearPublished++;
    }
    ```

15. Run the application. You should see the `TextBlock` showing **2000**. That's the default value we set in the `DependencyProperty.Register` call.

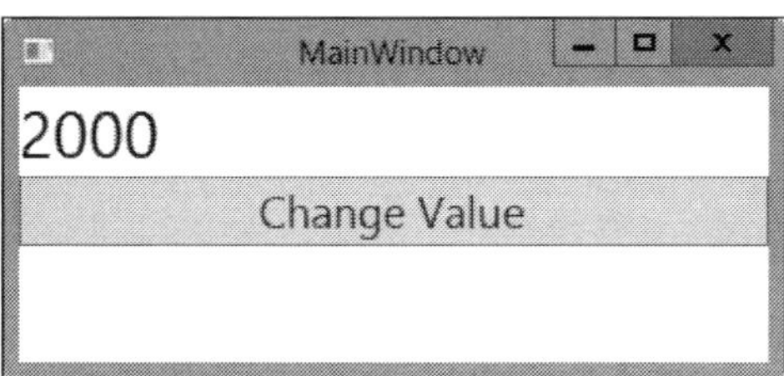

16. Now press the button **Change Value** a few times— the text should be incremented. This happened because of the change notifications raised by the dependency property system, to which the data binding system registered.

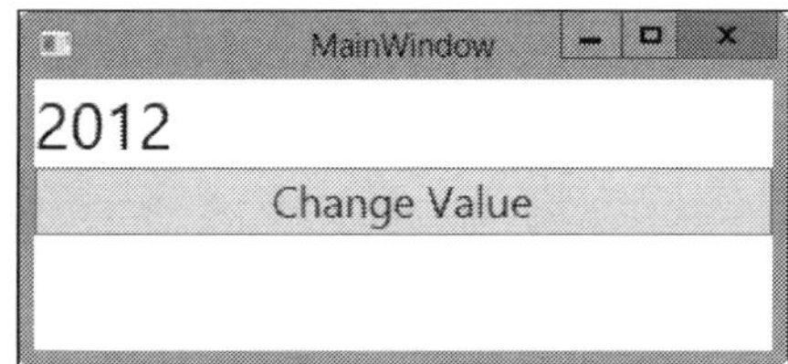

How it works...

A dependency property is managed by a `public static` (`readonly`) field named with the property name suffixed with `Property`; in our case it's `MyValueProperty`. This field manages the property value for any instance of the type it's declared in. The call to `DependencyProperty.Register` sets the property's name, its type, the owner type, and set of metadata for that property. The previous code uses an instance of `UIPropertyMetadata` (one of several possible types), that accepts (at least) the default value for the property (10 in our example).

The classic getter/setter method pair includes calls to `SetValue` and `GetValue`. These are defined in the `DependencyObject` base class, which means any type that wants to leverage the dependency property system must inherit from this class (directly or indirectly). For WPF elements, this is not a problem, as everything inherits from `DependencyObject` eventually.

When a new value is set for the property (as we did for our code), the `SetValue` method does "the right thing", meaning (for example), sending notifications to whoever is listening (such as the data binding system).

There's more...

When we register a dependency property, we can provide a property changed callback delegate, to be called when that property value changes for whatever reason:

```
public static readonly DependencyProperty
   YearPublishedProperty =   DependencyProperty.Register(
      "YearPublished", typeof(int), typeof(SimpleControl),
      new UIPropertyMetadata(2000, OnValueChanged));


private static void OnValueChanged(DependencyObject obj,
   DependencyPropertyChangedEventArgs e) {
   // do something when property changes
}
```

We'll examine this technique in a future recipe when we discuss attached properties.

This may seem unnecessary— after all, can't we just add code to the setter, and then just know when the property value is changed? No. The reason is that the property setter is just syntactic sugar—it's not always called directly. It is used by developers, as this is the familiar property syntax, but the XAML parser, for example, just calls `SetValue` directly—bypassing the property setter altogether. And it's not the only entity doing so. The setter should have nothing in it except the `SetValue` call.

Property value inheritance

User interface needs to be consistent, usually having the same fonts, sizes, and so on. Setting a font size, for example, on each and every element so they have the same value is tedious and unmaintainable. One of the ways WPF deals with that (not the only way; we'll see another powerful way in *Chapter 8*) is the idea of propagating a property value down the visual tree. This mechanism, property value inheritance, is supported by the dependency property infrastructure.

A canonical example is the font-related properties. If we set the `FontSize` property (for instance) on some container element, child elements (in any level) would use that property instead of the default:

```
<Window x:Class="CH01.InheritDemo.MainWindow"
        Title="MainWindow" FontSize="20"
        Width="400" Height="300">
    <StackPanel>
        <TextBlock Text="Text 1" />
        <TextBlock Text="Text 2" />
        <TextBlock Text="Text 3" />
    </StackPanel>
</Window>
```

Note the `FontSize` is set to `20` on the `Window` object. All the `TextBlock`s will now use the value of `20` for their font size instead of the default. This is a feature a dependency property may choose to use, specified at registration time. Here's an example of a dummy property:

```
public static readonly DependencyProperty DummyProperty =
   DependencyProperty.Register("Dummy", typeof(int),
      typeof(MainWindow), new FrameworkPropertyMetadata(0,
      FrameworkPropertyMetadataOptions.Inherits));
```

That last flag makes this property inheritable by default (same as the font related properties).

Why "dependency"?

What is the "dependency" part of dependency properties? In the previous section, we looked at visual inheritance. Suppose that one of those example `TextBlocks` sets a different `FontSize` values like so:

```
<Window x:Class="CH01.InheritDemo.MainWindow"
        Title="MainWindow" FontSize="20"
        Width="400" Height="300">
    <StackPanel>
        <TextBlock Text="Text 1" />
        <TextBlock Text="Text 2" FontSize="30"/>
        <TextBlock Text="Text 3" />
    </StackPanel>
</Window>
```

What will be the final result? It turns out 30 is the winner for the second `TextBlock`. What we see is a set of priorities for providers of values. The first (and lowest) priority is the default value registered with `DependencyProperty.Register`. A higher priority is the inheritance feature (if registered as such for that property). A higher still priority is a local value (30 in our example) that takes precedence over inheritance. So, a dependency property *depends* on one of several *levels* or *priorities* of value providers. In fact, there are about 11 different levels in all (we have seen three in this example). All provider values are not *lost*—they may become effective if the highest provider is cleared. Here's an example:

```
_text2.ClearValue(TextBlock.FontSizeProperty);
```

This clears the local value of the (for example) second `TextBlock`, reverting its `FontSize` value to 20 (the inherited value).

By the way, the highest priority provider (except for a coercion callback, explained in the next section) is an active animation. If this wasn't so, an animation would simply have no effect. Once the animation is removed, the property value reverts to its previous state (depending on the highest provider at that time).

We need to take this behavior into consideration. If a property does not seem to get the expected value, there's a good chance we missed some provider that's "stronger" than the one we expected to win. The Visual Studio debugger has a visualizer that can be used to view the current property values of elements, and (very important) the provider that's effectively providing this value. Here's an example for our famous second `TextBlock`:

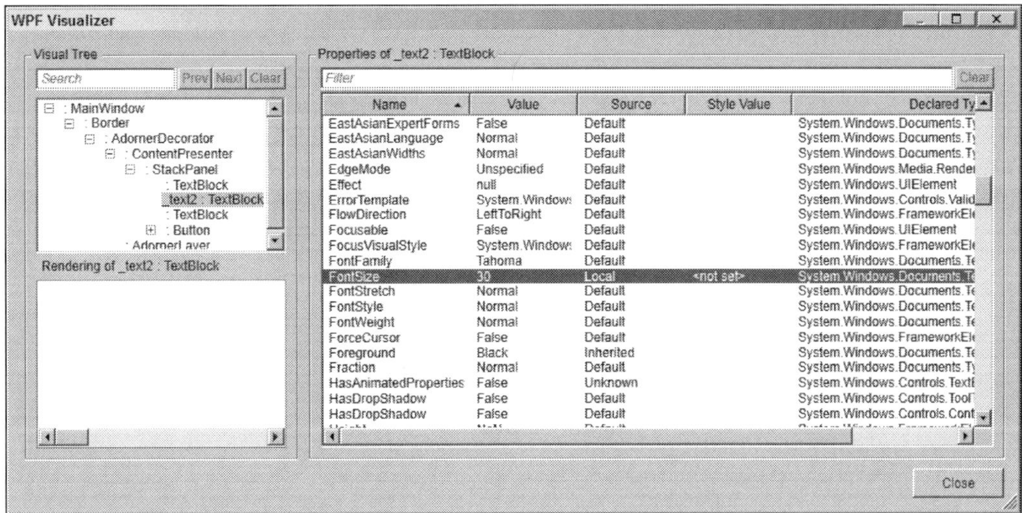

Note the **Local** reading of the **Source** column.

The `CH11.InheritDemo` project, available with the downloadable source for this chapter, can be used to test it out. To get to this dialog, set a breakpoint where you have easy access to the required variable (in this case it could be done in the `MainWindow` constructor after `InitializeComponent`), and then click on the small magnifying glass near the variable's value column:

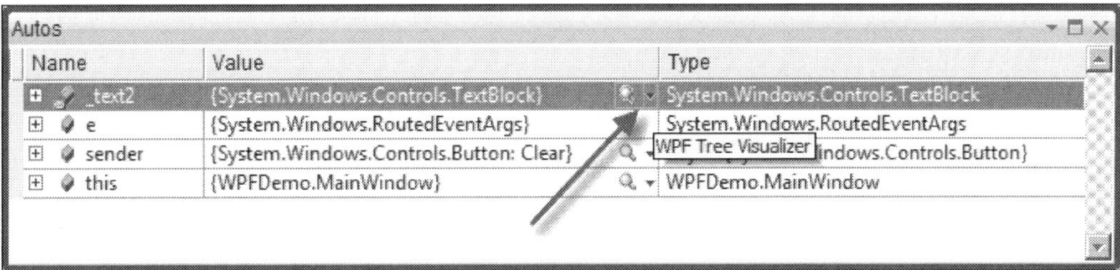

If we remove the `FontSize="30"` local value setting, and use the visualizer again, we get the following:

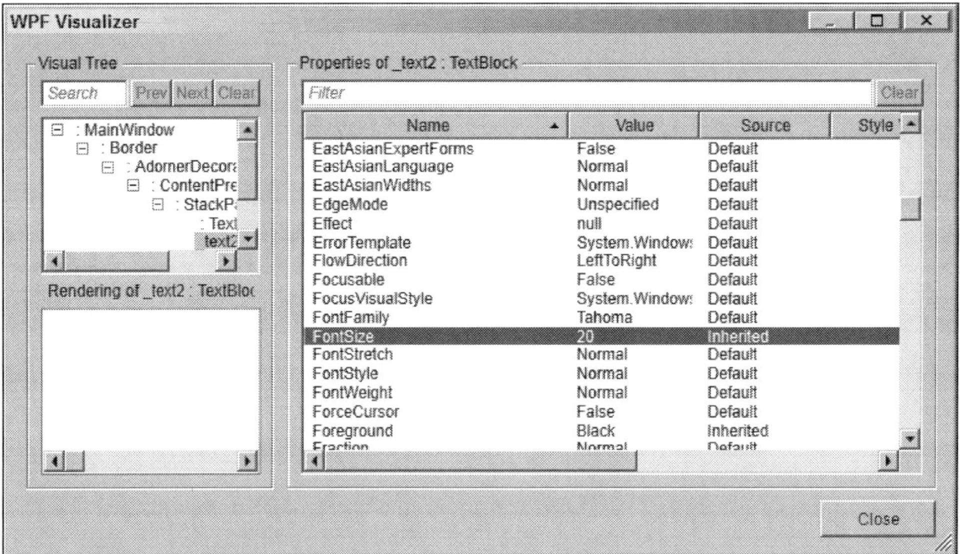

The **Source** column clearly indicates that the value was set because of visual inheritance.

This information is also available by using other tools that don't require Visual Studio or a debugger of any kind. One such free tool is Snoop (`http://snoopwpf.codeplex.com/`). This tool can look at any WPF window and drill down into the visual tree, showing property values (with their source); since it does not require anything special, it can be used in production environments, where tools such as Visual Studio are not typically found.

Dependency property levels

As mentioned, there are 11 levels, or priorities, of dependency property providers. Here's the complete list (highest to lowest precedence):

1. **Property coercion**: The coercion mechanism allows a delegate to execute before the final value is set for the property. That coercion delegate is provided as part of the property metadata at registration time. For example, if a property signifies an hour in the day, it should have a value between 0 and 23. The coercion callback can look at the suggested value, and if (say) it's greater than 23, return 23 as the final value.
2. **Active animation**: If an animation is active, it provides the property's current value.
3. **Local value**: Set through the property setter in code, or through XAML.
4. **Template parent properties**: If the control was created as part of a `ControlTemplate` or `DataTemplate`, these properties apply (we'll discuss data templates in *Chapter 6* and control templates in *Chapter 8*).

5. **Implicit style**: (We'll discuss implicit styles in *Chapter 8*).
6. **Style triggers** from Windows or the application (we'll discuss triggers in *Chapter 8*).
7. **Template triggers**: Triggers that are part of a template (again, *Chapter 8*).
8. **Style setters**: Values from styles defined in the Window or the application (styles are discussed in *Chapter 8*).
9. **Default style**: Set by the control creator and can be based on the current Windows theme.
10. **Inheritance**: As discussed in a previous section.
11. **Default value**: As set in the property metadata.

For a detailed look at all dependency property levels, you can refer to this link in the official MSDN documentation: `http://msdn.microsoft.com/en-us/library/1FBADA8E-4867-4ED1-8D97-62C07DAD7EBC(v=vs.100,d=loband).aspx`

Using an attached property

Attached properties are curious beings. There is no direct analogue to anything else in the .NET framework. The closest may be extension methods, introduced in C# 3.0. Extension methods are a way of extending a type without inheriting from it (even if that type is sealed). Attached properties are dependency properties that are defined by some type, but can be used by (almost) any other typed object. That is, they can extend a type's properties without code derivation. In this recipe, we'll see how to use an existing attached property, and in the next one we'll learn how to create a new attached property.

Getting ready

Make sure Visual Studio is up and running.

How to do it...

We'll create an application that creates a rectangle and places it inside a canvas at exact coordinates using attached properties:

1. Create a new WPF Application named `CH01.SimpleAttached`.
2. Open the `MainWindow.xaml` file and create the following basic layout:

```
<Grid>
   <Canvas>
      <RepeatButton Content="Move" />
   </Canvas>
</Grid>
```

3. This creates a grid which hosts a `Canvas` and that canvas hosts a `RepeatButton`. Let's add a `Rectangle` element to the `Canvas` and place it in some position:

```
<Canvas>
    <RepeatButton Grid.Row="1" Content="Move" />
    <Rectangle x:Name="_rect" Width="50" Height="50"
            Fill="Red" Stroke="Black" StrokeThickness="5"
            Canvas.Left="30" Canvas.Top="40" />
</Canvas>
```

4. Run the application. You should see something like this:

5. The `Canvas.Left` and `Canvas.Top` are attached properties. They are defined by the `Canvas` type, but they can be applied to any element (technically, anything that derives from `DependencyObject`). In this case, these two properties are applied to the `Rectangle`, essentially "extending" its property set with two new properties. The syntax `DefiningClassName.PropertyName` is the way to access an attached property in XAML.

6. Now let's try changing these properties in code. When the repeat button is clicked, let's move the rectangle a little bit to the right. First, let's name the `Rectangle`, so we can easily refer to it in code:

```
<Rectangle x:Name="_rect" Width="50" Height="50" Fill="Red"
           Stroke="Black" StrokeThickness="5"
           Canvas.Left="30" Canvas.Top="40" />
```

7. Add a `Click` event handler to the `RepeatButton`. In the handler, add the following code:

```
Canvas.SetLeft(_rect, Canvas.GetLeft(_rect) + 5);
```

8. An attached property is accessed in code using a set of static methods on the class declaring the property (in this case, the `Canvas`). The first argument to these methods is the intended target of the property (in this case the `Rectangle`). Run the application. Click on the button (and hold); you should see the rectangle moving along to the right, 5 units at a time.

How it works...

An attached property is first and foremost a dependency property, meaning it supports all the capabilities of dependency properties. However, as an attached property is "attached" to an object that did not define it, a simple property like syntax is not possible – as C# does not support the concept of attached properties natively. Instead, the declaring class provides two static methods, named `DeclaringType.SetPropertyName` and `DeclaringType.GetPropertyName`, that provide a way to set or get the property value for some object passed in as the first argument (as demonstrated in the last code snippet).

In XAML, things are simpler, as the XAML parser is aware of attached properties, and converts the simpler `DeclaringType.PropertyName` attribute to the aforementioned Set method.

There's more...

The actual implementation of the Set/Get static methods mentioned above is to call the regular `DependencyObject.SetValue/GetValue` as for a regular dependency property. This means that the code to move the rectangle could have been written as follows:

```
_rect.SetValue(Canvas.LeftProperty,
   (double)_rect.GetValue(Canvas.LeftProperty) + 5);
```

Why an attached property?

One may wonder why to go to all this trouble for the `Left` and `Top` properties. Would it not be simpler to define the `Left` and `Top` properties on the (for example) `UIElement` class and be done with it? These properties could have been *normal* dependency properties and enjoy the simpler syntax they carry.

The reason is, that a `Left` or `Top` property may not always make sense. In fact, it only makes sense when the element is placed within a `Canvas`. What if the rectangle is inside a `Grid`? Or a `StackPanel`? The `Left/Top` properties wouldn't make sense. This leads to the conclusion that attached properties are a kind of *contextual* property – they are relevant under particular circumstances, so they can be "attached" if and when actually needed.

Does the declaring type "own" the property?

The previous example may lead to a wrong conclusion. It seems `Canvas.Left` and the like are only relevant when the element is inside a `Canvas`. Similarly, the `Grid.Row` and `Grid.Column` attached properties only make sense for elements placed inside a `Grid`. Is this somehow necessary from an attached property point of view?

Not at all. This is just coincidence. The above properties in fact make sense only for elements placed inside their respective declaring type, but that does not have to be the case. For example, suppose we have a button with a tool tip defined:

```
<Button Content="Copy" ToolTip="Copy the Selected Items" />
```

If the button is disabled (`IsEnabled` set to true), the tool tip does not appear at runtime. To make it appear even if the control is disabled, we must set the `ToolTipService.ShowOnDisabled` attached property to `true`:

```
<Button Content="Copy" ToolTip="Copy the Selected Items"
        ToolTipService.ShowOnDisabled="True"/>
```

We set the property on the button, but it's defined in the `ToolTipService` class. This class is not an element (unlike the `Canvas` for example). In fact, it's a static class (instances of it cannot be created). So, there is no relationship between the button and the `ToolTipService` class, or between the `ToolTip` and `ToolTipService` classes, for that matter. The way this connection is established (so it can have some effect) will be revealed in the next recipe in this chapter.

See also

To create your own attached properties, refer to the next recipe, *Creating an attached property*.

Creating an attached property

An attached property can be used to somehow "enhance" or extend another object. In the case outlined in the previous recipe, *Using an attached property*, an element was placed at exact coordinates within a `Canvas` using the attached `Canvas.Left` and `Canvas.Top` properties. An attached property is a powerful tool for extending the behavior of any object without the need to inherit from the type of the object. In this task, we'll see this in action.

Getting ready

Make sure Visual Studio is up and running.

How to do it...

We'll create an attached property that would rotate any element it's attached to:

1. Create a new WPF Application named `CH01.CustomAttached`.

2. Open `MainWindow.xaml`. Add some elements in a `Canvas` (replace the default `Grid`) as follows:

```
<Canvas>
   <Ellipse Fill="Red" Width="100" Height="60" />
   <Rectangle Fill="Blue" Width="80" Height="80"
              Canvas.Left="100" Canvas.Top="100" />
   <Button Content="Hello" Canvas.Left="130" Canvas.Top="30"
    FontSize="20" />
</Canvas>
```

3. Suppose we want to rotate a particular element around its center. We would have to write something like this (example for the `Ellipse`):

```
<Ellipse Fill="Red" Width="100" Height="60"
        RenderTransformOrigin=".5,.5">
   <Ellipse.RenderTransform>
      <RotateTransform Angle="30" />
   </Ellipse.RenderTransform>
</Ellipse>
```

   Although this is certainly possible, this makes for a lot of typing. Now imagine doing something similar for other elements. Let's make it shorter by defining and using an attached property.

4. Add a new class to the project named `RotationManager`.

5. We'll register a new attached property within this class; a property any other object can use. To do that, we'll take advantage of a Visual Studio code snippet, `propa` (similar in concept to `propdp` discussed in the task *Creating a dependency property* in this chapter). Inside the class definition, type `propa` (without the quotes). This is how it should look at this point:

```
class RotationManager {
    propa
}   propa          Define an attached DependencyProperty
                   Code snippet for an attached property using DependencyProperty as the backing store
```

6. Press *Tab* once, and fill in the property details as follows: the property type should be double, its name should be `Angle`, its owner class `RotationManager`, and its default value zero. You'll have to add a `using` statement for `System.Windows` namespace. The generated code should look as follows (after removing the comment and some formatting):

```
class RotationManager : DependencyObject {
   public static double GetAngle(DependencyObject obj) {
      return (double)obj.GetValue(AngleProperty);
   }
```

```
    public static void SetAngle(DependencyObject obj,
       double value) {
       obj.SetValue(AngleProperty, value);
    }

    public static readonly DependencyProperty AngleProperty =
          DependencyProperty.RegisterAttached("Angle",
          typeof(double), typeof(RotationManager),
          new UIPropertyMetadata(0.0));

}
```

7. Now that we have an attached property definition, let's use it. We'll set it on our various elements. The first step is mapping an XML namespace to our namespace (as we learned in the recipe *Creating custom type instances in XAML* in this chapter). Open `MainWindow.xaml` and add a mapping on the root element, as in the following code snippet:

```
xmlns:local="clr-namespace:CH01.CustomAttached"
```

8. Now let's set the property with various values on the various elements. Here's an example for the `Ellipse` (notice the intellisense popping up to help):

```
 <Ellipse Fill="Red" Width="100" Height="60"
          local:RotationManager.Angle="45"/>
```

9. Add similar settings for the `Rectangle` and `Button` like as follows:

```
<Rectangle Fill="Blue" Width="80" Height="80"
           Canvas.Left="100" Canvas.Top="100"
           local:RotationManager.Angle="30" />
<Button Content="Hello" Canvas.Left="130" Canvas.Top="30"
        FontSize="20"
        local:RotationManager.Angle="90"/>
```

10. Notice that the designer preview shows no change. If you run the application, nothing happens. And why would anything happen? We declared a property and nothing else. Let's add some behavior logic if the property is actually used. For that, we'll add a property changed handler notification. Go back to `RotationManager.cs` and modify the property registration as follows:

```
public static readonly DependencyProperty AngleProperty =
      DependencyProperty.RegisterAttached("Angle",
      typeof(double), typeof(RotationManager),
      new UIPropertyMetadata(0.0, OnAngleChanged));
```

11. The `OnAngleChanged` method will be called for any change in the property value on any object it's applied to. Let's add some simple logic that will rotate the element:

```
private static void OnAngleChanged(DependencyObject obj,
   DependencyPropertyChangedEventArgs e) {
   var element = obj as UIElement;
   if(element != null) {
      element.RenderTransformOrigin = new Point(.5, .5);
      element.RenderTransform = new RotateTransform(
      (double)e.NewValue);
   }
}
```

12. If we switch back to the designer, we'll see the elements rotated according to the specified angles. If we run the application, we'll see something like this:

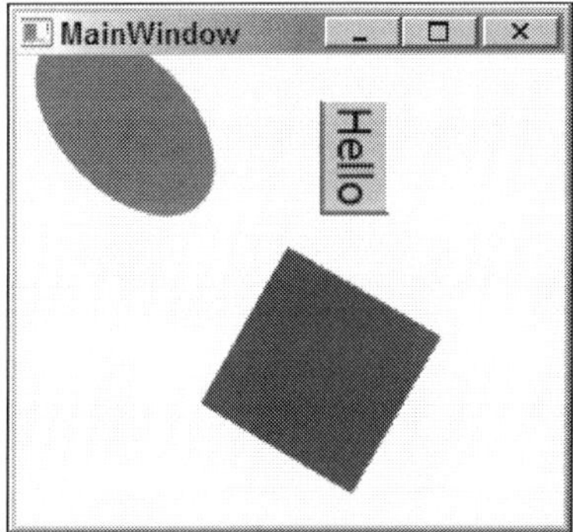

There we have it. An easy way to rotate any element by using an attached property.

How it works...

Attached properties are registered similarly to regular dependency properties. In terms of functionality, they *are* dependency properties. This means they support everything a dependency property supports: data binding, animation, and so on. An attached property can be defined by any class (`RotationManager` in our example) and can be applied to any object whose type derives from `DependencyObject`.

Simply registering an attached property has no effect on its own. There must be some "extra" code that looks for that property and does something when it's applied or changed. In the example shown, this is done by specifying a property changed handler, called by WPF whenever the property is changed on any object. In the example code, we restrict using a `UIElement`-derived type, as this is the first type that supports `RenderTransform` and `RenderTransformOrigin`. This also shows the weakness of attached properties: it's not possible to know whether specifying the property on some object is beneficial. We could have thrown an exception if the object was not `UIElement`-derived to somewhat rectify this (albeit at runtime rather than compile time), but this is not typically employed (although we could have written something with `Debug.WriteLine` to indicate this needs attention), as there may be other code that does not consider this an invalid setting.

There's more...

The property change notification scheme is typically used by WPF with attached properties that are defined by panels, such as `Canvas`, `DockPanel`, and `Grid`. Note that the panels only look for the relevant attached properties on their immediate children (and not grandchildren). This is not a limitation of attached properties, it's simply the way these panels work. Although attached properties within panels are common, there are other ways these properties can be used.

One possibility is to use the existence of these property values within styles (a complete treatment of styles is in given *Chapter 8*) or templates (templates are discussed in *Chapter 6* and *Chapter 8*). For now, think of a style as a grouping of related settings that can be applied as a group to an element. For example, the following style accomplishes roughly the same thing as our property change handler:

```
<Style TargetType="Button">
   <Setter Property="RenderTransformOrigin" Value=".5,.5" />
   <Setter Property="RenderTransform">
      <Setter.Value>
         <RotateTransform Angle="{Binding Path=(local:RotationManager.
Angle), RelativeSource={RelativeSource Mode=FindAncestor,
AncestorType=Button}}" />
      </Setter.Value>
   </Setter>
</Style>
```

Of course, this example works with buttons only because of the targeted style (style that works on buttons only), but the result is the same. Note the parentheses around the attached property name. This is essential - otherwise the XAML parser does not understand this to be an attached property; it interprets `local:RotationManager` as the property name (and expects `Angle` to be a sub-property). Also, leaving out the `"Path="` (as is customary in binding expressions), causes the expression to fail (for a similar reason).

Reusing existing attached properties

An attached property is (paradoxically) a detached entity. It has no special affinity to the declaring type. This means we can use an already defined attached property if it's typed appropriately, named appropriately, and has no use in the needed situation. In our example, we need an attached property that is of type `double`, has an intuitive enough name (maybe something with "angle" or "rotate"), and is unused in scenarios where the use of our property makes sense.

Clearly, it's not easy finding such a property, but sometimes one may get lucky. For instance, if we elect to go for the attached property `ToolTipService.HorizontalOffset` (typed as `double`), we can achieve the same effect as previously (with a style setter) without defining a new attached property. This is not a good choice in this case, as an offset is not an angle, and clearly tooltips have nothing to do with rotation. The worse problem here is that there may be a legitimate reason to place that property on a button (to cater offsetting a tooltip), so that reusing for rotation purposes would collide with the tooltip, making only one a winner. Still, the general concept holds - any attached property can be reused.

Attached property reuse is possible in styles, templates (data template and control template), and triggers (within styles and templates).

See also

For background on dependency properties, check out the recipe *Creating a dependency property* in this chapter.

Accessing a static property from XAML

XAML provides an easy way to set values of properties—type converters and the extended property syntax allow for flexible setting of values. However, some things cannot be expressed as a simple value, such as setting a property to the value of some static property.

Getting ready

Make sure Visual Studio is up and running.

How to do it...

We'll create an application that uses a static property from within XAML:

1. Create a new WPF Application named `CH01.StaticProperties`.
2. Open `MainWindow.xaml`. Replace the `Grid` element with a `StackPanel`.

3. Add some shapes as shown in the following code block:

```
<StackPanel>
    <Ellipse Stroke="Black" Height="50" />
    <Rectangle Stroke="Black" Height="50" />
</StackPanel>
```

4. Suppose we want to fill the ellipse with the desktop color selected by the user in Windows. WPF provides the `SystemColors` class, with many static properties that return a `Brush` representing the user's choice. For the desktop, this is a `DesktopBrush` property. We can try the following:

```
<Ellipse Stroke="Black" Height="50"
Fill="SystemColors.DesktopBrush" />
```

5. This throws an exception at runtime, as it cannot be converted to any "known" color (such as Red or Blue). To access a static property, we must use the `{x:Static}` markup extension, as follows:

```
<Ellipse Stroke="Black" Height="50"
Fill="{x:Static SystemColors.DesktopBrush}" />
```

6. This works. You can verify this by going to **Control Panel**, then selecting **Personalization** (on Windows 7 or 8).

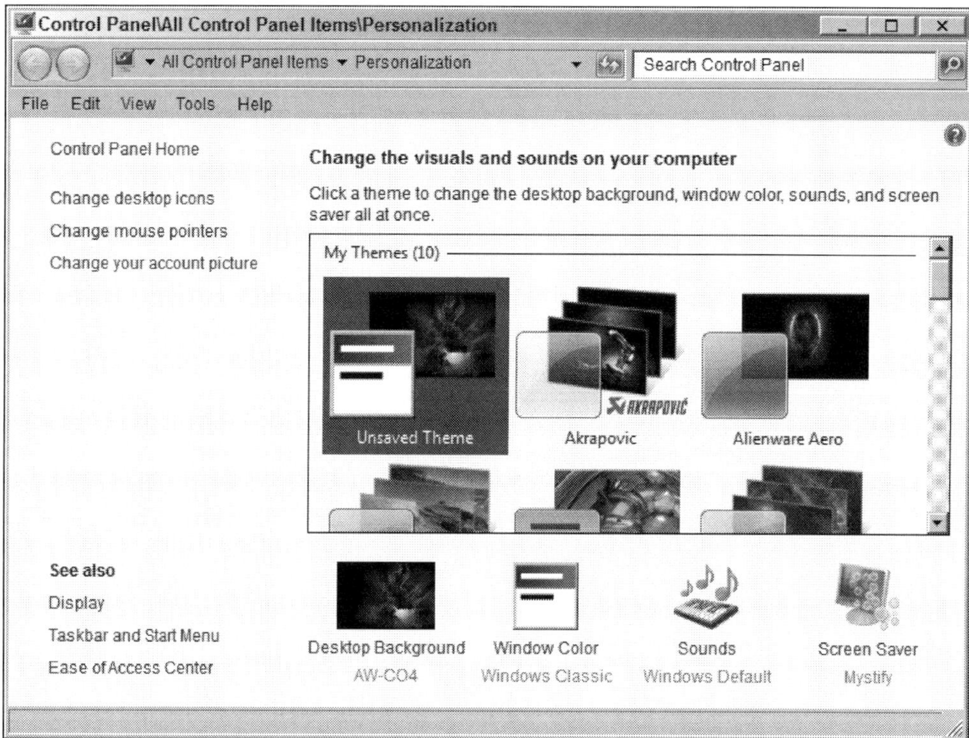

7. Select **Window Color** (switch to the classic theme first if the following window is shown differently). The **Window Color and Appearance** dialog is displayed:

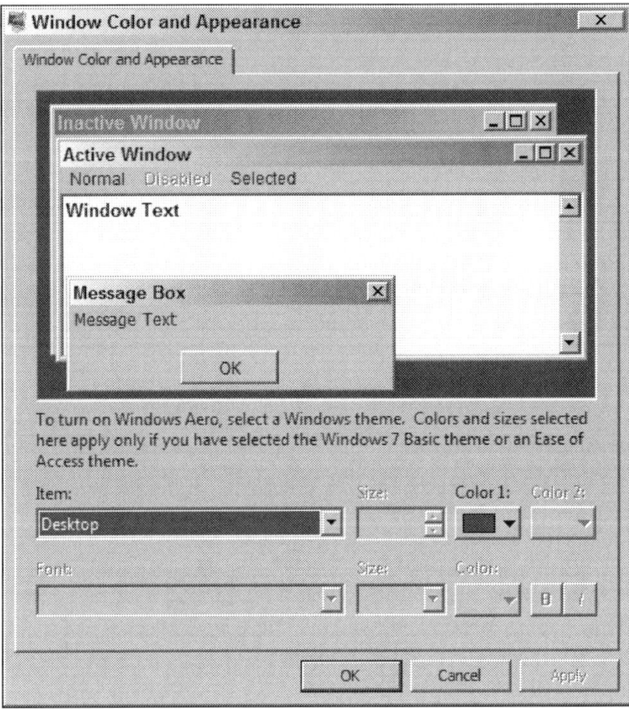

8. Change the desktop color and run the application again. You should see the ellipse filled with the new color.
9. Similarly, let's fill the rectangle with the active window caption color:

```
<Rectangle Stroke="Black" Height="50"
Fill="{x:Static SystemColors.ActiveCaptionBrush}"/>
```

10. Running the application shows something like the following:

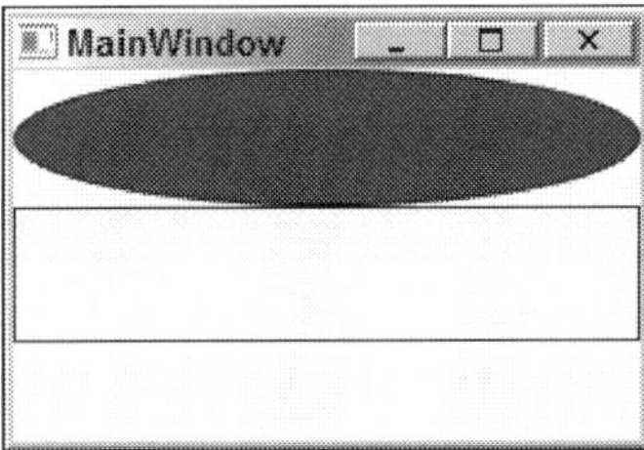

11. In this case, the active caption color on my system is a gradient, so the `ActiveCaptionBrush` provides the left side. The right side is provided by the `GradientActiveCaptionBrush` property. They are both brushes. If we wanted to recreate the caption gradient within the rectangle, we would need color objects, not brushes. Fortunately, these are provided via properties in the same class, named `ActiveCaptionColor` and `GradientActiveCaptionColor`. Let's combine these in a `LinearGradientBrush`:

```
<Rectangle Stroke="Black" Height="50">
   <Rectangle.Fill>
      <LinearGradientBrush EndPoint="1,0">
         <GradientStop Offset="0"
Color="{x:Static SystemColors.ActiveCaptionColor}" />
         <GradientStop Offset="1"
Color="{x:Static SystemColors.GradientActiveCaptionColor}" />
      </LinearGradientBrush>
   </Rectangle.Fill>
</Rectangle>
```

12. This is the final result:

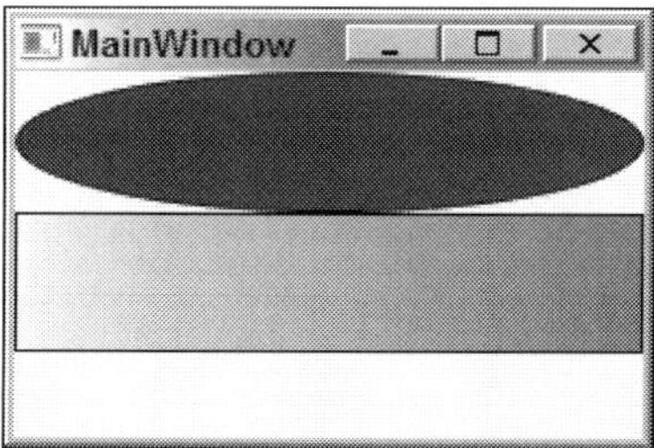

How it works...

XAML basically has very few capabilities. It can create objects, set values for properties, and set up event handlers. This is intentional, as XAML is declarative in nature. It cannot, for instance, call methods. That would make it closer to an imperative language (such as C#), which would make its existence dubious at best.

Sometimes, however, declarative operations require more than setting up properties. A method may be involved, or some other unusual construct, but the intent may still be declarative. This is where markup extensions come in. They provide a way to extend XAML with new (hopefully declarative) capabilities.

A markup extension is a class that derives from `System.Windows.Markup.MarkupExtension` and implements a single method, `ProvideValue`. In this example we have used the `{x:Static}` markup extension, which allows accessing any static property (whether it belongs to WPF or not; if not, a XAML namespace mapping is required as explained in the recipe *Creating custom type instances in XAML* in this chapter). `{x:Static}` is implemented by the `System.Windows.Markup.StaticExtension` class. Note that if the markup extension class ends with "Extension" we can remove it when referring to it in XAML – the XAML compiler will search with and without the word "Extension". This means `{x:Static}` can be written `{x:StaticExtension}`. In fact, most markup extensions end with "Extension" (a notable exception is the `Binding` markup extension).

There's more...

There are other built in markup extensions. Here are some of the simplest:

- `{x:Null}` specifies the null reference
- `{x:Type SomeType}` is the equivalent to the `typeof(SomeType)` operator in C#

We'll look at other markup extensions in subsequent chapters.

Creating a custom markup extension

Markup extensions are used to extend the capabilities of XAML, by providing declarative operations that need more than just setting some properties. These can be used to do pretty much anything, so caution is advised – these extensions must preserve the declarative nature of XAML, so that non-declarative operations are avoided; these should be handled by normal C# code.

Getting ready

Make sure Visual Studio is up and running.

How to do it...

We'll create a new markup extension that would provide random numbers and use it within a simple application:

1. First, we'll create a class library with the markup extension implementation and then test it in a normal WPF application. Create a new Class Library project named `CH01.CustomMarkupExtension`. Make sure the checkbox **Create directory for solution** is checked, and click on **OK**:

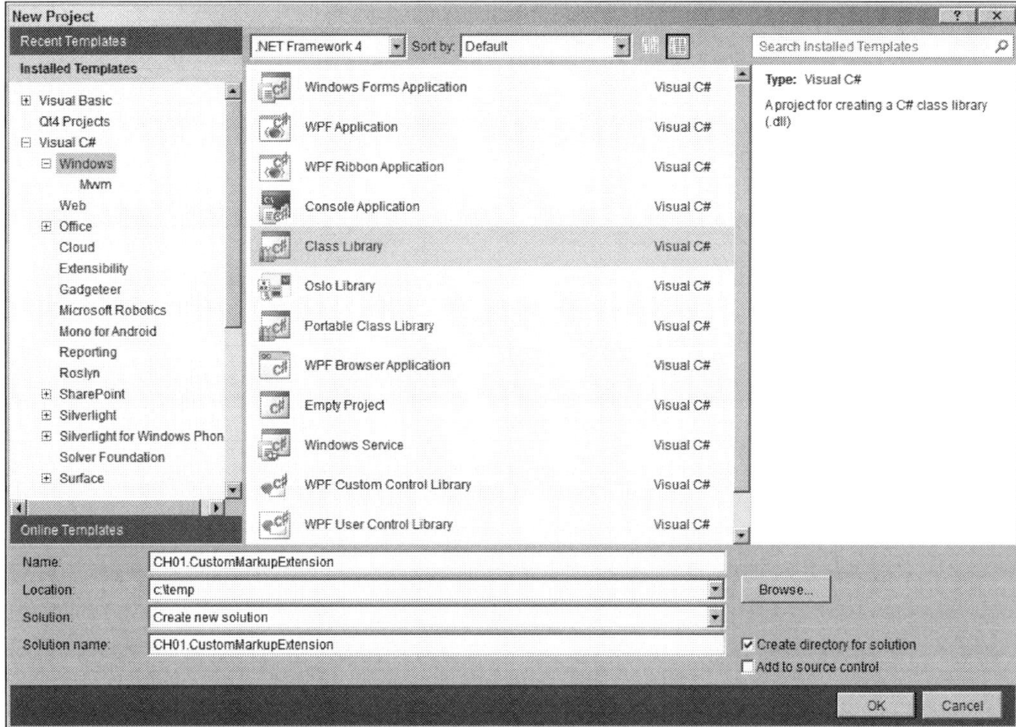

2. The base `MarkupExtension` class resides in the `System.Xaml` assembly. Add a reference to that assembly by right-clicking the **References** node in the **Solution Explorer**, and selecting **Add Reference....** Scroll down to `System.Xaml` and select it.
3. Delete the file `Class1.cs` that was created by the wizard.

4. Right-click the project node, and select **Add Class...**. Name the class `RandomExtension` and click on **Add**. This markup extension will generate a random number in a given range.
5. Mark the class as public and inherit from `MarkupExtension`.
6. Add a `using` statement to `System.Windows.Markup` or place the caret somewhere over `MarkupExtension`, click on the smart tag (or press *Ctrl* + . (dot), and allow the smart tag to add the using statement for you. This is how the class should look right now:

    ```
    public class RandomExtension : MarkupExtension {
    }
    ```

7. We need to implement the `ProvideValue` method. The easiest way to get the basic prototype is to place the caret over `MarkupExtension` and use the smart tag again, this time selecting Implement abstract class. This is the result:

    ```
    public class RandomExtension : MarkupExtension {
       public override object ProvideValue(IServiceProvider sp) {
          throw new NotImplementedException();
       }
    }
    ```

8. Before we create the actual implementation, let's add some fields and constructors:

    ```
    readonly int _from, _to;
    public RandomExtension(int from, int to) {
       _from = from; _to = to;
    }
    public RandomExtension(int to)
       : this(0, to) {
    }
    ```

9. Now we must implement `ProvideValue`. This should be the return value of the markup extension - a random number in the range provided by the constructors. Let's create a simple implementation:

    ```
    static readonly Random _rnd = new Random();
    public override object ProvideValue(IServiceProvider sp) {
       return (double)_rnd.Next(_from, _to);
    }
    ```

10. Let's test this. Right-click on the solution node in **Solution Explorer** and select **Add** and then **New Project...**.

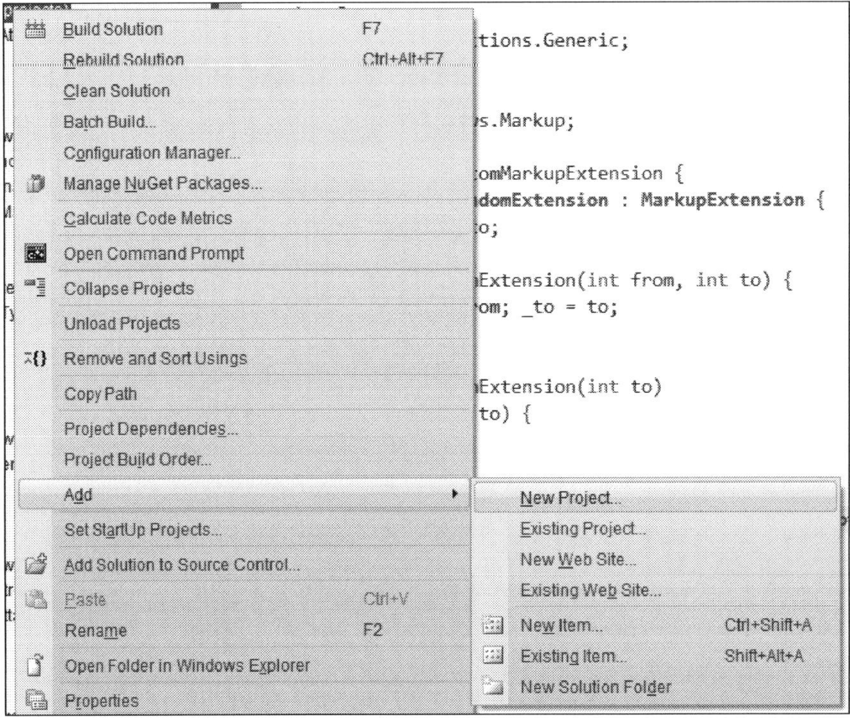

11. Create a WPF Application project named `CH01.TestRandom`.
12. Add a reference to the class library just created.
13. Open `MainWindow.xaml`. We need to map an XML namespace to the namespace and assembly our `RandomExtension` resides in:

```
xmlns:mext="clr-namespace:CH01.CustomMarkupExtension;
assembly=CH01.CustomMarkupExtension"
```

14. Replace the `Grid` with a `StackPanel` and a couple of `TextBlocks` as follows:

```
<StackPanel>
   <TextBlock FontSize="{mext:Random 10, 100}" Text="Hello"
              x:Name="text1"/>
   <TextBlock Text="{Binding FontSize, ElementName=text1}" />
</StackPanel>
```

15. The result is a TextBlock that uses a random font size between 10 and 100. The second TextBlock shows the generated random value.

How it works...

A markup extension is a class inheriting from MarkupExtension, providing some service that cannot be done with a simple property setter. Such a class needs to implement one method: ProvideValue. Whatever is returned provides the value for the property. ProvideValue accepts an IServiceProvider interface that allows getting some "context" around the markup extension execution. In our simple example, it wasn't used.

Any required arguments are passed via constructor(s). Any optional arguments can be passed by using public properties (as the next section demonstrates).

Let's try using our markup extension on a different property:

```
<TextBlock Text="{mext:Random 1000}" />
```

We hit an exception. The reason is that our ProvideValue returns a double, but the Text property expects a string. We need to make it a bit more flexible. We can query for the expected type and act accordingly. This is one such service provided through IServiceProvider:

```
public override object ProvideValue(IServiceProvider sp) {
   int value = _rnd.Next(_from, _to);
   Type targetType = null;
   if(sp != null) {
      var target = sp.GetService(typeof(IProvideValueTarget))
         as IProvideValueTarget;
      if(target != null) {
         var clrProp = target.TargetProperty as PropertyInfo;
         if(clrProp != null)
            targetType = clrProp.PropertyType;
         if(targetType == null) {
            var dp = target.TargetProperty
               as DependencyProperty;
            if(dp != null)
```

```
                    targetType = dp.PropertyType;
                }
            }
        }
        return targetType != null ?
            Convert.ChangeType(value, targetType) :
            value.ToString();
    }
```

You'll need to add a reference for the `WindowsBase` assembly (where `DependencyProperty` is defined). `IServiceProvider` is a standard .NET interface that is a kind of "gateway" to other interfaces. Here we're using `IProvideValueTarget`, which enables discovering what property type is expected, with the `TargetProperty` property. This is either a `PropertyInfo` (for a regular CLR property) or a `DependencyProperty`, so appropriate checks must be made before the final target type is ascertained. Once we know the type, we'll try to convert to it automatically using the `Convert` class, or return it as a string if that's not possible.

For more information on other interfaces that can be obtained from this `IServiceProvider`, check this page on the MSDN documentation: `http://msdn.microsoft.com/en-us/library/B4DAD00F-03DA-4579-A4E9-D8D72D2CCBCE(v=vs.100,d=loband).aspx`.

There's more...

Constructors are one way to get parameters for a markup extension. Properties are another, allowing optional values to be used if necessary. For example, let's extend our random extension, so that it is able to provide fractional values and not just integral ones. This option would be set using a simple public property:

```
public bool UseFractions { get; set; }
```

The implementation of `ProvideValue` should change slightly; specifically, calculation of the value variable:

```
double value = UseFractions ?
    _rnd.NextDouble() * (_to - _from) + _from :
    (double)_rnd.Next(_from, _to);
```

To use it, we set the property after the mandatory arguments to the constructor:

```
<TextBlock Text="{mext:Random 1000, UseFractions=true}" />
```

Don't go overboard

Markup extensions are powerful. They allow arbitrary code to run in the midst of XAML processing. We just need to remember that XAML is, and should remain, declarative. It's pretty easy to go overboard, crossing that fine line. Here's an example: let's extend our `RandomExtension` to allow modifying the property value at a regular interval. First, a property to expose the capability:

```
public TimeSpan UpdateInterval { get; set; }
```

Now, some modifications to the `ProvideValue` implementation:

```
if(UpdateInterval != TimeSpan.Zero) {
   // setup timer...
   var timer = new DispatcherTimer();
   timer.Interval = UpdateInterval;
   timer.Tick += (sender, e) => {
      value = UseFractions ?
         _rnd.NextDouble() * (_to - _from) + _from :
         (double)_rnd.Next(_from, _to);
      finalValue = targetType != null ?
         Convert.ChangeType(value, targetType) :
         value.ToString();
      if(dp != null)
         ((DependencyObject)targetObject).SetValue(
            dp, finalValue);
      else if(pi != null)
         pi.SetValue(targetObject, value, null);
   };
   timer.Start();
}
```

`targetObject` is obtained by calling `IProvideValueTarget.TargetObject`. This is the actual object on which the property is to be set.

And the markup:

```
<TextBlock Text="This is funny"
FontSize="{mext:Random 10, 50, UpdateInterval=0:0:1}" />
```

This is certainly possible (and maybe fun), but it's probably crossing the line.

Handling routed events

Events are essentially notifications from an object to the outside world – a variation on the "observer" design pattern. Most of the time an object is told what to do via properties and methods. Events are its way of talking back to whoever is interested. The concept of events existed in .NET since its inception, but WPF has something to say about the way events are implemented. WPF introduces routed events, an enhanced infrastructure for raising and handling events, which we'll look at in this recipe.

Getting ready

Make sure Visual Studio is up and running.

How to do it...

We'll create a simple drawing application that uses routed events to handle user interaction:

1. Create a new WPF Application named `CH01.SimpleDraw`. This will be a simple drawing program.
2. Add some markup to `MainWindows.xaml` that includes a `Canvas` and some rectangle objects to select drawing brushes:

   ```
   <Canvas Background="White" Name="_root">
   </Canvas>
   ```

3. To do some drawing, we'll handle the `MouseLeftButtonDown`, `MouseMove`, and `MouseUp` events on the canvas object. Within the `Canvas` tag, type `MouseLeftButtonDown=`. Intellisense will pop up, suggesting to add a default handler name. Resist the temptation, and type `OnMouseDown`:

   ```
   <Canvas Background="White" Name="_root"
       MouseLeftButtonDown="OnMouseDown">
   ```

4. Right-click on **OnMouseDown** and select **Navigate to Event Handler**. Visual Studio will add the required handler method in the code behind file (`MainWindow.xaml.cs`) and jump straight to it:

   ```
   private void OnMouseDown(object sender,
      MouseButtonEventArgs e) {
   }
   ```

5. Add similar handlers for the `MouseMove` and `MouseUp` events, named `OnMouseMove` and `OnMouseUp`, respectively.

6. Let's add simple drawing logic. First, add the following fields to the `MainWindow` class:

   ```
   Point _pos;
   bool _isDrawing;
   Brush _stroke = Brushes.Black;
   ```

7. Now the `OnMouseDown` event handler:

   ```
   void OnMouseDown(object sender, MouseButtonEventArgs e) {
      _isDrawing = true;
      _pos = e.GetPosition(_root);
      _root.CaptureMouse();
   }
   ```

8. Next, we'll handle mouse movement, like in the following code snippet:

   ```
   void OnMouseMove(object sender, MouseEventArgs e) {
      if(_isDrawing) {
         Line line = new Line();
         line.X1 = _pos.X;
         line.Y1 = _pos.Y;
         _pos = e.GetPosition(_root);
         line.X2 = _pos.X;
         line.Y2 = _pos.Y;
         line.Stroke = _stroke;
         line.StrokeThickness = 1;
         _root.Children.Add(line);
      }
   }
   ```

9. If we're in drawing mode, we create a `Line` object, set its two points locations and add it to the `Canvas`.
10. Finally, when the mouse button is released, just revert things to normal:

    ```
    void OnMouseUp(object sender, MouseButtonEventArgs e) {
       _isDrawing = false;
       _root.ReleaseMouseCapture();
    }
    ```

11. Run the application. We now have a functional little drawing program. Event handling seemed to be as simple as expected.

12. Let's make it a little more interesting, with the ability to change drawing color. We'll add some rectangle elements in the upper part of the canvas. Clicking any of them should change the drawing brushing from that point on. First, the rectangles:

```
<Rectangle Stroke="Black" Width="25" Height="25"
           Canvas.Left="5" Canvas.Top="5" Fill="Red" />
<Rectangle Stroke="Black"  Width="25" Height="25"
           Canvas.Left="35" Canvas.Top="5" Fill="Blue" />
<Rectangle Stroke="Black" Width="25" Height="25"
           Canvas.Left="65" Canvas.Top="5" Fill="Yellow" />
<Rectangle Stroke="Black" Width="25" Height="25"
           Canvas.Left="95" Canvas.Top="5" Fill="Green" />
<Rectangle Stroke="Black" Width="25" Height="25"
           Canvas.Left="125" Canvas.Top="5" Fill="Black" />
```

13. How should we handle clicks on the rectangles? One obvious way is to attach an event handler to each and every rectangle. But that would we wasteful. Events such as `MouseLeftButtonDown` "bubble up" the visual tree and can be handled at any level. In this case, we'll just add code to the `OnMouseDown` method:

```
void OnMouseDown(object sender, MouseButtonEventArgs e) {
    var rect = e.Source as Rectangle;
    if(rect != null) {
       _stroke = rect.Fill;
    }
    else {
       _isDrawing = true;
       _pos = e.GetPosition(_root);
       _root.CaptureMouse();
    }
}
```

14. Run the application and click the rectangles to change colors. Draw something nice.

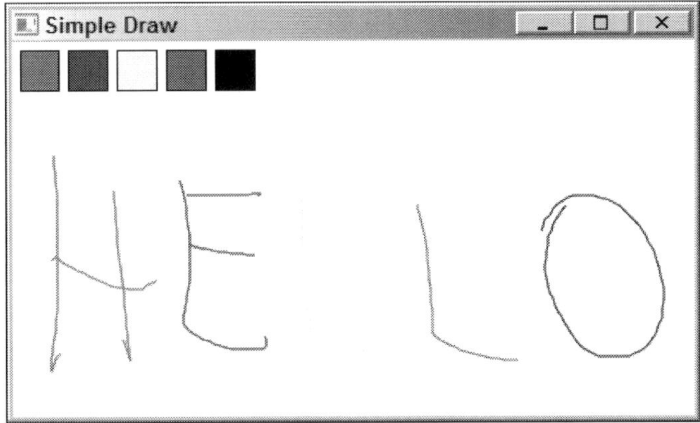

How it works...

WPF events are called **routed events** because most can be handled by elements that are not the source of the event. In the preceding example, the `MouseLeftButtonDown` was handled on the `Canvas` element, even though the actual event may have triggered on a particular `Rectangle` element. This is referred to as a routing strategy of **bubbling**.

When the left mouse button is pressed, we make a note that the drawing has started by setting `_isDrawing` to `true` (step 7). Then, we record the current mouse position relative to the canvas (`_root`) by calling the `MouseButtonEventArgs.GetPosition` method. And finally, although not strictly required, we "capture" the mouse, so that subsequent events will be sent to the `Canvas` and not any other window, even if the mouse pointer technically is not over the `Canvas`.

To properly ascertain which element was actually the source of the event, the `RoutedEventArgs.Source` property should be used (and not the `sender`, in our example the sender is always the `Canvas`).

There's more...

Bubbling is not the only routing strategy WPF supports. The opposite of bubbling is called **tunneling**; events with a tunneling strategy are raised first on the top level element (typically a `Window`), and then on its child, and so on, towards the element that is the actual source of the event. After the tunneling event has finished (calling any handlers along the way), its bubbling counterpart is raised, from the source up the visual tree towards the top level element (window).

A tunneling event always has its name starting with **Preview**. Therefore, there is `PreviewMouseLeftButtonDown` and its bubbling counterpart is simply `MouseLeftButtonDown`.

A third routing strategy is supported, called Direct. This is the simplest strategy; the event is raised on the source element of the event and that's it. No bubbling or tunnelling occurs. By the way, only very few events use the Direct strategy (for example, `MouseEnter` and `MouseLeave`).

Stopping bubbling or tunneling

After a bubbling event is handled by some element - it continues to bubble. The bubbling can be stopped by setting the `RoutedEventArgs.Handled` property to true.

If the event is a tunneling one - setting `Handled` to `true` stops the tunneling, but it also prevents the buddy-bubbling event from ever firing.

Attached events

Suppose we want to write a simple calculator application:

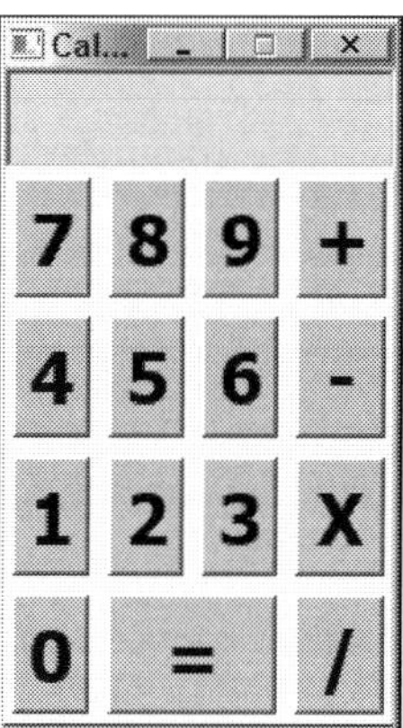

This is a `Grid` that contains various `Button` controls.

We would like to use as few handlers as we can. For the "=" button, we can attach a specific handler and prevent further bubbling:

```
void OnCalculate(object sender, RoutedEventArgs e) {
   // do operation
   e.Handled = true;

}
```

What about the digit buttons? Again, we could add a click handler to each one, but that would be wasteful. A better approach would be to leverage the `Click` event's bubbling strategy and set a single handler on the container `Grid`.

Typing **"Click="** on the `Grid` tag seems to fail. Intellisense won't help and in fact this won't compile. It may be obvious - a `Grid` has no `Click` event. `Click` is specific to buttons. Does this mean we can't set a `Click` handler on the `Grid`? Fortunately, we can.

WPF provides the notion of attached events. Such events can be handled by any element, even if that element's type does not define any such event. This is achieved through attached event syntax (similar to attached properties), such as the following code snippet:

```
<Grid ButtonBase.Click="OnKeyPressed">
```

The `Click` event is defined on the `ButtonBase` class, although `Button.Click` works just as well, because `Button` inherits from `ButtonBase`. Now we can look at the actual source of the click with the same `RoutedEventArgs.Source` described previously:

```
int digit;
string content = ((Button)e.Source).Content.ToString();
if(int.TryParse(content, out digit)) {
   // a digit
}
```

You can find the complete calculator sample in the `CH01.Calculator` project, available with the downloadable source for this chapter.

2

Resources

In this chapter we will cover:

- Using logical resources
- Dynamically binding to a logical resource
- Using user selected colors and fonts
- Using binary resources
- Accessing binary resources in code
- Accessing binary resources from another assembly
- Managing logical resources

Introduction

Traditional application resources consist of binary chunks of data, typically representing things such as icons, bitmaps, strings, and XML. In fact, the .NET framework provides generic support for these through the `ResourceManager` class.

WPF is no different—binary resources play an important role in a typical application. However, WPF goes a lot further with another kind of resource: **logical resources**. These are objects, any objects, which can be shared and used in a multitude of locations throughout the application; they can even be accessed across assemblies. Some of WPF's features, such as implicit (automatic) styles and type-based data templates, rely on the logical resources system.

In this chapter, we'll take a look at resources, binary and logical, their definition, and usage in XAML and code, and discuss various options and typical scenarios, such as combining resources (even across assemblies) and resource lookup and modifications.

Using logical resources

WPF introduces the concept of logical resources, objects that can be shared (and reused) across some part of a visual tree or an entire application. Logical resources can be anything, from WPF objects such as brushes, geometries, or styles, to other objects defined by the .NET Framework or the developer, such as `string`, `List<>`, or some custom typed object. This gives a whole new meaning to the term *resources*. These objects are typically placed inside a `ResourceDictionary` and located at runtime using a hierarchical search, as demonstrated in this recipe.

Getting ready

Make sure Visual Studio is up and running.

How to do it...

We'll create a simple application that demonstrates creating and using logical resources:

1. Create a new WPF Application named `CH02.SimpleResources`.
2. Open `MainWindow.xaml` and replace the `Grid` element with a `StackPanel`.
3. Add a `Rectangle` element to the `StackPanel`, as shown in the following code snippet:

    ```
    <Rectangle Height="100" Stroke="Black">
        <Rectangle.Fill>
            <LinearGradientBrush>
                <GradientStop Offset="0" Color="Yellow" />
                <GradientStop Offset="1" Color="Brown" />
            </LinearGradientBrush>
        </Rectangle.Fill>
    </Rectangle>
    ```

4. Now we want to add an `Ellipse` element, whose `Stroke` is the same as the previous `LinearGradientBrush`. One way to do that is to simply make a copy:

    ```
    <Ellipse StrokeThickness="20" Height="100">
        <Ellipse.Stroke>
            <LinearGradientBrush>
                <GradientStop Offset="0" Color="Yellow" />
                <GradientStop Offset="1" Color="Brown" />
            </LinearGradientBrush>
        </Ellipse.Stroke>
    </Ellipse>
    ```

This is wasteful – duplication of code causes a maintenance headache (and eventually a nightmare). More subtly, two brushes are created instead of one. Using a logical resource can solve this. Cut the `LinearGradientBrush` tag and paste it into the `Resources` property of the Window, as follows:

```
<Window.Resources>
    <LinearGradientBrush x:Key="brush1">
        <GradientStop Offset="0" Color="Yellow" />
        <GradientStop Offset="1" Color="Brown" />
    </LinearGradientBrush>
</Window.Resources>
```

The `Resources` property is a dictionary, so a key must be provided using the `x:Key` XAML attribute.

5. To use the brush in XAML, we need the `StaticResource` markup extension. Here's the revised markup for the rectangle and ellipse:

```
<Rectangle Height="100" Stroke="Black"
            Fill="{StaticResource brush1}" />
<Ellipse StrokeThickness="20" Height="100"
            Stroke="{StaticResource brush1}" />
```

6. Running the application shows the following:

How it works...

Every element (deriving from `FrameworkElement`) has a `Resources` property of type `ResourceDictionary`. This means that every element can have resources associated with it. In XAML, the `x:Key` attribute must be specified (most of the time; exceptions to this rule will be discussed in relation to styles and data templates). The preceding defined resource looks as follows inside the `Resources` collection of the `Window`:

```
<Window.Resources>
    <LinearGradientBrush x:Key="brush1">
        <GradientStop Offset="0" Color="Yellow" />
```

```
        <GradientStop Offset="1" Color="Brown" />
    </LinearGradientBrush>
</Window.Resources>
```

Using this resource in XAML requires the `StaticResource` markup extension (the "static" part will become clear after the next recipe, *Dynamically binding to a logical resource*) with the resource key provided:

```
<Rectangle Fill="{StaticResource brush1}" />
```

This causes a search from the current element (the `Rectangle`) up the element tree, looking for a resource with the key `brush1`; if found, its associated object is used as the property's value. If not found on any element up to the root `Window`, the search continues within the resources of `Application` (typically located in the `App.xaml` file). If not found even there, a runtime exception is thrown. This is depicted in the following diagram:

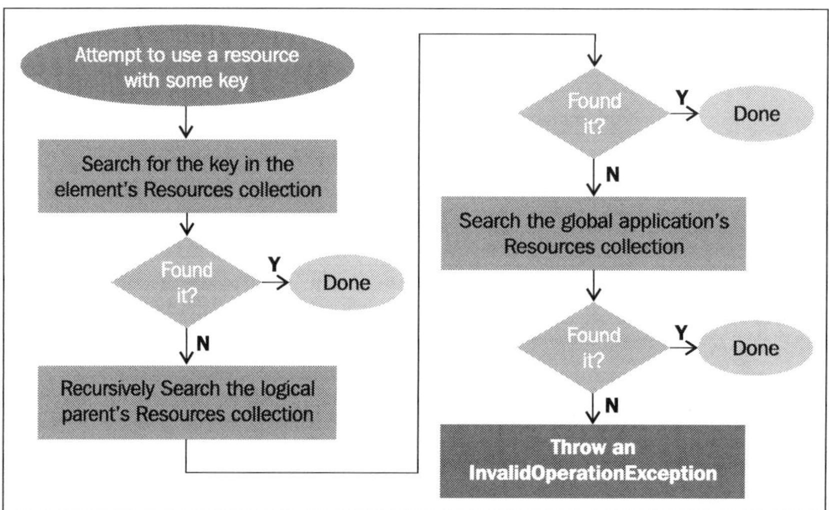

There's more...

The same lookup effect can be achieved in code by using the `FrameworkElement.FindResource` method, as follows:

```
Brush brush = (Brush)x.FindResource("brush1");
```

This has the same effect as using {StaticResource}. If an exception is undesirable in case of a non-existent resource, the TryFindResource can be used instead:

```
Brush brush = (Brush)x.TryFindResource("brush1");
if(brush == null) {    // not found
}
```

This method returns null if the specified resource does not exist.

A resource can also be directly accessed using an indexer, provided we know on which object it's actually defined. In our example, the brush is defined on the resources of Window, so can be accessed directly as follows:

```
Brush brush = (Brush)this.Resources["brush1"];
```

Adding or deleting resources dynamically

The Resources dictionary can be manipulated at runtime, by adding or removing resources. Here's how to add a new resource:

```
this.Resources.Add("brush2", new SolidColorBrush(
   Color.FromRgb(200, 10, 150)));
```

This adds a new resource (a Brush) to the Window's resources collection. Later, calls to FindResource can locate the new resource. A resource can be removed as well:

```
this.Resources.Remove("brush1");
```

It's important to realize that any object bound to the resource with {StaticResource} does not *lose* the resource in any way—it's still being referenced by it. However, future FindResource calls will fail to find that resource.

Modifying resources

All {StaticResource} (or FindResource) lookups with a specific key use the same object instance. This means that modifying the resource properties (not replacing the resource with a different one), impacts automatically all properties using that resource.

For example, if we modify the brush resource as follows:

```
var brush = (LinearGradientBrush)this.Resources["brush1"];
brush.GradientStops.Add(new GradientStop(Colors.Blue, .5));
```

This causes immediate changes to the output:

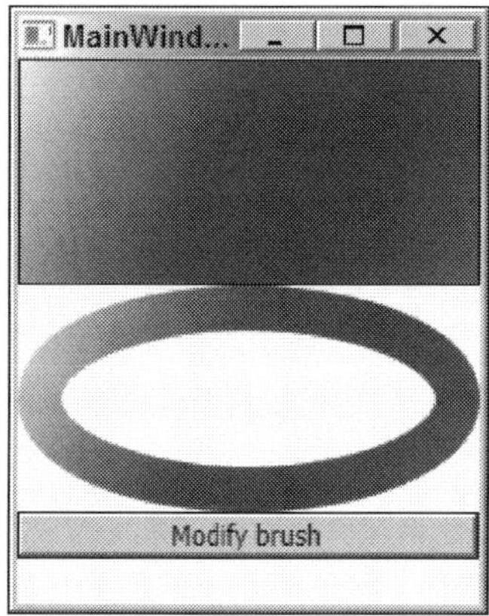

Resources that use other resources

A resource can use (as part of its definition) another resource. Here's an example:

```
<LinearGradientBrush x:Key="brush3">
    <GradientStop Offset="0" Color="Red" />
    <GradientStop Offset="1" Color="Orange" />
</LinearGradientBrush>
<DataTemplate x:Key="temp1">
    <Rectangle Fill="{StaticResource brush3}"
               StrokeThickness="4" Stroke="DarkBlue" />
</DataTemplate>
```

The `Rectangle` inside the `DataTemplate` uses the `LinearGradientBrush` defined just above it. The important point is that the resource, `brush3` must be declared before referencing it using `{StaticResource}`; this is due to the way the XAML parser hunts down resources.

Non-shared resources

Resources are shared by default, meaning there's only one instance created no matter how many lookups exist for that resource. Sometimes it's useful to get new instances for every lookup of a particular resource. To do that, we can add the attribute `x:Shared="False"` in defining the resource. Note there's no intellisense for that, but it works.

Other locations for resources

Elements are not the only objects that have the `Resources` property (a `ResourceDictionary`). Other objects that are not elements may have them as well. The canonical example is the template types (deriving from `FrameworkTemplate`): `DataTemplate`, `ControlTemplate`, and `ItemsPanelTemplate`. They can have resources that are available when those templates are used (the exact way this works will be explained in *Chapter 6, Data Binding*, and *Chapter 8, Style, Triggers, and Control Templates*, where templates are discussed).

Dynamically binding to a logical resource

As we saw in the previous recipe, *Using logical resources*, binding to a resource is achieved in XAML by using the `StaticResource` markup extension. But what happens if we replace a specific resource? Would that be reflected in all objects using the resource? And if not, can we bind to the resource dynamically?

Getting ready

Make a copy of the previous recipe project `CH02.SimpleResources`, or create a new project named `CH02.DynamicVsStatic` and copy the Window XAML contents from the previous project to the new one.

How to do it...

We'll replace `StaticResource` with `DynamicResource` and see the effect:

1. Open `MainWindow.xaml`. Add a button to the end of the `StackPanel` labeled **Replace brush** and connect it to an event handler named `OnReplaceBrush`. This is the added markup:

   ```
   <Button Content="Replace brush"
      Click="OnReplaceBrush" />
   ```

2. In the event handler, we'll replace the brush resource named `brush1` with a completely new brush:

   ```
   void OnReplaceBrush(object sender, RoutedEventArgs e) {
      var brush = new RadialGradientBrush();
      brush.GradientStops.Add(new GradientStop(Colors.Blue, 0));
      brush.GradientStops.Add(new GradientStop(Colors.White, 1));
      this.Resources["brush1"] = brush;
   }
   ```

3. Run the application and click on the button. You'll notice nothing happens. Now change the `StaticResource` markup extension to `DynamicResource` on the `Rectangle`:

```
<Rectangle Height="100" Stroke="Black"
           Fill="{DynamicResource brush1}" />
```

4. Now run the application and click on the button. You'll see the `Fill` property of `Rectangle` has changed to the new resource value:

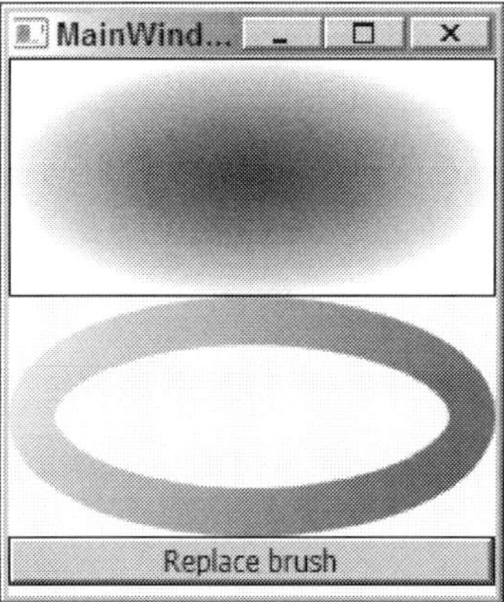

How it works...

The `DynamicResource` markup extension binds to a resource dynamically, which means that if the object itself is replaced with a new object (with the same key), the new resource is used. `StaticResource` bound properties keep referencing the *old* object.

This dynamic behavior allows for interesting effects. For instance, *themes* can be changed by swapping resources as long as the keys are the same.

There's more...

The `StaticResource` markup extension causes binding to the resource to occur at construction time (in the call to `InitializeComponent` of the `Window`). `DynamicResource`, on the other hand, is only bound when actually needed. This means that `DynamicResource` is a bit faster at `Window` load time, while consuming (naturally) more resources, as it needs to be notified when the resource is replaced.

Also, `DynamicResource` does not throw an exception if the key does not exist. If that key appears later, it will bind to the resource correctly.

`StaticResource` should be used most of the time unless there is a need to replace resources on the fly, in which case `DynamicResource` should be used.

Using user-selected colors and fonts

Sometimes it's useful to use one of the selected colors or fonts the user has chosen in the Windows **Control Panel Personalization** applet (or the older **Display Settings** in Windows XP), such as **Window caption**, **Desktop color**, and **Selection color**. Furthermore, an application may want to react dynamically to changes in those values. This can be achieved by accessing special resource keys within the `SystemColors` and `SystemFonts` classes.

Getting ready

Make sure Visual Studio is up and running. Go to the **Control Panel Personalization** applet and change the theme to **Classic**. This will make it easy to see the dynamic changes when colors of fonts change.

How to do it...

We'll create an application that uses some user-selected color and font, and reacts automatically to changes in those:

1. Create a new WPF Application named `CH02.UserSelectedColorsFonts`.
2. Open `MainWindow.xaml`. Add two rows to the grid.
3. Add a `Rectangle` covering the first row and a `TextBlock` in the lower row. The entire markup should look as follows:

```
<Grid>
    <Grid.RowDefinitions>
        <RowDefinition />
        <RowDefinition Height="Auto" />
    </Grid.RowDefinitions>
    <Rectangle Margin="10" />
    <TextBlock Grid.Row="1"
            Text="Hello from Active Caption Font"
    />
</Grid>
```

4. We want the rectangle filled with the color of the desktop as selected by the user in **Control Panel**. Add the following markup for the `Fill` rectangle property:

```
Fill="{DynamicResource {x:Static SystemColors.DesktopBrushKey}}"
```

5. The fill color should turn to the one set in **Control Panel | Personalization**. Now let's set the font family and font size to those for the window caption as defined in **Control Panel**. Add the following markup within the `TextBlock`:

```
FontFamily="{DynamicResource {x:Static SystemFonts.
CaptionFontFamilyKey}}"
FontSize="{DynamicResource {x:Static SystemFonts.
CaptionFontSizeKey}}"/>
```

6. Run the application. This is how it may look (yours may be different depending on the settings in **Control Panel**):

7. Let's check if this is, in fact, dynamic. Open **Control Panel** and find the **Personalization** applet (you may need to show all control panel items before you can locate it):

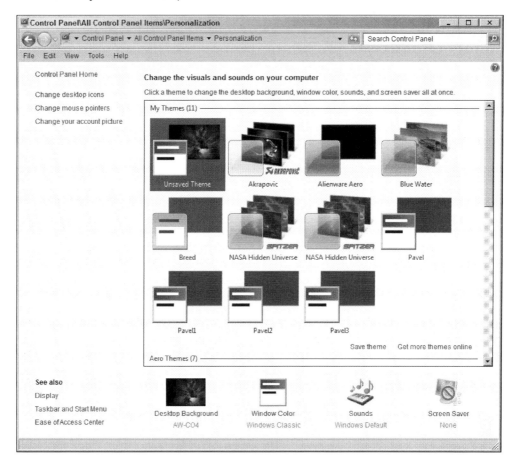

8. Select **Window Color** at the bottom of the window:

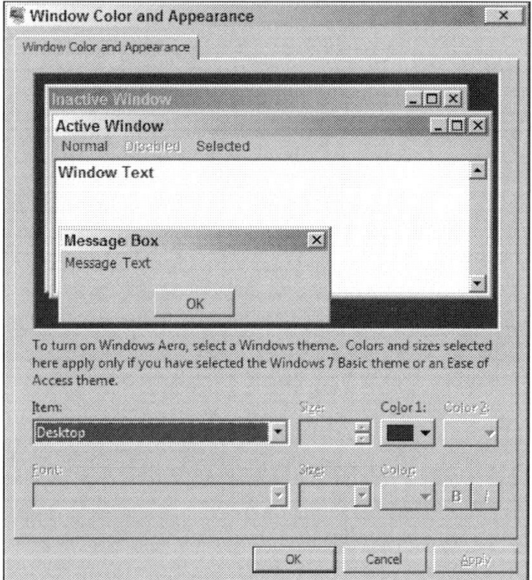

9. Change the desktop color to something else, and click on **Apply**:

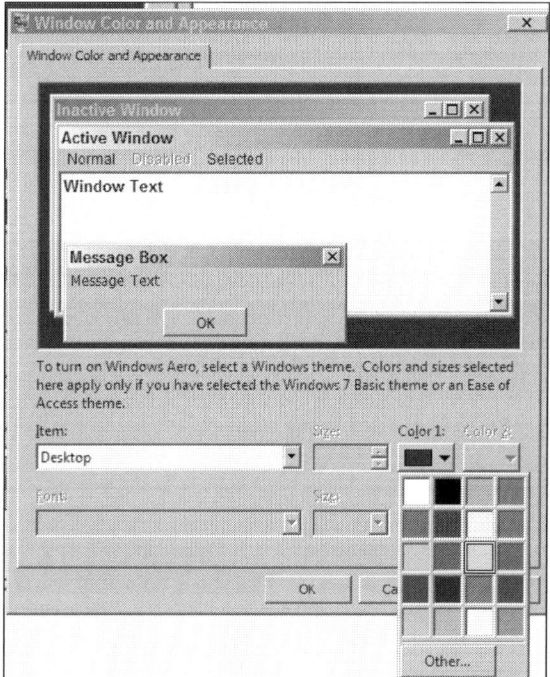

10. Note the rectangle fill is immediately updated without the need to restart the application:

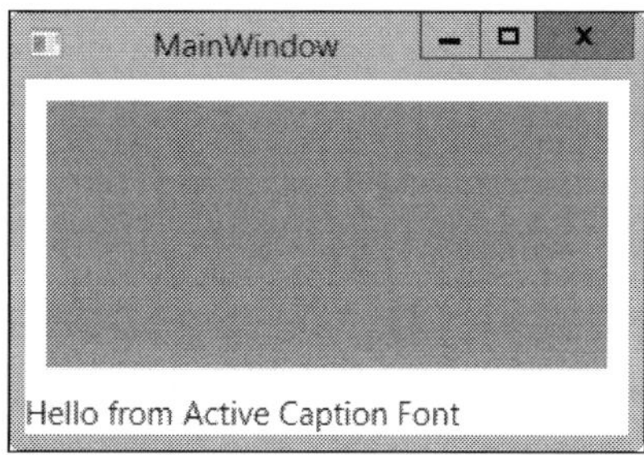

How it works...

The resource key supplied as part of an entry in a `ResourceDictionary` need not be a string. In fact, it's typed as an object. The following piece of XAML indicates that the key to a `DynamicResource` is a static property named `SystemColors.DesktopBrushKey`:

```
Fill="{DynamicResource {x:Static SystemColors.DesktopBrushKey}}"
```

Looking at this property reveals it's type as `ResourceKey`, which is an abstract class, so this must be something that derives from it (the exact type is not important, it's internal to the `PresentationFramework` assembly).

This means that this key object can do whatever is necessary behind the scenes, to be notified of changes in the system colors and reflect those changes back through the *standard way* when using a `DynamicResource`.

The font properties use the same idea. There are static properties ending with "Key" for every setting the user can change via the **Personalization** dialog. A similar class, `SystemParameters`, contains a bunch of other general properties (with a "Key" suffix), that may be changed (some via the **Personalization** dialog, some with code only). An example is `SystemParameters.CaptionHeightKey`, which indicates the current standard height of a caption of a window. This can help (for example) when constructing our own window "template" (meaning it doesn't have to look like a standard window); we may want to use some of these key properties to make our window unique on the one hand, but still have consistent (for example) caption height. We'll see an example of that in *Chapter 5, Application and Windows*.

There's more...

The aforementioned classes, `SystemColors`, `SystemFonts`, and `SystemParameters` expose the current values of the various properties as regular static properties. This means we could have used the following line to get the current brush color of the desktop:

```
Fill="{x:Static SystemColors.DesktopBrush}"
```

Although this is much simpler, and appears to work, it is not dynamic. This means the value is read at runtime, when the XAML is parsed (typically, when the window is constructed), but will remain with that value until that window is recreated (typically, when the application is restarted).

The advantage of this scheme (apart from its simplicity) is that it's lighter; WPF does not have to *monitor* that color for changes. This may suffice in scenarios when immediate response to colors/fonts/metrics changes is not necessary (and is probably unlikely to happen anyway).

Using binary resources

Binary resources are just that: chunks of bytes that typically mean something to the application, such as image or font files. In this recipe, we'll cover the basics of adding and using a binary resource.

Getting ready

Make sure Visual Studio is up and running.

How to do it...

We'll create a simple application that uses an image file added as a binary resource:

1. Create a new WPF Application named `CH02.BinaryResources`.
2. Let's add a logical images folder to the project. Right-click the project node in **Solution Explorer**, and select **Add | New Folder**.

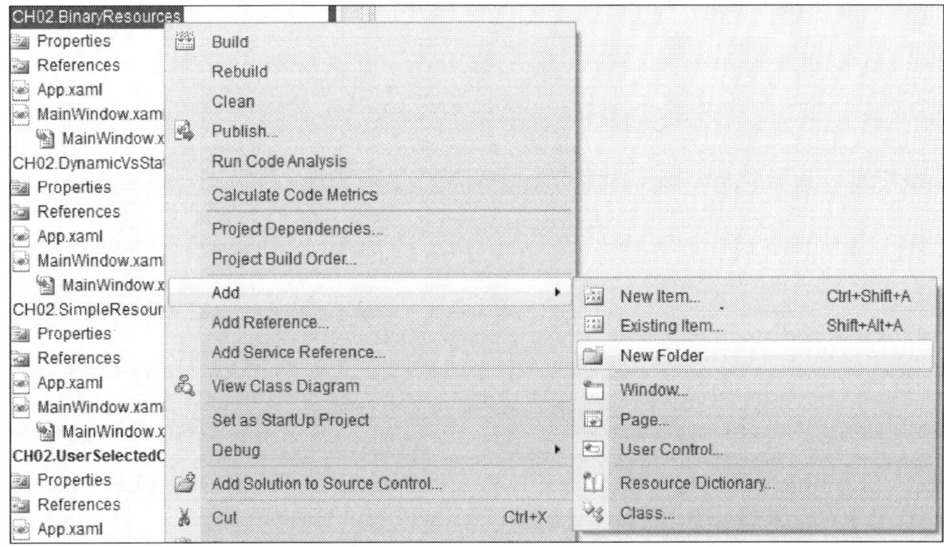

3. The folder is created as `NewFolder1`. Change its name to `Images`.
4. Right-click on the newly created **Images** folder, and select **Add** | **Existing Item...**:

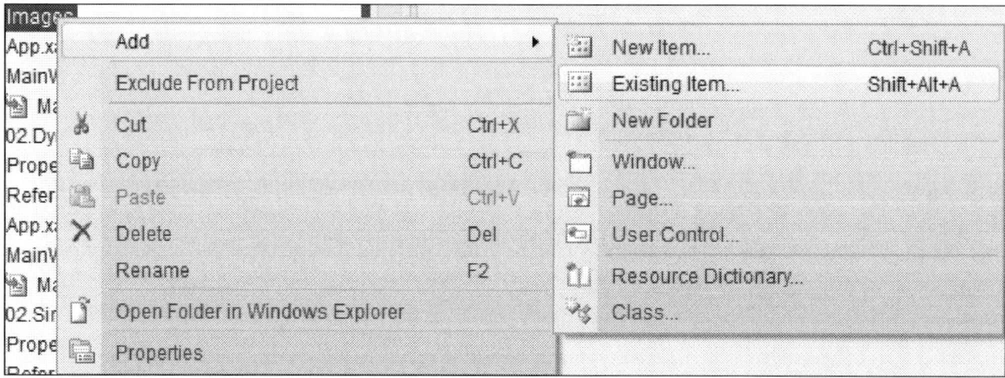

5. Navigate to some image file on your system (don't forget to change the file type filter to **Image files** at the bottom of the open file dialog box). I've used `apple.png` (found in the downloadable source for this chapter), but any image will do, preferably no larger than 48 x 48 pixels. The solution explorer should look something as follows:

6. Right-click on the newly added file and select **Properties**:

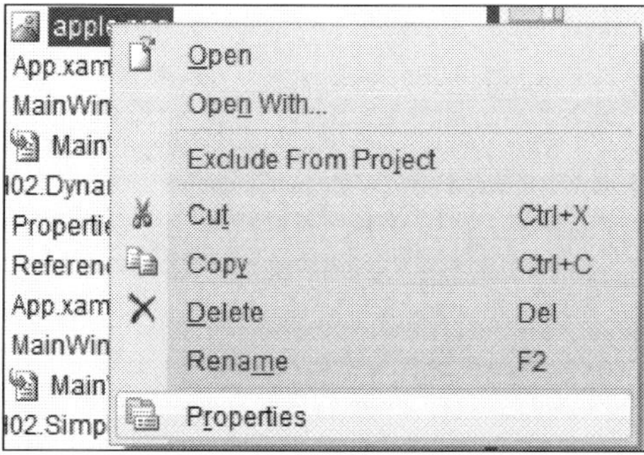

7. In the **Properties** windows, make sure the **Build Action** is set to **Resource**:

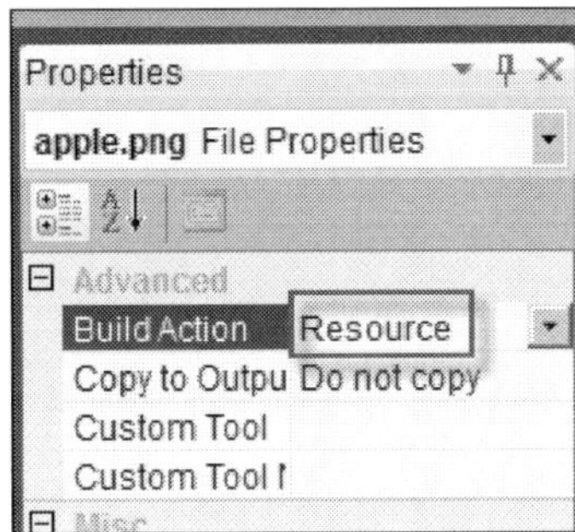

8. Open `MainWindow.xaml`, and replace the `Grid` panel with a `StackPanel`.
9. Add a `Button` control with the following markup:

```
<Button Margin="10" HorizontalAlignment="Center" Padding="4">
   <StackPanel Orientation="Horizontal">
      <Image Source="Images/apple.png" />
      <TextBlock VerticalAlignment="Center" Margin="10,0,0,0"
          FontSize="16" Text="Click me, please!" />
   </StackPanel>
</Button>
```

10. If the image you selected is large, change the `Image` element's `Width` and `Height` properties to something like 32 x 32 units.
11. Notice the button shows in the designer with the selected image and text. Running the application produces the following output:

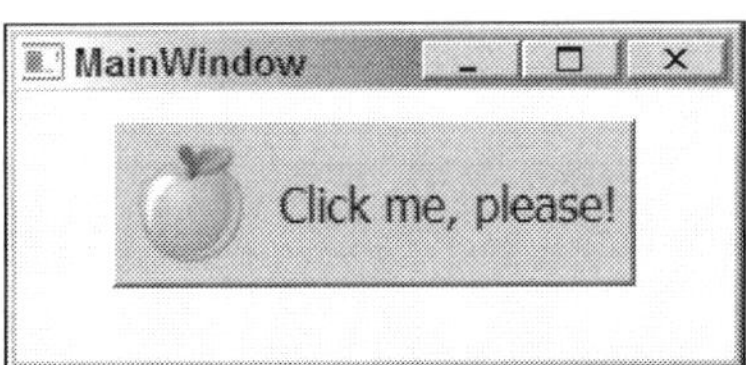

12. Add another image to the `Images` folder, such as `Jellyfish.jpg` from the `{My Pictures}\Sample Pictures` folder.
13. Right-click on the newly added image and select **Properties**.
14. Change the **Build Action** to **Content**.

15. Change the **Copy to Output Directory** property to **Copy if newer**:

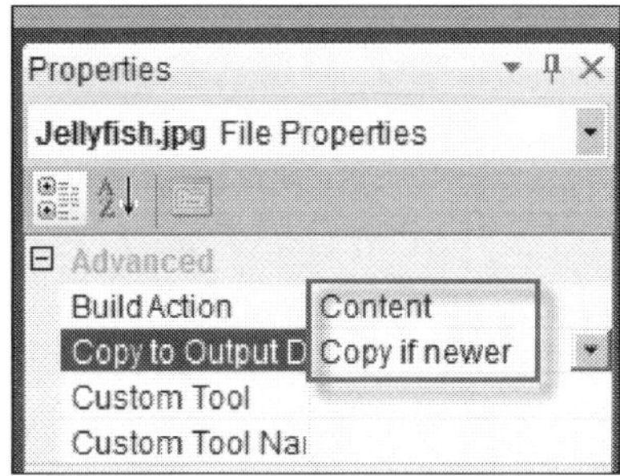

16. Add a property markup for the `Window.Background` property as follows:

```
<Window.Background>
    <ImageBrush ImageSource="Images/jellyfish.jpg" />
</Window.Background>
```

17. Run the application. You should see the window background turning into a jellyfish image:

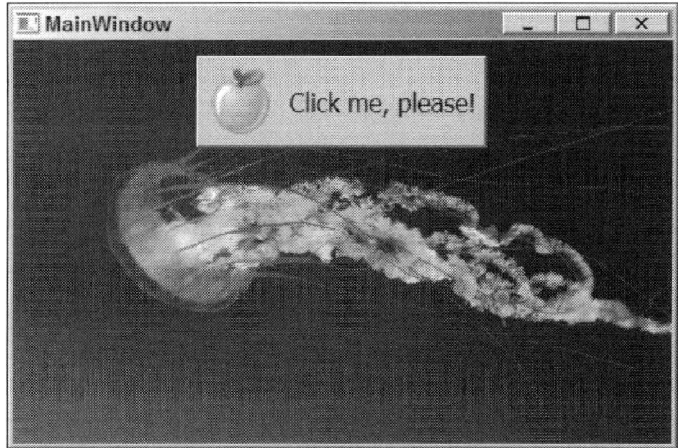

18. Close the application.
19. Right-click on the project node in **Solution Explorer** and select **Open Folder in Windows Explorer**:

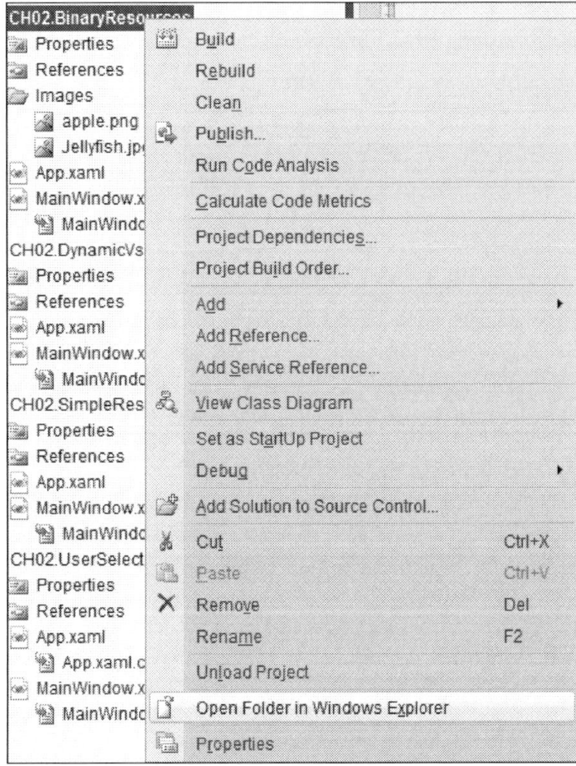

20. Navigate to the `Bin\Debug\Images` subfolder. Note the `Jellyfish.jpg` file.
21. Delete the file.
22. Copy the file `desert.jpg` from the `{My Pictures}\Sample Pictures` folder (or some other image to the currently open folder).
23. Rename the file to `Jellyfish.jpg`:

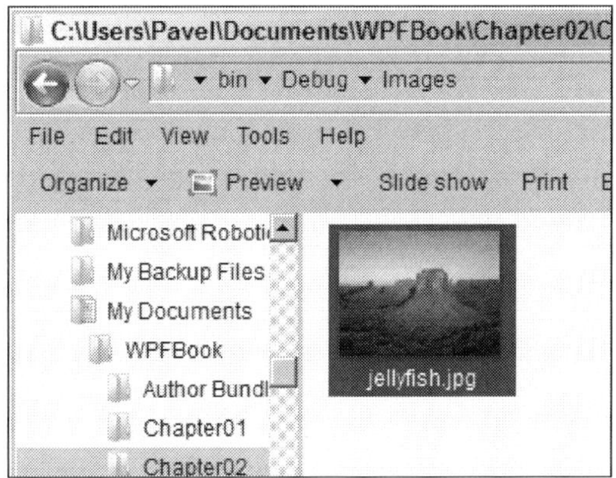

24. Navigate back to the `Debug` folder and run the application directly from Windows Explorer (without doing any rebuilding).
25. You should see the window background as the desert image instead of a jellyfish:

26. Try the same approach on the `apple.png` file stored in the main project folder under `Images`. Note that running the application from Windows Explorer (without rebuilding) does not change the image.

How it works...

The first added binary resource (the image file) is stored as a resource inside the compiled assembly. This is because the **Build Action** was set to **Resource** on the image. This makes the actual image file unnecessary when deploying the application.

These resources are part of the assembly and are stored in a resource named `MyApplication.g.resources`, where `MyApplication` is the name of the assembly. Here's a snapshot from .NET Reflector:

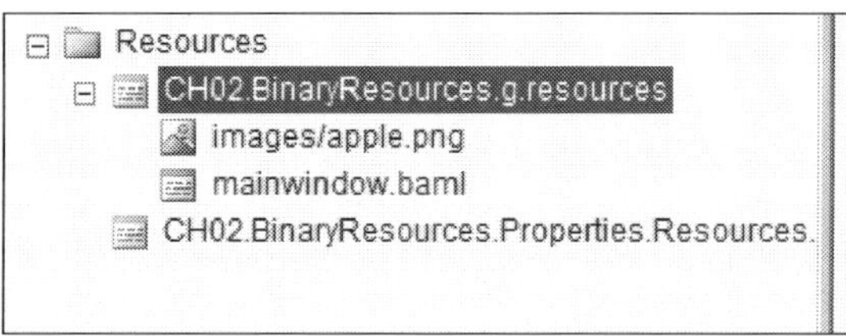

Accessing the resource in XAML can be done in several ways. In the previous example, an `Image` was used with the `Source` property set to the relative URI of the image (`Images/apple.png`). This works because the `Source` property (of type `ImageSource`) has an appropriate type converter. This relative URI can also be used in code, as follows:

```
_image.Source = new BitmapImage(
  new Uri("Images/apple.png", UriKind.Relative));
```

When the **Build Action** is set to **Content** (as in the jellyfish example), the resource is not included in the assembly. This makes it more appropriate when the resource needs to change often (perhaps by a designer) and a rebuild would be undesirable. Also, if the resource is large, and not always needed, it's better to leave it off to the resulting assembly. Note that to access the resource, the exact same syntax is used. This is possible because WPF adds the `AssemblyAssociatedContentFile` attribute to the assembly, specifying the name of the resource file. Here's a view with .NET Reflector:

```
[assembly: AssemblyConfiguration("")]
[assembly: CompilationRelaxations(8)]
[assembly: AssemblyAssociatedContentFile("images/jellyfish.jpg")]
[assembly: TargetFramework(".NETFramework,Version=v4.0,Profile=Client",
[assembly: AssemblyTitle("CH02.BinaryResources")]
[assembly: AssemblyCompany("")]
```

That's why we were able to replace the jellyfish image with a desert image and get it to show correctly given the name `jellyfish.jpg` without doing any kind of rebuilding.

There's more...

The relative URI is actually a shortcut to a more elaborate (and complete) URI scheme, called pack URI. The following markup:

```
Source="Images/apple.png"
```

Is equivalent to this (more verbose) markup:

```
Source="pack://application:,,,/Images/apple.png"
```

This seems to add no value, but is actually necessary in other cases where no nice type converter exists.

The pack URI scheme is borrowed from the **XML Paper Specification** (**XPS**), and the strange three commas are not optional values with some defaults, but rather escaped slashes. The reason is that this is a URI embedded inside another URI, so some disambiguation is required. You can find more information on pack URIs in the MSDN docs at `http://msdn.microsoft.com/EN-US/library/aa970069(VS.110).aspx`. We'll see examples of usage of this scheme in later recipes.

Embedded Resource

The **Build Action** options include something called **Embedded Resource**. Although resources are embedded by definition, this setting cannot be used with WPF and should be avoided.

Accessing binary resources in code

Accessing a binary resource in XAML is pretty straightforward, but this works for standard resources such as images. Other types of resources may be used in code, and this requires a different approach.

Getting ready

Make sure Visual Studio is up and running.

How to do it...

We'll create an application that shows book information read programmatically from an XML file stored as a resource:

1. Create a new WPF Application named `CH02.BinaryResourcesInCode`.
2. Add the `books.xml` (found in the downloadable source for this chapter) file as a resource (make sure **Build Action** is set to **Resource**). As an alternative, you can create the file yourself and type its contents as shown in the next step.
3. The `books.xml` file looks something like the following:

```
<Books>
   <Book Name="Windows Internals" Author="Mark Russinovich" />
   <Book Name="Essential COM" Author="Don Box" />
   <Book Name="Programming Windows with MFC"
         Author="Jeff Prosise" />
</Books>
```

4. Open `MainWindow.xaml`. Add two rows to the `Grid` with a `TextBox` and a `Button`:

```
<Grid>
    <Grid.RowDefinitions>
        <RowDefinition Height="Auto" />
        <RowDefinition />
    </Grid.RowDefinitions>
    <Button Content="Read Book Data" FontSize="14" />
    <TextBox Grid.Row="1" IsReadOnly="True" x:Name="_text"
             FontSize="16" Margin="4"/>
</Grid>
```

5. Add a `Click` event handler to the button.

6. Inside the `Click` event handler, we want to get to the `books.xml` resource. Add the following code:

```
var info = Application.GetResourceStream(new Uri("books.xml",
    UriKind.Relative));
```

7. This returns a `StreamResourceInfo`. Now we can access the `Stream` property and use it in any way we want. Here's an example (you'll need to add a `using System.Xml.Linq` statement):

```
var books = XElement.Load(info.Stream);
var bookList = from book in books.Elements("Book")
               orderby (string)book.Attribute("Author")
               select new {
                  Name = (string)book.Attribute("Name"),
                  Author = (string)book.Attribute("Author")
               };
foreach(var book in bookList)
   _text.Text += book.ToString() + Environment.NewLine;
```

8. Running the application and clicking the button produces the following:

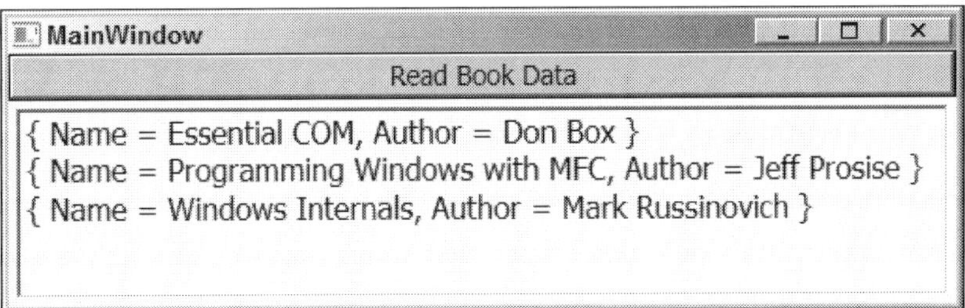

How it works...

The `Application.GetResourceStream` static method provides a programmatic way of accessing a resource using its relative URI (or absolute with the pack scheme). It returns a `StreamResourceInfo` object, which contains two properties: `ContentType` returns the MIME type (such as `image/jpeg` or `text/xml`) and, more importantly, the `Stream` property which provides access to the actual binary data.

If the resource has been marked with a **Build Action** of **Content**, then the similar looking `Application.GetContentStream` method should be used instead.

In the previous example, we've used the `XElement` class (from the relatively new LINQ to XML API) to turn the binary data into a `XElement` object. Then we use that object to query and display some data.

There's more...

There's actually another way to get to a resource while using core .NET types such as `ResourceManager` and `ResourceSet` (that have been around since .NET 1.0) instead of calling `Application.GetResourceStream`. Here's one way to get the `Stream` of a resource:

```
Stream GetResourceStream(string name) {
   string asmName = Assembly.GetExecutingAssembly().GetName().Name;
   var rm = new ResourceManager(asmName + ".g",
       Assembly.GetExecutingAssembly());
         using(var set = rm.GetResourceSet(
            CultureInfo.CurrentCulture, true, true)) {
      return (Stream)set.GetObject(name, true);
   }
}
```

This just shows that WPF has no special support for binary resources and in fact it leverages core .NET functionality in this regard.

Note that there's no counterpart for a resource on which **Build Action** was set to **Content**.

Accessing binary resources from another assembly

Sometimes binary resources are defined in one assembly (typically a class library), but are needed in another assembly (another class library or an executable). WPF provides a uniform and consistent way of accessing these resources using the pack URI scheme. Let's see how to do this.

Getting ready

Make sure Visual Studio is up and running.

How to do it...

We'll create two assemblies—one that holds resources, and another that needs to use those resources:

1. Create a new blank solution by selecting **File** | **New Project** from the main menu and then navigating to **Other Project Types** | **Visual Studio Solutions**. Name it `BinaryResourceAccess`:

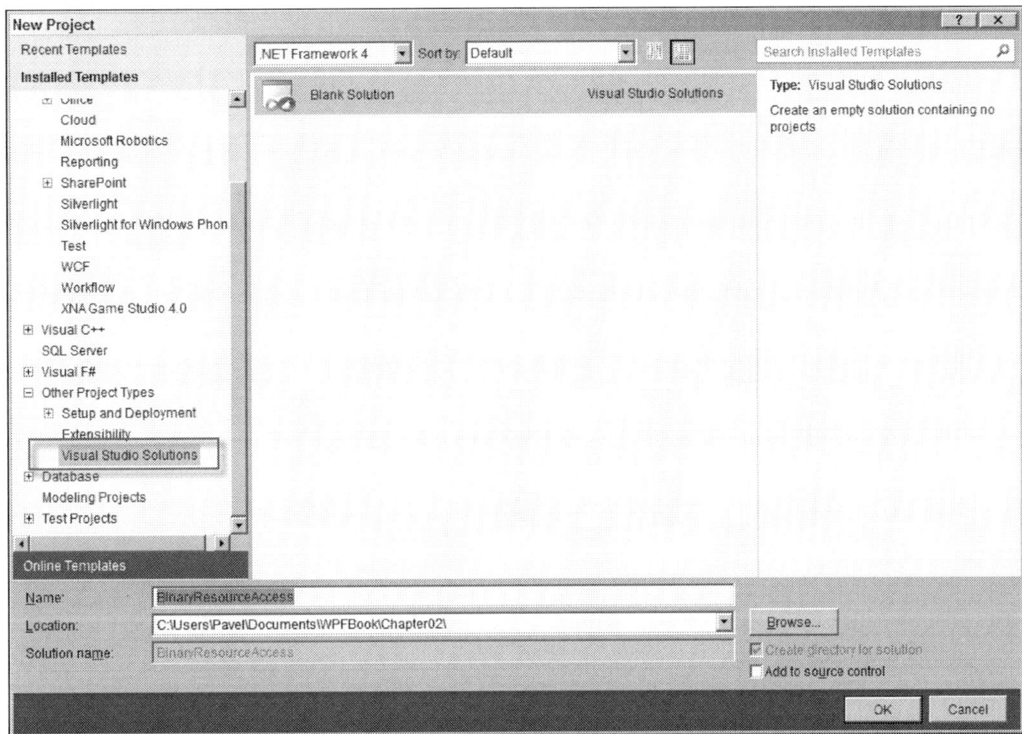

2. Right-click on the **Solution** node in **Solution explorer**, and select **Add | New Project...**:

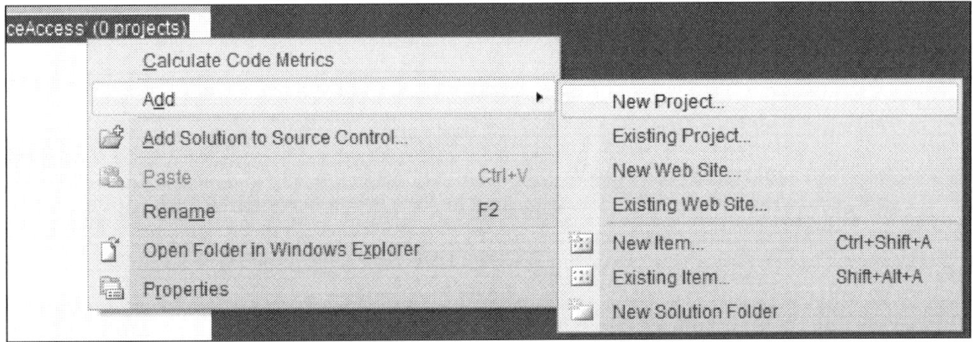

3. Select a **WPF User Control Library** project and name it `CH02.ClassLibraryResources`:

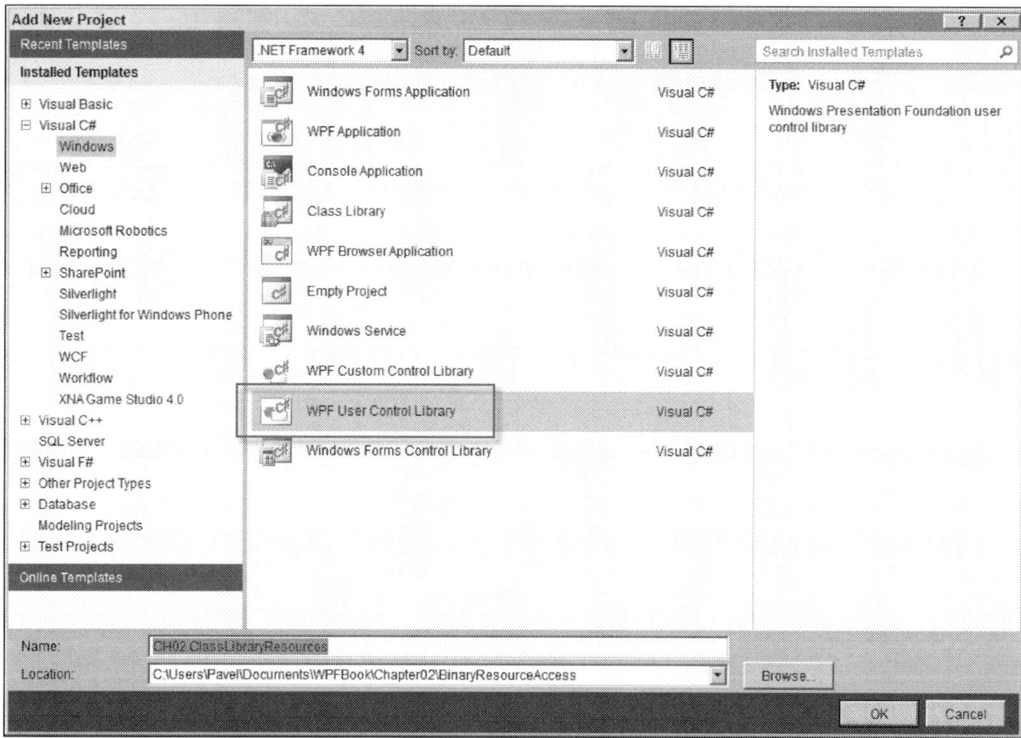

4. We're not going to actually use any user controls, but this is a simple way to create a class library with WPF references already included.
5. Delete the `UserControl1.xaml` file from the **Solution explorer**, as it's not needed.
6. Add a new folder to the project, named `Images`.
7. Add some image to the resulting folder, such as `apple.png` used in the recipe *Using logical resources*. Make sure its **Build Action** is set to **Resource**. The solution should look something like the following:

8. Right-click on the solution node and select **Add** | **New Project...**
9. Select a **WPF Application** and name it `CH02.UsingLibraryResources`.
10. Right-click on the **References** node in this new project in the **Solution explorer**, and select **Add Reference...**:

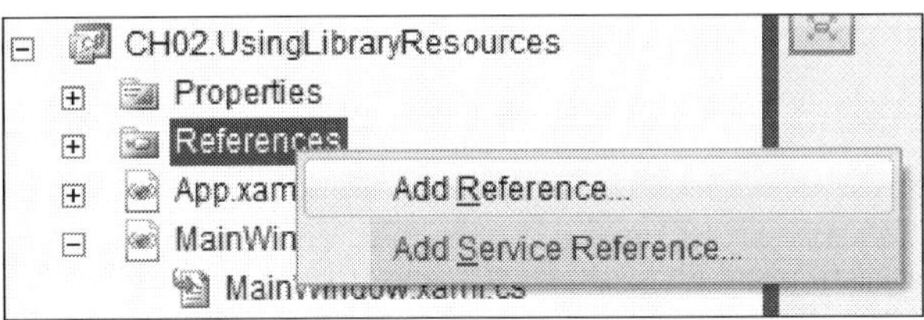

11. In the **Add Reference** dialog, click on the **Projects** tab and select the `CH02.ClassLibraryResources` project.
12. Open `MainWindow.xaml`. Create a two row `Grid` with the following markup:

```
<Grid>
    <Grid.RowDefinitions>
        <RowDefinition Height="Auto" />
        <RowDefinition />
    </Grid.RowDefinitions>
</Grid>
```

13. Add a `Button` to the `Grid` whose content is an `Image`, and a `TextBlock`. The image should point to the image file added to the class library project:

```
<Button HorizontalAlignment="Center" Margin="4" Padding="6">
   <StackPanel Orientation="Horizontal">
      <Image Source="/CH02.ClassLibraryResources;component/Images/
apple.png" />
      <TextBlock VerticalAlignment="Center" FontSize="14"
                 Text="Click me!" Margin="10,0,0,0" />
   </StackPanel>
</Button>
```

14. The image should show up in the designer preview. Running the application should also show the image correctly:

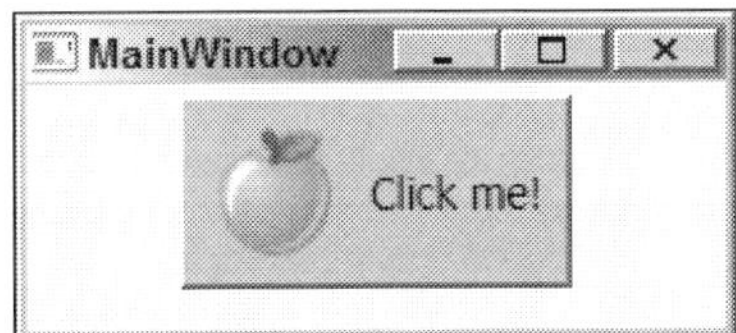

How it works...

WPF recognizes a pack URI to a referenced assembly in the form:

```
/AssemblyReference;component/ResourceName
```

Here, `AssemblyReference` may be a simple name (as in our example), but may also include a version (with a "v" prefix) and/or the public key token (if the assembly is strongly named). Here's an example:

```
/MyAssembly;v2.0;4ac42a7f7bd64f34;component/images/apple.png
```

This is a shorthand for a full pack URI (prefixed by `pack://application:,,,`), and can also be an argument to `Application.GetResourceStream`, as demonstrated in the recipe *Accessing binary resources in code*.

There's more...

This scheme does not work with resources marked with a **Build Action** of **Content**. A way around this is to use the full pack URI with a `siteOfOrigin` base. In the previous example turning the image into a **Content** requires modifying the `Source` property of `Image` to read as follows:

```
Source="pack://siteOfOrigin:,,,/images/apple.png"
```

Note that the Visual Studio designer fails to display the image and a squiggly will run under this line in the XAML editor, but it will work at runtime.

Managing logical resources

Logical resources may be of various types, such as brushes, geometries, styles, and templates. Placing all those resources in a single file such as `App.xaml` hinders maintainability. A better approach would be to separate resources of different types (or based on some other criteria) to their own files. Still, they must be referenced somehow from within a common file such as `App.xaml` so they are recognized. This recipe shows how to do just that.

Getting ready

Make sure Visual Studio is up and running.

How to do it...

We'll create an application that separates its resources across multiple files for convenience and manageability:

1. Create a new WPF Application named `CH02.ManagingResources`.
2. We want to create a separate file that would hold (for example) brush resources. Right-click on the **Project** node in **Solution explorer** and select **Add | ResourceDictionary...**:

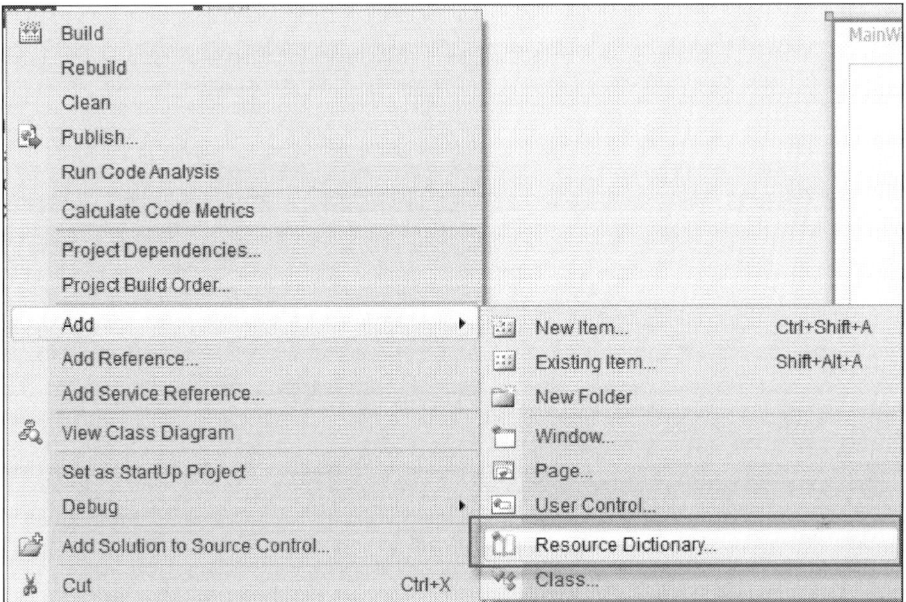

3. In the **Name** box, type `Brushes.xaml` and click on **Add**.
4. A XAML editor is opened with a `ResourceDictionary` as a root `elementVisual` studio shows no design surface, because a `ResourceDictionary` is just a collection of any typed objects, not elements. Let's add one fancy `Brush`:

```
<LinearGradientBrush EndPoint="1,0" x:Key="brush1">
    <GradientStop Color="Yellow" Offset="0" />
    <GradientStop Color="Orange" Offset=".7" />
    <GradientStop Color="DarkRed" Offset="1" />
</LinearGradientBrush>
```

5. Open `MainWindow.xaml`. Add an `Ellipse` within the `Grid` and set its `Fill` to be the fancy brush:

```
<Ellipse Fill="{StaticResource brush1}" />
```

   Notice the designer shows nothing. We want `Brushes.xaml` to be somehow part of the logical resource search.

6. Open `App.xaml`. We need to merge external resource dictionaries into the main application dictionary. Add the following inside the `<Application.Resources>` tag:

```
<ResourceDictionary>
    <ResourceDictionary.MergedDictionaries>
        <ResourceDictionary Source="Brushes.xaml" />
    </ResourceDictionary.MergedDictionaries>
</ResourceDictionary>
```

7. Now open `MainWindow.xaml`. The designer should show the brush used correctly (if it doesn't, build the project to refresh the designer). Running the application should show the following:

How it works...

A `ResourceDictionary` can incorporate other resource dictionaries using its `MergedDictionaries` property (a collection). This means a `ResourceDictionary` can reference as many resource dictionaries as desired and can have its own resources as well.

The `Source` property must point to the location of the `ResourceDictionary`. If that location is within a subfolder, that subfolder must be included. For example, if our `Brushes.xaml` was under a logical folder named **Resources**, merging that into `App.xaml` would look like as follows:

```
<ResourceDictionary Source="Resources/Brushes.xaml" />
```

There's more...

This idea can be also used to reference logical resources stored in other referenced assemblies. The `Source` property would have to be based on the pack URI syntax. Suppose that `Brushes.xaml` was placed in a class library within a **Resources** folder. The main application could merge it into another `ResourceDictionary` as follows:

```
<ResourceDictionary Source="/MyClassLibrary;component/Resources/
Brushes.xaml" />
```

Duplicated keys

Merging different resource dictionaries may cause an issue: two or more resources with the same keys that originate from different merged dictionaries. This is not an error and does not throw an exception. Instead, the selected object is the one from the last resource dictionary added (which has a resource with that key). Furthermore, if a resource in the current resource dictionary has the same key as the any of the resources in its merged dictionaries – it always wins out. Here's an example:

```
<ResourceDictionary>
   <SolidColorBrush Color="Blue" x:Key="brush1" />
   <ResourceDictionary.MergedDictionaries>
      <ResourceDictionary Source="Resources/Brushes2.xaml" />
      <ResourceDictionary Source="Resources/Brushes.xaml" />
   </ResourceDictionary.MergedDictionaries>
</ResourceDictionary>
```

With this markup, the resource named `brush1` is a blue `SolidColorBrush` because it appears in the `ResourceDictionary` itself. This "overrides" any resources named `brush1` in the merged dictionaries. If this blue brush did not exist, `brush1` would be looked up in `Brushes.xaml` first, as this is the last entry in the merged dictionaries collection.

3
Layout and Panels

In this chapter we will cover:

- Creating a table-like user interface
- Dynamically sizing grid rows/columns
- Creating a scrollable user interface
- Creating a border around panels and elements
- Placing elements in exact positions
- Adding/removing elements to a panel dynamically
- Creating a tabbed user interface
- Implementing drag-and-drop

Introduction

Layout is the process of element placement, and how their size and position changes in response to user interactions (such as a window resize). WPF offers a bunch of layout panels that provide different ways to lay out elements. By combining those panels in various ways, complex and adaptive layouts can be created.

The layout process

Layout is a two-step process. First, the layout container asks each of its children for its desired size. In the second step, it uses whatever logic is applicable to determine at what position and what size each child element should be – and places each child in that rectangular area. A more detailed look at this process can be found in the *Creating a custom panel* recipe in *Chapter 10, Custom Elements*.

Each element indicates to its parent its requirements. The following diagram summarizes the most important properties related to these requirements:

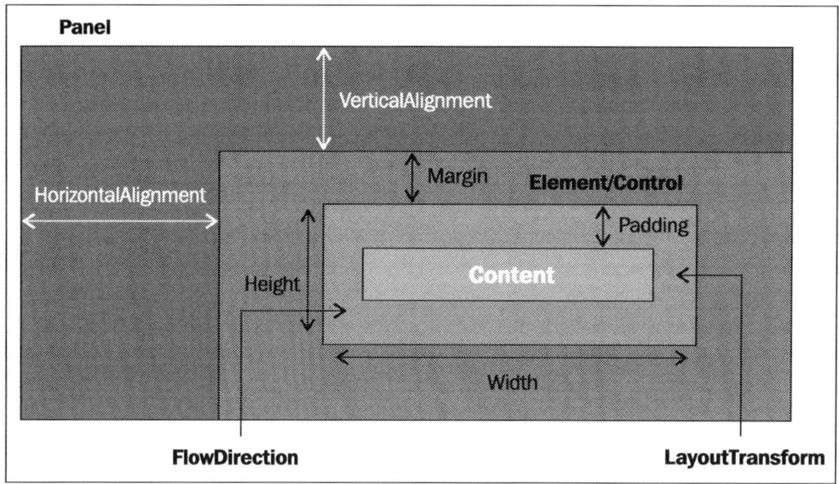

Here's a quick breakdown of these important properties:

- `Width/Height`: The width and height of the element in question. This is not typically set (`Double.NaN` being the default value), meaning the element can be as big as it needs to be. Nevertheless, it may be set if needed.
- `Margin`: A *breathing space* around the element. This is of type `Thickness` (a value type) that has four properties (`Left`, `Top`, `Right`, and `Bottom`) that determine the amount of space around the element. It can be specified in XAML using four numbers (left, top, right, and bottom), two numbers (the first is left and right, the second is top and bottom), or a single number (same distance in all four directions).
- `Padding`: The same idea as `Margin`, but determines the space between the outer edge of the element and its content (if any). This is of type `Thickness` as well, and is defined by the `Control` base class and some other special elements, such as `Border`.
- `HorizontalAlignment/VerticalAlignment`: Specifies how to align the element against its parent if extra space is available. Possible values are `Left`, `Center`, `Right`, and `Stretch` for `HorizontalAlignment`, and `Top`, `Center`, `Bottom`, and `Stretch` for `VerticalAlignment`.
- `HorizontalContentAlignment/VerticalContentAlignment` (not shown in figure): Same idea as `Horizontal/VecticalAlignment`, but for the `Content` of the element (if any).
- `LayoutTransform`: Allows a transformation (of type deriving from `Transform`) to be applied on the element before its layout requirements are communicated to its parent.

- `FlowDirection`: Can be used to switch the layout direction from the default (`LeftToRight`) to `RightToLeft`, suitable for right to left languages such as Hebrew and Arabic. This effectively turns every left to right and vice versa.

Coordinates systems in WPF

Every size or position in WPF is provided in units known as **Device Independent Units** (**DIU**). Contrary to other UI technologies, such as Windows Forms, these are not device units or pixels and they are not integers; rather, a WPF unit is 1/96 of an inch and always expressed as a double value.

This feature provides a more consistent way to present visuals. On a standard 96 DPI display device, 1 DIU = 1 pixel. With higher DPIs, for instance, a 96 unit line is still one inch long. It may require more pixels to paint because of the higher DPI, but the size is consistent. This helps in making WPF results consistent and predictable.

In XAML, it's possible to provide sizes in several formats. If just a number is provided, it's interpreted as a DIU value; however, some suffixes exist to change the unit of measurement: "in" for inch, "cm" for centimeters, and "pt" for points (1 point = 1/72 inch). If specified, a type converter (`LengthConverter`) converts the values to DIUs (for example, "2in" is turned into the value 192).

A consequence of using doubles rather than integers is that high precision is maintained if elements (or pure graphics) need to be transformed, for example, rotated or stretched.

In this chapter, we'll take a look at some of WPF's layout panels, including some layout related controls that are not technically panels, to get a better understanding of WPF's layout mechanism and user interface building approach.

Creating a table-like user interface

Table layout is a popular placement strategy, supported by the `Grid` panel. Let's examine the `Grid` and see what it's capable of.

Getting ready

Make sure Visual Studio is up and running.

How to do it...

We'll create a simple UI that benefits from a grid-like layout and demonstrate some of its features:

1. Create a new WPF application named `CH03.GridDemo`.
2. Open `MainWindow.xaml`. There's already a `Grid` placed inside the `Window`. That's because the `Grid` is typically used as the main layout panel within a window.
3. Change the `Title` of `Window` to `Grid Demo`.
4. Inside the `Grid`, add the following markup to create some rows and columns:

```
<Grid.RowDefinitions>
    <RowDefinition Height="Auto" />
   <RowDefinition Height="Auto" />
    <RowDefinition Height="Auto" />
    <RowDefinition />
</Grid.RowDefinitions>
<Grid.ColumnDefinitions>
    <ColumnDefinition Width="Auto" />
    <ColumnDefinition />
</Grid.ColumnDefinitions>
```

5. This creates a 4 rows by 2 columns `Grid`. Now let's add some elements and controls to host the grid:

```
<TextBlock Grid.ColumnSpan="2" HorizontalAlignment="Center"
           Text="Book Details" FontSize="20" Margin="4"/>
<TextBlock Grid.Row="1" HorizontalAlignment="Right"
           Text="Name:" Margin="4" />
<TextBlock Grid.Row="2" HorizontalAlignment="Right"
           Text="Author:" Margin="4" />
<TextBlock Grid.Row="1" Grid.Column="1"
           Text="Windows internals" Margin="4" />
<TextBlock Grid.Row="2" Grid.Column="1"
           Text="Mark Russinovich" Margin="4" />
<Rectangle Grid.Column="1" Grid.Row="3" Margin="4"
         StrokeThickness="4" Stroke="Black" Fill="Red" />
<TextBlock Grid.Column="1" Grid.Row="3"
           Text="Book Cover" VerticalAlignment="Center"
           FontSize="16"  HorizontalAlignment="Center"/>
```

6. Run the application. It should look as follows:

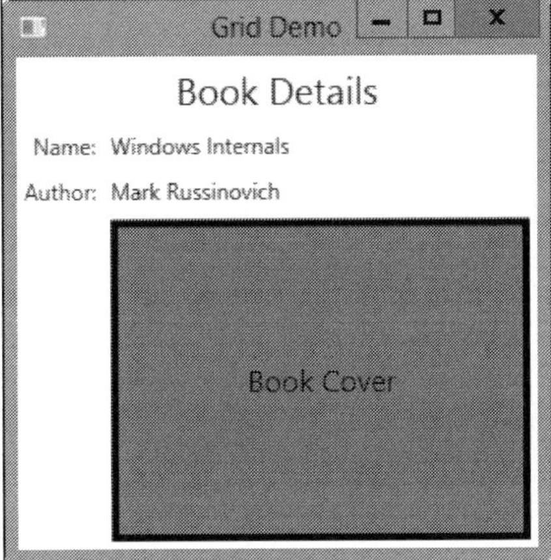

7. Resize the window and watch the layout changes. Note that the `Grid` rows marked with a `Height` of `Auto` remain fixed in size, while the row that has no `Height` setting fills the remaining space (it is the same idea for the columns):

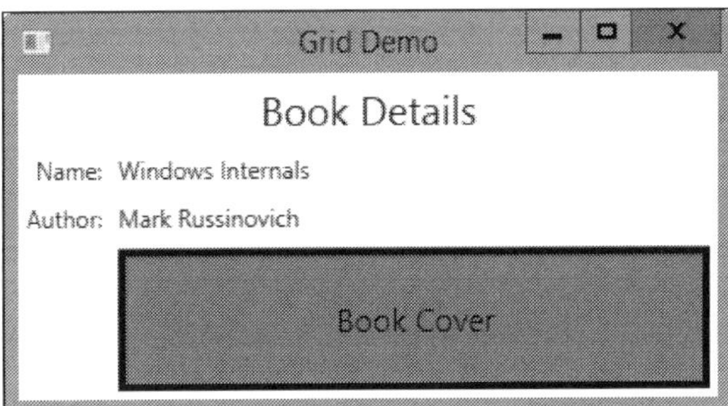

How it works...

The `Grid` panel creates a table-like layout of cells. The number of rows and columns is not specified by simple properties. Instead, it's specified using `RowDefinition` objects (for rows) and `ColumnDefinition` objects (for columns). The reason has to do with the size and behavior that can be specified on a row and/or column basis.

A `RowDefinition` has a `Height` property, while a `ColumnDefintion` has a `Width` property. Both are of type `GridLength`. There are three options for setting a `GridLength`:

- A specific length
- A "star" (relative) based factor (this is the default, and factor equals 1)
- Automatic length

Setting `Height` (of a `RowDefintion`) or `Width` (of a `ColumnDefinition`) to a specific number makes that row/column that particular size. In code it's equivalent to `new GridLength(len)`.

Setting `Height` or `Width` to `Auto` (in XAML) makes the row/column as high/wide as it needs to be based on the tallest/widest element placed within that row/column. In code, it's equivalent to `GridLength.Auto`.

The last option (which is the default) is setting `Height`/`Width` to `n*` in XAML, where n is some number (1 if omitted). This sets up a relationship with other rows/columns that have a "star" length. For example, here are three rows of a `Grid`:

```
<RowDefinition Height="2*" />
<RowDefinition />
<RowDefinition Height="3*" />
```

This means that the first row is twice as tall as the second row (`Height="*"`). The last row is three times taller than the second row and is one and a half times taller than the first row. These relations are maintained even if the window is resized.

There's more...

Elements are placed in grid cells using the attached `Grid.Row` and `Grid.Column` properties (both default to zero, meaning the first row/column).

Elements occupy one cell by default. This can be changed by using the `Grid.RowSpan` and `Grid.ColumnSpan` properties (these were set for the first `TextBlock` in the code). If we need an element to stretch to the end of the `Grid` (for example, through all columns from some starting column), it's ok to specify some large number (it will be constrained to the actual number of rows/columns of the `Grid`).

Shared row/column size

There may be times when more than one grid should have the same row height (or column width). This is possible using the `SharedSizeGroup` property of `DefinitionBase` (the base class of `RowDefinition` and `ColumnDefinition`). This is just a string; if `RowDefinition` or `ColumnDefinition` objects from two separate grids have the same value for this property, they would maintain identical length. To make this work, the attached property `Grid.IsSharedSizeScope` must be set to `true` on a common parent of those `Grid` instances.

This feature is most useful with `DataTemplate` properties (which are discussed in detail in *Chapter 6, Data Binding*) when binding to an `ItemsControl` control (or one of its derivatives).

Here's a quick example: A ListBox defines a DataTemplate for its items (ItemTemplate property) for displaying information on Person objects, defined as follows:

```
class Person {
   public string Name { get; set; }
   public int Age { get; set; }
}
```

The ListBox is defined with the following markup:

```
<ListBox ItemsSource="{Binding}"
    Grid.IsSharedSizeScope="True">
    <ListBox.ItemTemplate>
        <DataTemplate>
            <Grid>
                <Grid.ColumnDefinitions>
                    <ColumnDefinition Width="Auto"
                        SharedSizeGroup="abc" />
                    <ColumnDefinition />
                </Grid.ColumnDefinitions>
                <TextBlock Text="{Binding Name}" FontSize="20"
                           Margin="4"/>
                <TextBlock Grid.Column="1" FontSize="16"
          Text="{Binding Age, StringFormat=is {0} years old}"
                    VerticalAlignment="Bottom" Margin="4"/>
            </Grid>
        </DataTemplate>
    </ListBox.ItemTemplate>
</ListBox>
```

Note the attached property Grid.IsSharedSizeScope is set to true on a common parent of all involved Grid instances (the ListBox is an obvious choice) and the SharedSizeGroup property of RowDefinition is set to some string ("abc"). The string itself does not matter – what matters is that it's the same string for all relevant Grid instances. Since this is part of a DataTemplate, Grid instances are created for every item in the ListBox. Here's the result when binding to some collection of Person objects:

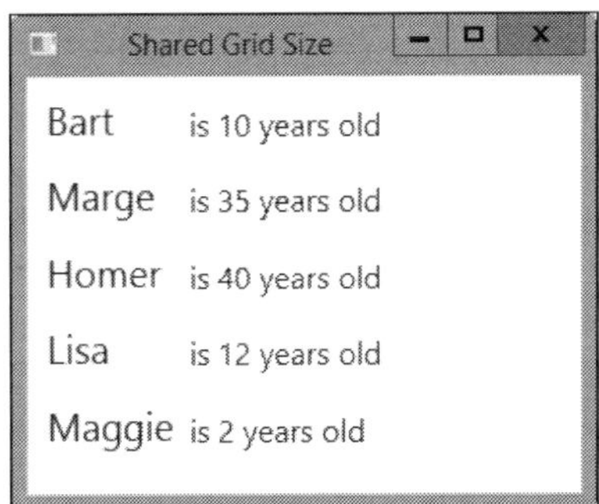

Here's what happens if one of the above properties is missing (note the misalignments):

The complete project is named `CH03.SharedGridSizeDemo` and is available in the downloadable source for this chapter.

Placement in the same cell

If more than one element is placed in the same cell, they sit one on top of the other – by default, elements appearing later in the XAML are on top. We can change that by using the attached `Panel.ZIndex` property (default is zero). Higher values make the element on top (negative values are accepted).

The power of the Grid

The `Grid` is so flexible, that it can emulate most of the standard WPF panels, all except the `WrapPanel` (which is too chaotic for the `Grid`), namely the `StackPanel`, `Canvas`, and `DockPanel`. This is why Visual Studio chooses the `Grid` as the default root layout panel when a new window is generated.

If the `Grid` can do almost anything, why use other panels at all? There are two reasons. The first is convenience: although a `Grid` can emulate a `StackPanel`, that's cumbersome and leads to increased markup with no real gains. The second reason is performance: the `StackPanel` (for instance) has very little to worry about, while the `Grid` has a lot. For a layout consisting of many elements the complexity of `Grid` may degrade performance, so it's usually best to use the lightest panel possible that gets the job done.

Adding rows/columns dynamically

Although `Grid` instances are typically constructed in XAML and have a fixed number of columns and rows, that doesn't have to be the case. It's possible to add (or remove) rows/columns at runtime if so desired. Here's an example that adds three rows to an existing `Grid` named `_grid`:

```
RowDefinition[] rows = {
   new RowDefinition { Height = new GridLength(100) },
```

```
        new RowDefinition { Height = GridLength.Auto },
        new RowDefinition { Height = new GridLength(2,
            GridUnitType.Star) }
    };
    Array.ForEach(rows, row => _grid.RowDefinitions.Add(row));
```

The first row has a fixed height of `100`, the second is auto-sized, and the third is a `star` row with a factor of `2`.

The UniformGrid

There is a simpler grid in WPF, the `UniformGrid` (in the `System.Windows.Controls.Primitives` namespace). This grid has two properties to set the grid size: `Rows` and `Columns` (both default to 1). Every cell in a `UniformGrid` is, well, uniform (same width and height). Every new element is placed in the next cell starting from the top left, moving left to right, and then down to the next row, starting from the left again.

The `UniformGrid` may be used as a simple shortcut for a full-blown grid (it's more lightweight), if the need arises. A more creative use of the `UniformGrid` is a custom panel hosting elements in an `ItemsControl`.

Here's a quick example: A `ListBox` holds a collection of numbers, displayed by default in a row layout (a `VirtualizingStackPanel`, similar to a `StackPanel` for our purposes, is the default panel for laying out items in an `ListBox`). Let's change that to a `UniformGrid`. Here's the complete `ListBox` markup:

```
<ListBox ItemsSource="{Binding}" FontSize="25"
    SelectionMode="Multiple">
    <ListBox.ItemsPanel>
        <ItemsPanelTemplate>
            <UniformGrid Rows="4" Columns="4" />
        </ItemsPanelTemplate>
    </ListBox.ItemsPanel>
</ListBox>
```

Here's the `ListBox` at runtime when bound to a list of numbers:

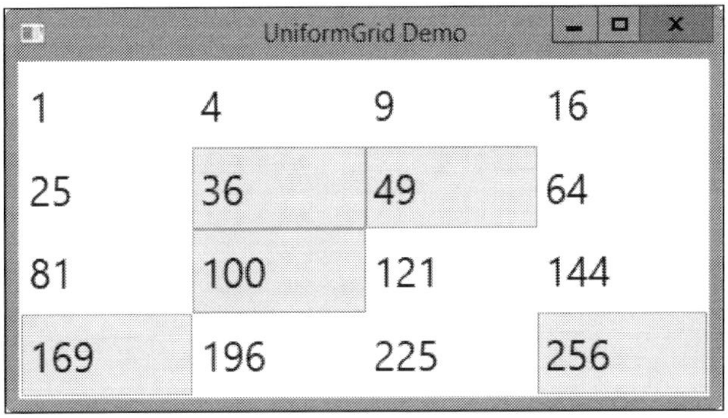

Despite appearances, this is still a regular `ListBox`! The complete source is in the `CH03.UniformGridLayout` project available in the downloadable source for this chapter.

Dynamically sizing grid rows/columns

A typical user interface contains multiple parts, each responsible for some UI features. Many times it's useful for the user to manually resize those parts, as she sees fit. It turns out the `Grid` supports dynamic resizing with the help of a `GridSplitter` element. Let's see how this can be done.

Getting ready

Make sure Visual Studio is up and running.

How to do it...

We'll create a simple two way splitter, similar to the main view in Windows Explorer, to demonstrate a typical `GridSplitter` usage:

1. Create a new WPF application named `CH03.DynamicGridSizing`.
2. Open `MainWindow.xaml`. Add two columns to the existing `Grid` as follows:

```
<Grid.ColumnDefinitions>
    <ColumnDefinition MinWidth="40"/>
    <ColumnDefinition Width="2*" MinWidth="50" />
</Grid.ColumnDefinitions>
```

3. Place two `Ellipse` elements in the created columns, so we'd have some content to work with:

```
<Ellipse Stroke="Black" StrokeThickness="2" Fill="Red" />
<Ellipse Stroke="Black" StrokeThickness="2" Fill="Green"
         Grid.Column="1"/>
```

4. Running the application at this point would maintain the 1:2 ratio between the widths of the two columns. Let's add a `GridSplitter` element to the grid to allow dynamic sizing:

```
<GridSplitter Grid.Column="1" HorizontalAlignment="Left"
       Width="3" Background="Blue" Margin="-1,0,0,0"/>
```

5. Run the application. You'll be able to resize the grid columns interactively with the mouse.

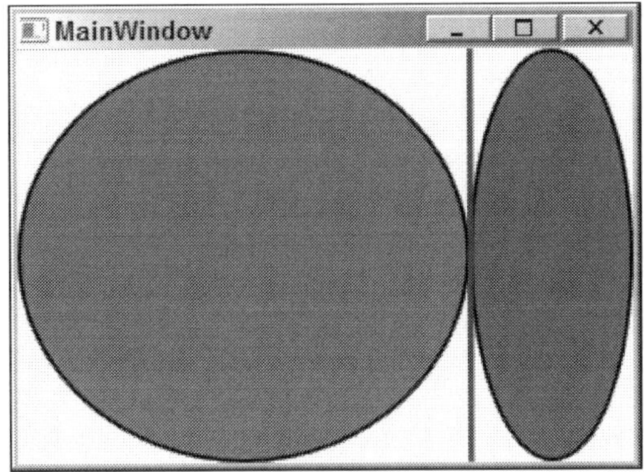

How it works...

A `GridSplitter` *attached* itself to two columns or rows, providing interactive sizing. How can something be placed between cells? It can't. It's placed in one cell (doesn't really matter which) and aligned to the *other* side. Here's a quick rundown for correct `GridSplitter` usage:

- Place the `GridSplitter` after the content within the resized content areas. This usually means placing it last in XAML (highest in the Z order).
- For a horizontal splitter, a `Width` must be set. For a vertical splitter, `Height` must be set.
- A `Background` is highly recommended. This can be any brush, not just a `SolidColorBrush`. This can also be set to `Transparent` if it's clear where the splitter is located.
- It must be placed in one of the two cells such that its sizing and its `HorizontalAlignment` (in the case of column resizing) are set to the align on the other side. In our example it's placed in the right cell, but aligned left.

There's more...

It's easy enough to *nest* `GridSplitter` instances, by placing more than one within the grid. We just need to make sure everything is set up correctly. For example, adding two rows to the previous example, we can set up another splitter for the bottom row (spanning works for the `GridSplitter` as well):

```
<GridSplitter Grid.Row="1" VerticalAlignment="Top"
            Margin="0,-1,0,0"
            Grid.ColumnSpan="2" HorizontalAlignment="Stretch"
            Height="3" Background="Blue" />
```

And this is the result (I've added a third `Ellipse`):

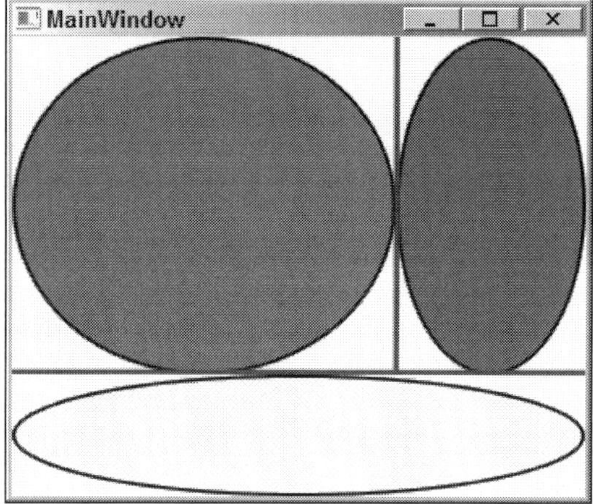

The complete source is available in the downloadable source for this chapter.

> `HorizontalAlignment` is set to `Stretch`. This is essential for a horizontal splitter (otherwise it won't be visible).

Creating a scrollable user interface

There are occasions when some data to display is larger than the display area; this requires scrolling capabilities. WPF provides that using a simple control, the `ScrollViewer`.

Getting ready

Make sure Visual Studio is up and running.

How to do it...

We'll create a simple image viewer that provides scrollbars if necessary when viewing a large image:

1. Create a new WPF application named `CH03.ScrollDemo`.
2. Add an image to the project. For example, you could select the `Penguins.jpg` file from the **Pictures** | **Sample Pictures** folder.
3. Open `MainWindow.xaml`. Add a `ScrollViewer` control inside the existing `Grid`.

4. Inside the `ScrollViewer`, add an `Image` element, and set its `Source` property to the image you added:

```
<ScrollViewer>
    <Image Source="penguins.jpg" Stretch="None" />
</ScrollViewer>
```

5. Set the `Image Stretch` property to `None`. This ensures the image is displayed in its original size.
6. Run the application. You should be able to scroll vertically as needed, but not horizontally:

7. Let's fix that. Set the `HorizontalScrollBarVisibility` on the `ScrollViewer` to `Auto`:

```
<ScrollViewer HorizontalScrollBarVisibility="Auto">
```

8. Run the application. You should be able to scroll in both directions:

How it works...

ScrollViewer is a content control (derived from ContentControl) that hosts a single child (its Content property) and uses a pair of ScrollBar controls to support scrolling. The most important properties are VerticalScrollBarVisibility and HorizontalScrollBarVisibility, which indicate the way scrolling should work and the way the scrollbars present themselves. There are four options (ScrollBarVisibility enumeration):

- Visible: The scroll bar is always visible. If the content requires a smaller space, the scroll bar is disabled.
- Auto: The scroll bar appears if needed and disappears if not needed.
- Hidden: The scroll bar is not shown, but scrolling is still possible using the keyboard or programmatically.
- Disabled: The scroll bar is hidden and no scrolling is possible. The ScrollViewer does not give more space than it has to the content (in that dimension).

The default values are Visible for VerticalScrollBarVisibility and Disabled for HorizontalScrollBarVisibility.

There's more...

The HorizontalScrollBarVisibility and VerticalScrollBarVisibility properties are exposed as attached properties as well, so they are relevant to other controls that internally use a ScrollViewer, such as ListBox. Here's a simple example that changes the way a horizontal scroll bar is presented in a ListBox:

```
<ListBox ScrollViewer.HorizontalScrollBarVisibility="Hidden">
```

Creating a border around panels and elements

Sometimes a simple decoration is required around some element or panel, such as a border. Luckily, the Border element does just that to anything placed inside it.

Getting ready

Make sure Visual Studio is up and running.

How to do it...

We'll create a simple border encompassing some text, to show most of the capabilities of Border:

1. Create a new WPF application named CH03.BorderDemo.
2. Open MainWindow.xaml. Replace the existing Grid with a StackPanel, and add a TextBlock inside it, like the following markup shows:

```
<StackPanel Margin="4">
    <TextBlock Text="Hello from Center" FontSize="25"
               HorizontalAlignment="Center" />
</StackPanel>
```

3. Running the application shows the text centered horizontally within the StackPanel.
4. Suppose we want to draw a border around the TextBlock. Add a Border element around the TextBlock as shown in the following markup:

```
<Border BorderThickness="3" BorderBrush="Blue"
        CornerRadius="6">
    <TextBlock Text="Hello from Center" FontSize="25"
HorizontalAlignment="Center" />
</Border>
```

5. Run the application. It should look as follows:

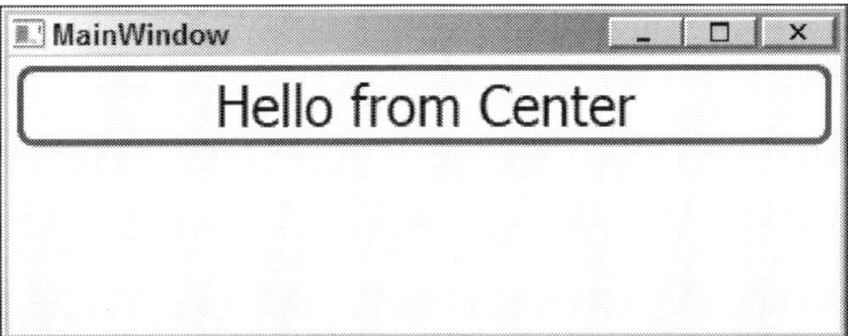

How it works...

The Border element is a type of decorator (derived from the Decorator class, implementing the so-called "Decorator" design pattern). It provides a simple border around whatever child element is provided (Child property). Typically, the child is a panel, because panels have no border related properties (unlike controls that do have those via the Control base class).

Border provides BorderBrush and BorderThickness properties, but also Background. The CornerRadius property is used to create a rounded rectangular border. The Padding property provides some breathing space between the inner border and the actual child (the same effect can be achieved with the Margin property on the child).

> The BorderThickness is of type Thickness, meaning it's possible to draw a border with different widths in the four directions or even remove any of the directions by specifying a value of zero for that direction.

Placing elements in exact positions

WPF's layout panels provide much flexibility in building a user interface. Furthermore, most of the panels adapt well to size and content changes of themselves and their child elements. This means that positions and sizes don't necessarily remain the same as the user resizes or otherwise manipulates the UI.

Most of the time that's a good thing; sometimes, however, we need to place elements in exact positions without them moving unexpectedly. This is typical of highly graphical content, such as graphs, charts, or animations. The Canvas panel provides a convenient container for such content.

Getting ready

Make sure Visual Studio is up and running.

How to do it...

We'll create a simple application that hosts a Canvas with some elements inside to demonstrate the way elements are positioned inside a Canvas:

1. Create a new WPF application named CH03.CanvasDemo.
2. Open MainWindow.xaml. Replace the existing Grid with a Canvas.
3. Add some elements to the Canvas as follows:

```
<Ellipse Stroke="Black" StrokeThickness="2"
         Fill="Red" Canvas.Right="50" Canvas.Top="40"
         Width="50" Height="50"/>
<TextBlock Text="Canvas Demo" FontSize="20"
           Canvas.Left="100" Canvas.Top="20" />
<Rectangle Stroke="Black" StrokeThickness="1" Fill="LightBlue"
           Canvas.Bottom="0" Canvas.Left="40"
           Width="30" Height="100" />
```

4. The Canvas.Left/Top/Right/Bottom attached properties place the elements exactly where they are needed. Run the application and resize the window to see the effects of these properties.

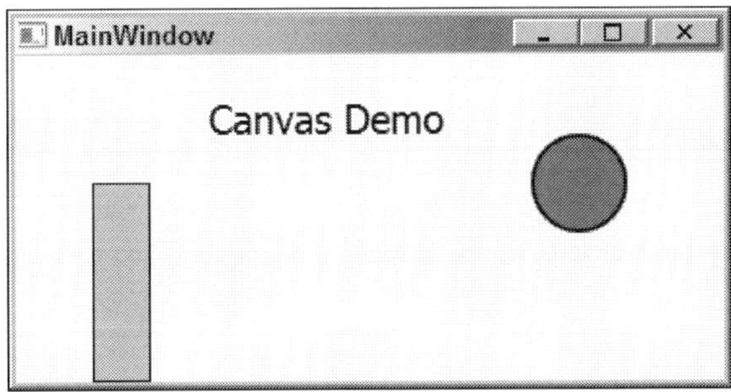

How it works...

The `Canvas` panel does very little layout (if one could call it that). Setting two (non-opposite) of the four attached properties it defines, sets the element with the requested distances from the requested sides of the `Canvas`.

If elements overlap, their Z order is considered. By default, later elements defined in XAML sit on top of previous ones. This can be changed (in XAML or code) using the attached `Panel.ZIndex` property.

There's more...

`Canvas` is by far the fastest panel, as it does practically very little layout. This makes it great for graphic intensive work and for running animations with a high frame rate. It's much less suitable for "traditional" user interface layouts (that's what the other panels are for).

Canvas has no background

If we try to intercept events such as mouse events on the `Canvas`, we get nothing. The reason is that the `Canvas` has a `null` background (this is the default setting for all panels), so all mouse events *fall through* to its containing element. If we need those events on the `Canvas`, we'll set its `Background` to something other than `null`. By the way, `Brushes.Transparent` works just fine for this purpose.

Canvas is not limited to its bounds

By default, if elements are placed or stretched beyond the `Canvas` boundaries, they are still drawn as usual, possibly on top of other elements adjacent to the `Canvas`. If this is undesirable, set the `ClipToBounds` property to `true`.

Adding/removing elements to a panel dynamically

Panels contain elements that are typically added in XAML as a base for the user interface. Sometimes, however, we need to add or remove elements dynamically at run time based on user actions or other criteria. Let's see how this can be done.

Getting ready

Make sure Visual Studio is up and running.

How to do it...

We'll create a simple circle drawing program. Every click adds a circle to a `Canvas`.

1. Create a new WPF application named `CH03.PaintingCircles`.
2. Open `MainWindow.xaml`. Replace the default `Grid` with a `Canvas`, name it `_canvas`, and set its `Background` to `White`.
3. Add an event handler for the `MouseUp` event to the `Canvas`:

```
<Canvas x:Name="_canvas" Background="White"
        MouseUp="OnClickCanvas">
</Canvas>
```

4. Navigate to the event handler you just created. We want a left-click to add an ellipse where the mouse pointer is and a right-click to make an `Ellipse` under the cursor disappear.
5. Add the following code to the event handler in case the left button was clicked:

```
void OnClickCanvas(object sender, MouseButtonEventArgs e) {
      switch(e.ChangedButton) {
         case MouseButton.Left:
            // add a random ellipse
            var circle = new Ellipse {
               Stroke = Brushes.Black,
               StrokeThickness = 3,
               Fill = Brushes.Red,
               Width = 30,
               Height = 30
            };
            var pos = e.GetPosition(_canvas);
            Canvas.SetLeft(circle, pos.X -
               circle.Width / 2);
```

```
                Canvas.SetTop(circle, pos.Y -
                   circle.Height / 2);
                _canvas.Children.Add(circle);
                break;
        }
    }
```

In the preceding code, an `Ellipse` object is created and positioned in a way that its center is at the point of clicking. Then, the `Ellipse` is added to the `Canvas`.

6. We want to remove an ellipse when the right mouse button is clicked. Add the following code as another `case` within the `switch` statement:

```
case MouseButton.Right:
   var ellipse = e.Source as Ellipse;
   if(ellipse != null)
      _canvas.Children.Remove(ellipse);
   break;
```

7. Run the application and draw some circles!

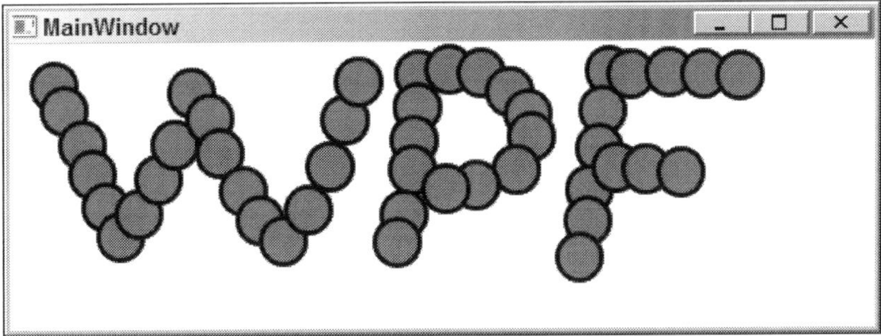

How it works...

Every panel maintains a `Children` property (its `ContentProperty` for easier usage in XAML) of type `UIElementCollection`, which is a collection of `UIElement` objects. This means that any object derived from `UIElement` can be a child in a `Panel`. The preceding code uses the `Add` and `Remove` methods to dynamically add or remove `Ellipse` objects to the `Canvas`.

Creating a tabbed user interface

The tabbed user interface has been popular in recent years, due to its screen real estate savings and ease of use. It replaces the older, MDI (Multiple Document Interface) model that exists within the Windows UI subsystem and popularized by frameworks such as MFC (Microsoft Foundation Classes). Visual Studio itself is a good example of tabbed interface usage (although Visual Studio can work in MDI mode as well). In this recipe, we'll see the basics of a tabbed user interface. Check out the *There's more...* section for a more realistic way of managing tabs.

Getting ready

Make sure Visual Studio is up and running.

How to do it...

We'll create a bare-bones application showing two simple tabs:

1. Create a new WPF application named `CH03.SimpleTabs`.
2. Open `MainWindow.xaml`. Replace the existing `Grid` with a `TabControl`.
3. Add a `TabItem` control to the `TabControl` as follows:

```
<TabControl>
    <Tabitem Header="Header 1">
        <Grid>
            <Ellipse Stroke="Black" Fill="Blue"
                     StrokeThickness="4" Margin="10"/>
            <TextBlock Text="Data 1" FontSize="30"
                       Foreground="White"
                       HorizontalAlignment="Center"
                       VerticalAlignment="Center" />
        </Grid>
    </Tabitem>
</TabControl>
```

4. A `TabItem` maintains a `Header` and some `Content` (its `ContentProperty`). Let's add another `TabItem` as follows:

```
<Tabitem>
    <Tabitem.Header>
        <StackPanel Orientation="Horizontal" Margin="2">
            <Rectangle Stroke="Black" Fill="Red"
                       StrokeThickness="2"
                       Width="20" Height="20" />
```

```
                <TextBlock Text="Header 2" Margin="4,0,0,0"
                           VerticalAlignment="Center" />
            </StackPanel>
        </TabItem.Header>
        <Grid>
            <Rectangle Stroke="Black" Fill="Green"
                       RadiusX="20" RadiusY="20"
                       StrokeThickness="4" Margin="10"/>
            <TextBlock Text="Data 2" FontSize="30"
                       Foreground="White"
                       HorizontalAlignment="Center"
                       VerticalAlignment="Center" />
        </Grid>
    </TabItem>
```

5. Run the application and click to move between the tabs:

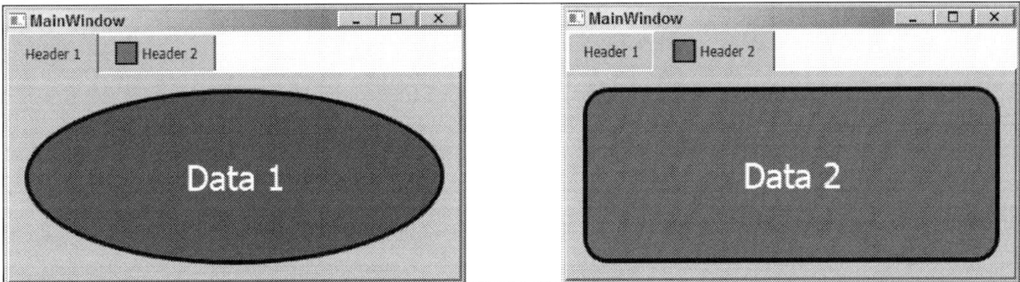

How it works...

The `TabControl` is an `ItemsControl` derivative (actually derives from `Selector`), which means it can host a bunch of objects. These should be `TabItem` controls, which are `HeaderedContentControls`. This means a `TabItem` has a `Header` (of type `object`, it can be anything) and `Content` (again can be anything).

The second tab is an example of a richer `Header`, consisting of a horizontal `StackPanel` hosting a `Rectangle` element and a `TextBlock`.

There's more...

Placing `TabItem` objects by hand is certainly possible, but a typical scenario would be using a `TabItem` per some data managed by the application. Consider Visual Studio as an example: the tabs are created dynamically based on the actual open documents.

One way to achieve this by using code is simply to use the Items property of the TabControl and call the Add method whenever a new tab is needed. However, this is a very inconvenient option, as the content of such a tab may be complex, or designed beforehand using a tool such as Expression Blend, thus available as XAML.

A more efficient and robust approach would be to leverage data binding, data templates, styles, and maybe even triggers. A detailed discussion of these topics can be found in *Chapter 6, Data Binding*.

Suppose our data is a simple type like the following:

```
class Dataitem {
   public string Header { get; set; }
   public string Text { get; set; }
}
```

We want to display the Header property somehow on the Header of a TabItem and the Text should be displayed within the Content of a TabItem. We can customize things by creating a Style for TabItem, and providing DataTemplate objects for the Header and Content properties. Further customization is possible via triggers (only one in the following example). First, the DataTemplates for the Header and Content (as resources):

```
<Window.Resources>
  <DataTemplate x:Key="tabHeaderTemplate">
     <StackPanel Orientation="Horizontal" Margin="4">
        <Ellipse Stroke="Black" StrokeThickness="1"
                  Fill="Blue" Width="16" Height="16" />
        <TextBlock Margin="4,0,0,0" VerticalAlignment="Center"
                   FontSize="15" Text="{Binding Header}" />
    </StackPanel>
  </DataTemplate>
  <DataTemplate x:Key="tabContentTemplate">
    <Grid>
      <TextBlock FontSize="30" VerticalAlignment="Center"
        HorizontalAlignment="Center" Text="{Binding Text}" />
    </Grid>
  </DataTemplate>
</Window.Resources>
```

Next, we need to plug these templates into a TabItem using the ItemContainerStyle property of the TabControl (inherited from ItemsControl):

```
<TabControl x:Name="_tabs">
   <TabControl.itemContainerStyle>
      <Style TargetType="Tabitem">
         <Setter Property="HeaderTemplate"
                 Value="{StaticResource tabHeaderTemplate}" />
```

```
            <Setter Property="ContentTemplate"
                   Value="{StaticResource tabContentTemplate}" />
            <Style.Triggers>
               <Trigger Property="IsSelected" Value="True">
                  <Setter Property="Background" Value="Yellow" />
               </Trigger>
            </Style.Triggers>
         </Style>
      </TabControl.ItemContainerStyle>
   </TabControl>
```

To test this, we'll add some data items in the constructor:

```
   _tabs.ItemsSource = new List<DataItem> {
      new DataItem { Header = "Header 1", Text = "Data 1 " },
      new DataItem { Header = "Header 2", Text = "Data 2 " },
      new DataItem { Header = "Header 3", Text = "Data 3 " },
   };
```

Running the application produces the following tabs:

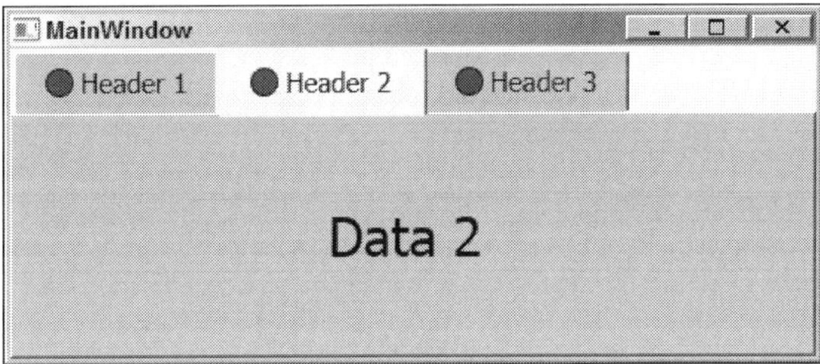

The complete source code is in the `CH03.ComplexTabs` project, available in the downloadable source for this chapter.

Implementing drag-and-drop

Drag-and-drop functionality is common in applications, where one object is held down and dragged to some other object with the mouse. This approach is not as common as it used to be, especially with a mouse, because it requires hand coordination skills. Recent tablet devices are touch enabled, where drag and drop makes a lot of sense. As a general rule, always provide an alternative to drag-and-drop. That said, this can be a handy feature for advanced users.

Getting ready

Make sure Visual Studio is up and running.

How to do it...

We'll create an application that allows dragging elements (circles and rectangles) from one part of the window to another container within the same window, showing the necessary steps to get drag-and-drop working properly:

1. Create a new WPF application named `CH03.SimpleDragDrop`.
2. Open `MainWindow.xaml`. Fill the existing `Grid` with the following markup:

```
<Grid>
    <Grid.ColumnDefinitions>
        <ColumnDefinition Width="2*"/>
        <ColumnDefinition Width="40" />
        <ColumnDefinition />
    </Grid.ColumnDefinitions>
    <Border BorderThickness="2" BorderBrush="Black">
        <Canvas x:Name="_source" Background="White" />
    </Border>
    <Border BorderBrush="Black" BorderThickness="2"
            Grid.Column="2" >
        <WrapPanel itemWidth="50" itemHeight="50"
                   x:Name="_target" Background="Yellow">
        </WrapPanel>
    </Border>
</Grid>
```

   This sets up a `Canvas` on which we'll place some objects, and a `WrapPanel`, to be used as the target of drag-and-drop.

3. To enable the `WrapPanel` to be a drag-and-drop target, set its `AllowDrop` property to `true`.
4. We'll fill the `Canvas` with some random shapes. Add the following method to the `MainWindow` class:

```
void initObjects() {
   var rnd = new Random();
   const int width = 45, height = 45;
   for(int i = 0; i < 30; i++) {
    var shape = rnd.Next(10) > 4 ? (Shape)new Ellipse() :
          (Shape)new Rectangle();
      shape.Stroke = Brushes.Black;
```

```
        shape.StrokeThickness = 2;
          shape.Fill = rnd.Next(10) > 4 ? Brushes.Red :
            Brushes.LightBlue;
        shape.Width = width;
        shape.Height = height;
        Canvas.SetLeft(shape, rnd.NextDouble() *
           (_source.ActualWidth - width));
        Canvas.SetTop(shape, rnd.NextDouble() *
           (_source.ActualHeight - height));
        _source.Children.Add(shape);
    }
}
```

This creates a bunch of ellipses and rectangles, placing them at random locations. The user should be able to drag any one of those to the `WrapPanel`.

5. Add the following code in the `MainWindow` constructor (after the call to `InitializeComponent`) to invoke `InitObjects` once the `Window` is loaded:

```
Loaded += delegate {
   InitObjects();
};
```

6. Add an event handler for the `MouseLeftButtonDown` (called `OnBeginDrag`) on the `Canvas` and place the following code inside:

```
void OnBeginDrag(object sender, MouseButtonEventArgs e) {
   var obj = e.Source as Shape;
   if(obj != null) {
      DragDrop.DoDragDrop(obj, obj, DragDropEffects.Move);
   }
}
```

The preceding code checks to see if the clicked object is a kind of shape, and if so, initiates a drag-and-drop operation, specifying that object as source and data (first and second arguments) and the allowed operations.

7. When the user drops the object, the `Drop` event is fired on the target element. Add an event handler for the `Drop` event on the `WrapPanel` and implement the event handler with the following code:

```
void OnDrop(object sender, DragEventArgs e) {
   var element = e.Data.GetData(e.Data.GetFormats()[0])
       as UIElement;
   if(element != null) {
      _source.Children.Remove(element);
      _target.Children.Add(element);
   }
}
```

The preceding code looks at the first data provided, and if it's a `UIElement`, removes it from the original `Canvas` and adds it to the `WrapPanel`.

8. Run the application and move some objects across to the `WrapPanel`:

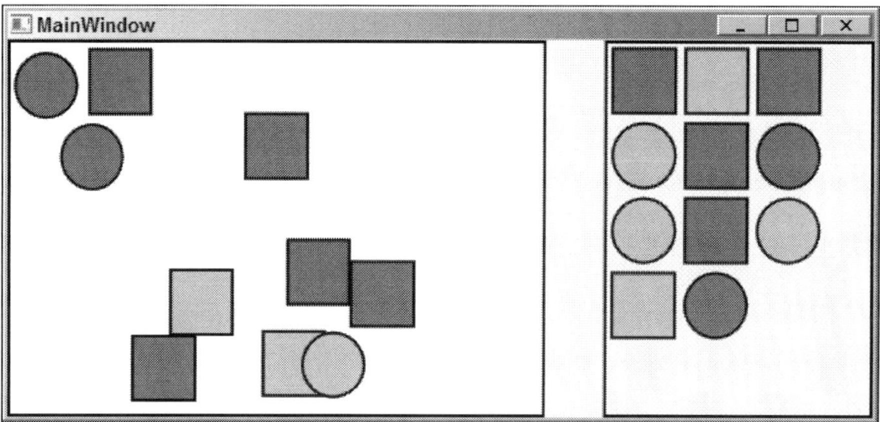

How it works...

Drag-and-drop support in WPF is pretty similar to that of WinForms. An element has to *agree* to be the target of a drag-and-drop operation by setting its `AllowDrop` property to `true` (it's false by default).

When the (typically left) mouse button is down, the drag-and-drop operation is initiated by using the static `DragDrop.DoDragDrop` method. This method is kind of weird, because the next statement in that event handler executes when the drag-and-drop operation completes or is canceled (by pressing *Esc*, for instance). Internally, it captures the mouse and handles mouse messages. One of those turns into the `Drop` event on a target element that has set itself to be a drop target.

Within `Drop`, the data object is queried to discover what's available. A sophisticated target may accept more than one type of data. Some types are defined by Windows itself, such as text, bitmap image, or a file drop. Other times, it's a custom object that makes sense within the application only.

To actually make the move from one container to another, the element is first removed from its parent (step 7) and then added to its new parent. This sequence is important, as an element can have a single parent at any one time; trying to add the element to the new parent before removing it from the old one would throw an exception.

The `Data` property in the `DragEventArgs` (of type `IDataObject`) is WPF's representation of things that are part of OLE (Object Linking and Embedding) and COM (Component Object Model) that lie underneath such operations. We typically do not need to concern ourselves with all that—just get the available data and use it appropriately.

In the code sample the data has been the `Shape` itself – its type is the `typeof` of that object. Since we had two kinds of shapes, it was easier to get the first data item and cast it to a `Shape`—we didn't really care what the exact shape is.

There's more...

In our example, all shapes were good enough. What if the drop target wants to somehow let users know whether the dragged object is actually valid for this target – before the actual drop? This is possible through the `DragEnter` event.

Suppose we decide that only ellipses are good for dropping, but not rectangles. In case the drop is not allowed, a *no drop* icon shows instead of an *allow drop* icon. Here's a `DragEnter` event handler for the `WrapPanel` that would achieve this:

```
void OnDragEnter(object sender, DragEventArgs e) {
   if(e.Data.GetDataPresent(typeof(Ellipse).FullName))
      e.Effects = DragDropEffects.Move;
   else
      e.Effects = DragDropEffects.None;
   e.Handled = true;
}
```

Curiously enough, you'll need to handle the `DragOver` and `DragLeave` events in a similar fashion for this to work properly (check out `MainWindow.xaml` in the downloadable source for this chapter).

The opposite of `DragEnter` is `DragLeave`. This indicates the mouse has moved out of the target element. A more useful event is `DragOver`. This is fired repeatedly while the cursor is within the target element. This may be useful if the target has different *zones* and not all zones can accept the source. The `DragEventArgs.GetPosition` method is helpful here, to determine exactly where the mouse cursor is, relative to the target element.

Built-in drag-and-drop

Some controls naturally support drag-and-drop of certain types of data. `TextBox`, for instance, and `RichTextBox` support dragging-and-dropping text, even to/from other applications, unrelated to WPF.

Drag-and-drop to other applications

When using standard formats (available through the `DataFormats` class), things work out as expected. However, if we're trying to pass custom objects, they must be marked with the `Serializable` attribute or implement the `IDataObject` interface (the former is far easier). This allows WPF to reconstruct the object within the target process (as it has a separate address space). The example of a `Shape` that we used would fail between processes (event two instances of our own executable) because `UIElement` derived objects are never **serializable**. This would force us to pass over other information, such as the type name, or some serializable object with all relevant data that would be enough to reconstruct the `Shape` on the other side.

4
Using Standard Controls

In this chapter we will cover:

- Working with text
- Using content controls
- Displaying images
- Creating tooltips
- Creating a list of items
- Creating a standard menu
- Creating a context menu
- Selecting options with checkboxes and radio buttons
- Manipulating tab order and focus

Introduction

Every UI framework must provide a set of standard controls, such as text boxes, buttons, and list boxes. WPF is no different.

The difference between elements and controls is not that important in practice, but it is useful to understand the distinction.

Elements derive from `FrameworkElement` (directly or indirectly), but not from `Control`. They have a certain look and provide some functionality that is customizable, mostly by changing properties. For example, an `Ellipse` is an element. There's no way to change the fundamental appearance of an `Ellipse` (and it would be illogical to be able to turn an `Ellipse` into (for example) a triangle). We can still customize an `Ellipse` in a few ways using properties such as `Stroke`, `StrokeThickness`, `Fill`, and `Stretch`.

Controls, on the other hand, derive (directly or indirectly) from the `Control` class. `Control` adds a bunch of properties, of which the most significant is the `Template` property. This allows complete changing of the control's appearance without affecting its behavior. And all that can be achieved with XAML alone, without code or any class derivation. This is a dramatic departure from previous UI technologies (such as WinForms) that require a derivation and custom (usually non-trivial) code.

The following class diagram shows some of the fundamental element-related classes in WPF:

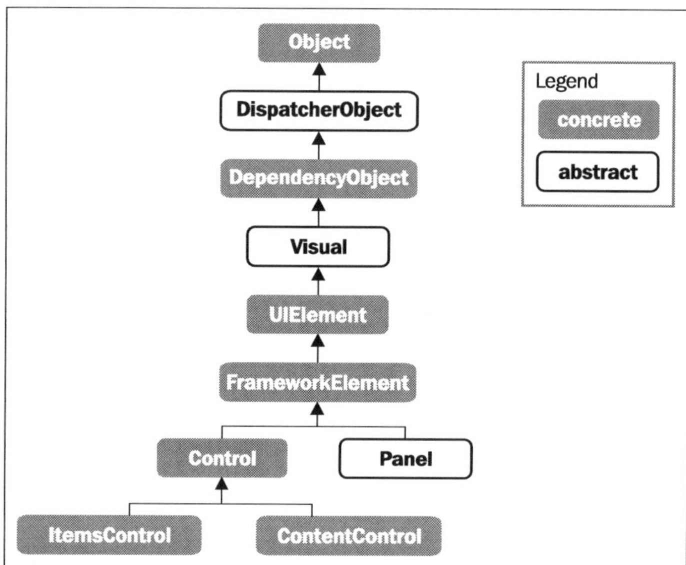

In this chapter, we'll take a closer look at some of WPF's standard controls.

Working with text

Text is the most fundamental way of conveying and inputting information. WPF provides a bunch of elements and controls that allow text display and input.

Getting ready

Make sure Visual Studio is up and running.

How to do it...

We'll create a simple application that uses the more common text related controls to demonstrate their usage:

1. Create a new WPF application named `CH04.TextControls`.
2. Open `MainWindow.xaml`. Add four rows and two columns to the existing `Grid`:

   ```
   <Grid.RowDefinitions>
       <RowDefinition Height="Auto" />
       <RowDefinition Height="Auto"/>
       <RowDefinition />
       <RowDefinition Height="Auto"/>
   </Grid.RowDefinitions>
   <Grid.ColumnDefinitions>
       <ColumnDefinition Width="Auto" />
       <ColumnDefinition />
   </Grid.ColumnDefinitions>
   ```

3. Add some controls to the grid as follows:

   ```
   <TextBlock FontSize="16" Text="User comment details"
              Margin="4"
              Grid.ColumnSpan="2" HorizontalAlignment="Center" />
   <Label Content="_Name:" Grid.Row="1" Target="_name" />
   <TextBox Grid.Row="1" Grid.Column="1"
            x:Name="_name" Margin="2"/>

   <Label Content="_Comment:" Grid.Row="2" Target="_comment" />

   <TextBox AcceptsReturn="True" Grid.Row="2"

            Grid.Column="1" x:Name="_comment" Margin="2"/>

   <Button HorizontalAlignment="Center" Margin="4"

           Grid.Row="3" Grid.ColumnSpan="2" FontSize="16"

           Content="Submit Comment"  />
   ```

   The `TextBox` controls allow input, while the `TextBlock` and `Label` display text that cannot be modified by the user.

The Visual Studio 2010 designer may report an exception in this window. This is due to the `Target` property setting (as explained in the *How it works...* section). In Visual Studio 2012, the designer survives, but there's still a squiggly under the `Target` property setting.

4. Add a `Click` event handler to the button and place the following simple code inside:

```
MessageBox.Show(string.Format("User: {0}, Comment:{1}{2}",
   _name.Text, Environment.NewLine, _comment.Text));
```

5. Running the application shows the following (after typing some text):

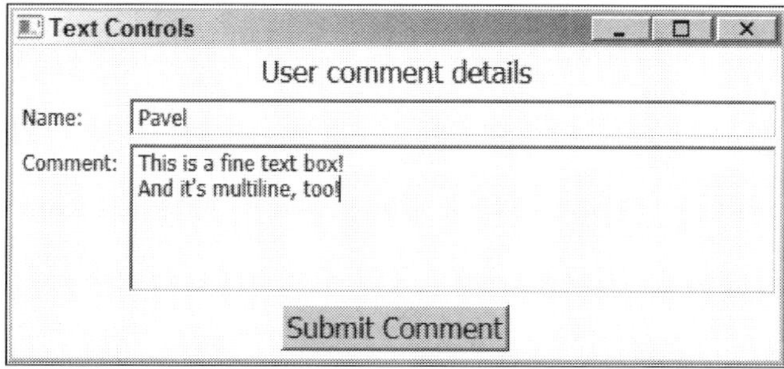

6. Pressing *Alt* + *N* places the caret inside the **Name** textbox, while pressing *Alt* + *C* places the caret inside the **Comment** textbox.
7. Clicking the button yields a simple message box:

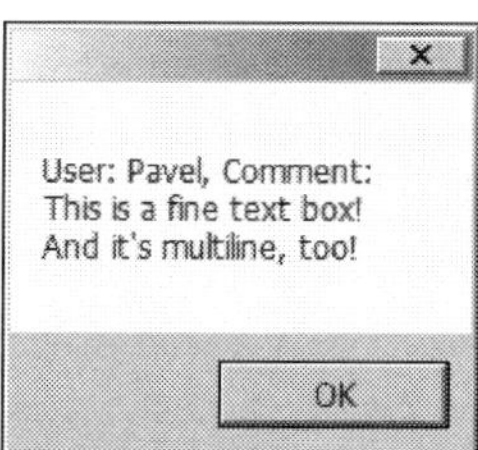

How it works...

This recipe explores the simplest (and most common) text-based controls. `TextBlock` displays some text via its `Text` property. It has many properties to control its actual output, such as font-related properties (`FontSize`, `FontFamily`, `FontWeight`, and so on), `Foreground` (a `Brush` used for the text glyphs), `TextAlignment`, and `TextWrapping`.

The `Label` control may seem very similar to a `TextBlock`, but there are at least two major differences.

The `Label` is actually a `ContentControl` (more on that in the *Using content controls* recipe later in this chapter), which means it can display anything, not just text. However, it's really useful only for text, as you'll see shortly.

It provides an access key feature. Any character in its `Content` string preceded by an underscore becomes an access key (with the *Alt* key). Pressing that access key (with *Alt*) causes the input focus to jump to the control designated by the `Target` property. In the preceding example, pressing *Alt* + *N* causes the **Name** `TextBox` to receive the input focus.

The access key character is an underscore (it's an ampersand (&) in other technologies—Windows Forms and Win32). The underscore was selected because it's XML friendly; otherwise something like "&" would have to be written instead of a simple ampersand.

The `Target` property of `Label` is of type `UIElement`. The reason the preceding code works is because an appropriate type converter does the right thing (curiously enough, Visual Studio 2010/2012 intellisense places a blue squiggly on the `Target` property, as noted previously; however, it does work correctly at runtime). Otherwise, a binding expression would have been required (this was the case in prior versions of WPF).

A `TextBox` is the simplest text input control. It provides the actual text via the `Text` property. It can support multiple lines by setting its `AcceptsReturn` property to `true` (programmatically, however, any `TextBox` can show multiline content if new line characters are embedded within the text).

`TextBox` provides the expected text related properties, similar to a `TextBlock`. It also provides methods for clipboard operations, such as `Copy`, `Cut`, `Paste`, `Undo`, and `Redo`. It also handles the (related) standard WPF commands for clipboard operations (more on commands in *Chapter 7, Commands and MVVM*).

There's more...

The `TextBlock` element is more complex than it seems. Its `Text` property is the simplest way to get it to display something, but it's not the only one. It actually contains an `Inlines` property (its `ContentProperty` for easier XAML entry), which is a collection of types inheriting from `Inline`, such as `Run`, `LineBreak`, `Bold`, `Italic`, `Underline`, and `Hyperlink`. The following is an example:

```
<TextBlock>
   <Run Foreground="Blue" Text="Hello TextBlock" />
   <LineBreak />
   <Bold><Italic FontSize="16">This is pronouned text</Italic></Bold>
```

```
        <LineBreak />
        <Run>Click the following link to go to search:</Run>
        <Hyperlink>Search in Database</Hyperlink>
    </TextBlock>
```

This markup produces the following result:

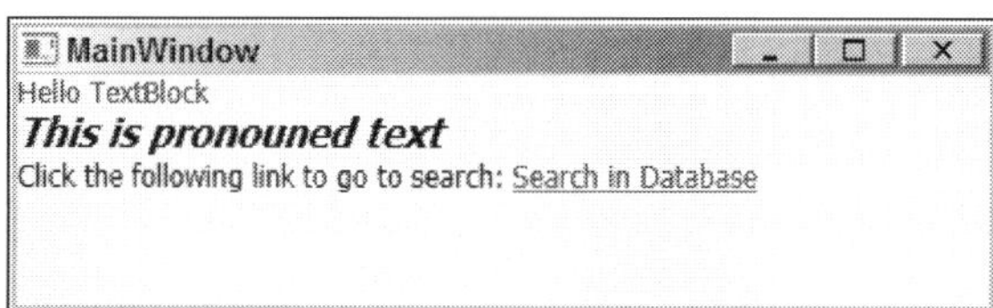

Although the same effect can be achieved by multiple `TextBlock` elements, this is much more economical – there's only one element here, which makes it easier on WPF when (for example) layout is concerned.

Here are the common inlines:

- `Run`: Represents some text (`Text` property) with its own formatting properties.
- `LineBreak`: Represents a line break.
- `Italic`, `Bold`, `Underline` (all deriving from `Span`): Encapsulate whatever is inside (any other inline) with the particular attribute represented by this inline.
- `Hyperlink` (derives from `Span`): Encapsulates its content in a hyperlink style rendering. The `NavigationUri` property can be set to indicate the link to activate upon clicking, but this only works if the `Hyperlink` has a `NavigationWindow` as a parent (not discussed in this book as it's not as useful as it sounds). Otherwise, the `Click` event can be used to do whatever is needed (such as activating a URL using `Process.Start` for example). Another nice feature of the `Hyperlink` is that it's a command source, having the `Command`, `CommandParameter`, and `CommandTarget` properties, meaning it can activate a command when clicked (see *Chapter 7, Commands and MVVM* for more information on these properties).

Using content controls

Content controls provide a flexible way of customizing the appearance of a control. The `ContentControl` class includes a `Content` property, of type object; meaning, it can be anything. A typical example is a `Button`. The `Button` inherits from `ContentControl` (not directly, but this is unimportant for this discussion). A typical button shows text, an image, or perhaps an image and text. But in fact, it can hold anything, such as a graphic drawing, a video playing, any combination of the above, or anything else. This is the power of `ContentControl`. Let's see how this works.

Getting ready

Make sure Visual Studio is up and running.

How to do it...

We'll create several buttons (which are ContentControls) and show the various ways their content can be set and viewed:

1. Create a new WPF Application named CH04.ContentControls.
2. Open MainWindow.Xaml. Change the root Grid to a StackPanel.
3. Add a Button to the StackPanel and set its Content to some string:

   ```
   <Button Content="Click me" Margin="4" Padding="4"
           FontSize="16" HorizontalAlignment="Left"/>
   ```

4. Add an image file to the project (the following XAML uses copy.png, included in the downloadable source for this chapter, but you can select any image).
5. Add another Button to the StackPanel that uses the image like so:

   ```
   <Button Margin="4" HorizontalAlignment="Left" Padding="4">
       <StackPanel Orientation="Horizontal">
           <Image Source="copy.png" Width="16" Height="16" />
           <TextBlock Text="Copy" Margin="10,0,0,0"
                      VerticalAlignment="Center" FontSize="16"/>
       </StackPanel>
   </Button>
   ```

   The Content is set implicitly to a horizontal StackPanel. This makes the button show the Image and TextBlock.

6. Let's create a simple data class, named Person:

   ```
   class Person {
      public int Age { get; set; }
      public string Name { get; set; }
      public override string ToString() {
         return string.Format("{0} is {1} years old", Name, Age);
      }
   }
   ```

7. Now let's create an instance of Person as a resource in the Window. First, we'll have to add an XML namespace mapping (as we did several times before). We'll call the prefix local and map it to the project's namespace:

   ```
   xmlns:local="clr-namespace:CH04.ContentControls"
   ```

8. Then we'll create the actual `Person`:

```
<Window.Resources>
    <local:Person Age="10" Name="Bart" x:Key="p1" />
</Window.Resources>
```

9. Add another `Button` to the `StackPanel` whose content is the `Person` resource:

```
<Button Content="{StaticResource p1}" FontSize="16"
        Margin="4" Padding="4" HorizontalAlignment="Left"/>
```

10. Running the application shows the following:

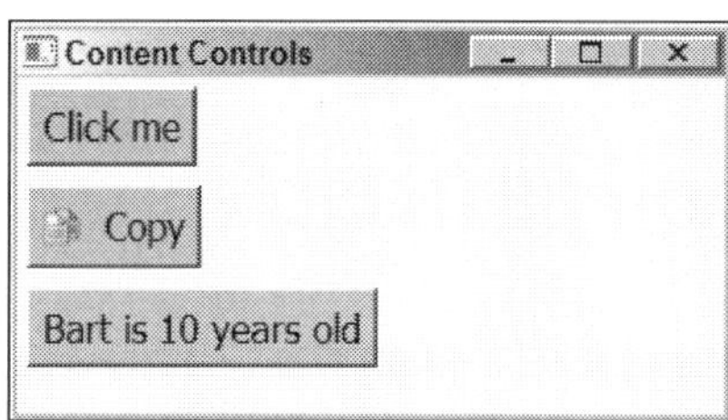

11. Let's add another `Button` that also has its `Content` set to the same `Person`, but shows it differently. This requires setting `ContentTemplate` to a `DataTemplate` object and using some data bindings:

```
<Button Content="{StaticResource p1}" FontSize="16"
        Margin="4" Padding="4" HorizontalAlignment="Left">
    <Button.ContentTemplate>
        <DataTemplate>
            <Grid TextBlock.FontSize="16">
                <Grid.ColumnDefinitions>
                    <ColumnDefinition Width="Auto" />
                    <ColumnDefinition />
                </Grid.ColumnDefinitions>
                <Grid.RowDefinitions>
                    <RowDefinition Height="Auto" />
                    <RowDefinition Height="Auto" />
                </Grid.RowDefinitions>
                <TextBlock Text="Name:" />
                <TextBlock Text="{Binding Name}"
                           Margin="6,0,0,0"
                           Foreground="Blue" Grid.Column="1" />
                <TextBlock Text="Age:" Grid.Row="1"/>
                <TextBlock Text="{Binding Age}"
                             Margin="6,0,0,0" Grid.Row="1"
                             Foreground="Red" Grid.Column="1"
                             TextAlignment="Right"/>
```

```
                </Grid>
            </DataTemplate>
        </Button.ContentTemplate>
    </Button>
```

12. Run the application. It should look as follows:

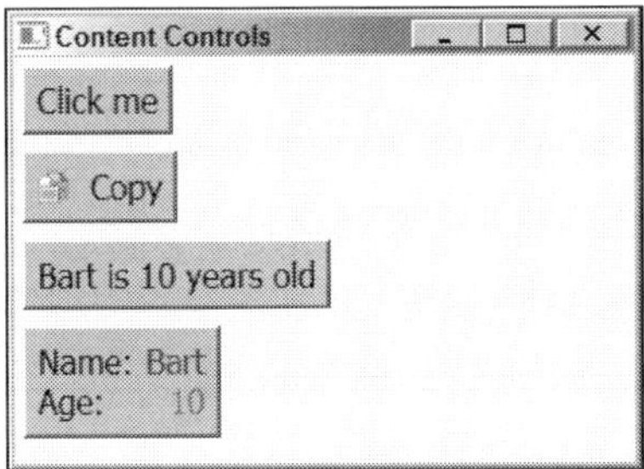

How it works...

A ContentControl-derived type renders its Content using the following rules:

- If it's a string, a TextBlock is rendered with its Text set to the string value.
- If it derives from UIElement, it's rendered as is (its OnRender method is called).
- If ContentTemplate is null, then it's rendered as a TextBlock with its Text set to the ToString of the Content. Otherwise, the supplied DataTemplate is used for rendering.

The preceding code uses all of these options.

The first button just holds a string in its Content, so it's rendered as a TextBlock.

The second button is used to show an image and text. As the Content property is a single one, multiple items require a Panel – in this case a StackPanel. This corresponds to the second rule – StackPanel (like any Panel) derives (eventually) from UIElement, so is rendered as is.

The third button's Content is a data object (a Person). Without a DataTemplate, it's rendered as a TextBlock with the ToString as its Text. As we created a sensible override for Person.ToString(), this shows the name and age of the person.

The fourth (and last) button is the most interesting one. Its `Content` is set to a data object (our `Person`) as well, but this time a `DataTemplate` object is provided via the `ContentTemplate` property. This allows for a custom way of rendering a `Person`. A `DataTemplate` must contain a single root element (typically some `Panel`). To use the actual property values, data binding is required (the source of the binding is (implicitly) always the `Content`). The `DataTemplate` objects are powerful constructs; they and other data binding features will be discussed fully in *Chapter 6, Data Binding*.

There's more...

`ContentControl` itself is not an abstract class. It's sometimes used to bind to something else through its `Content` property.

There are many `ContentControl`-derived types (some of which we'll see in later recipes in this chapter), but they all support the same basic concepts: `Content` and an optional `ContentTemplate`. The preceding code used buttons, but there are many others, such as `ScrollViewer`, `Label`, `CheckBox`, `RadioButton`, and `ToolTip`.

Headered content controls

One common base class deriving from `ContentControl` is `HeaderedContentControl`. This adds a `Header` property (of type `object`) and an associated optional template (`HeaderTemplate` property). These two properties serve the same purpose as `Content` and `ContentTemplate`. In a sense, these controls have two *contents* and two *content templates*. Here's an example with a `GroupBox`:

```
<GroupBox Margin="10" >
    <GroupBox.Header>
        <StackPanel Orientation="Horizontal">
            <Image Source="cup.png" />
            <TextBlock Text="Tea options"
                       Margin="6,0,0,0"/>
        </StackPanel>
    </GroupBox.Header>
    <StackPanel>
        <CheckBox Margin="4">Sugar</CheckBox>
        <CheckBox Margin="4">Mint</CheckBox>
        <CheckBox Margin="4">Milk</CheckBox>
        <CheckBox Margin="4">Cinnamon</CheckBox>
    </StackPanel>
</GroupBox>
```

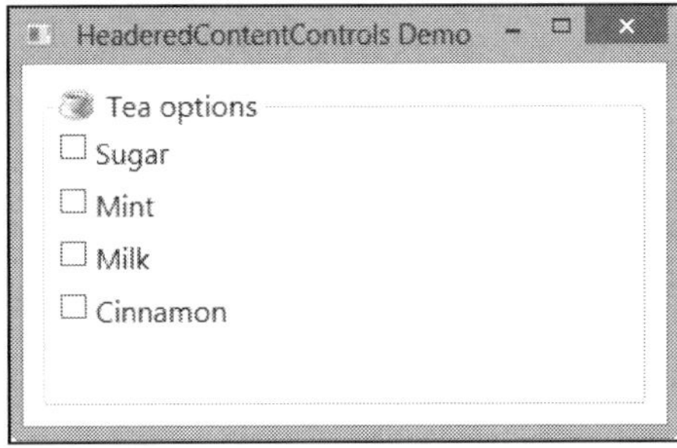

And a similar example with an `Expander` (using templates):

```
<Expander Margin="10" x:Name="_bookInfo"
           ExpandDirection="Down">
    <Expander.HeaderTemplate>
        <DataTemplate>
            <Border BorderBrush="Blue" BorderThickness="1"
                    Padding="4">
                <TextBlock Text="{Binding Name,
                    StringFormat=Book: {0}}" />
            </Border>
        </DataTemplate>
    </Expander.HeaderTemplate>
    <Expander.ContentTemplate>
        <DataTemplate>
            <Border BorderBrush="Blue" BorderThickness="2"
                    Padding="4">
                <StackPanel>
                    <TextBlock Text="{Binding Name,
                      StringFormat=Name: {0}}" />
                    <TextBlock Text="{Binding Author,
                      StringFormat=Author: {0}}" />
                    <TextBlock Text="{Binding YearPublished,
                      StringFormat=Published: {0}}" />
                </StackPanel>
            </Border>
        </DataTemplate>
    </Expander.ContentTemplate>
</Expander>
```

And the code behind (sets the book info to the `Header` and `Content`):

```
_bookInfo.Content = _bookInfo.Header = new Book {
   Name = "Windows Internals",
   Author = "Mark Russinovich",
   YearPublished = 2009
};
```

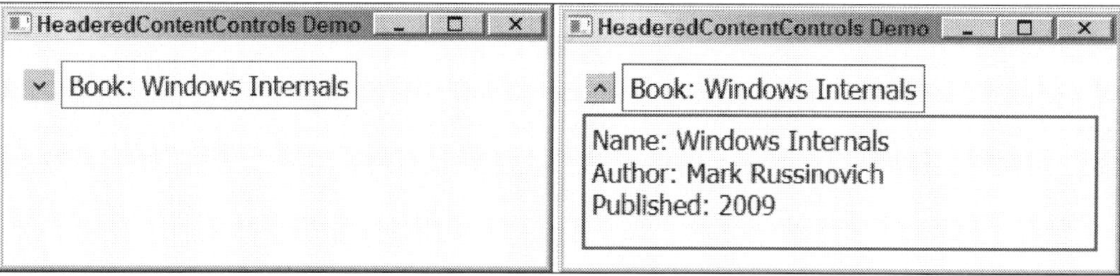

See also

For more information on data templates, check out *Chapter 6, Data Binding*.

Displaying images

Images are a common way to convey information, application options, or just make things look pretty. The `Image` element is typically used to show images, whether they originate from static image files or are generated dynamically. Let's take a look at how this works.

Getting ready

Make sure Visual Studio is up and running.

How to do it...

We'll create a simple image viewer, where the user can browse the file system, select an image and view it.

1. Create a new WPF Application named `CH04.Images`.
2. Add an existing image to the project, to serve as an icon. The downloadable source for this chapter includes an `open.png` image, but you can use any (preferably small) image.
3. Open `MainWindow.xaml`. Replace the existing `Grid` with a `DockPanel`.

4. Add a single `Button` to the `DockPanel`, dock it at the top, and place the added image inside the button using an `Image` element (with some text):

```
<Button DockPanel.Dock="Top" FontSize="20" Margin="4"
        Padding="4">
    <StackPanel Orientation="Horizontal">
        <Image Source="open.png" Stretch="None" />
        <TextBlock Text="Open Image File..." Margin="20,0,0,0"
                   VerticalAlignment="Center" />
    </StackPanel>
</Button>
```

5. Add a `ScrollViewer` to the `DockPanel`. Inside it place another `Image` element, but don't set any `Source`:

```
<ScrollViewer BorderBrush="Black" Margin="4"
              BorderThickness="1"
              HorizontalScrollBarVisibility="Auto"
              VerticalScrollBarVisibility="Auto">
    <Image x:Name="_image" Stretch="None" />
</ScrollViewer>
```

6. This is how it should look now when run:

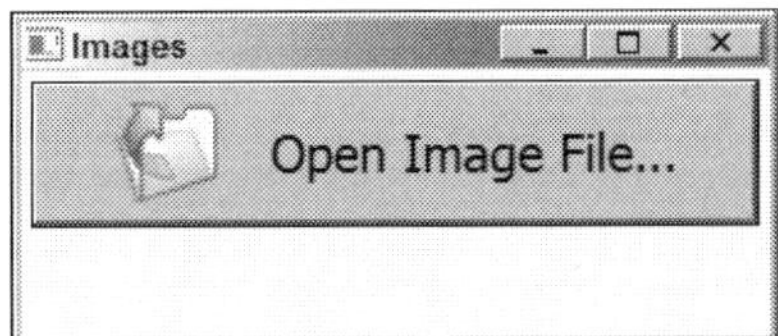

7. When the button is clicked, we want to allow the user to select an image file, so that it's shown by the `Image` inside the `ScrollViewer`. Add a `Click` event handler to the button and place the following code in it (you'll need to add a `using` statement for the `Microsoft.Win32` namespace):

```
void OnOpenImage(object sender, RoutedEventArgs e) {
   var dlg = new OpenFileDialog();
   dlg.Filter = "Images|*.jpg;*.gif;*.bmp;*.png";
   if(dlg.ShowDialog() == true) {
      try {
         var bmp = new BitmapImage(new Uri(dlg.FileName,
            UriKind.Absolute));
         _image.Source = bmp;
      }
      catch(Exception ex) {
         MessageBox.Show("Error loading image: " +
         ex.Message);
      }
   }
}
```

8. Run the application, click the button, and select an image file. This is the result:

How it works...

The `Image` element is capable of displaying an image pointed to by its `Source` property. This property is of type `ImageSource`, which is abstract. In step 4, a simple string (`open.png`) was provided to `Source`. This works because a type converter has created a `BitmapImage` (an `ImageSource` derivative) object out of the image resource.

In step 7, an actual `BitmapImage` is created in code, as required, to read an image file.

The way an `Image` is displayed depends on the `Stretch` property. This indicates how an image is stretched, as the actual size of the `Image` element typically differs from the natural size of the image source. There are four possible values, `Uniform` being the default. Here's how setting `Stretch` affects the displayed image (of the famous penguins):

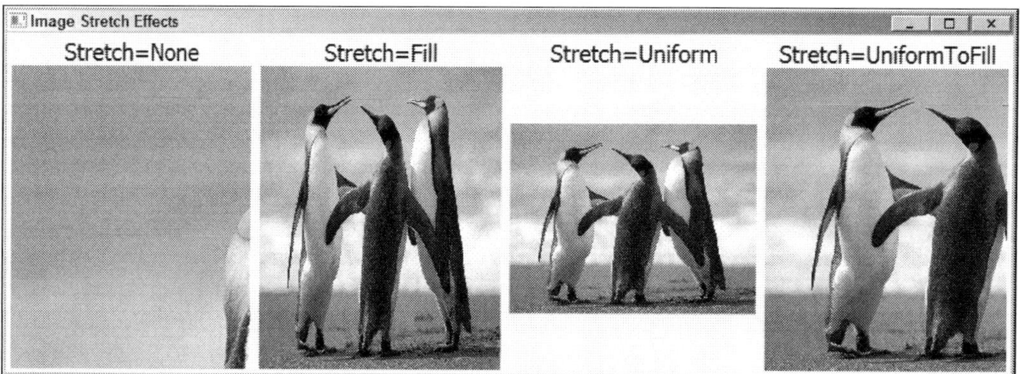

With Stretch=None, the image is displayed in its original size. In the code sample, a ScrollViewer was used to allow scrolling through large images. Uniform and UniformToFill preserve the aspect ratio (the original image width divided by the height), while Fill simply stretches the image to fill the available space for the Image. UniformToFill may cut out content if the available space has a different aspect ratio than the original.

Do not confuse Image with ImageSource. The Image is an element, so can be placed somewhere in the visual tree. An ImageSource is the actual data; an Image element simply shows the image data in some way. The original image data (ImageSource) is unchanged.

There's more...

ImageSource has some interesting derivatives. One of them is DrawingImage, which is an ImageSource that uses a Drawing object (not to be confused with ImageDrawing, which is a Drawing that uses an ImageSource). A Drawing is a representation of a 2D drawing. Drawing itself is abstract and has some concrete implementations. The following class diagram shows some of the classes deriving from ImageSource:

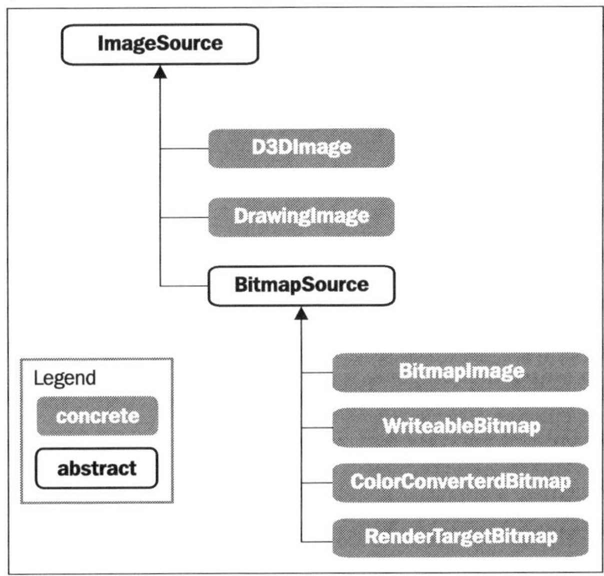

The following is an example of building a `Drawing` as a resource, based on a `Geometry` (more information on geometries can be found in *Chapter 9, Graphics and Animation*):

```
<CombinedGeometry x:Key="ringGeometry"
                  GeometryCombineMode="Exclude">
    <CombinedGeometry.Geometry1>
        <EllipseGeometry Center="100,100"
            RadiusX="100" RadiusY="100" />
    </CombinedGeometry.Geometry1>
    <CombinedGeometry.Geometry2>
        <EllipseGeometry Center="100,100"
            RadiusX="80" RadiusY="80" />
    </CombinedGeometry.Geometry2>
</CombinedGeometry>
<GeometryDrawing x:Key="ringDrawing"
    Geometry="{StaticResource ringGeometry}"
    Brush="LightBlue">
    <GeometryDrawing.Pen>
        <Pen Brush="Black" Thickness="3" />
    </GeometryDrawing.Pen>
</GeometryDrawing>
```

A `Drawing` is not an element, so it cannot be part of a visual tree – it needs to be hosted somehow. One way is to use a `DrawingImage` as the `ImageSource` of an `Image`, like so:

```
<Image>
   <Image.Source>
      <DrawingImage Drawing="{StaticResource ringDrawing}" />
   </Image.Source>
</Image>
```

It will look as follows like when run:

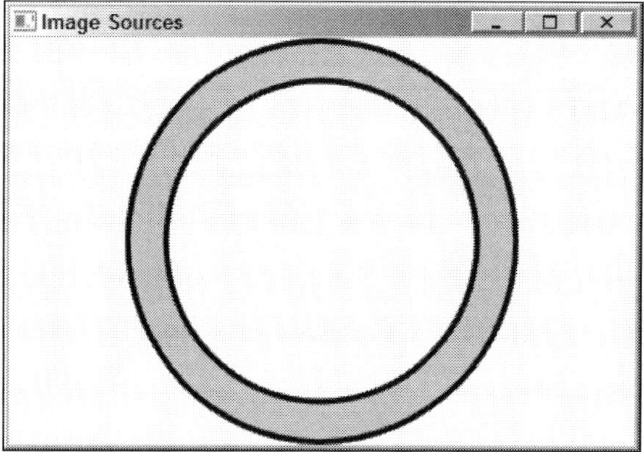

Another ImageSource derivative is BitmapSource, which is abstract as well. It's the base class of BitmapImage used in the code example. There are many other derivatives. One I'd like to mention here is WriteableBitmap. This is a bitmap with accessible pixels. The application can manipulate those pixels as desired by calling WritePixels. The following an example of creating a WriteableBitmap and attaching it as a Source of an Image (named _image):

```
public partial class MainWindow : Window {
   WriteableBitmap _bmp;
   DispatcherTimer _timer;
   Random _rnd = new Random();
   int[] _pixel = { 255 };
   public MainWindow() {
      InitializeComponent();
      _bmp = new WriteableBitmap(100, 100, 0, 0,
          PixelFormats.Gray8, null);
      _image.Source = _bmp;
      _timer = new DispatcherTimer();
      _timer.Interval = TimeSpan.FromMilliseconds(20);
      _timer.Tick += delegate {
         int x = _rnd.Next(_bmp.PixelWidth);
         int y = _rnd.Next(_bmp.PixelHeight);
         _bmp.WritePixels(new Int32Rect(x, y, 1, 1), _pixel,
             _bmp.BackBufferStride, 0);
      };
      _timer.Start();
   }
}
```

The code fills up the bitmap with random white pixels using a timer, 50 times per second. This is how it looks at some captured point:

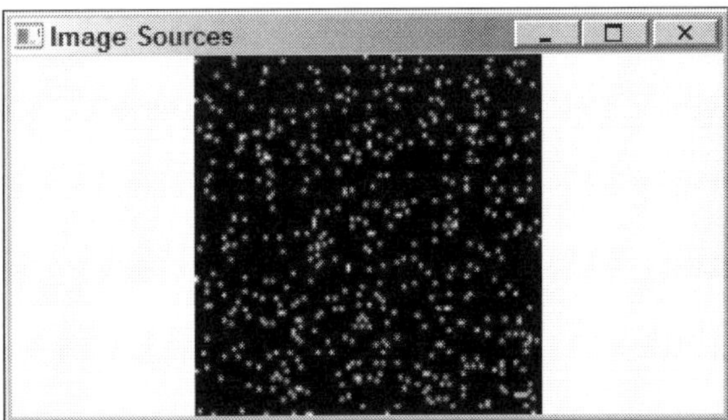

The complete source code is available in the downloadable source for this chapter under the `CH04.ImageSources` project.

See also

For more information on `WriteableBitmap`, check out the *Manipulating a bitmap programmatically* recipe in *Chapter 9, Graphics and Animation*.

Creating tooltips

Tooltips are typically those yellowish (or another color, depending on the Windows theme and user customization) pop ups that show up when the mouse pointer hovers over something important within the UI, providing some extra information relevant to that something. WPF makes it easy to create tooltips, either standard ones, or custom.

Getting ready

Make sure Visual Studio is up and running.

How to do it...

1. Create a new WPF application named `CH04.ToolTips`.
2. Open `MainWindow.xaml`. Add two rows to the existing `Grid` as follows:

```
<Grid.RowDefinitions>
    <RowDefinition Height="Auto" />
    <RowDefinition />
</Grid.RowDefinitions>
```

3. Add a `ToolBar` to the `Grid`, with two buttons in it:

```
<ToolBar>
    <Button Content="Copy" FontSize="16" Margin="4"
            Padding="4" Command="Copy" />
    <Button Content="Paste" FontSize="16" Margin="4"
            Padding="4" Command="Paste" />
</ToolBar>
```

   The `Command` properties used will make the buttons work correctly on the `TextBox` we'll add in the next step. For more information on commands, check out *Chapter 7, Commands and MVVM*.

4. Add a `TextBox` to the second row of the `Grid` and make it multiline:

```
<TextBox AcceptsReturn="True" Grid.Row="1" FontSize="14"
         VerticalScrollBarVisibility="Auto"
         HorizontalScrollBarVisibility="Auto"/>
```

5. Running the application allows for simple copying and pasting of text. This works because of the commands bound to the buttons. Now let's add a simple tool tip to the **Copy** button. We'll do this by setting the `ToolTip` property of the `Button` to some text:

```
<Button Content="Copy" FontSize="16" Margin="4"
        Padding="4" Command="Copy"
        ToolTip="Copy the selected text to the clipboard"/>
```

6. Run the application. Type some text in the `TextBox`, then select some text (the **Copy** button should become enabled) and hover over the button with the mouse:

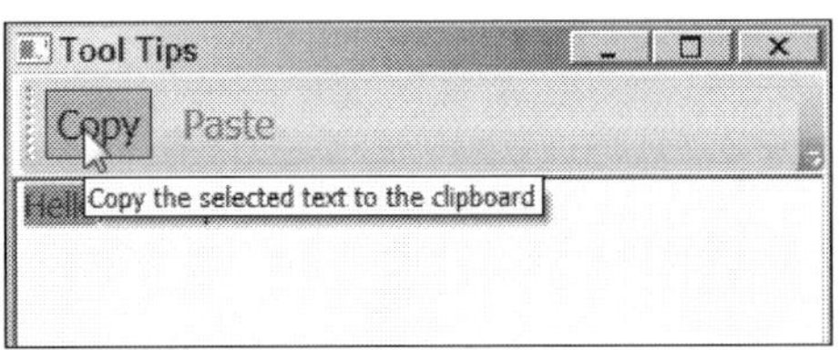

7. Now let's try something more ambitious. Add a custom tool tip for the **Paste** button by setting its `ToolTip` property to something more fancy:

```
<Button.ToolTip>
  <ToolTip>
    <Border CornerRadius="10" BorderThickness="2"
       BorderBrush="Black" Padding="4" Background="LightBlue">
       <Grid Width="120">
         <TextBlock FontSize="15" TextWrapping="Wrap"
                    Text="Paste text from the clipboard" />
       </Grid>
    </Border>
  </ToolTip>
</Button.ToolTip>
```

8. Run the application and make sure some text is in the clipboard. Then hover over the **Paste** button:

This certainly looks more interesting, although not perfect (the yellowish background sips through). We'll see in the *There's more...* section how to remedy that.

How it works...

The `ToolTip` control is a `ContentControl`, so can have any content, with the same rules as any other `ContentControl` (see the *Using content controls* recipe earlier in this chapter). The `ToolTip` property (on `FrameworkElement`) is of type `object`. If a non-`ToolTip` control is supplied, WPF automatically creates a `ToolTip` control to wrap the actual content provided.

The tooltip background originates in the Windows theme and can also change because of user preferences. For example, with the Windows Classic theme, the color can be changed using the personalization options within the Windows **Control Panel**. Here's how to do it: Open the Control Panel **Personalization** item, and select **Windows Color** at the bottom. The following dialog box should appear:

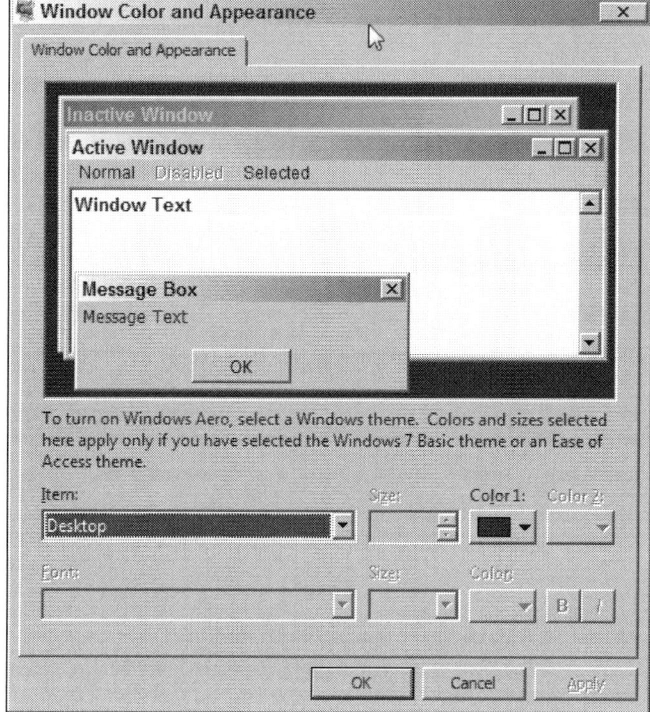

Open the **Item** combo box, and select **ToolTip**:

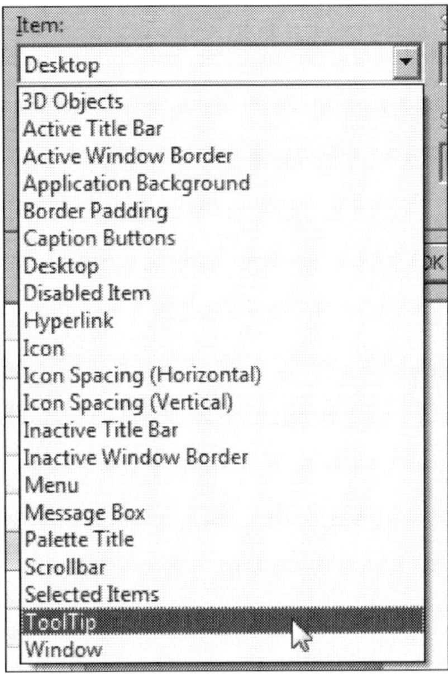

Here we can change the background (and foreground) color of tooltips (as well as the default font). For some themes there's no UI to do this, such as when using the Aero theme in Windows 7.

There's more...

More tooltip customization is possible using the `ToolTipService` class. This class provides a bunch of attached properties that can be applied to elements on which tooltips exist. For example, in our code sample, the tooltips don't appear if a button is disabled. To make the tooltip appear no matter what the enabled state is, set the `ToolTipService.ShowOnDisabled` property to `true`. Other properties you can change include `ShowDuration`, `HasDropShadow`, `IsEnabled`, and `InitialShowDelay`, to name a few; most of them are self-explanatory.

Deeper tooltip customization

As was evident in the example code, the non-textual tooltip was sitting on top of the default yellowish (or whatever color) background. This is because of the default control template of the `ToolTip`. Fortunately, there's a way to fix this (without replacing the control template) by setting some properties via a `Style` (styles will be discussed in *Chapter 8*). Here's a complete new button which uses this idea:

```
<Button Content="Undo" Command="Undo" FontSize="16"
        Margin="4" Padding="4"
        ToolTipService.HasDropShadow="False">
    <Button.Resources>
       <Style TargetType="ToolTip">
         <Setter Property="Background" Value="Transparent" />
         <Setter Property="BorderBrush" Value="Transparent" />
       </Style>
    </Button.Resources>
    <Button.ToolTip>
       <Border CornerRadius="10" BorderThickness="2"
               BorderBrush="Black" Padding="4"
               Background="LightBlue">
            <Grid>
                <TextBlock FontSize="15" TextWrapping="Wrap"
                           Text="Undo the last action" />
            </Grid>
        </Border>
    </Button.ToolTip>
</Button>
```

Using the above markup, the tooltip now looks polished, and becomes independent of the Windows theme or the user's preference:

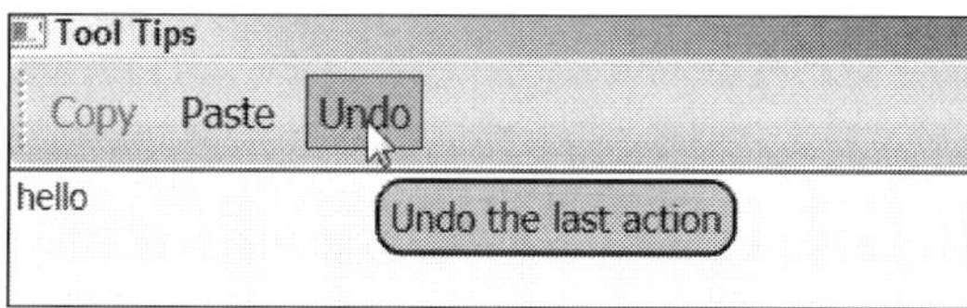

Realistic tooltips

The preceding example is fun enough, but it's impractical to customize every single tooltip in this way. The "proper" way to do this is by defining a `DataTemplate` that uses data binding expressions to get to the actual text (and maybe other things like images) of that tooltip. Data binding is discussed in *Chapter 6*.

Creating a list of items

Lists are typically used to show a collection of related objects. WPF provides several controls which can be used for that purpose, such as `ListBox` and `ComboBox` (which can be considered *classic*). All these derive from `ItemsControl`, which defines some basic functionality, such as an `Items` property. In this recipe, we'll take a quick look at `ListBox` and `ComboBox`. We'll reserve a more detailed explanation for *Chapter 6, Data Binding*, as this is the typical way list-based controls are used in WPF.

Getting ready

Make sure Visual Studio is up and running.

How to do it...

1. Create a new WPF application named `CH04.Lists`.
2. Open `MainWindow.Xaml`. Add two rows to the existing `Grid`, as follows:

```
<Grid.RowDefinitions>
    <RowDefinition Height="Auto" />
    <RowDefinition />
</Grid.RowDefinitions>
```

3. Add a `ComboBox` to the `Grid` with some string items:

```
<ComboBox Margin="4" x:Name="_langCombo">
    <ComboBoxItem>C++</ComboBoxItem>
    <ComboBoxItem>C#</ComboBoxItem>
    <ComboBoxItem>Visual Basic</ComboBoxItem>
    <ComboBoxItem>F#</ComboBoxItem>
</ComboBox>
```

4. Add a `GroupBox` containing an empty `ListBox` to the second row:

```
<GroupBox Header="Some Keywords" Grid.Row="1" Margin="4">
    <ListBox x:Name="_keywordList" Margin="4">
    </ListBox>
</GroupBox>
```

5. When the selection in the `ComboBox` changes, we'll populate the `ListBox` with some keywords from that language. Add an event handler for the `SelectionChanged` event for the `ComboBox` and place the following code in the handler:

```
void OnLangChanged(object s, SelectionChangedEventArgs e) {
   _keywordList.Items.Clear();
   string[] keywords = null;
```

```
        switch(_langCombo.SelectedIndex) {
           case 0: // C++
              keywords = new string[] {
                 "for", "auto", "mutable", "explicit",
                 "class", "volatile"
              };
              break;

           case 1: // C#
              keywords = new string[] {
                 "while", "var", "implicit", "return",
                 "where", "enum"
              };
              break;

           case 2: // VB
              keywords = new string[] {
                 "Dim", "Select", "While",
                 "Property", "Function", "If"
              };
              break;

           case 3: // F#
              keywords = new string[] {
                 "let", "rec", "mutable",
                 "module", "yield", "type"
              };
              break;
        }
        if(keywords != null)
           Array.ForEach(keywords,
              keyword => _keywordList.Items.Add(keyword));
     }
```

6. Run the application. You should be able to select a language from the drop down `ComboBox` and view a selected set of keywords for that particular language:

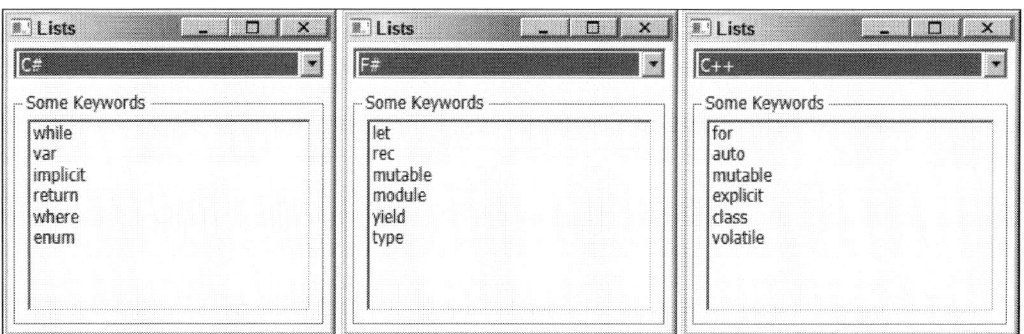

How it works...

`ItemsControl` is the base class of all multiple-item containing controls. It provides for some basic properties, such as Items (a collection of objects) and some customization hooks we'll look at in *Chapter 8*. The following class diagram depicts the important classes derived from `ItemsControl` class:

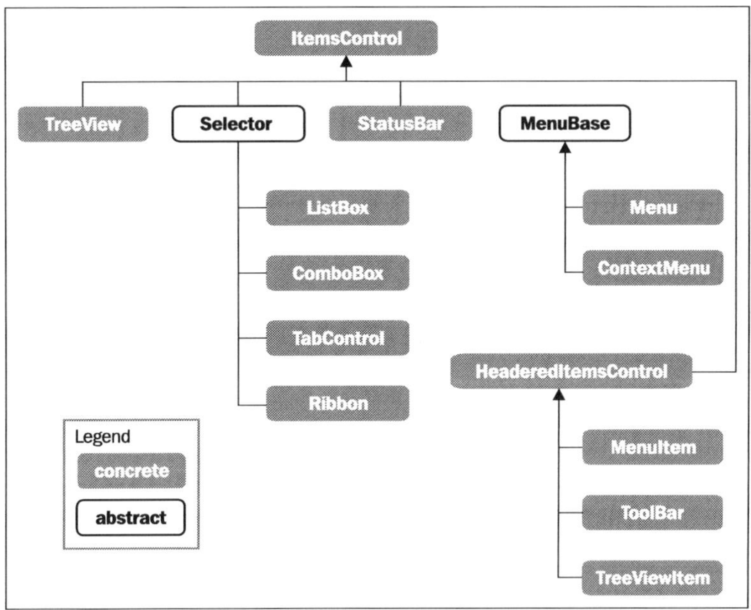

`ListBox` and `ComboBox` both inherit from (the abstract) `Selector` class (which inherits from `ItemsControl`). `Selector` adds the notion of selection. `ItemsControl` itself is not abstract, but does not support selection of any kind), with properties such as `SelectedIndex` (an integer) and `SelectedItem` (the actual object) and an event (`SelectionChanged`), which is leveraged in the preceding code. Another useful property of `Selector` is `SelectedValue`, which is based on another property, `SelectedValuePath`. For example, if the `Selector` holds `Person` objects and `SelectedValuePath` is `Name`, then `SelectedValue` would be the currently selected person's `Name` property.

`ListBox` adds the idea of multiple selections, with the `SelectedItems` property and a `SelectionMode` property. `SelectionMode` of `Single` signifies single item selection (the default), while `Multiple` allows selection/de-selection with mouse clicks and `Extended` allows multi-selection with the *Ctrl* and *Shift* keys to quickly select/deselect range of items.

In the `SelectionChanged` event handler, we switch on the currently selected item index, clear the `ListBox` items, and then add the required strings using the `Items` property's `Add` method (this is done with `Array.ForEach` that simply calls some delegate – in this example provided as a lambda function—for each item in the array, a string in this case).

There's more...

ListBox wraps every object it gets in a ListBoxItem, while ComboBox does the same with ComboBoxItem. These wrapper controls are created automatically for each object added to the ListBox / ComboBox. Both are types of ContentControl, meaning they can hold anything, with the usual rules of ContentControls. A DataTemplate may be provided using the ItemTemplate property (from ItemsControl). This means that the ComboBox in the preceding code sample could have looked as follows:

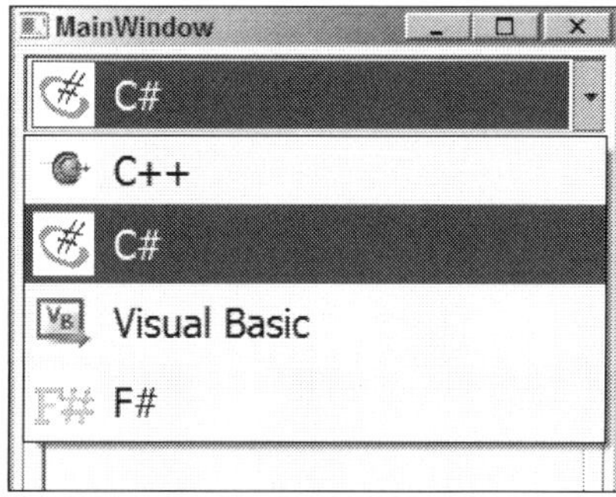

This can be achieved in two ways: first, by hard coding a horizontal StackPanel with an image and text inside every ComboBoxItem, as follows (the full code sample is in the CH04.Lists2 project available with the downloadable source for this chapter):

```
<ComboBoxItem Padding="4">
    <StackPanel Orientation="Horizontal" >
        <Image Source="Images/CS.jpg" Width="32"
               Stretch="Uniform" />
        <TextBlock Text="C#" VerticalAlignment="Center"
                   FontSize="20" Margin="10,0,0,0" />
    </StackPanel>
</ComboBoxItem>
```

The second is by using a data object with an appropriate DataTemplate. We'll look at this more closely in *Chapter 6, Data Binding*, as it's the typical way of working, especially when data binding is involved.

Creating a standard menu

A drop-down menu is one of the most (if the not the most) recognizable aspects of graphical user interfaces. Not as popular today as it was in the early days of GUIs, it's still a vital part of many applications. Let's see how to create one with WPF.

Getting ready

Make sure Visual Studio is up and running.

How to do it...

We'll create a simple Notepad-like text editor with a typical menu:

1. Create a new WPF application named `CH04.Menus`.
2. Open `MainWindow.xaml`. Add two rows to the existing `Grid` as follows:

```
<Grid.RowDefinitions>
    <RowDefinition Height="Auto"/>
    <RowDefinition />
</Grid.RowDefinitions>
```

3. Add a `TextBox` to the second row:

```
<TextBox Grid.Row="1" AcceptsReturn="True" />
```

4. Add a `Menu` control to the first row with `MenuItem` objects underneath:

```
<Menu>
    <MenuItem Header="_File">
        <MenuItem Header=" _Exit" />
    </MenuItem>
    <MenuItem Header="_Edit">
        <MenuItem Command="Copy" />
        <MenuItem Header="_Paste" Command="Paste" />
        <Separator />
        <MenuItem Header="_Undo" Command="Undo" />
    </MenuItem>
</Menu>
```

5. Running the application shows two top level menu items, **File** and **Edit**. You can type in the text box and use the **Copy**, **Paste**, and **Undo** menu items, which work as expected. Selecting **File** | **Exit** does nothing. Let's change that.
6. Add a **Click** event handler to the **Exit** `MenuItem`. Add the following code to the handler:

```
void OnExit(object sender, RoutedEventArgs e) {
   Close();
}
```

7. Run the application. Note that clicking **File** | **Exit** closes the application (by closing the `Window`).

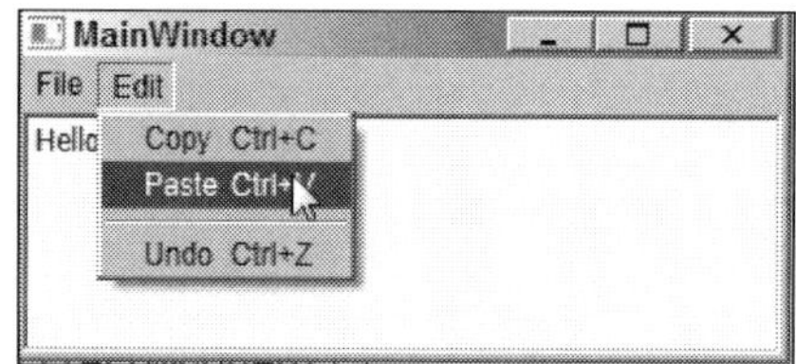

How it works...

The menu derives from `MenuBase` (an abstract class that is also the base of `ContextMenu`), which derives from `ItemsControl`. This is not surprising, as a menu holds child objects, which technically can be anything, but really should be `MenuItem` objects.

`MenuItem` itself derives from `HeaderedItemsControl`, which is an `ItemsControl` with a header (similar to a `HeaderedContentControl`). The `Header` property (along with `HeaderTemplate`) typically provides the menu item text (but can be anything, as `Header` is of type object). A `Command` property allows binding to a command – in the code sample it was the **Copy**, **Paste**, and **Undo** built-in commands which, that a `TextBox` handles automatically (as demonstrated in the *Creating tooltips* recipe in this chapter). Note that if the `Command` is attached to a `RoutedUICommand` (as all built-in commands are), the `Header` text is unnecessary. It's automatically supplied by the `Text` property of `RoutedUICommand` (more on commands in *Chapter 7, Commands and MVVM*), as can be seen with the **Copy** menu item.

A `MenuItem` raises the `Click` event when that item is selected. This is used in the preceding code to handle the **File** | **Exit** menu item.

A `Separator` element can be used as a simple separator between items, as shown between **Paste** and **Undo**. It serves no other function, and can never receive focus.

There's more...

A `MenuItem` has an `Icon` property that is typically used to supply a small image that is placed to the left of the `Header`. However, `Icon` is of type `object`, thus can be anything (there's no `IconTemplate` property, however).

The underscore character can be used to allow an *Alt* + *Key* combination to select a particular menu item. This is similar to the rule for a `Label` (discussed in the recipe *Working with text* in this chapter).

`MenuItem` is an `ItemsControl`, so can use the same facilities, such as data templates and other customization hooks, as demonstrated in *Chapter 6, Data Binding*.

Other MenuItem properties and events

`MenuItem` objects can be checked by setting `IsCheckable` to true. This provides for a toggling behavior. The current state is available via the `IsChecked` property. It also fires the `Checked` and `Unchecked` events for similar reasons.

The `InputGestureText` allows a text to be appended to the `Header`, indicating the keyboard shortcut that fires this item. This, however, does not actually bind the key gesture to anything. Typically, this is done with the `RoutedCommand` that is attached via the `Command` property, as a `RoutedCommand` can be associated with a keyboard gesture (described in *Chapter 7* in more detail).

Creating a context menu

Context menus are typically invoked when the user right clicks a certain area or element (or presses *Shift* + *F10* or a designated key on some keyboards). They are called "context" menus because different situations may call for different menus, or at least different available options. The `ContextMenu` class (a derivative of `MenuBase`) can host a bunch of `MenuItem` controls (and separators). Let's see how this works.

Getting ready

Open the `CH04.Lists` project from the *Creating a list of items* recipe.

How to do it...

We'll continue with the `CH04.Lists` project and enhance it to make a context menu available:

1. Open `MainWindow.xaml`.
2. Set the `ContextMenu` property of the `ListBox` to a `ContextMenu` object with some `MenuItem` instances:

```
<ListBox.ContextMenu>
    <ContextMenu>
        <MenuItem Header="_Language" >
            <MenuItem Header="C++" Tag="0" />
            <MenuItem Header="C#" Tag="1" />
            <MenuItem Header="Visual Basic" Tag="2" />
            <MenuItem Header="F#" Tag="3" />
        </MenuItem>
        <Separator />
        <MenuItem Header="_Save..." />
        <MenuItem Header="_Load..." />
    </ContextMenu>
</ListBox.ContextMenu>
```

3. Let's add a `Click` handler for changing a language. We'll add that to the **Language** `MenuItem`, taking advantage of the bubbling routing strategy of the `Click` event. In the handler, add the following code:

```
void OnChangeLanugage(object sender, RoutedEventArgs e) {
   var item = e.Source as MenuItem;
   _langCombo.SelectedIndex = Convert.ToInt32(item.Tag);
}
```

4. Running the application allows changing language by right-clicking somewhere inside the `ListBox`:

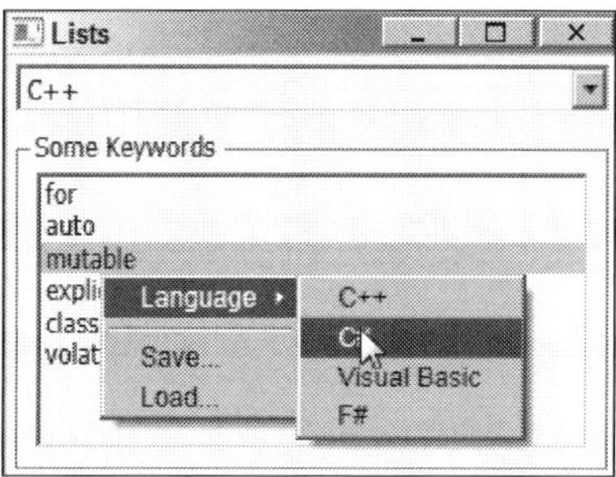

How it works...

A `ContextMenu` object holds `MenuItem` objects, similar to a regular `Menu`. `ContextMenu`. However, cannot be a direct part of a visual tree; instead, it must be placed with the appropriate property (usually `FrameworkElement.ContextMenu`). This is exactly how it's done in the preceding code sample. Any right-click inside the `ListBox` triggers opening the context menu. Any `Click` event handlers or `Command` objects are invoked when the user actually selects an item.

The preceding `Click` event handler leverages the `Tag` property that every element has for application defined purposes – in this case, the correct selected index in the `ComboBox` to change the current programming language.

There's more...

There are many properties in `ContextMenu` to change its placement (by default the top-left corner appears at the mouse pointer location), such as `Placement`, `HorizontalOffset`, and `VerticalOffset`. A bunch of attached properties (that can be set on elements) for `ContextMenu` customization exist in the `ContextMenuService` class. For example, the `ShowOnDisabled` property can be set to `true` to allow the `ContextMenu` to open even if the element is disabled. The relationship between `ContextMenu` and `ContextMenuService` classes is similar to the one between `ToolTip` and `ToolTipService` (as discussed in the *Creating tooltips* recipe in this chapter). Note that `ContextMenuService` settings override `ContextMenu` settings if they conflict.

Selecting options with checkboxes and radio buttons

Checkboxes and radio buttons are some of the most recognizable and useful controls. Checkboxes allow selecting or unselecting options, while radio buttons allow selecting one option out of several. Let's see how to use them in WPF.

Getting ready

Make sure Visual Studio is up and running.

How to do it...

We'll create a simple tea choosing application that uses checkboxes and radio buttons to make some tea:

1. Create a new WPF application named `CH04.SelectingOptions`.
2. Open `MainWindow.xaml`. Replace the `Grid` with a `StackPanel`.
3. Add a `GroupBox` with some tea type options to the `StackPanel`, as follows:

```
<GroupBox Header="What kind of tea would you like?">
    <StackPanel Margin="4" x:Name="_teaTypePanel">
        <RadioButton Content="Earl Grey" IsChecked="True"/>
        <RadioButton Content="Mint" />
        <RadioButton Content="Chinese Green" />
        <RadioButton Content="Japanese Green" />
    </StackPanel>
</GroupBox>
```

4. Add another `GroupBox` to allow options for tea supplements:

```
<GroupBox Header="Select tea supplements">
    <StackPanel Margin="4">
        <CheckBox Content="Sugar" x:Name="_isSugar" />
        <CheckBox Content="Milk" x:Name="_isMilk" />
        <CheckBox Content="Lemon" x:Name="_isLemon" />
    </StackPanel>
</GroupBox>
```

5. Add a `Button` to the `StackPanel` that would make the actual tea:

```
<Button Content="Make Tea!" Margin="4" FontSize="20"
        HorizontalAlignment="Center" Padding="4"/>
```

6. Add a `Click` event handler to the button with the following code:

```
void OnMakeTea(object sender, RoutedEventArgs e) {
   var sb = new StringBuilder("Tea: ");
   foreach(RadioButton rb in _teaTypePanel.Children)
      if(rb.IsChecked == true) {
         sb.AppendLine(rb.Content.ToString());
         break;
      }
   if(_isSugar.IsChecked == true)
      sb.AppendLine("With sugar");
   if(_isMilk.IsChecked == true)
      sb.AppendLine("With milk");
   if(_isLemon.IsChecked == true)
      sb.AppendLine("With lemon");
   if(_isLemon.IsChecked == true && _isMilk.IsChecked == true)
      sb.AppendLine("Very unusual!");
   MessageBox.Show(sb.ToString(), "Tea Maker");
}
```

7. Run the application and select some tea options, then click the button. You should see something like the following:

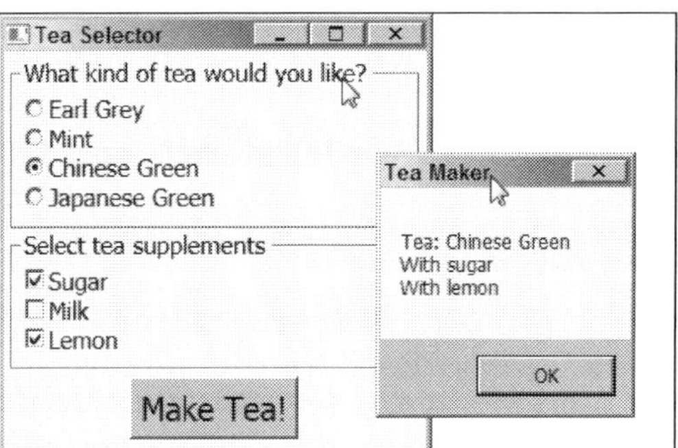

How it works...

Both `CheckBox` and `RadioButton` derive from `ToggleButton`, which defines their basic behavior. Specifically, it defines the `IsChecked` property, typed as `Nullable<bool>` (`bool?` in C#). This means it can have three values: `true`, `false`, and `null`. `null` indicates an intermediate state (useful for scenarios where the `CheckBox` is used to indicate something for multiple items, and not all have the same value; a classic example is the Read Only checkbox in Windows Explorer's folder properties). This is applicable to checkboxes, but has no real meaning for radio buttons. `ToggleButton` also defines appropriate events (`Checked`, `Unchecked`, and `Indeterminate`).

The preceding code uses the `IsChecked` property to make decisions. For radio buttons, selecting one button automatically deselects all others within the group. A radio button group is implicit when all radio buttons are within the same container (`StackPanel` in this case). However, if groups of radio buttons need to be defined within the same container, the `GroupName` property (a `string`) should be set to the same value for a specific group. In fact, `GroupName` is the only property `RadioButton` adds with respect to its base class; this should be used with caution, as `GroupName` takes effect even between panels.

`CheckBox` adds no new properties – it just provides a different appearance from `ToggleButton`.

Manipulating tab order and focus

The *Tab* key in a typical user interface can be used to move the keyboard focus from one control to another (with *Shift* + *Tab* working in the reverse order), providing keyboard navigation capabilities without the need to use the mouse. This has to be logical – that is, the focus should not jump erratically all over the place, but rather move to the next logical control within the UI. The following recipe shows how to set the tab order and how to set the focus to a given control.

Getting ready

Make sure Visual Studio is up and running.

How to do it...

We'll create a personal information entry form that uses tab order in a logical manner, and places the keyboard focus where it makes sense when the form first appears:

1. Create a new WPF application named `CH04.TabAndFocus`.
2. Open `MainWindow.xaml`. Add some rows and columns to the `Grid` and some elements, as follows:

```
<Grid Margin="4">
    <Grid.RowDefinitions>
        <RowDefinition Height="Auto" />
        <RowDefinition Height="10" />
        <RowDefinition Height="Auto" />
        <RowDefinition Height="10" />
        <RowDefinition Height="Auto" />
        <RowDefinition Height="Auto" />
    </Grid.RowDefinitions>
    <Grid.ColumnDefinitions>
        <ColumnDefinition Width="Auto" />
```

```
            <ColumnDefinition Width="20" />
            <ColumnDefinition />
        </Grid.ColumnDefinitions>
        <Button Grid.Row="5" FontSize="16" Content="Send Comment"
                Grid.ColumnSpan="3" HorizontalAlignment="Center"
                Margin="0,20,0,0" Padding="4"/>
        <TextBlock Text="Name:" VerticalAlignment="Center"/>
        <TextBox Grid.Column="2" x:Name="name"/>
        <TextBlock Text="Birthday:" Grid.Row="2"
                   VerticalAlignment="Center"/>
        <DatePicker Grid.Row="2" Grid.Column="2" />
        <TextBlock Text="Comments:" Grid.Row="4" />
        <TextBox AcceptsReturn="True" Grid.Row="4"
                    Grid.Column="2" Height="100" />
    </Grid>
```

3. Run the application. Press *Tab* and watch the keyboard focus move.

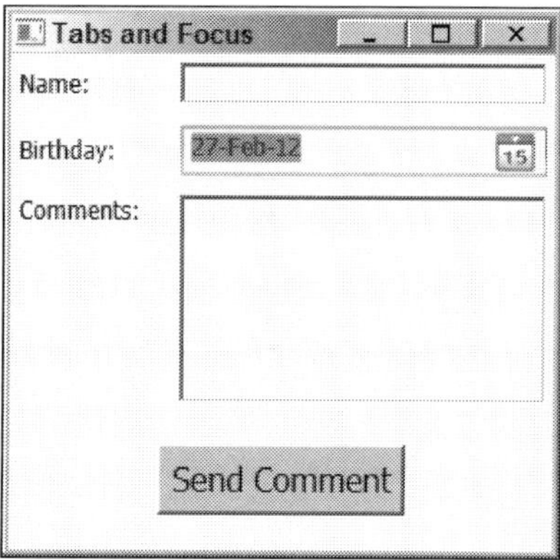

4. The focus moves first to the button, then the top text box, then the date picker, then the large text box. Let's make the top text box first in the tab order by setting its `TabIndex` property to 0:

```
<TextBox Grid.Column="2" TabIndex="0"/>
```

5. We can do the same, incrementing the `TabIndex`, for other controls in the required order. When the window starts up, no control has the focus. Let's make the top text box get the focus automatically, in XAML.
6. Add the following attached property on the `Grid`:

```
<Grid FocusManager.FocusedElement="{Binding ElementName=name}"
```

7. Run the application. The keyboard focus should start at the top `TextBox`. Note that its `TabIndex` doesn't have to be zero now.

How it works...

The default tab order is based on the order of elements as they are defined in XAML (or the order they are added to a `Children` element of `Panel` in code). The `TabIndex` property (from `Control`) allows changing the tab order (the default value is `Int32.MaxValue`), where lower values are first in the tab order.

The `IsTabStop` property indicates whether a control is included in tab navigation (`true` by default).

Most of the time, the order of control placement should be enough to achieve the required tab order, but in case it's not, the aforementioned properties should help.

The keyboard focus can be changed at any time by calling the static `Keyboard.Focus` method, passing the control that should have keyboard focus (that control must have its `Focusable` property set to `true`). The `Keyboard.FocusedElement` static property returns the current control that has keyboard focus (or `null` if no control has focus at this time, for example, the focus is in some other application).

There's more...

The preceding code sample uses the `FocusManager.FocusedElement` attached property to set the focus to the top `TextBox` (using a data binding expression). Curiously enough, setting this property on the `Window` itself does not achieve the same result. The following section explains why.

Keyboard focus versus logical focus

Keyboard focus is a well-known concept. Only one control at a time can have the keyboard focus in the entire desktop. WPF defines another concept called logical focus. A control can have logical focus in some container that is a focus scope. That is, only one control can have logical focus in a given focus scope, but another control can have logical focus if placed in a different focus scope. What this means is that when the keyboard focus leaves a focus scope, that scope still "remembers" the last control which had keyboard focus. When focus returns to that focus scope, that control will receive keyboard focus.

By default, `Window`, `Menu`, `ContextMenu`, and `ToolBar` are focus scopes. A focus scope can be set using the `FocusManager.IsFocusScope` attached property.

In our example, the `Window` is a focus scope (we did not change that), so its only child (the `Grid`) becomes the target of keyboard focus. Naturally, the `Grid` is useless as such. Setting the name textbox to be focused within the `Window` is pointless, because the `Grid` is not a focus scope.

We can solve that in several ways. One way is setting the logical focus within the `Grid` (as was done in the code sample). Another way is keeping the setting on the `Window`, but marking the `Grid` with `Focusable="False"`. Yet another way is to remove the focus scope property of `Window` by setting `FocusManager.IsFocusScope` to `false`.

The logical focus is important in particular when dealing with `RoutedCommand` objects, as we'll discuss in *Chapter 7*.

5
Application and Windows

In this chapter we will cover:

- Creating a window
- Creating a dialog box
- Using the common dialog boxes
- Creating ownership between windows
- Creating a custom shaped window
- Creating a single instance application
- Handling an unhandled exception

Introduction

In the preceding chapters, we dealt with a lot of WPF details, concerning various aspects of its features, such as resources and controls. In this chapter, we'll take a broader look at WPF's application model, including the use of windows within an application.

Creating a window

Windows are the typical top level controls in WPF. By default, a `MainWindow` class is created by the application wizard and automatically shown upon running the application. In this recipe, we'll take a look at creating and showing other windows that may be required during the lifetime of an application.

Getting ready

Make sure Visual Studio is up and running.

How to do it...

We'll create a new class derived from `Window` and show it when a button is clicked:

1. Create a new WPF application named `CH05.NewWindows`.
2. Right-click on the project node in **Solution explorer**, and select **Add | Window...**:

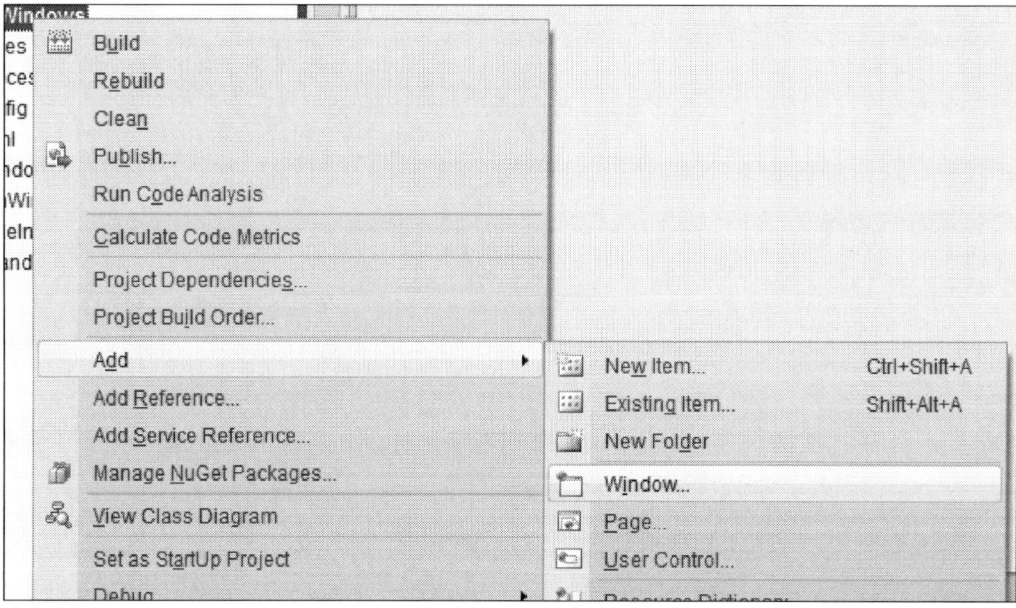

3. In the resulting dialog, type `OtherWindow` in the **Name** textbox and click on **Add**.
4. A file named `OtherWindow.xaml` should open in the editor. Add a `TextBlock` to the existing `Grid`, as follows:

```
<TextBlock Text="This is the other window" FontSize="20"
   VerticalAlignment="Center" HorizontalAlignment="Center" />
```

5. Open `MainWindow.xaml`. Add a `Button` to the `Grid` with a `Click` event handler:

```
<Button Content="Open Other Window" FontSize="30"
        Click="OnOpenOtherWindow" />
```

6. In the `Click` event handler, add the following code:

```
void OnOpenOtherWindow(object sender, RoutedEventArgs e) {
   var other = new OtherWindow();
   other.Show();
}
```

7. Run the application, and click the button. The other window should appear and live happily alongside the main window:

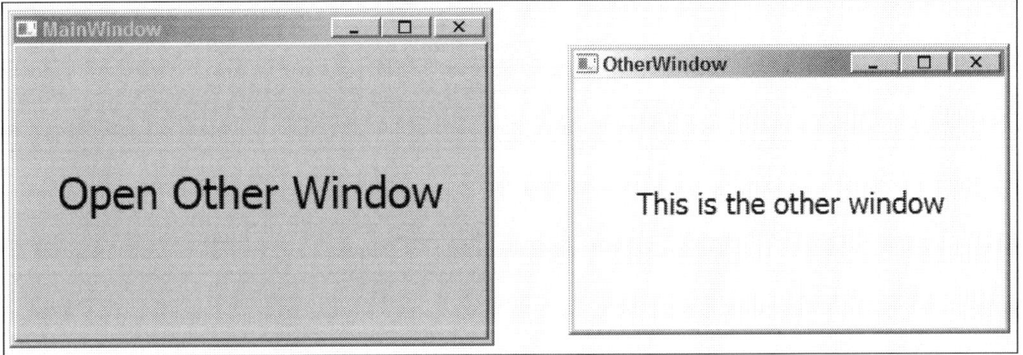

How it works...

A `Window` is technically a `ContentControl`, so can contain anything. It's made visible using the `Show` method. This keeps the window open as long as it's not explicitly closed using the classic close button, or by calling the `Close` method. The `Show` method opens the window as **modeless**—meaning the user can return to the previous window without restriction.

We can click the button more than once, and consequently more `Window` instances would show up.

There's more...

The first window shown can be configured using the `Application.StartupUri` property, typically set in `App.xaml`. It can be changed to any other window. For example, to show the `OtherWindow` from the previous section as the first window, open `App.xaml` and change the `StartupUri` property to `OtherWindow.xaml`:

```
StartupUri="OtherWindow.xaml"
```

Selecting the startup window dynamically

Sometimes the first window is not known in advance, perhaps depending on some state or setting. In this case, the `StartupUri` property is not helpful. We can safely delete it, and provide the initial window (or even windows) by overriding the `Application.OnStartup` method as follows (you'll need to add a reference to the `System.Configuration` assembly for the following to compile):

```
protected override void OnStartup(StartupEventArgs e) {
   Window mainWindow = null;
   // check some state or setting as appropriate
         if(ConfigurationManager.AppSettings["AdvancedMode"] == "1")
      mainWindow = new OtherWindow();
   else
      mainWindow = new MainWindow();
   mainWindow.Show();
}
```

This allows complete flexibility in determining what window or windows should appear at application startup.

Accessing command line arguments

The WPF application created by the New Project wizard does not expose the ubiquitous `Main` method. WPF provides this for us – it instantiates the `Application` object and eventually loads the main window pointed to by the `StartupUri` property.

The `Main` method, however, is not just a starting point for managed code, but also provides an array of strings as the command line arguments passed to the executable (if any). As `Main` is now beyond our control, how do we get the command line arguments?

Fortunately, the same `OnStartup` method provides a `StartupEventArgs` object, in which the `Args` property is mirrored from `Main`. The downloadable source for this chapter contains the project `CH05.CommandLineArgs`, which shows an example of its usage. Here's the `OnStartup` override:

```
protected override void OnStartup(StartupEventArgs e) {
   string text = "Hello, default!";
   if(e.Args.Length > 0)
      text = e.Args[0];

   var win = new MainWindow(text);
   win.Show();
}
```

The `MainWindow` instance constructor has been modified to accept a string that is later used by the window. If a command line argument is supplied, it is used.

Creating a dialog box

A dialog box is a `Window` that is typically used to get some data from the user, before some operation can proceed. This is sometimes referred to as a modal window (as opposed to modeless, or non-modal). In this recipe, we'll take a look at how to create and manage such a dialog box.

Getting ready

Make sure Visual Studio is up and running.

How to do it...

We'll create a dialog box that's invoked from the main window to request some information from the user:

1. Create a new WPF application named `CH05.Dialogs`.
2. Add a new `Window` named `DetailsDialog.xaml` (a `DetailsDialog` class is created).
3. Visual Studio opens `DetailsDialog.xaml`. Set some `Window` properties: `FontSize` to `16`, `ResizeMode` to `NoResize`, `SizeToContent` to `Height`, and make sure the `Width` is set to `300`:

```
ResizeMode="NoResize" SizeToContent="Height" Width="300"
FontSize="16"
```

4. Add four rows and two columns to the existing `Grid`, and add some controls for a simple data entry dialog as follows:

```
<Grid.RowDefinitions>
    <RowDefinition Height="Auto" />
    <RowDefinition Height="Auto"/>
    <RowDefinition Height="Auto"/>
    <RowDefinition Height="Auto"/>
</Grid.RowDefinitions>
<Grid.ColumnDefinitions>
    <ColumnDefinition Width="Auto" />
    <ColumnDefinition />
</Grid.ColumnDefinitions>
<TextBlock Text="Please enter details:" Grid.ColumnSpan="2"
            Margin="4,4,4,20" HorizontalAlignment="Center"/>
<TextBlock Text="Name:" Grid.Row="1" Margin="4"/>
<TextBox Grid.Column="1" Grid.Row="1" Margin="4"
         x:Name="_name"/>
```

```
<TextBlock Text="City:" Grid.Row="2" Margin="4"/>
<TextBox Grid.Column="1" Grid.Row="2" Margin="4"
         x:Name="_city"/>
<StackPanel Grid.Row="3" Orientation="Horizontal"
            Margin="4,20,4,4" Grid.ColumnSpan="2"
            HorizontalAlignment="Center">
    <Button Content="OK" Margin="4"  />
    <Button Content="Cancel" Margin="4" />
</StackPanel>
```

5. This is how it should look in the designer:

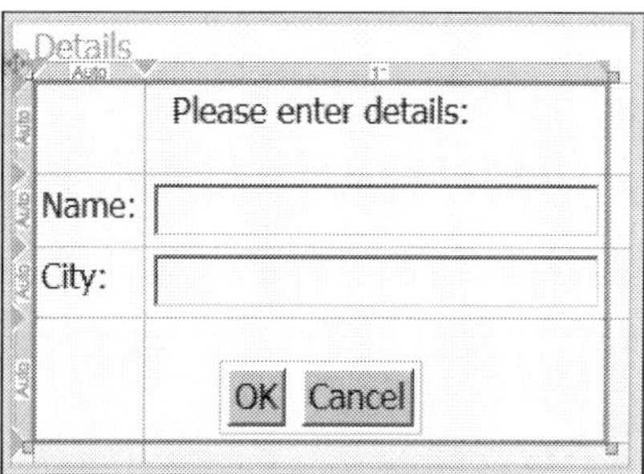

6. The dialog should expose two properties for the name and city the user has typed in. Open `DetailsDialog.xaml.cs`. Add two simple properties:

```
public string FullName { get; private set; }
public string City { get; private set; }
```

7. We need to show the dialog from somewhere in the main window. Open `MainWindow.xaml`, and add the following markup to the existing `Grid`:

```
<Grid.RowDefinitions>
    <RowDefinition Height="Auto" />
    <RowDefinition />
</Grid.RowDefinitions>
<Button Content="Enter Data" Click="OnEnterData"
        Margin="4" FontSize="16"/>
<TextBlock FontSize="24" x:Name="_text" Grid.Row="1"
    VerticalAlignment="Center" HorizontalAlignment="Center"/>
```

8. In the `OnEnterData` handler, add the following:

```
private void OnEnterData(object sender, RoutedEventArgs e) {
   var dlg = new DetailsDialog();
   if(dlg.ShowDialog() == true) {
      _text.Text = string.Format(
          "Hi, {0}! I see you live in {1}.",
          dlg.FullName, dlg.City);
   }
}
```

9. Run the application. Click the button and watch the dialog appear. The buttons don't work yet, so your only choice is to close the dialog using the regular close button. Clearly, the return value from `ShowDialog` is not true in this case.

10. When the **OK** button is clicked, the properties should be set accordingly. Add a **Click** event handler to the **OK** button, with the following code:

    ```
    private void OnOK(object sender, RoutedEventArgs e) {
       FullName = _name.Text;
       City = _city.Text;
       DialogResult = true;
       Close();
    }
    ```

    The `Close` method dismisses the dialog, returning control to the caller. The `DialogResult` property indicates the returned value from the call to `ShowDialog` when the dialog is closed.

11. Add a **Click** event handler for the **Cancel** button with the following code:

    ```
    private void OnCancel(object sender, RoutedEventArgs e) {
       DialogResult = false;
       Close();
    }
    ```

12. Run the application and click the button. Enter some data and click on **OK**:

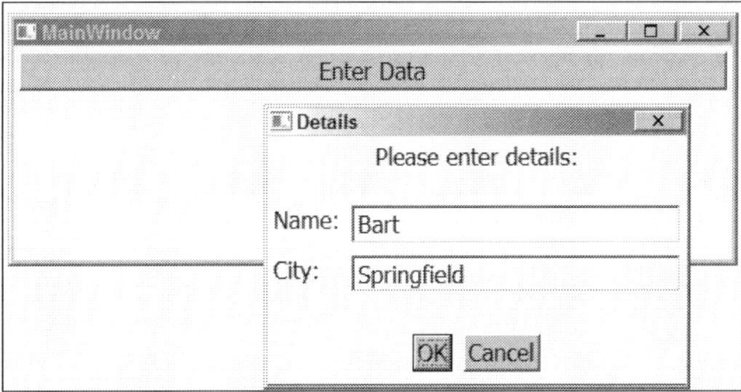

13. You will see the following window:

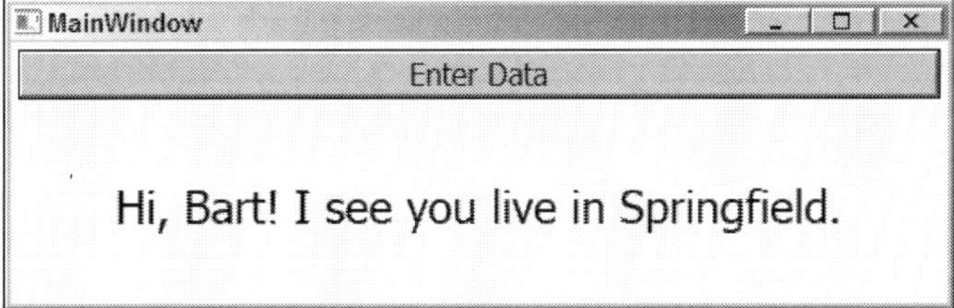

How it works...

A dialog box in WPF is nothing more than a regular window shown using `ShowDialog` instead of `Show`. This forces the user to dismiss the window before she can return to the invoking window. `ShowDialog` returns a `Nullable<bool>` (can be written as `bool?` in C#), meaning it can have three values: `true`, `false`, and `null`. The meaning of the return value is mostly up to the application, but typically `true` indicates the user dismissed the dialog with the intention of making something happen (usually, by clicking some **OK** or other confirmation button), and `false` means the user changed her mind, and would like to abort. The `null` value can be used as a third indicator to some other application-defined condition.

The `DialogResult` property indicates the value returned from `ShowDialog` because there is no other way to convey the return value from the dialog invocation directly. That's why the **OK** button handler sets it to `true` and the **Cancel** button handler sets it to `false` (this also happens when the regular close button is clicked, or *Alt* + *F4* is pressed).

Most dialog boxes are not resizable. This is indicated with the `ResizeMode` property of the `Window` set to `NoResize`. However, because of WPF's flexible layout, it certainly is relatively easy to keep a dialog resizable (and still manageable) where it makes sense (such as when entering a potentially large amount of text in a `TextBox` – it would make sense if the `TextBox` could grow if the dialog is enlarged).

There's more...

Most dialogs can be dismissed by pressing *Enter* (indicating the data should be used) or pressing *Esc* (indicating no action should take place). This is possible to do by setting the **OK** button's `IsDefault` property to `true` and the **Cancel** button's `IsCancel` property to `true`. The default button is typically drawn with a heavier border to indicate it's the *default* button, although this eventually depends on the button's control template.

If these settings are specified, the handler for the **Cancel** button is not needed. Clicking **Cancel** or pressing *Esc* automatically closes the dialog (and sets `DiaglogResult` to `false`). The **OK** button handler is still needed as usual, but it may be invoked by pressing *Enter*, no matter what control has the keyboard focus within the `Window`. The `CH05.DefaultButtons` project from the downloadable source for this chapter demonstrates this in action.

Modeless dialogs

A dialog can be show as **modeless**, meaning it does not force the user to dismiss it before returning to other windows in the application. This is done with the usual `Show` method call – just like any `Window`. The term dialog in this case usually denotes some information expected from the user that affects other windows, sometimes with the help of another button labeled "Apply".

The problem here is mostly logical—how to convey the information change. The best way would be using data binding, rather than manually modifying various objects. We'll take an extensive look at data binding in the next chapter.

Using the common dialog boxes

Windows has its own built-in dialog boxes for common operations, such as opening files, saving a file, and printing. Using these dialogs is very intuitive from the user's perspective, because she has probably used those dialogs before in other applications. WPF wraps some of these (native) dialogs. In this recipe, we'll see how to use some of the common dialogs.

Getting ready

Make sure Visual Studio is up and running.

How to do it...

We'll create a simple image viewer that uses the Open common dialog box to allow the user to select an image file to view:

1. Create a new WPF Application named `CH05.CommonDialogs`.
2. Open `MainWindow.xaml`. Add the following markup to the existing `Grid`:

```
<Grid.RowDefinitions>
    <RowDefinition Height="Auto" />
    <RowDefinition />
</Grid.RowDefinitions>
<Button Content="Open Image" FontSize="20" Click="OnOpenImage"
        HorizontalAlignment="Center" Margin="4" />
<Image Grid.Row="1" x:Name="_img" Stretch="Uniform" />
```

3. Add a `Click` event handler for the button. In the handler, we'll first create an `OpenFileDialog` instance and initialize it (add a `using` to the `Microsoft.Win32` namespace):

```
void OnOpenImage(object sender, RoutedEventArgs e) {
   var dlg = new OpenFileDialog {
      Filter = "Image files|*.png;*.jpg;*.gif;*.bmp",
      Title = "Select image to open",
      InitialDirectory = Environment.GetFolderPath(
        Environment.SpecialFolder.MyPictures)
   };
```

4. Now we need to show the dialog and use the selected file (if any):

```
if(dlg.ShowDialog() == true) {
   try {
      var bmp = new BitmapImage(new Uri(dlg.FileName));
      _img.Source = bmp;
   }
   catch(Exception ex) {
      MessageBox.Show(ex.Message, "Open Image");
   }
}
```

5. Run the application. Click the button and navigate to an image file and select it. You should see something like the following:

How it works...

The `OpenFileDialog` class wraps the Win32 open/save file dialog, providing easy enough access to its capabilities. It's just a matter of instantiating the object, setting some properties, such as the file types (`Filter` property) and then calling `ShowDialog`. This call, in turn, returns `true` if the user selected a file and `false` otherwise (`null` is never returned, although the return type is still defined as `Nullable<bool>` for consistency).

> The look of the Open file dialog box may be different in various Windows versions. This is mostly unimportant unless some automated UI testing is done. In this case, the way the dialog looks or operates may have to be taken into consideration when creating the tests.

The filename itself is returned in the `FileName` property (full path). Multiple selections are possible by setting the `MultiSelect` property to `true` (in this case the `FileNames` property returns the selected files).

There's more...

WPF similarly wraps the **Save As** common dialog with the `SaveFileDialog` class (in the `Microsoft.Win32` namespace as well). Its use is very similar to `OpenFileDialog` (in fact, both inherit from the abstract `FileDialog` class).

What about folder selection (instead of files)? The WPF `OpenFileDialog` does not support that. One solution is to use Windows Forms' `FolderBrowseDialog` class. Another good solution is to use the Windows API Code Pack described shortly.

Another common dialog box WPF wraps is `PrintDialog` (in `System.Windows.Controls`). This shows the familiar print dialog, with options to select a printer, orientation, and so on. The most straightforward way to print would be calling `PrintVisual` (after calling `ShowDialog`), providing anything that derives from the `Visual` abstract class (which include all elements). General printing is a complex topic and is beyond the scope of this book.

What about colors and fonts?

Windows also provides common dialogs for selecting colors and fonts. However, these are not wrapped by WPF. There are several alternatives:

- Use the equivalent Windows Forms classes (`FontDialog` and `ColorDialog`, both from `System.Windows.Forms`)
- Wrap the native dialogs yourself
- Look for alternatives on the Web

The first option is possible, but has two drawbacks: first, it requires adding reference to the `System.Windows.Forms` assembly; this adds a dependency at compile time, and increases memory consumption at run time, for very little gain. The second drawback has to do with the natural mismatch between Windows Forms and WPF. For example, `ColorDialog` returns a color as a `System.Drawing.Color`, but WPF uses `System.Windows.Media.Color`. This requires mapping a GDI+ color (WinForms) to WPF's color, which is cumbersome at best.

The second option of doing your own wrapping is a non-trivial undertaking and requires good interop knowledge. The other downside is that the default color and font common dialogs are pretty old (especially the color dialog), so there's much room for improvement.

The third option is probably the best one. There are more than a few good candidates for color and font pickers. For a color dialog, for example, you can use the `ColorPicker` or `ColorCanvas` provided with the Extended WPF toolkit library on CodePlex (`http://wpftoolkit.codeplex.com/`). Here's how these may look (`ColorCanvas` on the left-hand side, and one of the possible views of `ColorPicker` on the right-hand side):

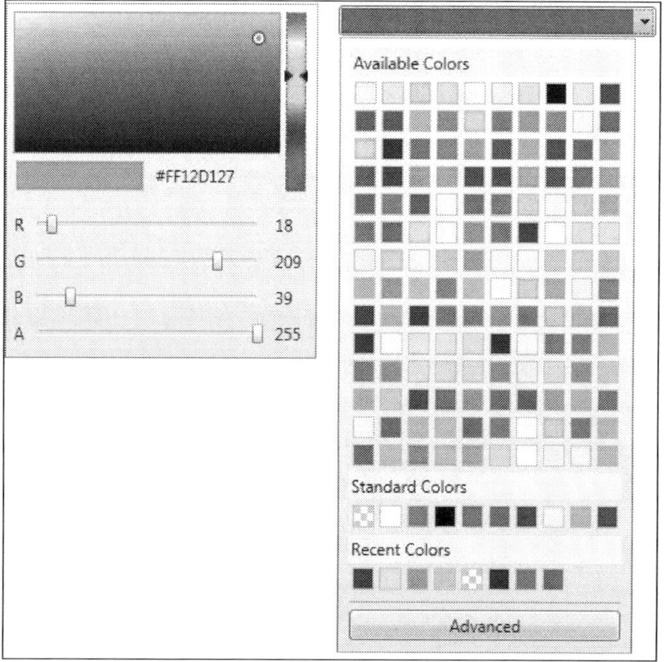

The Windows API Code Pack

The Windows API Code Pack is a Microsoft project on CodePlex (`http://archive.msdn.microsoft.com/WindowsAPICodePack`) that provides many .NET wrappers to native Windows features, in various areas, such as shell, networking, Windows 7 features (this is less important now as WPF 4 added first class support for Windows 7), power management, and DirectX. One of the Shell features in the library is a wrapper for the Open dialog box that allows selecting a folder instead of a file. This has no dependency on the WinForms assembly.

Creating ownership between windows

`Window` objects are self-sufficient by default, and are independent of other windows in the application. Sometimes, however, it's useful to connect two (or more) windows in an owner-owned relationship. An owned window obeys the following rules:

- Closed automatically if its owner is closed
- Minimized automatically if its owner is minimized
- Always appears on top of its owner, but unconstrained to its surface (unlike traditional Win32 child windows)
- Never shown in the task bar if it's currently minimized

In this recipe, we'll see how to create such ownership and show a typical use case.

Getting ready

Make sure Visual Studio is up and running.

How to do it...

We'll create a tool-like window that is owned by the main window, demonstrating a typical usage of window ownership:

1. Create a new WPF Application project named `CH05.OwnerWindows`.
2. Right-click on the project node in **Solution Explorer** and select **Add** | **Window...**.
3. Type **ToolsWindow** in the **Name** text box and click on **Add**.
4. The `ToolsWindow.xaml` file should be open. Set the following properties on the `Window` object:

   ```
   SizeToContent="WidthAndHeight" ResizeMode="NoResize"
   ```

5. Replace the existing `Grid` with a `ToolBar` and add some buttons as follows:

   ```
   <ToolBar FontSize="20">
       <RadioButton Content="Pointer" Margin="4"
                    IsChecked="True"/>
       <RadioButton Content="Pencil" Margin="4"/>
       <RadioButton Content="Brush" Margin="4"/>
       <RadioButton Content="Eraser" Margin="4"/>
       <RadioButton Content="Selection" Margin="4"/>
   </ToolBar>
   ```

6. Open `App.xaml`. Remove the `StartupUri` property value from the `Application` object.
7. Open `App.xaml.cs`. Override the `OnStartup` method as follows:

   ```
   protected override void OnStartup(StartupEventArgs e) {
      var mainWindow = new MainWindow();
      var toolWindow = new ToolsWindow();
      mainWindow.Show();
      toolWindow.Owner = mainWindow;
      toolWindow.Show();
   }
   ```

8. Run the application. Note that the **Tool** window is always on top of the main window. Minimize the main window – the tool window is minimized as well. Restore it – both windows are restored.

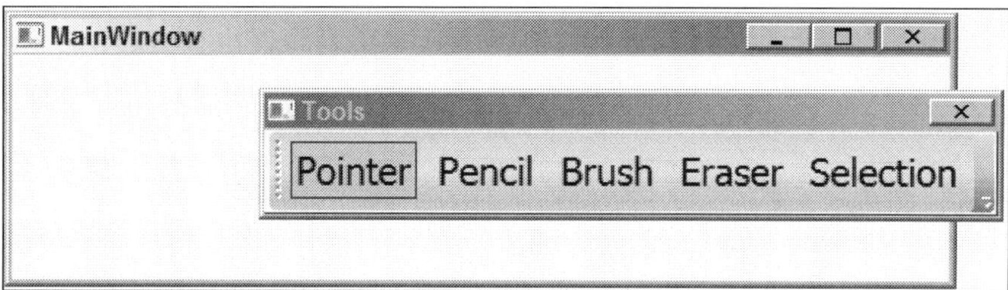

How it works...

Window ownership is not a WPF specific feature – it's a capability exposed by the Win32 user API. WPF simply makes it easily accessible.

Every `Window` object has an `Owner` property. By default, it's `null`, meaning the `Window` is unowned, independent of other windows. If an owner is set, the `Window` now obeys ownership rules, as described in the introduction section of this recipe.

> A `Window` (not a `NavigationWindow` hosted in a browser) can be removed from the Task Bar by specifying `false` for the `ShowInTaskBar` property.

There's more...

Ownership can be removed simply by reverting the `Owner` property back to `null`, freeing the window once again.

Each `Window` also has an `OwnedWindows` property, which is a collection of that `Window`'s owned windows (of type `WindowCollection`). This may be useful when some operation needs to be performed on all or some of windows owned by `Window`.

Creating a custom shaped window

A typical window has several aspects that are not directly controllable by a WPF application, such as the look of the title bar, minimize, maximize, and close buttons; its shape is always rectangular, and so on. These settings (called the non-client area of the window) are defined by the current Windows theme selected by the user using the **Control Panel**, with some customization possible for font sizes, colors, caption color, and so on, but the basic appearance characteristics of the window remain.

An application may want to customize the way a window looks from the outside. Canonical examples of this are media players. The built-in Windows Media Player, for instance, can be switched to *skin mode* where its shape becomes something that is far from rectangular (this particular skin was downloaded from Microsoft's website; in Windows Media Player, open the **View | Skin** chooser menu and click **More Skins**):

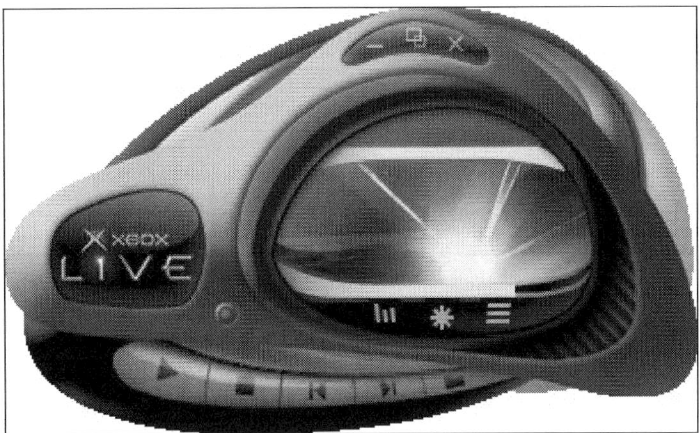

Let's see how we can create a custom shaped window with WPF.

Getting ready

Make sure Visual Studio is up and running.

How to do it...

We'll create a custom shaped window and make it function just like a regular window for moving and closing:

1. Create a new WPF Application project named `CH05.CustomShapeWindow`.
2. Open `MainWindow.xaml`. Set the following properties of the `Window` object to remove the default window appearance so we can provide our own:

```
AllowsTransparency="True" WindowStyle="None"
    Background="Transparent"
```

3. At this point, the window is pretty much invisible. It's time to provide some irregular content. Add the following markup in the existing `Grid`:

```
<Rectangle RadiusX="30" RadiusY="30">
    <Rectangle.Fill>
        <LinearGradientBrush EndPoint="0,1">
            <GradientStop Color="DarkBlue" Offset="0" />
```

```
            <GradientStop Color="#80000080" Offset="1" />
        </LinearGradientBrush>
    </Rectangle.Fill>
</Rectangle>
<TextBlock TextAlignment="Center" VerticalAlignment="Top"
    Margin="4" Text="My Window Title" FontSize="18"
    Foreground="White" FontWeight="Bold" />
<Button Content="X" HorizontalAlignment="Right"
    FontWeight="Bold" VerticalAlignment="Top"
    Margin="20,4" FontSize="16" />
<TextBlock Text="Welcome to the new Window!"
    Foreground="Yellow" FontSize="25"
    VerticalAlignment="Center" HorizontalAlignment="Center" />
```

4. Running the application now shows the following:

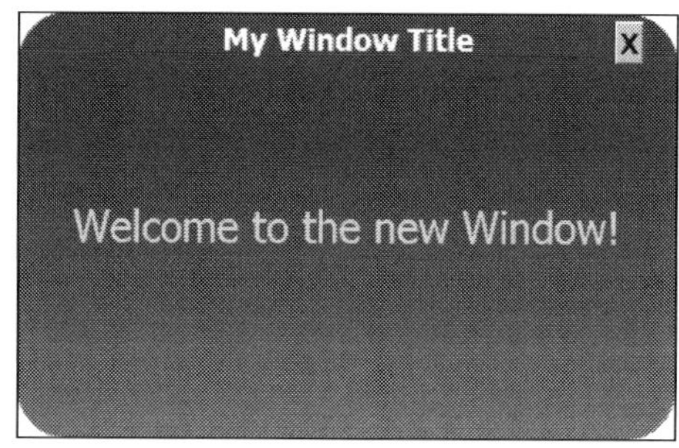

   The window cannot be moved with the mouse (but can be moved by pressing *Alt* + Space and selecting **Move**), and cannot be closed with the mouse (but can be closed with *Alt* + *F4* or *Alt* + Space and then **Close**).

5. To make the window work as expected with the mouse, we'll add two event handlers.
6. The first is a **Click** handler for the "X" button. Enter the following in the handler:

```
private void OnClose(object sender, RoutedEventArgs e) {
   Close();
}
```

7. The second is a `MouseLeftButtonDown` handler for the `Grid`. Add the following code in the handler:

```
private void OnMove(object sender, MouseButtonEventArgs e) {
   DragMove();
}
```

8. Run the application. You should be able to move the window with the mouse and close it by clicking the button.

How it works...

The `AllowsTransparency` and `WindowStyle` settings shown above are the mandatory ingredients that tell windows not to paint anything in the so-called non-client area of the window. Setting `Background` to `Transparent` allows other content to show through and flesh out the real look of the window.

In the preceding XAML, a `Rectangle` with rounded corners is placed first, followed by two `TextBlock` instances, one for some kind of title and the other to simulate the actual content of the window. A `Button` is added as well, to provide a convenient way to close the window.

One consequence of the title bar removal is losing the ability to move or close the window with the mouse. Usually such features are desirable, so we need to implement them ourselves. Fortunately, this is not difficult. To close the window, we just wire up some control (in this case a `Button`) to call the regular `Window.Close` method. Moving the window seems more complex, and technically it is, but WPF makes this easy with the `Window.DragMove` method. We just need to call it in a `MouseLeftButtonDown` event handler; the rest is done for us as part of `DragMove`.

There's more...

What about custom shaped windows that look like the previous Media Player skin? The trick here is to use an image with transparency (typically a PNG file) as the window's background. The downloadable source for this chapter contains a project named `CH05.ImageShapeWindow` that shows this in action. This is the required XAML to make this work (apart from the two required property settings):

```
<Window.Background>
    <ImageBrush ImageSource="invader.png" />
</Window.Background>
```

The `invader.png` is an image with transparent areas. This is how the window looks when running:

We can add the ability to move and close the window in much the same way as previously shown (check out the source of this example).

What about reusability?

The above examples are fine for a single window that is required to be different. What if we wanted all of an application's windows to have a unique shape? Placing the same XAML and event handlers is not very reusable and becomes a maintenance headache.

A better approach would be to create a custom control template for a window and derive a new class from `Window` that would handle closing and moving, but potentially also minimizing and restoring. This custom class would be able to expose other special properties if needed. We'll discuss control templates in *Chapter 8, Styles, Triggers, and Control Templates*.

Creating a single instance application

We may sometimes want to limit the number of running instances of some application to just one. Running some executable creates a new Windows process to host that executable, with its own address space, tables, resources, and so on. Sometimes this is not desirable; if the executable tries to run while another instance is already running, it should quit and optionally make the other instance's main window active. A canonical example in Windows is Windows Media Player. An attempt to open a second media player activates the first Media Player window (although it's debatable whether such behavior is desired for Media Player).

Let's see how this can be achieved.

Getting ready

Make sure Visual Studio is up and running.

How to do it...

We'll create a simple application that will not run with more than one process. A second run will transfer activation to the running instance's window, and quit:

1. Create a new WPF Application project named `CH05.SingleInstApp`.
2. Open `MainWindow.xaml`. Give the window a distinct `Title`, such as **Single Instance**.

3. Open `App.xaml.cs`. We'll need to use some Win32 functions. Add the following to the `App` class:

```
[DllImport("user32", CharSet = CharSet.Unicode)]
static extern IntPtr FindWindow(string cls, string win);
[DllImport("user32")]
static extern IntPtr SetForegroundWindow(IntPtr hWnd);

[DllImport("user32")]
static extern bool IsIconic(IntPtr hWnd);
[DllImport("user32")]
static extern bool OpenIcon(IntPtr hWnd);
```

4. Override the `OnStartup` method as follows:

```
bool isNew;
var mutex = new Mutex(true, "MySingleInstMutex", out isNew);
if(!isNew) {
   ActivateOtherWindow();
   Shutdown();
}
```

5. Add the implementation of `ActivateOtherWindow`:

```
Private static void ActivateOtherWindow() {
   var other = FindWindow(null, "Single Instance");
   if(other != IntPtr.Zero) {
      SetForegroundWindow(other);
      if(IsIconic(other))
         OpenIcon(other);
   }
}
```

6. Run the application without the debugger (*Ctrl* + *F5* or **Debug** | **Start Without Debugging** menu). The main window should appear. Now run the application again (you can also use Windows Explorer). The previous window should activate. If it was minimized, it should be restored and activated.

How it works...

A `Mutex` is a synchronization object, typically used to synchronize access to a shared resource (such as a file), so that only one thread can access the resource at a time, thus preventing data corruption or other inconsistencies within the shared resource. Under the covers it wraps a Win32 Mutex object (represented as a handle), so it's a true kernel object, capable of cross AppDomain and cross process synchronization—something that the roughly equivalent `Monitor.Enter/Exit` (or the C# `lock` keyword) cannot do.

In this case the `Mutex` is not used because of its synchronization capabilities, but simply as a way to identify a singleton object in the user's session. The name string argument passed to its constructor should be unique, to not confuse objects with other processes (its creation may also fail as a result). The `isNew` returned value indicates whether this is a brand new kernel mutex or another handle to an existing one. If it already exists, then it was created by an already running application instance, so we want to kill this new instance. But before we do that we want to activate the main window of the running instance. This is where `ActivateOtherWindow` comes in.

`ActivateOtherWindow` uses the Win32 function `FindWindow` to look for the other window based on its `Title`; if found, it brings it to the foreground (`SetForegroundWindow`). If it's also minimized (`IsIconic`)—it restores it (`OpenIcon`).

There's more...

Locating the existing window may be tricky. In the preceding example, the title is a constant string, so that's easily located with `FindWindow`. What if the window title is something like "My App - somefile.dat", meaning it starts the same ("My App"), but continues with the active file the user is working on? `FindWindow` can't handle this.

An alternative would be to call the Win32 `EnumWindows` function, go over each top level window looking for the title (using the Win32 `GetWindowText` function), and match to the expected pattern.

In an extreme case, the title of the main window may be too unpredictable even for iterating with `EnumWindows`. A more robust alternative is possible by hosting a WCF service within the application (using the `NetNamedPipeBinding` binding). The service would expose an operation that instructs the app to activate its main window. All that would be needed now is to connect to the service (easy to do with WCF and Visual Studio) and invoke the operation (a decent treatment of WCF is well beyond the scope of this book). This gives the added benefit of providing a way to send parameters to the other running instance (such as a file name provided as a command line argument); a example of the parameters to pass are Microsoft Word (the file to open) and Media Player (the file to play). The downloadable project for this recipe includes an example WCF hosting for just this purpose.

First, define the service contract:

```
[ServiceContract]
interface IActivateWindow {
   [OperationContract]
   void Activate(string[] args);
}
```

Second, implement:

```
class ActivationService : IActivateWindow {
   public void Activate(string[] args) {
      var helper = new WindowInteropHelper(
         Application.Current.MainWindow);
      if(App.IsIconic(helper.Handle))
         App.OpenIcon(helper.Handle);
      App.SetForegroundWindow(helper.Handle);
      // use args...
   }
}
```

Check for another instance; if it exists, switch to it by calling the service. Otherwise, we're the first, so open a WCF host to listen for clients (all in the `App` class):

```
const string _pipeAddress =
   "net.pipe://127.0.0.1/pipe/activation";

protected override void OnStartup(StartupEventArgs e) {
   bool isNew;
   var mutex = new Mutex(true, "MySingleInstanceMutex",
      out isNew);
   if(!isNew) {       // use the service
      var svc = ChannelFactory<IActivateWindow>.CreateChannel(
         new NetNamedPipeBinding(),
         new EndpointAddress(_pipeAddress));
      svc.Activate(e.Args);
      Shutdown();
   }
   else {
      CreateHost();
   }
}

ServiceHost _host;
void CreateHost() {
   _host = new ServiceHost(typeof(ActivationService));
   _host.AddServiceEndpoint(typeof(IActivateWindow),
      new NetNamedPipeBinding(), _pipeAddress);
   _host.Open();
}
```

Handling an unhandled exception

If a .NET exception goes unhandled, the process crashes with an unpleasant dialog presented to the user by Windows. Unpleasantness aside, the user may lose data as a result of the crash.

WPF provides a way to catch unhandled exceptions and perhaps handle them in some meaningful way. At the very least, the application may present a friendlier looking crash report and perhaps write the exception information to some log. At best, the application may recover from the error and continue running normally. Let's see how this can be done.

Getting ready

Make sure Visual Studio is up and running.

How to do it...

We'll create a simple application that throws an unhandled exception and see how we can catch it even if it's unhandled:

1. Create a new WPF Application project named `CH05.UnhandledExceptions`.
2. Open `MainWindow.xaml`. Add a `Button` to the `Grid` as follows:

   ```
   <Button Content="Throw Exception" FontSize="20" Margin="10" />
   ```

3. Add a `Click` handler to the button. In the handler, add the following:

   ```
   private void OnClick(object sender, RoutedEventArgs e) {
      throw new InvalidOperationException("something has gone
   wrong");
   }
   ```

4. Running the application now without the debugger and clicking the button would crash the process, producing the default crash dialog.
5. Open `App.xaml.cs`. Add an event handler for the `DispatcherUnhandledException` event (in the constructor):

   ```
   public App() {
      DispatcherUnhandledException += OnUnhandledException;
   }
   ```

6. Add a `using` statement for the `System.Diagnostics` namespace.

7. Add the following code to the handler:

```
Trace.WriteLine(string.Format("{0}: Error: {1}", DateTime.Now,
    e.Exception));
MessageBox.Show("Error encountered! Please contact support."
    + Environment.NewLine + e.Exception.Message);
Shutdown(1);
e.Handled = true;
```

8. Run the application and click the button. You should see the following message box. Click on **OK** and the application is shut down without the unpleasant Windows dialog:

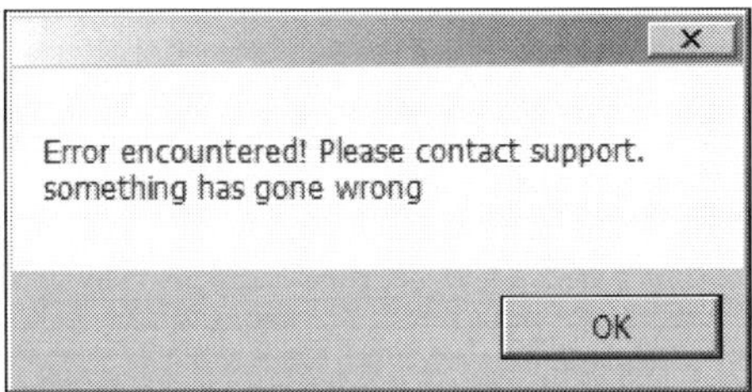

How it works...

The `DispatcherUnhandledException` event of the `Application` object is fired when an exception escapes handling, meaning no method on the main thread's call stack has elected to handle the exception. Without this event, the process would crash.

The event allows last minute handling of an error. If the `Handled` property of the `DispatcherUnhandledExceptionEventArgs` provided is set to `true`, the process does not terminate (returning to pumping messages). However, it's usually too dangerous in this situation to let the application continue running as usual, because the application may be in some inconsistent state – after all, an exception has occurred somewhere, and this may have resulted in partial work being done. It's usually safer to shut down the app and inform the user he/she should run the app again. At least the user won't see the disturbing Windows dialog and the application gets to save information about the exception and perhaps some other state before going down.

The preceding code sets `Handled` to `true` to prevent crashing, but calls `Application.Shutdown` to terminate the application, deemed too dangerous to continue running from this point. The call to `Trace.WriteLine` would show up in any configured `TraceListener` properties (tracing configuration is beyond the scope of this book); by default, it would go to the debugger window (if a debugger is attached). Otherwise, it can be captured by a custom tool, such as **DebugView** available from the **SysInternals** tools (`http://www.sysinternals.com`).

There's more...

This event can only be used to catch exceptions occurring on the UI thread (usually the main thread). Exceptions occurring on other threads (such as threads from the thread pool) will still crash the process (and not go through the event handler).

This means that letting exceptions *slide* to the `DispatcherUnhandledException` event is not generally a good idea. It should be an excepted situation that gets there – and it will never happen from a non-UI thread. Remember, this is a WPF mechanism; WPF has control of the UI thread, but not other threads. If such behavior is desired, we can use standard .NET mechanisms to be notified when an unhandled exception has occurred, such as registering with the `UnhandledException` event of the `AppDomain` class (registered on the current domain with `AppDomain.CurrentDomain`).

6
Data Binding

In this chapter we will cover:

- Element to element binding
- Binding to a single object
- Binding to collections
- Using data templates
- Using value converters
- Creating a master-details view
- Sorting and filtering bound collections
- Grouping bound collections
- Binding to multiple properties
- Binding hierarchical data to a TreeView
- Presenting data in a grid
- Validating data

Introduction

WPF is usually advertised as having great graphics and animation capabilities. This is certainly true, as one of the most powerful features of WPF has nothing to do with graphics directly: data binding. This feature is so powerful, that a new way of thinking is required, especially for those coming from a more "traditional" background, such as WinForms or MFC.

Data binding is essentially simple: one property changes in an object – another property in another object reflects the change in some meaningful way. That's the short story. The longer story involves a lot of possible customizations, such as value converters and binding modes. Coupled with data templates, data binding provides a compelling and powerful way to visualize and interact with data.

A new pattern has emerged for WPF (and Silverlight) applications because of the power of data binding, called Model View View-Model (MVVM); it's based on similar ideas from patterns known as Model View Controller (MVC), and Model View Presenter (MVP). The main difference, however, is the zealous use of data binding to declaratively connect objects without resorting to fragile coding and maintenance headaches. We'll take a look at MVVM in the next chapter, but for now we have to get a strong grip on data binding and how to use it, which is the focus of this chapter.

Element to element binding

Data binding is classically done between a user interface element and a data object. Sometimes, however, it's useful to bind one element's property to another's property. This can reduce (or even eliminate) the need for handling conventional events. Let's see how to make this work. This will also serve as a good start for doing bindings of any kind.

Getting ready

Make sure Visual Studio is up and running.

How to do it...

We'll create a `Slider` that affects the font size of a `TextBlock` without using any code.

1. Create a new WPF application named `CH06.ElementToElementBindings`.
2. Open `MainWindow.xaml`. Add the following markup to the existing `Grid`:

```
<Grid.RowDefinitions>
    <RowDefinition />
    <RowDefinition Height="Auto" />
    <RowDefinition Height="Auto" />
</Grid.RowDefinitions>
<TextBlock Text="This is a sizing text"
           TextAlignment="Center" VerticalAlignment="Center"/>
<Slider x:Name="_slider" Grid.Row="1" Minimum="10"
        Maximum="80" Value="30"/>
```

3. We'd like the `FontSize` property of `TextBlock` to match the `Value` property of `Slider`. The traditional approach would be to use an event (`ValueChanged`), but let's use data binding instead. Set the `FontSize` property of `TextBlock` as follows:

```
FontSize="{Binding Path=Value, ElementName=_slider}"
```

4. Run the application. Move the slider and watch the font size change.

5. Add a `TextBox` to the last row of the `Grid` and connect its `Text` property to the `Value` property of `Slider`:

```
<TextBox  Text="{Binding Value, ElementName=_slider}"
          Grid.Row="2" FontSize="20"/>
```

6. Run the application. Move the slider and watch the text change. Now type a value into the `TextBox` (for example, 60); nothing happens until you move the focus of the `TextBox` (for example, press *Tab*). The font size and slider change to reflect the new value.

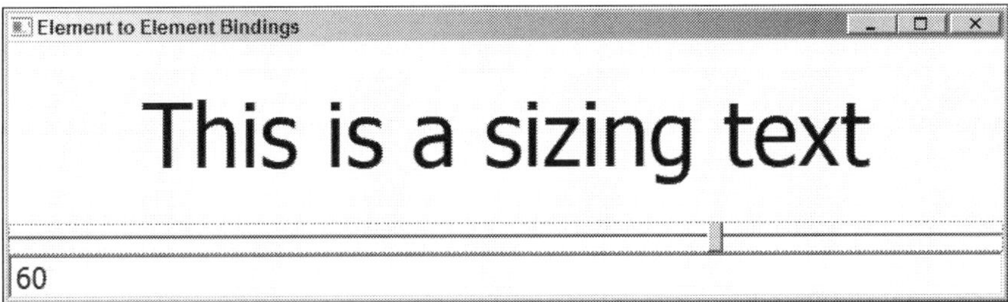

How it works...

Data binding connects a source property on a source object to a target property on a target object. Whenever the source changes, the target is updated. This is the classical model, but as we'll see other options are available in WPF. In the example code, both the source and target objects are elements (not plain data).

Binding is specified in XAML using the `Binding` markup extension, placed on the target property (this property must be a dependency property). The `Binding` properties we need to set are (at least) the source object and the source property, if any binding is to actually take place.

In the preceding code, the source object is set using the `ElementName` property and the source property is set through the `Path` property. Note in the `TextBox` example, the source property is set implicitly as a constructor argument (omitting `Path=`). The result is the same, but is usually more convenient, especially when we use Data Templates in the *Using data templates* recipe later in this chapter.

There's more...

We can hook up the binding in code as well as in XAML. The following is the equivalent code to the `FontSize` property of `TextBox` binding to the `Slider`:

```
var binding = new Binding("Value");
binding.ElementName = "_slider";
_text.SetBinding(TextBlock.FontSizeProperty, binding);
```

Why would we want to do that? Most of the time we wouldn't. Creating bindings in code is useful mostly when writing custom controls, as we'll see in *Chapter 10, Custom Elements*.

Binding mode

The `Binding` class has numerous properties to customize the binding process. We saw the `ElementName` and `Path` properties. Let's take a look at another useful one, `Mode` (of the type `BindingMode` enum).

The canonical data binding flow is from a source to a target. This is referred to as one way binding. WPF supports other modes, such as two way (if the target changes, the source is updated). In fact, in our example, the `TextBox Text` property (target) was bound to the `Value` property of `Slider` (source), but writing a new value to the `TextBox` (and getting the focus out) also moved the slider; this is a two way binding.

By default, the `Mode` is set to `BindingMode.Default`. The `Default` mode here means whatever the target dependency property has been stated at registration time (`DependencyProperty.Register`) with a `FrameworkPropertyMetadata` (`BindsTwoWayByDefault` property, as discussed in *Chapter 1*). For the `TextBox.Text` property the default is a two way binding; for the `TextBlock.Text` property it's one way (as with most properties).

WPF supports two other (less useful) binding modes:

- `OneTime`: Indicates the binding should occur only when the properties are first connected. Any further changes to the source are not reflected on the target. This is sometimes useful for properties that don't really change after first being bound, such as commands (discussed in the next chapter).
- `OneWayToSource`: Similar to one way, but works from the target to the source. This is sometimes useful when the required target property is not a dependency property, but the source property is.

Update source trigger

In the preceding example, changing the text in the TextBox did not trigger an immediate change in the source (the slider); we had to move the keyboard focus out of the TextBox. The reason for that is tucked in another Binding property, UpdateSourceTrigger; it's only relevant in a TwoWay or OneWayToSource binding mode, with the following possible values:

- LostFocus: The source is updated when the target element loses focus (which is exactly why the TextBox only updated the Slider after it had lost focus)
- PropertyChanged: The source is updated as soon as the target property changes. This is the default for most properties
- Explicit: The source is updated if the UpdateSource method is called on the binding expression (more on that in the next section)
- Default: This is the default (if not explicitly set otherwise) set by the target property at registration time with the FrameworkPropertyMetadata.DefaultUpdateSourceTrigger property

Updating the source or target manually

Data binding typically occurs automatically, which is usually the desired behavior. Sometimes, however, we may want to "force" data flow from source to target or vice versa (typically in a OneTime binding mode, or when UpdateSourceTrigger is set to Explicit). This is possible with the BindingExpression.UpdateSource and BindingExpression.UpdateTarget methods. Here's an example:

```
var expr = BindingOperations.GetBindingExpression(_text,
    TextBox.TextProperty);
expr.UpdateSource();
```

Binding to a single object

Although element to element binding is occasionally useful, the classic data binding scenario involves an element bound to pure data. One of the benefits of this kind of binding is a decoupling of data from the way it's presented (if at all). All later changes are performed on the data only, letting the binding take care of updating whatever elements are bound to this data. In this recipe, we'll look at binding to a single data object.

Getting ready

Make sure Visual Studio is up and running.

How to do it...

We'll create some controls that bind to a single `Person` object, showing the basics of element to data binding.

1. Create a new WPF application named `CH06.SingleObjectBinding`.
2. Open `MainWindow.xaml`. Change the existing `Grid` to a `StackPanel`.
3. Add two `TextBlock` elements with their `Text` property set with binding expressions like so:

```
<StackPanel>
    <TextBlock Text="{Binding Name}" />
    <TextBlock Text="{Binding Age}" />
</StackPanel>
```

4. Running the application at this time shows nothing. That's because the bindings are missing a source object. Let's fix that.
5. Add a new class to the project named `Person`. Create two automatic properties, like so:

```
class Person {
   public string Name { get; set; }
   public int Age { get; set; }
}
```

6. Open `MainWindow.xaml.cs`. Add a private field of type `Person` to the `MainWindow` class.
7. In the `MainWindow` constructor, create an instance of `Person` and set it to the private field. Then set the `DataContext` property to this value:

```
_person = new Person { Name = "Bart", Age = 10 };
DataContext = _person;
```

8. Run the application. The property values are reflected in the `TextBlock`s because the `DataContext` is the default source for the binding.

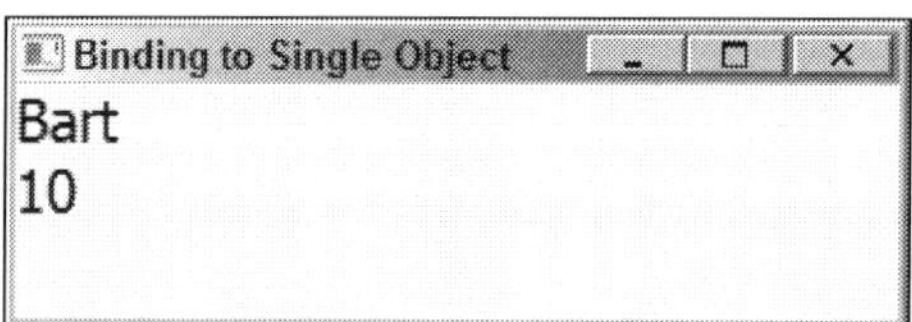

9. Open `MainWindow.xaml`. Add a `Button` to the `StackPanel` with a `Click` event handler. Enter the following code inside the handler:

```
private void OnChange(object sender, RoutedEventArgs e) {
   _person.Age++;
}
```

10. Run the application and click the button. Notice the displayed age doesn't change. The property actually changed, but WPF didn't know about it.

11. Open `Person.cs` and make the `Person` class implement the `INotifyPropetryChanged` interface (in the `System.ComponentModel` namespace). It contains a single event, `PropertyChanged`:

```
class Person : INotifyPropertyChanged {
   public string Name { get; set; }
   public int Age { get; set; }

   public event PropertyChangedEventHandler PropertyChanged;
}
```

12. We need to raise the event when a property changes. We'll have to remove the automatic property and implement it ourselves. Delete the `Age` property implementation and add the following code:

```
int _age;
public int Age {
   get { return _age; }
   set {
      _age = value;
      var pc = PropertyChanged;
      if(pc != null)
         pc(this, new PropertyChangedEventArgs("Age"));
   }
}
```

13. Run the application and click the button several times. The age is changed and displayed correctly.

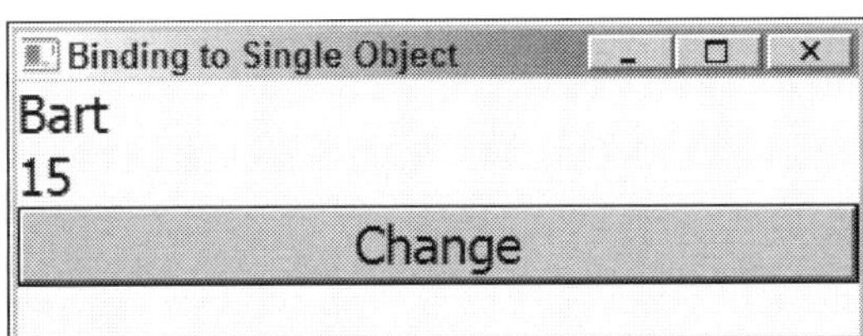

How it works...

A binding needs a source object. In the previous recipe, we used the `ElementName` property to get to a source object. For binding to data, `ElementName` is not appropriate.

The most useful (and common) option is to use the `DataContext` property. It's defined on `FrameworkElement` (and `FrameworkContentElement`) and indicates the default source object for bindings if none is specified in some other way (such as `ElementName`). When a binding expression is not given an explicit source, the source becomes the closest non-null `DataContext` starting from the target object up the visual tree. If none is found, then the binding simply fails.

There's more...

Data binding may seem like magic, but underneath some code does the actual job. In the preceding example, the binding worked initially, but it failed to track changes to the source object until we implemented the `INotifyPropertyChanged` interface on the data object (`Person`).

The problem is that with a property implemented as a thin wrapper around a private field, there's no way WPF (or any other entity for that matter) can come to know that it changed. This may require some polling of the property, but that's too expensive. The object must somehow notify interested parties that the property changed.

There are two common ways to do that. The first is to turn the property into a dependency property, which naturally supports change notifications. Although this seems attractive at first, it has two problems:

- It requires the data object to inherit from `DependencyObject`, which may be inconvenient; the class may already inherit from something, so the base class is taken (as .NET supports single inheritance only).
- Even if the base class is not an issue, the data object must now incur a dependency on WPF; this is far from ideal, as the same data object may also be needed in another type of application, such as ASP.NET or WinForms. Adding this dependency is cumbersome at the very least.

The second option, which is commonly used, is to implement the `INotifyPropertyChanged` interface. As this is an interface, it does not take the place of an optional base type that may be needed. And this interface is not defined by WPF, but rather is part of `System.Dll`, one of the core .NET assemblies.

When bindings fail

If a data binding expression has incorrect data, the binding operation may fail; for example, if the name `TextBlock` in the previous XAML is modified as follows:

```
<TextBlock Text="{Binding Name1}" />
```

The property name is somehow misspelled. Running the application throws no exceptions; the binding silently fails. This may seem strange, but this is generally a good thing. To find out about possible failures, we can run the application with the debugger, and watch the Output window (**View** | **Output** in the Visual Studio menu). This is what you'll get in this case:

System.Windows.Data Error: 40 : BindingExpression path error: 'Name1' property not found on 'object' ''Person' (HashCode=37814994)'. BindingExpression:Path=Name1; DataItem='Person' (HashCode=37814994); target element is 'TextBlock' (Name=''); target property is 'Text' (type 'String')

This shows the exact error, so it's usually easy to spot and correct.

Why is no exception thrown? The reason is that a data binding may fail at some point in time, and that's ok, because the conditions for this binding have not been met yet; there may be some information that is retrieved from a database, or from a web service, for instance; when the data is finally available, those bindings suddenly begin to work correctly. We'll discuss other ways of debugging data bindings in later recipes.

Other ways of getting a source binding object

There are two more ways of specifying a source object for binding. One of them is a `Source` property, which seems simple enough, but in fact is almost useless. `Source` expects some object, but as bindings are mostly expressed in XAML, `Source` must be something that the XAML parses can see at XAML parsing time. This is usually problematic, as XAML is unable to express dynamic connections to data that may not even be available yet; it is sometimes useful when binding to data from a resource (using `Source={StaticResource resourceName}`).

The last option is using the `RelativeSource` property. This allows binding the target object to something that is related to it in some way. `RelativeSource` offers a `Mode` property (an enum, also available as a constructor argument) that specifies the relativity kind. Specifying a `RelativeSource` is done with a `RelativeSource` markup extension. The possible modes are:

- `Self`: The source object is the target object itself, meaning binding one property to another property on the same object. Here's an example of binding a content of the `Button` to its current width:

  ```
  <Button Content="{Binding ActualWidth, RelativeSource=
      {RelativeSource Self}}" />
  ```

- `FindAncestor`: The source object is a parent (not necessarily the immediate one) of the target object. You can specify the kind of parent via the `AncestorType` property (and the *N*th ancestor of that type with the `AncestorLevel` property (default is 1)). Here's an example of binding a text of the `TextBlock` to the height of its containing window:

  ```
  <TextBlock Text="{Binding ActualHeight, RelativeSource=
   {RelativeSource FindAncestor, AncestorType=Window}}" />
  ```

- `PreviousData`: Makes the source the previous data object when binding to a collection (as we'll see in the next recipe)
- `TemplatedParent`: Indicates the source object is the control whose template is being built. This is relevant inside a control template only (as we'll see in *Chapter 8*)

Implementing INotifyPropertyChanged

The `INotifyPropertyChanged` implementation shown is simple enough, but it has its drawbacks. First, most of this code would have to be duplicated in every property, so placing it in a common base class would be beneficial:

```
public abstract class ObservableObject :
   INotifyPropertyChanged {
   public event PropertyChangedEventHandler PropertyChanged;

   protected virtual void OnPropertyChanged(string propName) {
      var pc = PropertyChanged;
      if (pc != null)
         pc(this, new PropertyChangedEventArgs(propName));
   }
}
```

This is certainly better, and the `Person` class can be refactored:

```
class Person : ObservableObject {
   public string Name { get; set; }

   int _age;
   public int Age {
      get { return _age; }
      set {
         if(_age != value) {
            _age = value;
            OnPropertyChanged("Age");
         }
      }
   }
}
```

Note the check for a new value that is actually different from the current one.

The most severe problem is the use of a property name as a string, which is at least inelegant, but more importantly can lead to subtle errors if the property name is misspelled or later changed.

One way to improve this is to check at runtime that the property with that name actually exists as the first line in `OnPropertyChanged`:

```
Debug.Assert(GetType().GetProperty(propName) != null);
```

Another way to improve the code is to do the inequality check within a common method. A further improvement would be not specifying the actual property name, but letting the code infer it automatically. Check out the following method:

```
protected void SetProperty<T>(ref T field, T value,
                      Expression<Func<T>> expr) {
   if(!EqualityComparer<T>.Default.Equals(field, value)) {
      field = value;
      var lambda = (LambdaExpression) expr;
      MemberExpression memberExpr;
      if (lambda.Body is UnaryExpression) {
         var unaryExpr = (UnaryExpression)lambda.Body;
         memberExpr = (MemberExpression)unaryExpr.Operand;
      }
      else {
         memberExpr = (MemberExpression)lambda.Body;
      }

      OnPropertyChanged(memberExpr.Member.Name);
   }
}
```

The first check uses `EqualityComparer<T>.Default` object to check for equality. This property returns a default equality comparer that calls `object.Equals` if it has to, but if the target object implements `IEquatable<T>`, it uses that implementation (for more information on this please check out the MSDN documentation).

`SetProperty<>` accepts as the last argument, a lambda expression that the compiler provides for the method in the form of an `Expression` object, which is a way to look at code as data. This allows the extraction of the property name provided by the caller. A complete look at expressions (`System.Linq.Expressions`) is beyond the scope of this book; check the MSDN docs or the Web. Bottom line – using this method in a data object becomes safer if not simpler:

```
int _age;
public int Age {
   get { return _age; }
   set { SetProperty(ref _age, value, () => Age); }
}
```

Now the property name is deduced automatically, so any errors will be evident at compile time, rather than runtime.

Implementing SetProperty with Visual Studio 2012 and C# 5.0

With Visual Studio 2012 and C# 5.0, the preceding code can be simplified further, thanks to a C# 5.0 feature that provides the caller member name automatically. This is how it looks:

```
protected void SetProperty<T>(ref T field, T value,
     [CallerMemberName] string propName = null) {
    if(!EqualityComparer<T>.Default.Equals(field, value)) {
       field = value;
       var pc = PropertyChanged;
       if(pc != null)
          pc(this, new PropertyChangedEventArgs(propName));
    }
}
```

The new `CallerMemberName` attribute makes the compiler provide the calling member name. This means that the property setter is now simplified:

```
set { SetProperty(ref _age, value); }
```

That's about as simple as we can get.

Binding to a collection

The previous recipe showed how to bind various properties to a single object, using single data controls, such as `TextBlock`, `TextBox`, or `Button`. Some controls, however, are capable of displaying multiple object data, such as a `ListBox`. These controls can bind to a collection of data objects, and with the help of data templates and value converters (to be covered in later recipes), become a powerful visualization tool. Let's examine the basic ideas of binding to collection of objects.

Getting ready

Make sure Visual Studio is up and running.

How to do it...

We'll create a collection of `Person` object and bind them to a `ListBox`, showing the details we need to take care of.

1. Create a new WPF Application named `CH06.BindingToCollection`.
2. Open `MainWindow.xaml`. Add a `ListBox` to the existing `Grid` and give it a name:

```
<ListBox x:Name="_list">
</ListBox>
```

3. Create a new `Person` class, with two properties, `Name` and `Age`, similar to the previous recipe (no need for `INotifyPropertyChanged` for this example).
4. Open `MainWindow.xaml.cs`. Add a private field of type `List<Person>` to `MainWindow`.
5. In the `MainWindow` constructor, after the call to `InitailizeComponent`, create a list of `Person` objects as follows:

```
_people = new List<Person> {
   new Person { Name = "Bart", Age = 10 },
   new Person { Name = "Homer", Age = 45 },
   new Person { Name = "Marge", Age = 35 },
   new Person { Name = "Lisa", Age = 12 },
   new Person { Name = "Maggie", Age = 1 }
};
```

6. Set the `ItemsSource` property of `ListBox` to refer to that list:

```
_list.ItemsSource = _people;
```

7. Run the application. You should see the following:

8. Clearly, the default `ToString` of `Person` is called for each object. We can change the `ToString` implementation to something more useful:

```
public override string ToString() {
   return string.Format("{0} is {1} years old", Name, Age);
}
```

9. Running the application now shows:

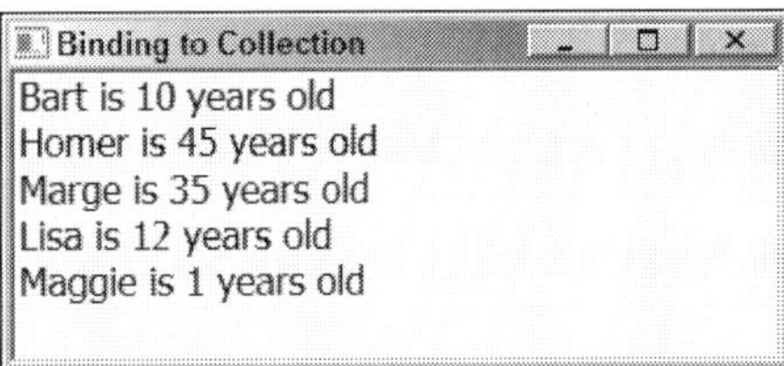

10. Another way to customize the view is set the `DisplayMemebrPath` property of the `ListBox`. Open `MainWindow.xaml` and set the property as follows:

```
<ListBox x:Name="_list" DisplayMemberPath="Name">
```

11. Running the application shows only the names.
12. Create two rows for the `Grid`:

```
<Grid.RowDefinitions>
    <RowDefinition />
    <RowDefinition Height="Auto" />
</Grid.RowDefinitions>
```

13. Add a `Button` to the second row, with a `Click` event handler as follows:

```
<Button Content="Add" Click="OnAdd" Grid.Row="1" />
```

14. In the event handler, add a `Person` object to the existing collection:

```
_people.Add(new Person { Name = "Moe", Age = 40 });
```

15. Run the application and click on the button. No person is added to the `ListBox`. That's because when an object is added to a `List<>`, no notification is sent.
16. To solve that, replace `List<Person>` with `ObservableCollection<Person>` (in the `System.Collections.ObjectModel` namespace).
17. Now run the application and click the button. **Moe** is added to the `ListBox`.

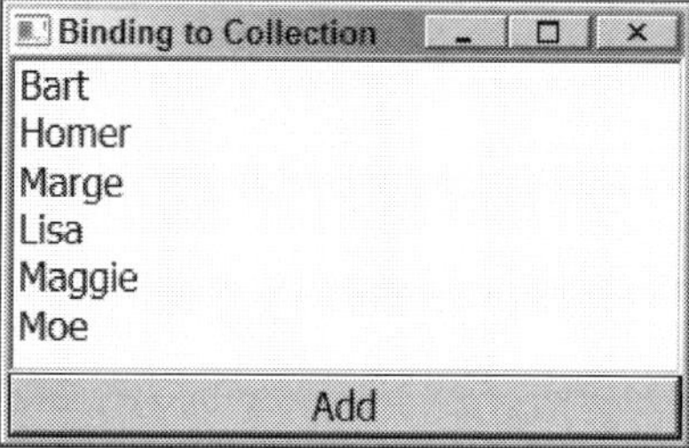

How it works...

All controls inheriting from `ItemsControl` provide an `ItemsSource` property that should be set to some collection object (implementing at least `IEnumerable`), which sets up the source of the binding.

By default, items are displayed as `TextBlocks` using the `ToString` values for each object. One way to change that is using the `DisplayMemberPath` property. This is a property path, meaning we can use sub-properties, including indexers, to get the actual property we want to display.

Using `List<T>` is usually not good enough because when objects are added or removed from the list, no notification is sent, so no bound control can be updated. WPF looks for an interface, `INotifyCollectionChanged`, to be implemented in the source collection object. `List<T>` does not implement this interface, but an alternative class, `ObservableCollection<T>`, does.

There's more...

Can we use a `DataContext` in this case? Certainly. We can set the `DataContext` of some object which is a parent of the `ItemsControl` in question and then use an empty binding expression to find it. This will allow us to bind the same collection to other objects. Here's an example with a `ComboBox` within the same `Grid`:

```
<ComboBox ItemsSource="{Binding}" Grid.Row="2"/>
```

Note the binding expression. Omitting it will fail the binding, as it means the source is a null reference, which means no source. Now we need to set the `DataContext` in code:

```
DataContext = _people;
```

Synchronizing selected items

With the previous example, a `ComboBox` and a `ListBox` are bound to the same exact data. If the selection is changed in the `ListBox`, it does not affect the selected item in the `ComboBox` and vice versa. If we wanted the selected item to be synchronized between Selector controls that bind to the same data, we could set the `IsSynchronizedToCurrentItem` property on the `ComboBox` and `ListBox` to true:

```
IsSynchronizedWithCurrentItem="True"
```

Now moving the selection in one control updates it in the other. How does this work? We'll discuss that in a future recipe in this chapter, *Sorting and filtering bound collections*.

Data binding and the Items property are mutually exclusive

Using data binding with `ItemsControl` and its derivatives makes using the `Items` property for adding or removing elements throw an exception. And with good reason too - with data binding we want to deal with the data itself, and not have to think about which control it's bound to (if any). It is possible to use the `Items` property in a read-only manner, but it's bad practice to do so; we want to deal with the data only and not with controls that may disappear or be replaced in the future.

What about "real" data?

The preceding code uses collections of objects created locally, but many applications get their data from an external source, such as a relational database or some web service. WPF, however, does not care about that. The result is a collection, obtained in some way, for example, using the Entity Framework (EF) to access a SQL Server database, or by calling some Windows Communication Foundation (WCF) service. The net result is a collection (at least `IEnumerable<T>`), which is all WPF needs for binding to work correctly.

Using data templates

In previous recipes we showed some `Person` objects as strings, whether it's the `ToString` implementation or some specific property. Text is not the only option. Even with text, we may want to change its properties, such as fonts and colors. WPF provides a powerful way to visualize data using the concept of data templates. In this recipe, we'll see how to create and use such templates.

Getting ready

Make sure Visual Studio is up and running.

How to do it...

We'll create a simple application that shows `Person` objects in a more interesting way using data templates.

1. Create a new WPF Application named `CH06.DataTemplates`.
2. Add a new class named `Person`, with an `Age` and `Name` properties, similar to the previous recipe.
3. Open `MainWindow.xaml`. Add two rows to the grid like so:

```
<Grid.RowDefinitions>
    <RowDefinition Height="Auto"/>
    <RowDefinition />
</Grid.RowDefinitions>
```

4. Add a `Button` to the first row, with its `Content` bound to whatever `DataContext` is effective at the moment:

```
<Button Content="{Binding}" />
```

5. Open `MainWindow.xaml.cs`. Add the following to the constructor after the call to `InitializeComponent`:

```
DataContext = new Person { Age = 10, Name = "Bart" };
```

6. Run the application. You should see the button display the default `ToString` of the `Person` instance. We can change that by overriding `ToString`, but let's try something different.

7. Set the `ContentTemplate` property of the `Button` to a `DataTemplate` instance and add inside that some markup with binding expressions. The entire `Button` XAML might look something like this:

```
<Button Content="{Binding}">
    <Button.ContentTemplate>
        <DataTemplate>
            <Border BorderBrush="Green" BorderThickness="2">
                <StackPanel Margin="4">
                    <TextBlock Foreground="Red" FontSize="20"
                         Text="{Binding Name}"
                         TextAlignment="Center" />
                    <TextBlock FontSize="16"
                         Text="{Binding Age}"
                         TextAlignment="Right" />
                </StackPanel>
            </Border>
        </DataTemplate>
    </Button.ContentTemplate>
</Button>
```

8. Running the application shows the following:

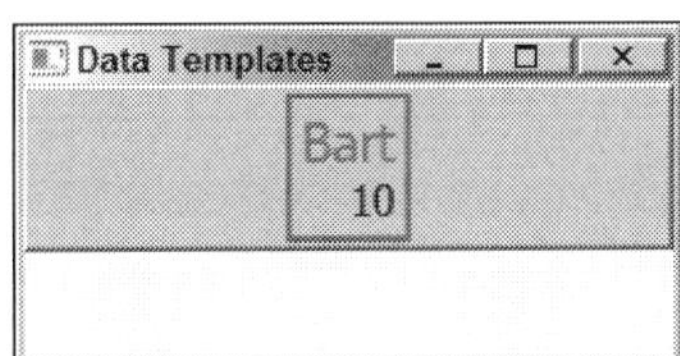

9. Open `MainWindow.xaml`. Add a `ListBox` to the second row of the `Grid` and give it a name:

```
<ListBox Grid.Row="1" x:Name="_list"
    HorizontalContentAlignment="Stretch" />
```

10. Open `MainWindow.xaml.cs`. In the constructor, create a bunch of `Person` objects, and set the `ItemsSource` property of `ListBox` to that collection:

```
_list.ItemsSource = new ObservableCollection<Person> {
   new Person { Name = "Bart", Age = 10 },
   new Person { Name = "Homer", Age = 45 },
   new Person { Name = "Marge", Age = 35 }
};
```

11. Running the application shows each person in the list with its `ToString` representation. We want to use the `DataTemplate` previously defined.
12. To avoid copy/paste, move the previous `DataTemplate` to a resource in the Window with a key `personTemplate`:

```
<Window.Resources>
    <DataTemplate x:Key="personTemplate">
...
    </DataTemplate>
</Window.Resources>
```

13. Change the `ContentTemplate` property of `Button` to use the resource:

```
<Button Content="{Binding}"
  ContentTemplate="{StaticResource personTemplate}" />
```

14. Set the `ItemTemplate` property of `ListBox` to that same resource:

```
<ListBox Grid.Row="1" x:Name="_list"
    HorizontalContentAlignment="Stretch"
    ItemTemplate="{StaticResource personTemplate}" />
```

15. Run the application. Every person object is displayed in the same way based on the data template.

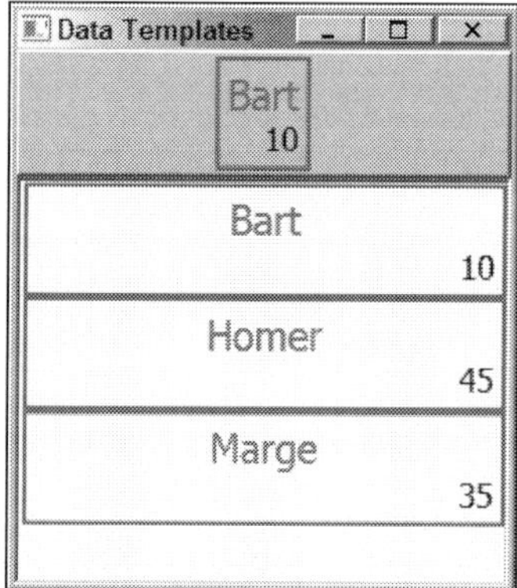

How it works...

Data templates are just what they sound like: templates for visualizing data; these are in contrast to control templates (which we'll see in *Chapter 8*), that are templates for controls.

Content controls have a Content property (of type Object) that is rendered as TextBlocks if that object does not derive from UIElement. If, however, their ContentTemplate is non-null, then that DataTemplate provides the visual appearance of that object. This can be a single element only, typically a Panel, which can host just about anything. Binding expressions inside the template should not include a specific Source or ElementName, because the default Source (or DataContext if you will) is the actual data object (a specific person in the preceding code example). This means that the following markup sets the text to be the value of the Name property of the currently bound object (whether this is a Person or not).

```
<TextBlock Foreground="Red" Text="{Binding Name}" />
```

If the property does not exist, then the binding fails. This means that for every such Person a copy of the visual tree represented by the DataTemplate is instantiated (that's why it's called "template").

The ItemsControl class and its derivatives provide a property called ItemTemplate that serves the exact same purpose, but affects each item in the collection it's bound to.

The HeaderedContentControl (and its derivatives) provide an additional HeaderTemplate to customize the way the value set to the Header property is displayed.

There's more...

Data templates are not directly connected to data binding; that is, it's possible to use the regular Items property to add or remove objects from, say, a ListBox and still be able to use data templates. Using ItemsControl and its derivatives without data binding is rare, and should be avoided.

Data type based data templates

Providing data templates via the relevant properties (as was done in the preceding code samples) is easy enough, and the use of resources simplifies this further. There is another option, though. We can specify generally that whenever some type is encountered anywhere in the application, a specific DataTemplate should be used without the need to specify it directly via properties.

To do that, we must create the DataTemplate as a resource, setting the DataType property to the required type, but omitting the usual x:Key property. Here's an example for our trusty Person (assuming the XML prefix local points to the current assembly defining the Person type):

```
<Window.Resources>
    <DataTemplate DataType="{x:Type local:Person}">
...
    </DataTemplate>
</Window.Resources>
```

The resource can be placed in `App.xaml` for a more global effect. A `ListBox` bound to some `Person` objects can be written as follows:

```
<ListBox HorizontalContentAlignment="Stretch"
         ItemsSource="{Binding}" />
```

Note the lack of the `ItemTemplate` property. It's set automatically because of the resource definition.

The real benefit from this feature is its automatic polymorphism. Suppose there's a class deriving from `Person`:

```
class Employee : Person {
   public string Department { get; set; }
}
```

We can build a `DataTemplate` for displaying employees as follows:

```
<DataTemplate DataType="{x:Type local:Employee}">
   <Border BorderBrush="Black" BorderThickness="1">
      <StackPanel Margin="4" Orientation="Horizontal">
         <TextBlock Foreground="Blue" FontSize="20"
             Text="{Binding Name}" TextAlignment="Center" />
         <TextBlock Foreground="Red" FontSize="16"
             Text="{Binding Department}"
             Margin="20,0,0,0" VerticalAlignment="Center"/>
        </StackPanel>
    </Border>
</DataTemplate>
```

Now suppose we create a few objects and bind them to a `ListBox`, as follows:

```
DataContext = new ObservableCollection<Person> {
   new Person { Name = "Bart", Age = 10 },
   new Employee { Name = "Homer", Age = 45,
      Department = "Nuclear" },
   new Person { Name = "Marge", Age = 35 },
   new Employee { Name = "Lisa", Age = 12,
      Department = "Accounting" },
   new Person { Name = "Maggie", Age = 1 }
};
```

Some of these are `Person` objects and some `Employee` objects, but the `DataTemplate` is selected correctly based on the actual type:

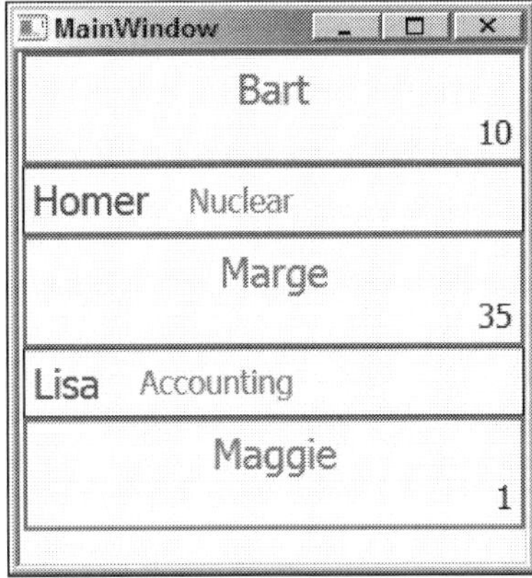

The complete example is available in the downloadable source for this chapter in the `CH06.DataTypedDataTemplates` project.

Data template selectors

Another way to select different data templates is based on the concept of a template selector. This is an object that receives each data object bound to an `ItemsControl` (or its derivatives) and returns the required `DataTemplate` for this instance. This allows the selecting of different templates for different objects of the same type (something the data type based technique can't do).

To achieve this, we need to create a class deriving from the abstract `DataTemplateSelector` and override its `SelectTemplate` abstract method. Here's a selector class that uses different templates for displaying `Process` objects:

```
class ProcessTemplateSelector : DataTemplateSelector {
   public string SystemProcessTemplate { get; set; }
   public string UserProcessTemplate { get; set; }

   public override DataTemplate SelectTemplate(object item,
      DependencyObject container) {
      Process process = (Process)item;
      return ((FrameworkElement)container).FindResource(
         process.SessionId == 0 ?
         SystemProcessTemplate : UserProcessTemplate)
         as DataTemplate;
   }
}
```

The selector method is called for each and every item when it's first bound to the control. This particular implementation uses the `SessionId` property of the `Process` class to decide what template to use. For flexibility, it exposes two possible template names as properties, which is useful for trying out different templates dynamically. The item argument is the actual object on which decisions should be made (a `Process` in our case); the container property is the actual control (a `ListBox` in our case as we shall see in a moment), that may be useful – as it is in this case - it's used as a base element for hunting a `DataTemplate` resource based on the custom properties.

This is just a class, so an instance should be created somehow and used by an `ItemsControl` object. First, we create two alternative `DataTemplate`s for `Process` objects in a `Resources` dictionary:

```
<DataTemplate x:Key="systemTemplate">
    <Border Background="Red" BorderBrush="Black"
            BorderThickness="1" Margin="2" Padding="4">
        <TextBlock HorizontalAlignment="Center"
            VerticalAlignment="Center"
            FontSize="16" Text="{Binding ProcessName}" />
    </Border>
</DataTemplate>
<DataTemplate x:Key="userTemplate">
    <Border Background="White" BorderBrush="Blue"
            BorderThickness="1" Margin="2">
        <StackPanel Orientation="Horizontal"
                    TextBlock.FontSize="15" Margin="2">
            <TextBlock Text="{Binding ProcessName}" />
            <TextBlock Margin="10,0,0,0"
  Text="{Binding Id, StringFormat='ID: 0'}" />
            <TextBlock Margin="10,0,0,0"
  Text="{Binding Threads.Count, StringFormat='Threads: 0'}" />
        </StackPanel>
    </Border>
</DataTemplate>
```

Now for the selector object itself. As a control needs to access it, it's easiest to create it as a resource as well:

```
<local:ProcessTemplateSelector x:Key="_selector"
        SystemProcessTemplate="systemTemplate"
        UserProcessTemplate="userTemplate" />
```

All that's left is to create a `ListBox` that chooses to use the selector:

```
<ListBox HorizontalContentAlignment="Stretch"
         ItemsSource="{Binding}"
         ItemTemplateSelector="{StaticResource _selector}"/>
```

The processes themselves are bound to the `ListBox` using the usual `DataContext`:

```
DataContext = Process.GetProcesses();
```

That's it. Running this example on my machine produces the following:

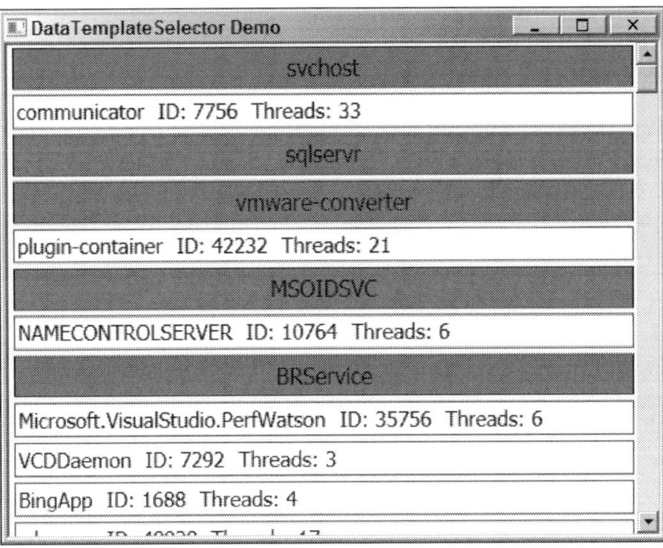

The complete example is available with the downloadable source for this chapter in a project named `CH06.DataTemplateSelectors`.

It's important to realize the `SelectTemplate` is only called once per object. This means that if an object changes internally that would mandate a different data template to be used, this won't happen. In cases like these, a value converter may be more appropriate (as we'll see in the next recipe). It is possible, however, to force the control to re-evaluate all its templates by explicitly setting `ItemTemplateSelector` to `null` and then to an actual instance (which could be the same one); this will force the `ItemsControl` to re-create the items while using the selector to get the chosen `DataTemplate` for each object.

Using value converters

Data templates provide a powerful way to visualize any data. We discussed a few ways to customize the appearance of data templates. In this recipe, we'll look at value converters, which is a flexible mechanism to customize data bindings in general, and data templates in particular. Their power ranges from simple data transformations to significant visual changes.

Getting ready

Make sure Visual Studio is up and running.

How to do it...

We'll create a weather forecast application that uses a value converter to convert a general weather outlook into a brush.

1. Create a new WPF application named `CH06.WeatherForecast`.
2. We'll create a simple weather forecasting application. Add a new class named `Forecast` with some simple properties:

```
enum GeneralForecast {
   Sunny,
   Rainy,
   Snowy,
   Cloudy,
   Dry
}

class Forecast {
   public GeneralForecast GeneralForecast { get; set; }
   public double TemperatureHigh { get; set; }
   public double TemperatureLow { get; set; }
   public double Percipitation { get; set; }
}
```

3. Open `MainWindow.xaml`. Add three rows in the `Grid` and some controls:

```
<Grid.RowDefinitions>
    <RowDefinition Height="Auto" />
    <RowDefinition Height="Auto" />
    <RowDefinition />
</Grid.RowDefinitions>
<StackPanel Orientation="Horizontal">
    <TextBlock Text="Select number of days to forecast:"
        FontSize="15" VerticalAlignment="Center" Margin="4"/>
    <ComboBox x:Name="_days" SelectedIndex="0" Width="50"/>
    <Button Margin="4" Content="Get Forecast" FontSize="16" />
</StackPanel>
<StackPanel Orientation="Horizontal" Grid.Row="1" Margin="4"
         TextBlock.FontSize="15">
    <TextBlock Text="Select units:" Margin="4"/>
    <RadioButton Content="Celsius" IsChecked="True"
```

```
                Margin="10,4"/>
        <RadioButton Content="Fahrenheit" Margin="20,4"/>
    </StackPanel>
    <ListBox ItemsSource="{Binding}" Grid.Row="2"
        HorizontalContentAlignment="Stretch">
    </ListBox>
```

4. We'll generate a dummy forecast when the button is clicked. Add a `Click` event handler for the button. Inside, add the following code:

```
var data = new List<Forecast>();
int days = (int)_days.SelectedItem;
var rnd = new Random();
for(int i = 0; i < days; i++) {
   double temp = rnd.NextDouble() * 40 - 10;
   var forecast = new Forecast {
      GeneralForecast = (GeneralForecast)rnd.Next(
         Enum.GetValues(typeof(GeneralForecast)).Length),
      TemperatureLow = temp,
      TemperatureHigh = temp + rnd.NextDouble() * 15,
      Percipitation = rnd.Next(10)>5 ? rnd.NextDouble()*10 : 0
   };
   data.Add(forecast);
}
DataContext = data;
```

5. `_days` is the `ComboBox` instance for selecting the number of days. To populate it, add the following to the `MainWindow` constructor:

```
_days.ItemsSource = Enumerable.Range(1, 10);
```

6. The call to `Enumerable.Range` returns a collection of integers (1 to 10 in this case). The `ListBox` is bound to the `DataContext`, but to see something useful, we need a `DataTemplate` for the `ListBox`. Add the following to the `ListBox` markup:

```
<ListBox.ItemTemplate>
    <DataTemplate>
        <Border Margin="4" BorderBrush="Black" Padding="4"
            BorderThickness="2" Background="White">
            <StackPanel Orientation="Horizontal">
                <TextBlock FontSize="20" FontWeight="Bold"
                    Text="{Binding GeneralForecast}" />
                <TextBlock FontSize="16" Margin="10,0,0,0"
                    VerticalAlignment="Bottom"
                    Text="{Binding TemperatureLow,
                    StringFormat='Low: \{0:N2\}'}" />
                <TextBlock FontSize="16" Margin="10,0,0,0"
```

```
                        VerticalAlignment="Bottom"
                        Text="{Binding TemperatureHigh,
                         StringFormat='High: \{0:N2\}'}" />
                    <TextBlock FontSize="16" Margin="20,0,0,0"
                         VerticalAlignment="Bottom"
                         Text="{Binding Percipitation,
                         StringFormat='Percip: \{0:N2\}'}" />
                </StackPanel>
            </Border>
        </DataTemplate>
    </ListBox.ItemTemplate>
```

7. Run the application. Select a number of days from the `ComboBox` and click the button. Here's a sample output:

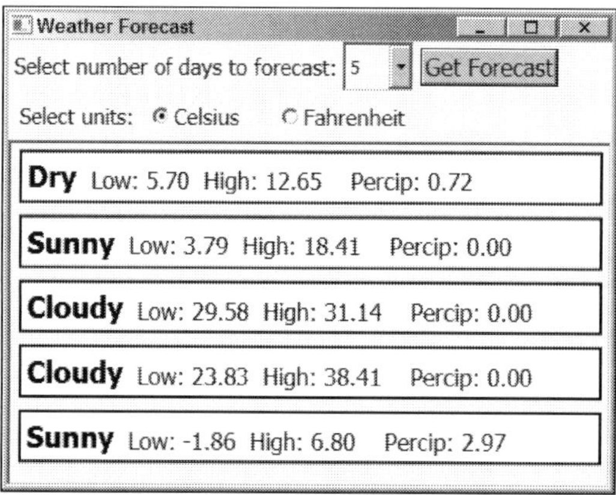

8. We'd like to change the background of each day's forecast based on the general forecast (for example, a yellow background for sunny weather). For that we'll create a value converter. Add a new class to the project named `GeneralForecastToBrushConverter`.

9. Implement the `IValueConverter` interface on that class (in the `System.Windows.Data` namespace). This is what the skeleton looks like:

```
class GeneralForecastToBrushConverter : IValueConverter {
   public object Convert(object value, Type targetType, object 
parameter, System.Globalization.CultureInfo culture) {
      throw new NotImplementedException();
   }

   public object ConvertBack(object value, Type targetType, 
object parameter, System.Globalization.CultureInfo culture) {
      throw new NotImplementedException();
   }
}
```

10. We need to convert a `GeneralForecast` enum value to a `Brush` with the appropriate color. Add the following to the `Convert` method (delete the `throw` statement):

```
var gf = (GeneralForecast)value;
switch(gf) {
   case GeneralForecast.Cloudy:
      return Brushes.LightGray;
   case GeneralForecast.Dry:
      return Brushes.LightYellow;
   case GeneralForecast.Rainy:
      return Brushes.LightGreen;
   case GeneralForecast.Snowy:
      return Brushes.LightBlue;
   case GeneralForecast.Sunny:
      return Brushes.Yellow;
}
return Binding.DoNothing;
```

11. To set everything up, we need to create an instance of the converter and wire it up to a binding expression. We'll create it as a resource in the `Window` (the `local` XML namespace maps to the project namespace):

```
<Window.Resources>
    <local:GeneralForecastToBrushConverter x:Key="gf2brush" />
</Window.Resources>
```

12. Now we need to change the `Background` property of (for example) the `Border` element within the `DataTemplate` to take the converter into consideration, passing the `GeneralForecast` value:

```
Background="{Binding GeneralForecast,
   Converter={StaticResource gf2brush}}"
```

13. Run the application. Here's a sample output:

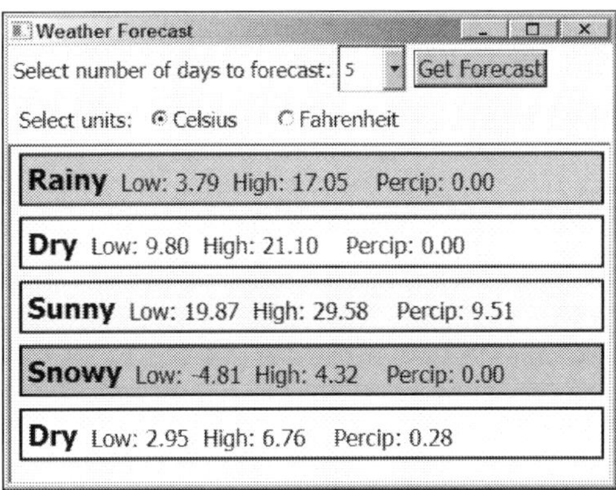

How it works...

A value converter is an object implementing the `IValueConverter` interface. It provides a way to convert, or project, one value to another. The values may be of incompatible types (as in the preceding example – an enum converted into a `Brush`), or they may be of the same type, but require some transformation that is not possible declaratively.

Value converters are powerful, because they are written in code, not just markup. An instance of the converter is typically created in XAML as a resource and are provided via binding expressions with the `Converter` property. Whenever the source property changes, the converter gets the opportunity to return a different result through the `Convert` method.

The `ConvertBack` method is called in a two way binding, where the roles of source and target are reversed. In a one-way binding, there's no need to implement `ConvertBack`.

There's more...

The `Convert` and `ConvertBack` methods accept other arguments beside the actual bound value. Here's the prototype for `Convert`:

```
public object Convert(object value, Type targetType,
   object parameter,  CultureInfo culture);
```

`targetType` indicates the expected return type for the binding to work. In our example, that target property is `Background`, which is a type of `Brush`, so `targetType` is `typeof(Brush)`. This argument can serve several purposes:

- Provide a way to validate that the converter is in fact used in the correct context. In our example, the following code is added as the first line to make sure a `Brush` is what's requested:

  ```
  if(targetType != typeof(Brush))
     throw new ArgumentException("targetType");
  ```

- To differentiate between several ways a single converter may work. For instance, a converter may be able to return a `Brush` or a `Color`, depending on its exact placement. This would give the method a way to distinguish between the possible return types it supports.

The parameter argument can be specified with the `ConverterParameter` property of the `Binding`, providing a way to customize the current requested conversion. This is application specific; WPF does nothing with this argument.

The last culture argument allows specifying a `CultureInfo` object through the `ConverterCulture` property of the `Binding`. This is specified in the usual `CultureInfo` way, for example, "en", "en-US", "fr-CA", and so on. This allows the converter to base its operation on culture specific information, such as date and time formats and currency type. By default, the system UI culture is provided.

Using converters for debugging

Debugging data bindings is naturally hard, as everything is so "automatic". There's no location to place a breakpoint, for example (in Silverlight 5, however, it is possible to place a breakpoint in XAML bindings, but this feature is unavailable at this time in WPF). One way to get around that is to create a simple converter, which does nothing, but provides a way to set a breakpoint. With that breakpoint in place, you can examine the value coming in, the target type, and so on.

Formatting strings

Strings are a common data type to show in bindings, whether a converter is involved or not. Suppose we want to show the temperature in our forecast, but want to prefix a text, such as `Temp:` in front of the actual value. One way to do that is to create another `TextBlock` that shows that constant text. Or we can use a `TextBlock` with `Inline` elements, consisting of `Run` elements that bind to values and simple `Span` elements that don't.

Another common example is displaying values that have several formats, such as date or time. By default, the `ToString` method will be called on (for example) a `DateTime` object. How would we display just the time? Or the date? Or perhaps the date in the long format?

One possible solution is to use a converter, which clearly can do anything. However, for these scenarios there's a simpler way that does not require code: the `StringFormat` property of a `Binding`. This is similar to the `ToString` methods that accept a format string. In the preceding example, each value of the forecast was prefixed with some text using `StringFormat`. For example:

```
Text="{Binding TemperatureLow, StringFormat='Low: \{0:N2\}'}"
```

This indicates that the word `Low:` should be displayed as is, and the format specifier `N2` means (for double values) the number should be displayed with 2 decimal digits. The strange backslashes are escapes for the curly braces; otherwise they might confuse the XAML parser. The single quote is not strictly required in this case, but the intent seems clearer.

Customizing with data triggers

Converters are certainly one of the most powerful tools in the binding toolbox, because they use code, which naturally can do anything. Some changes, however, can be made with XAML alone. One such change was shown in the previous section with `StringFormat`. What about non-string related customizations?

Data triggers can be applied to `DataTemplate` objects (via the `Triggers` property) to make certain changes under certain conditions, with no code needed. For example, our forecast `DataTemplate` can be rewritten with the use of data triggers to have the same effect without any converter:

```
<DataTemplate>
    <Border x:Name="_border" Margin="4" BorderBrush="Black"
   BorderThickness="2" Padding="4" Background="LightGray">
        <StackPanel Orientation="Horizontal">
            <TextBlock FontSize="20" FontWeight="Bold"
    Text="{Binding GeneralForecast}" />
            <TextBlock FontSize="16" Margin="10,0,0,0"
    VerticalAlignment="Bottom"
    Text="{Binding TemperatureLow,
        StringFormat=Low: \{0:N2\}}" />
            <TextBlock FontSize="16" Margin="10,0,0,0"
    VerticalAlignment="Bottom"
    Text="{Binding TemperatureHigh,
        StringFormat='High: \{0:N2\}'}" />
            <TextBlock FontSize="16" Margin="20,0,0,0"
    VerticalAlignment="Bottom" Text="{Binding Percipitation,
        StringFormat='Percip: \{0:N2\}'}" />
        </StackPanel>
    </Border>
    <DataTemplate.Triggers>
        <DataTrigger Binding="{Binding GeneralForecast}"
                     Value="Sunny">
            <Setter Property="Background" Value="Yellow"
                    TargetName="_border"/>
        </DataTrigger>
        <DataTrigger Binding="{Binding GeneralForecast}"
                     Value="Snowy">
            <Setter Property="Background" Value="LightBlue"
                    TargetName="_border"/>
        </DataTrigger>
        <DataTrigger Binding="{Binding GeneralForecast}"
                     Value="Rainy">
            <Setter Property="Background" Value="LightGreen"
                    TargetName="_border"/>
        </DataTrigger>
        <DataTrigger Binding="{Binding GeneralForecast}"
                     Value="Dry">
            <Setter Property="Background" Value="LightYellow"
                    TargetName="_border"/>
        </DataTrigger>
    </DataTemplate.Triggers>
</DataTemplate>
```

The changes are marked in bold. A full discussion of triggers in general, and data triggers in particular, is provided in *Chapter 8, Styles, Triggers, and Control Templates*, but here we can see the basics.

A `DataTrigger` object checks a property for equality to a value; the required property is specified using the `Binding` property of `DataTrigger`, which should be a binding expression. The comparison is always with an equality operator; there's no way to use something like greater than, less then, and so on; this is one of the shortcomings of triggers. In our case, however, this is good enough – we compare values of the `GeneralForecast` property to the various enum values. If there is a match, a bunch of `Setter` objects can be used that set a value to some property on some object (using the `TargetName` property). Note that our famous `Border` is named `_border`, which all setters reference.

The end result is the same – no converter needed. The complete project is named `CH06.WeatherForecastWithTriggers` and is available with the downloadable source for this chapter.

Creating a master-detail view

A master-detail view is a common way to display lots of information. The master shows a compressed view of some objects, while the detail view shows the selected object (from the master) in greater detail, as appropriate. Let's examine a typical way to achieve this in WPF.

Getting ready

Make sure Visual Studio is up and running.

How to do it...

We'll create an application that shows a list of processes and a detailed look of a selected process.

1. Create a new WPF application named `CH06.MasterDetail`.
2. Open `MainWindow.xaml`. Add the following markup to the existing `Grid`, creating two columns with first holding a `ListBox`:

```
<Grid.ColumnDefinitions>
    <ColumnDefinition Width="200"/>
    <ColumnDefinition  />
</Grid.ColumnDefinitions>
<ListBox ItemsSource="{Binding}" FontSize="16"
         DisplayMemberPath="ProcessName" x:Name="_master"/>
```

3. The `ListBox` will serve as the master view, showing a flat list of all running processes on the system. Now we need the detail view. This will be a simple `Grid` hosting some `TextBlock` elements bound to various properties of a process:

```
<Grid Grid.Column="1" TextBlock.FontSize="16">
    <Grid.RowDefinitions>
        <RowDefinition Height="Auto" />
        <RowDefinition Height="Auto" />
        <RowDefinition Height="Auto" />
        <RowDefinition Height="Auto" />
        <RowDefinition Height="Auto" />
    </Grid.RowDefinitions>
    <TextBlock Margin="6" Text="{Binding ProcessName,
StringFormat='Name: \{0\}'}" />
    <TextBlock Grid.Row="1" Margin="6" Text="{Binding Id,
StringFormat='ID: 0'}" />
    <TextBlock Grid.Row="2" Margin="6" Text="{Binding
PriorityClass, StringFormat='Priority Class: \{0\}'}" />
    <TextBlock Grid.Row="3" Margin="6" Text="{Binding Threads.
Count, StringFormat='Threads: 0'}" />
    <TextBlock Grid.Row="4" Margin="6" Text="{Binding
TotalProcessorTime, StringFormat='Processor Time: \{0:G\}'}" />
</Grid>
```

4. Let's add the collection of processes as the base for the `ListBox` binding. Open `MainWindow.xaml.cs` and add the following in the constructor:

```
DataContext = Process.GetProcesses();
```

5. Running the application now shows the details of the first process in the list, regardless of selection. To actually view the details of the currently selected process, we need to set the `DataContext` that the detail `Grid` sees. Add the following as a property of the inner `Grid`:

```
DataContext="{Binding SelectedItem, ElementName=_master}"
```

6. Run the application. You should be able to see details of the currently selected process.

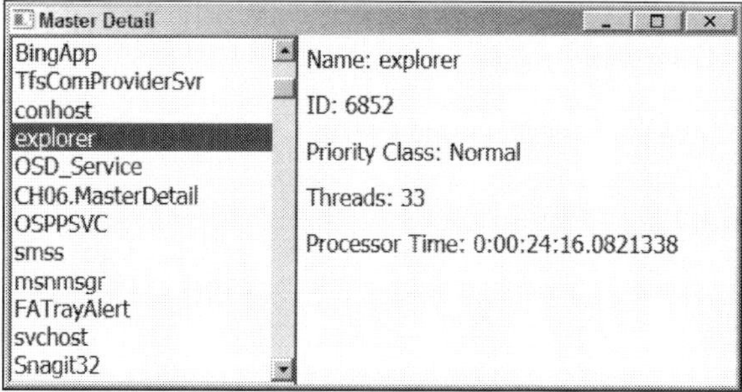

How it works...

The source to a binding is typically supplied with a `DataContext`. In this case, a top level `DataContext` is used for the "master" `ListBox`, and an inner `DataContext` is used for the "details" by binding to the `ListBox.SelectedItem` property. This is very convenient, making the inner binding expressions simple. Naturally, a converter can be used if appropriate.

There's more...

Binding the `SelectedItem` of the `ListBox` is a viable option, but there is another way to achieve this, and it's a bit more elegant.

First, we set the `IsSynchronizedWithCurrentItem` property of the `ListBox` to `true`. Then, we set the inner `DataContext` to bind to the `CurrentItem` property like so:

```
DataContext="{Binding CurrentItem}"
```

This works without any changes to the inner bindings. It seems odd, though: where did that property come from? And what is the source object? It can't be the nearest `DataContext`, because that's a list of processes.

The answer lies with a data view object, which always exists between the control and the actual collection. It implements the `ICollectionView` interface (in the `System.ComponentModel` namespace). This interface will be discussed more fully in the next recipe, but for now there is a property called `CurrentItem` on this interface and we're binding to it. Setting `IsSynchronizedWithCurrentItem` to `true` on the `ListBox` is necessary so that the current item on the `ICollectionView` is actually tracked.

A simpler selected item binding

We can even simplify the use of `CurrentItem`. We simply drop the inner `DataContext` expression (with the binding to `CurrentItem`), but instead we add a forward slash to all the property paths in the inner bindings. For example, the `ProcessName` property is bound as follows:

```
Text="{Binding /ProcessName, StringFormat='Name: \{0\}'}"
```

Note the forward slash before `ProcessName`. This slash is shorthand for `CurrentItem`; that's why the inner `DataContext` is unnecessary.

The full source of this example is in the `CH06.MasterDetail2` project available within the downloadable source for this chapter.

Sorting and filtering bound collections

Data templates provide a powerful way to present data using text, images, and anything else WPF is capable of. Often, we need to present the data in some order, typically sorted by some property (or properties). Sometimes we don't want to show all data, but a part of it, such as when a user searches for something and we want to show the result of the search, which maybe just a subset of the original data.

One way to go about it is to operate on the data itself. We can certainly apply sorting on lists (`List<T>.Sort`, `Array.Sort`, and so on), as well as filtering (`List<T>.FindAll`), and by using **Language Integrated Query** (**LINQ**) it's even easier (and more versatile) to sort (`orderby` clause) and/or filter (`where` clause) to get a new collection. Although this works, it requires explicitly binding the resulting collection to the correct controls (some may show the original collection, some may show sorted/filtered data).

WPF provides an alternative: using a view object that sits between the original data and the control, we can specify sorting and filtering (and as we'll see later, grouping as well), without ever touching the original data collection.

Getting ready

Make sure Visual Studio is up and running.

How to do it...

We'll create an application that shows all processes running on the system and provide for sorting and filtering.

1. Create a new WPF application named `CH06.SortingAndFiltering`.
2. Open `MainWindow.xaml`. Add two rows to the existing `Grid`. The first holds a `ListBox`, and the second holds a horizontal `StackPanel`:

```
<Grid.RowDefinitions>
    <RowDefinition />
    <RowDefinition Height="Auto" />
</Grid.RowDefinitions>
<ListBox HorizontalContentAlignment="Stretch"
         ItemsSource="{Binding}">
</ListBox>
<StackPanel Grid.Row="1" Orientation="Horizontal" Margin="4"
            TextBlock.FontSize="14">
</StackPanel>
```

3. The `ListBox` should display information for `System.Diagnostics.Process` objects. Add the following data template to the `ListBox`:

```
<ListBox.ItemTemplate>
   <DataTemplate>
      <Border Margin="2" Padding="4" BorderBrush="Black"
              BorderThickness="1">
         <StackPanel Orientation="Horizontal"
                     TextBlock.FontSize="16">
            <TextBlock Foreground="Black" FontWeight="Bold"
                       Text="{Binding ProcessName}" />
            <TextBlock Margin="10,0,0,0" Foreground="Blue"
            Text="{Binding Id, StringFormat='(\{0\})'}" />
                <TextBlock Margin="20,0,0,0" Foreground="Red"
Text="{Binding Threads.Count, StringFormat='Threads: \{0\}'}"
/>
         </StackPanel>
      </Border>
   </DataTemplate>
</ListBox.ItemTemplate>
```

4. Open `MainWindow.xaml.cs`. Add the following to the constructor to set up the binding:

```
DataContext = Process.GetProcesses();
```

5. Running the application now shows the processes in the order they provided by `Process.GetProcesses`:

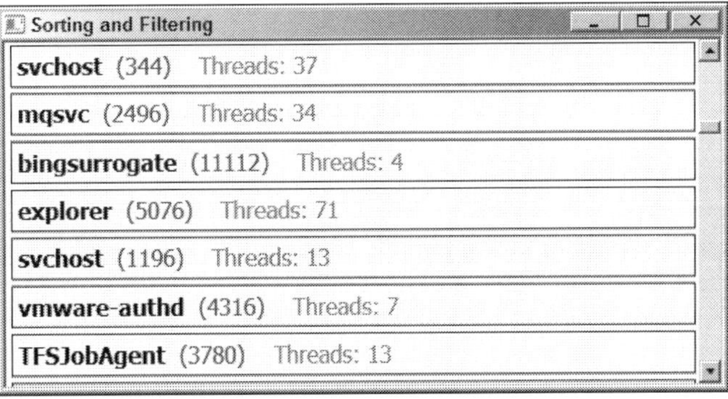

6. Open `MainWindow.xaml`. Add the following controls to the `StackPanel` to be used for sorting purposes:

```
<TextBlock Text="Sort by" VerticalAlignment="Center"/>
<ComboBox Width="150" Margin="6,0,0,0" x:Name="_sortField"
          SelectedIndex="0">
</ComboBox>
<CheckBox Margin="10,0,0,0" Content="Ascending"
           VerticalAlignment="Center"
           IsChecked="true" x:Name="_ascending"/>
<Button Margin="4,0,0,0" Content="Sort" />
```

7. The `ComboBox` should display allowed properties for sorting. Add a new class named `SortField` as follows:

```
class SortField {
   public string DisplayName { get; set; }
   public string PropertyName { get; set; }
}
```

8. A bunch of `SortField` objects would be required for all the properties we may wish to sort. To create a list of such objects in XAML, we need a non-generic class. Add the following simple class just below the `SortField` class:

```
class SortFieldList : List<SortField> {
}
```

9. Open `MainWindow.xaml`. Add an XML namespace mapping to the `CH06.SortingAndFiltering` namespace on the `Window` root element:

```
xmlns:local="clr-namespace:CH06.SortingAndFiltering"
```

10. Create an instance of `SortFiledList` as a `Resource` and add some `SortField` objects to be used for sorting:

```
<Window.Resources>
    <local:SortFieldList x:Key="sortFields">
        <local:SortField DisplayName="(Unsorted)" />
        <local:SortField DisplayName="Process Name"
                         PropertyName="ProcessName" />
        <local:SortField DisplayName="Process ID"
                         PropertyName="Id" />
        <local:SortField DisplayName="# Threads"
                         PropertyName="Threads.Count" />
    </local:SortFieldList>
</Window.Resources>
```

11. Now bind the `ComboBox` to use the list, by adding the following properties:

```
ItemsSource="{StaticResource sortFields}"
  DisplayMemberPath="DisplayName"
  SelectedValuePath="PropertyName"
```

12. Add a `Click` event handler for the **Sort** button. Inside the handler, add the following:

```
var view = CollectionViewSource.GetDefaultView(DataContext);
view.SortDescriptions.Clear();
if(_sortField.SelectedValue != null)
   view.SortDescriptions.Add(new SortDescription((string)
     _sortField.SelectedValue,_ascending.IsChecked == true ?
     ListSortDirection.Ascending :
     ListSortDirection.Descending));
```

13. Run the application. Use the `ComboBox` to select the property to sort and click on **Sort**.

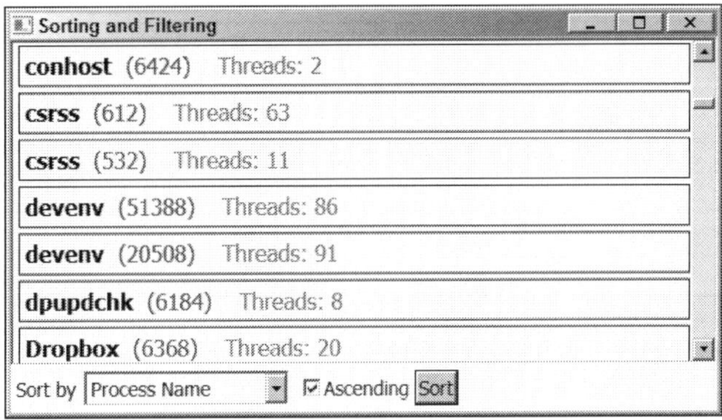

14. Now let's add filtering. Open `MainWindow.xaml` and add the following elements to the `StackPanel`:

```
<TextBox Margin="10,0,0,0" x:Name="_filterText" Width="120" />
<Button Margin="4,0,0,0" Content="Filter" />
```

15. Add a `Click` event handler for the **Filter** button. Add the following code in the handler:

```
var view = CollectionViewSource.GetDefaultView(DataContext);
if(string.IsNullOrWhiteSpace(_filterText.Text))
   view.Filter = null;
else
   view.Filter = obj => ((Process)obj).ProcessName.IndexOf(
     _filterText.Text,
     StringComparison.InvariantCultureIgnoreCase) > -1;
```

16. Run the application. Enter some text in the filter `TextBox` and click on **Filter**. You can also combine that with sorting.

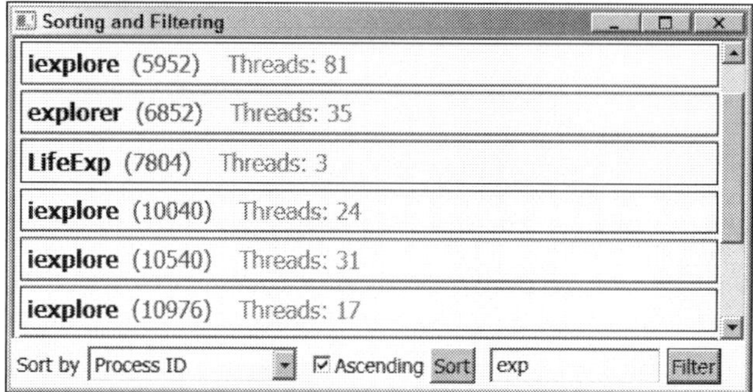

How it works...

The view that sits between the data collection and a bound control is an object implementing the `ICollectionView` interface. A default view always exists and is obtained by the static `CollectionViewSource.GetDefaultView` method, passing the data collection itself.

With an `ICollectionView` in hand, sorting is possible by using the `SortDescriptions` property, which is a collection of `SortDescription` objects. We can use this collection to set properties to sort (more than one is possible for sub-sorting; for example, we can sort by process name, and if several processes have the same process name we can sort by (for example) process ID), and the direction of the sort (ascending or descending). Note that we don't touch the actual data – just manipulate the view.

To remove the sorting, we call the `Clear` method on the `SortDescriptions` property.

Filtering is achieved by setting the `Filter` property of `ICollectionView`. This property is of type `Predicate<object>`, which is a delegate that accepts an object (which is a single data item) and returns `true` (to display that data in bound controls) or `false` (to hide it). Naturally, this delegate can be specified by an actual method, an anonymous method, or a lambda expression (just like any other delegate). The delegate is called for each and every item to determine if that particular item is to be shown.

To clear the filter, we set the `Filter` property to `null`.

As we can see, sorting and filtering are orthogonal, meaning they can be used in isolation or together for a combined effect.

There's more...

In the preceding example, a single control (`ListBox`) was bound to the data collection. What would happen if another control (say a `ComboBox`, or any control derived from `ItemsControl`) was bound to the same data collection? The sorting and/or filtering would occur in both controls.

This may not be the desired behavior. Perhaps one control should show everything, and another control should show some filtered data. With the previous approach this won't work.

The solution is to create a new view, and use that instead of the default view. To create a new view, we need to create an instance of a `CollectionViewSource`, set its `Source` property to the actual data, and use its `View` property (`ICollectionView`) to do the sorting/filtering. Creating the `CollectionViewSource` can be done in XAML or code. Let's see a code-based approach first. We add a field of type `CollectionViewSource` to the `Window` and set it up in the constructor:

```
_cvs = new CollectionViewSource();
_cvs.Source = Process.GetProcesses();
DataContext = _cvs;
```

The `Source` property is set to the actual collection. Note that the `DataContext` is set to the `CollectionViewSource` instance, and not to the actual data (if it did, the default view would have been used). The binding expressions, however, are completely unchanged, as if binding directly to the data source; this makes it very convenient to use.

To do the actual sorting or filtering, we use the view that's exposed through the View property of `CollectionViewSource`. The rest of the code remains unchanged:

```
var view = _cvs.View;
```

The complete source is in the `CH06.SortingAndFiltering2` project available in the downloadable source for this chapter.

Creating a `CollectionViewSource` in XAML is possible (as a `Resource`). For example:

```
<CollectionViewSource x:Key="_cvs" />
```

Then, we can get it in code and manipulate it in much the same way:

```
_cvs = Resources["_cvs"] as CollectionViewSource;
_cvs.Source = Process.GetProcesses();
DataContext = _cvs;
```

The advantage of creating a `CollectionViewSource` in XAML is that we can create `SortDescription` objects in XAML as well, especially if there are some fixed sorting criteria.

The project `CH06.SortingAndFiltering2` project, available in the downloadable source for this chapter has the full source code for this example.

More features of ICollectionView

As we saw in the previous recipe, `ICollectionView` can track a single selected item using the properties `CurrentItem` (the actual data item) and `CurrentPosition` (the numerical index). For the default view, the Selector-derived control must set `IsSynchronizedWithCurrentItem` to `true`, but it's automatically tracked for explicitly created views. This feature can help stay detached from actual controls, and not really care what controls (if any) are bound using that view.

Another feature supported by `ICollectionView` is navigation. It's occasionally useful to add controls that allow moving forward or backwards through a collection, or moving to the start or end of the collection. Again, this can be done on a control by control basis, but we want to stay clear of the actual controls (this will be more evident in the next chapter when we discuss the MVVM pattern) bound to the data. For this, `ICollectionView` exposes a bunch of self-explanatory methods: `MoveCurrentToFirst`, `MoveCurrentToLast`, `MoveCurrentToNext`, `MoveCurrentToPrevious`, `MoveCurrentToPosition` (to the specified index), `MoveCurrentTo` (to the specified data object), and two properties that can be used to enable/disable navigating controls (`IsCurrentAfterLast`, `IsCurrentBeforeFirst`).

The last useful feature of `ICollectionView` is grouping. As this is a little more complicated, we'll treat it in its own recipe.

Live shaping

WPF 4.5 introduces a new feature called "live shaping" that reflects dynamic changes in sorting/filtering/grouping. Suppose we create a `ListBox` that shows stock item values. These values are sorted when the application starts up. Then these values change rapidly – the sorting does not operate dynamically unless we remove the sorting and apply it again.

In WPF 4.5 we can instruct the view to keep things "alive" and update the position of items based on dynamic changes. Let's create a simple `StockItem` class to represent our data item:

```
class StockItem : INotifyPropertyChanged {
   public event PropertyChangedEventHandler PropertyChanged =
      delegate { };

   public string Name { get; set; }

   double _value;

   public double Value {
      get { return _value; }
      set {
         _value = value;
```

```
            PropertyChanged(this,
               new PropertyChangedEventArgs("Value"));
         }
      }
   }
```

Here's the extra code needed, assuming `_items` is a collection of `StockItem` objects bound to some `ListBox`:

```
var view = CollectionViewSource.GetDefaultView(_items);
view.SortDescriptions.Add(
   new SortDescription("Value", ListSortDirection.Ascending));
var liveview = (ICollectionViewLiveShaping)
   CollectionViewSource.GetDefaultView(_items);
liveview.IsLiveSorting = true;
```

The new `ICollectionViewLiveShaping` interface is the key. Setting `IsLiveSorting` to `true` makes sorting aware of dynamic value changes. Similar properties exist for filtering and grouping (`IsLiveFiltering` and `IsLiveGrouping`). The `CH06.LiveShaping` project (which must be opened in Visual Studio 2012), which is available in the downloadable source for this chapter, shows this in action.

Grouping bound collections

The previous recipe used the `ICollectionView` source for sorting, filtering, and navigating. Another useful feature of `ICollectionView` is grouping. This allows the partitioning of the data into groups based on some criteria (typically a property). Each such group is subject to sorting and/or filtering, if used.

Getting ready

Make sure Visual Studio is up and running.

How to do it...

We'll use the same collection of process objects used previously, but this time we'll group them by some criteria.

1. Create a new WPF Application named **CH06.GroupingData**.
2. Open `MainWindow.xaml`. Add a `ListBox` to the existing grid, with a simple data template to display information on process objects:

```
<ListBox ItemsSource="{Binding}" HorizontalContentAlignment="Stret
ch">
   <ListBox.ItemTemplate>
```

```
        <DataTemplate>
            <UniformGrid Rows="1" Columns="2">
                <TextBlock Text="{Binding ProcessName}" />
<TextBlock Text="{Binding Id,
                    StringFormat=ID: \{0\}}" />
            </UniformGrid>
        </DataTemplate>
    </ListBox.ItemTemplate>
</ListBox>
```

3. Open `MainWindow.xaml.cs`. Add the following in the constructor:

```
var processes = Process.GetProcesses().Where(CanAccess);
DataContext = processes;
```

4. `CanAccess` is a simple method that is used to filter out all the inaccessible processes (we'll use a property for grouping that needs access permissions normally given only to the `LocalSystem` account):

```
public static bool CanAccess(Process process) {
   try {
      var h = process.Handle;
      return true;
   }
   catch {
      return false;
   }
}
```

5. Running the application now shows a simple process view:

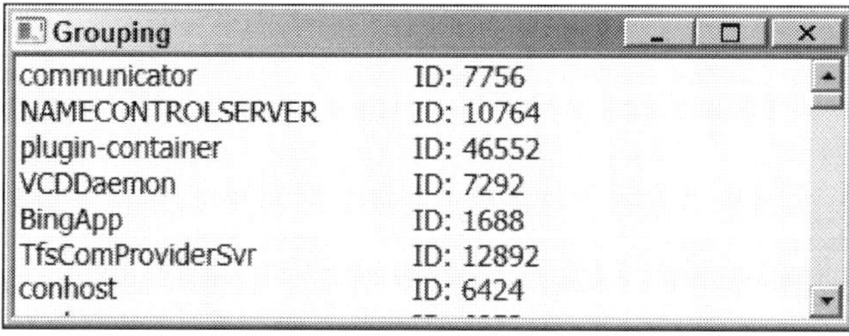

6. Now let's add grouping. We'll group the processes by their `PriorityClass` property. Open the `MainWindow` constructor. Add the following lines after the initialization of the `processes` local variable:

```
var view = CollectionViewSource.GetDefaultView(processes);
view.GroupDescriptions.Add(new PropertyGroupDescription(
    "PriorityClass"));
```

7. This sets up grouping based on the `PriorityClass` property. Run the application. The display shows no visible grouping, but note that the order of processes is different:

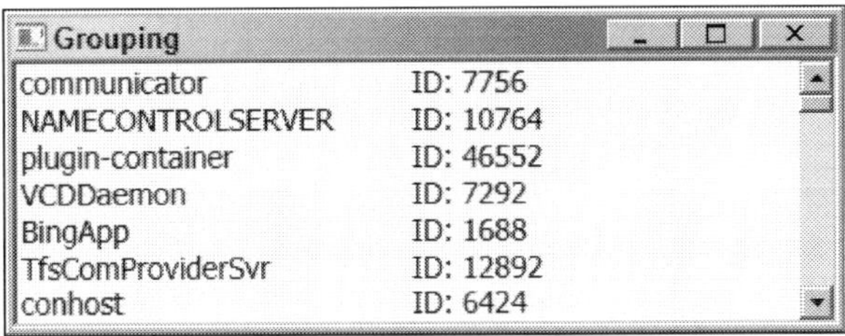

8. Grouping is happening, but the `ListBox` disregards that. To make the groups obvious, we'll add a `GroupStyle` control as the `GroupStyle` property of the `ListBox`:

```
<ListBox.GroupStyle>
   <GroupStyle>
      <GroupStyle.HeaderTemplate>
         <DataTemplate>
            <Border BorderBrush="Red" BorderThickness="2"
                  Background="White" Margin="2">
               <TextBlock Text="{Binding Name,
                    StringFormat=Priority: {0}}"
                    FontSize="16" FontWeight="Bold"
                    Margin="4" />
            </Border>
         </DataTemplate>
      </GroupStyle.HeaderTemplate>
   </GroupStyle>
</ListBox.GroupStyle>
```

9. This indicates what each group is going to look like. Run the application now and scroll to see more groups:

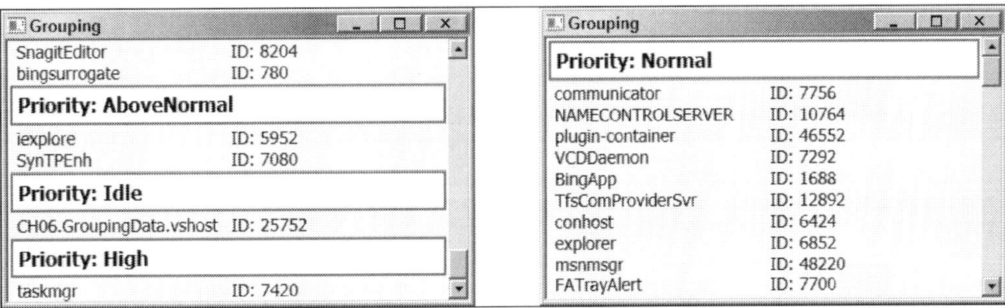

How it works...

The `ICollectioView` interface discussed in the previous recipe supports grouping with the `GroupDescriptions` property. It accepts a type derived from `GroupDescription` (`GroupDescription` is abstract), `PropertyGroupDescription` being the only concrete class provided by WPF. The simplest useful constructor accepts a property name (a property path, in fact, so it's possible to use a nested property).

The bound control (in this example a `ListBox`) rearranges the items to be consistent with the grouping criteria (as well as sorting and filtering if used). However, there is no default visual cue indicating grouping is actually taking place.

To remedy that, all controls derived from `ItemControls` support the `GroupStyle` property, which is of type `System.Windows.Controls.GroupStyle` (not really a control or a `Style`). This is a kind of group descriptor, with various properties we can utilize. The most useful is `HeaderTemplate` that we can set with a `DataTemplate` to indicate how a group header is to look like. The `DataContext` property of `HeaderTemplate` is a n object derived from `CollectionViewGroup` created by WPF. The misleadingly named `Name` property in the `CollectionViewGroup` is actually the value of the property that's used for grouping (`PriorityClass` in our example). All items in that particular group are available through the `Items` property; this means the `Name` property in this case is roughly equivalent to `Items[0].PriorityClass`.

There's more...

There are other properties in `GroupStyle` that can be used to further customize the group appearance. The `HeaderTemplateSelector` property can be used for selecting a `DataTemplate` as a `HeaderTemplate` based on some group criteria (this is similar to the `ItemTemplateSelector` property of `ItemsControl`). `HeaderStringFormat` may be useful to customize the header if it's a string. The `Panel` property can change the way groups are laid out (by default using a vertical `StackPanel`). For example, let's change the `Panel` property to use a horizontal `StackPanel`:

```
<GroupStyle.Panel>
   <ItemsPanelTemplate>
      <StackPanel Orientation="Horizontal" />
   </ItemsPanelTemplate>
</GroupStyle.Panel>
```

This is the result when running:

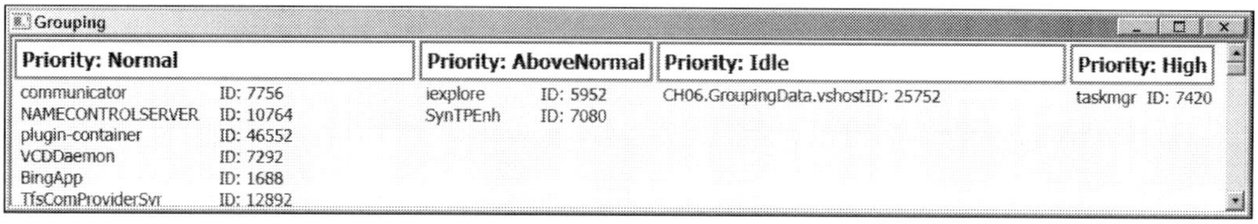

Amazingly enough, this is still a `ListBox`!

Grouping by a non-property

Adding a `PropertyGroupDescription` object based on a property is easy enough, but what about using some criteria that is not reflected in a property?

Fortunately, `PropertyGroupDescirption` supports another constructor, accepting a property name and a value converter. The converter has the opportunity to return some value that is indicative of the group based on the property value provided.

For example, suppose we want to group processes by their threads count, but not with a single thread variance, but by groups of 10 threads; the first group is 1-9 threads, the second 10-19, the third 20-29, and so on. Here's the call to create the grouping:

```
view.GroupDescriptions.Add(new PropertyGroupDescription(
    "Threads.Count", new ThreadsToGroupConverter()));
```

Here's a converter's `Convert` method that consolidates every 10 threads to one group integer:

```
public object Convert(object value, Type targetType,
   object parameter, CultureInfo culture) {
   int count = (int)value;
   return count / 10;
}
```

The `CollectionViewGroup.Name` property has now become that calculated integer. The `HeaderTemplate` in this case may need a converter as well, to turn that number into some useful group name. Its `Convert` method may look like the following:

```
public object Convert(object value, Type targetType,
   object parameter,  CultureInfo culture) {
   int count = (int)value;
   string text = string.Format("{0}-{1}",
       count == 0 ? 1 : count * 10, count * 10 + 9);
   return text;
}
```

After creating the converter in XAML, the data template can use it:

```
<TextBlock Text="{Binding Name, Converter=
    {StaticResource threadsToGroupName},
    StringFormat=Threads: {0}}"
```

Here's the result:

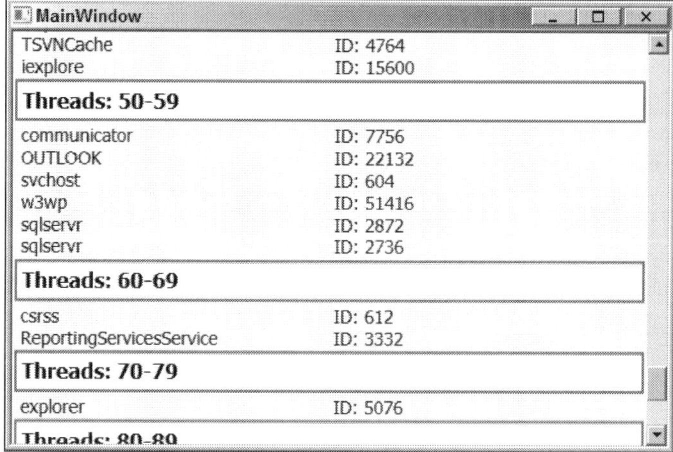

The full source code is in the `CH06.GroupingData2` project available in the downloadable source for this chapter.

See also

For a full discussion of value converters, refer to the *Using value converters* recipe in this chapter.

Binding to multiple properties

So far we've seen data binding occur for a target property base on a single source property. Sometimes, however, a target property depends on changes of more than one source property. This is supported in WPF through multi binding. Let's see how it's done.

Getting ready

Make sure Visual Studio is up and running.

How to do it...

We'll create a simple color selector using a multi-binding.

1. Create a new WPF application named `CH06.MultiBindings`.

2. Open `MainWindow.xaml`. Add the following to the existing `Grid`:

```
<Grid.RowDefinitions>
    <RowDefinition />
    <RowDefinition Height="Auto" />
    <RowDefinition Height="Auto" />
    <RowDefinition Height="Auto" />
</Grid.RowDefinitions>
<Rectangle Stroke="Black" StrokeThickness="1" Margin="4" >
</Rectangle>
<Slider Minimum="0" Maximum="255" Margin="4"
    x:Name="_red" Grid.Row="1" />
<Slider Minimum="0" Maximum="255" Margin="4"
    x:Name="_green" Grid.Row="2" />
<Slider Minimum="0" Maximum="255" Margin="4"
    x:Name="_blue" Grid.Row="3" />
```

3. We'd like to use the three sliders to change the RGB color fill of the rectangle. This means we need to set one property (`Rectangle.Fill`) based on three properties (`Slider.Value` for each one). Since there's no default way to convert more than one property to a single property we need a converter. Add a new class named `RGBConverter`.

4. This class should implement the `IMultiValueConverter` interface. Implement the class as follows:

```
class RGBConverter : IMultiValueConverter {
   SolidColorBrush _brush = new SolidColorBrush();

   public object Convert(object[] values, Type targetType,
      object parameter, CultureInfo culture) {
      _brush.Color = Color.FromRgb(System.Convert.ToByte(
          values[0]), System.Convert.ToByte(values[1]),
          System.Convert.ToByte(values[2]));
      return _brush;
   }

   public object[] ConvertBack(object value, Type[] tTypes,
      object parameter, CultureInfo culture) {
      throw new NotImplementedException();
   }
}
```

5. Open `MainWindow.xaml`. We need to create a `MultiBinding` and connect to the source properties and the converter. First, add an XML namespace mapping for the application namespace with prefix `local`, and create an instance of the converter:

```
<Window.Resources>
    <local:RGBConverter x:Key="rgbConverter" />
</Window.Resources>
```

6. Add the following as `Rectangle.Fill`:

```
<Rectangle.Fill>
    <MultiBinding Converter="{StaticResource rgbConverter}">
        <Binding Path="Value" ElementName="_red" />
        <Binding Path="Value" ElementName="_green" />
        <Binding Path="Value" ElementName="_blue" />
    </MultiBinding>
</Rectangle.Fill>
```

7. Run the application and move the sliders. The rectangle changes color accordingly.

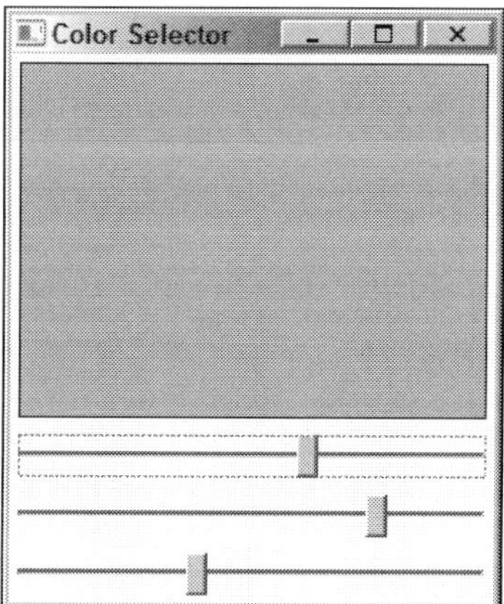

How it works...

A `MultiBinding` object collects a set of property bindings and funnels them through a converter to get the final target property value. This means a `MultiBinding` must have a converter, as WPF has no way of knowing how to map a set of properties to a single property value.

Each object within a `MultiBinding` is a `Binding` in itself, reaching out to a desired source property (in our case using `ElementName`). Note that we must supply the `Binding` objects in element syntax. There's no way to provide them with the `Binding` markup extension.

The converter must implement the `IMultiValueConverter` interface. It's a different interface than the regular converter, because the `Convert` method must accept an array of values that are provided in the exact same order they are specified in the XAML. In our example, the red component value is first because the red slider element is used first in the list of child bindings. Also, `ConvertBack` (much less useful) returns an array of objects and accepts an array of types.

There's more...

`MultiBinding` has a `StringFormat` property that can be used to format a string based on strings provided by the individual bindings. For example, suppose we wanted to add a `TextBlock` on top of the `Rectangle` to show the exact RGB values currently selected. Here's a `MultiBinding` that does the trick:

```
<TextBlock FontSize="18" VerticalAlignment="Center"
    HorizontalAlignment="Center">
    <TextBlock.Text>
        <MultiBinding
      StringFormat="R: {0:N0}, G: {1:N0}, B: {2:N0}">
            <Binding Path="Value" ElementName="_red" />
            <Binding Path="Value" ElementName="_green" />
            <Binding Path="Value" ElementName="_blue" />
        </MultiBinding>
    </TextBlock.Text>
</TextBlock>
```

Note that a converter is not needed in this special case, because the result is a string. Also, note the use of the indices `{0}`, `{1}`, `{2}` to extract the results from the specific child binding.

Binding hierarchical data to a TreeView

A `TreeView` is a common control for viewing hierarchical data. It derives from `ItemsControl`, but it's a bit more complex than standard controls derived from, `ItemsControl`, such as `ListBox`, because of its hierarchical nature, although it's possible to use a `TreeView` without data binding. Binding provides an elegant way to fill the tree with data. Let's examine this in more detail.

Getting ready

Make sure Visual Studio is up and running.

How to do it...

We'll create an application that shows a tree view with processes as the top level objects. For each process, child tree view items will show the modules loaded into that process.

1. Create a new WPF Application named `CH06.TreeViewBinding`.
2. Open `MainWindow.xaml.cs`. In the constructor, set the `DataContext` to the collection of processes on the system:

   ```
   DataContext = Process.GetProcesses();
   ```

3. We'd like to show a `TreeView` of processes with each tree node expanding to show all modules loaded into that process. Open `MainWindow.xaml` and add a `TreeView` to the existing `Grid`:

   ```
   <TreeView ItemsSource="{Binding}">
   </TreeView>
   ```

4. Let's add a data template for displaying processes. Add an `ItemTemplate` property to the `TreeView` as follows:

   ```
   <TreeView.ItemTemplate>
       <DataTemplate ItemsSource="{Binding Modules}">
           <StackPanel Orientation="Horizontal" Margin="2">
               <TextBlock Text="{Binding ProcessName}"
                  FontWeight="Bold" FontSize="16" />
               <TextBlock Margin="5,0,0,0" FontSize="16"
             Text="{Binding Id, StringFormat=(\{0\})}" />
           </StackPanel>
       </DataTemplate>
   </TreeView.ItemTemplate>
   ```

5. Running this just shows a list of processes. To show a hierarchy, we'll first turn the `DataTemplate` to a `HierarchicalDataTemplate` with an `ItemsSource`:

   ```
   <TreeView.ItemTemplate>
       <HierarchicalDataTemplate ItemsSource="{Binding Modules}">
   ```

6. Now we need an inner `DataTemplate` to indicate how modules are shown. Add the following before the closing tag of `HierarchicalDataTemplate`:

   ```
   <HierarchicalDataTemplate.ItemTemplate>
       <DataTemplate>
           <StackPanel Orientation="Horizontal" Margin="2">
               <TextBlock Text="{Binding ModuleName}"
                          FontSize="14" FontWeight="Bold"/>
               <TextBlock Margin="5,0,0,0" FontSize="12"
            Text="{Binding FileName, StringFormat=(\{0\})}"
                           VerticalAlignment="Center"/>
           </StackPanel>
       </DataTemplate>
   </HierarchicalDataTemplate.ItemTemplate>
   ```

7. Run the application. Expand some processes and watch the module list unfold (processes that cannot be expanded are those that require system level access to view such information).

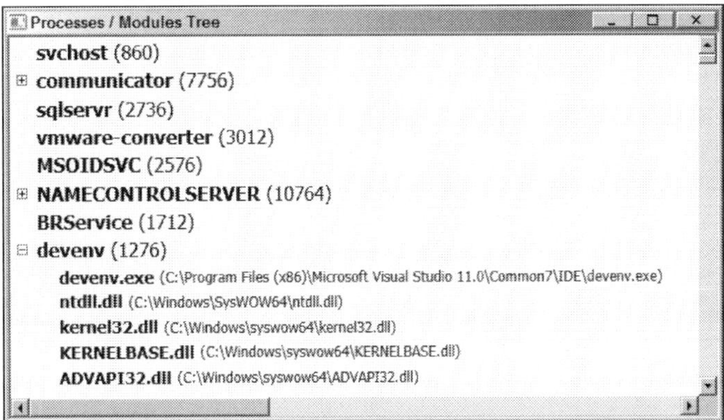

How it works...

As an `ItemsControl`, a `TreeView` may use its `ItemTemplate` property to set a `DataTemplate` for its bound data. However, how should the inherent hierarchy be handled? It's done with the help of a `DataTemplate` derivative - `HierarchicalDataTemplate`. `HierarchicalDataTemplate` is a `DataTemplate` that can contain a child `DataTemplate` that specifies how a child object should be presented. This can go on as needed, because that child `DataTemplate` can be in itself a `HierarchicalDataTemplate`. The way a `HierarchicalDataTemplate` indicates what collection its child is bound to is with its `ItemsSource` property. In the preceding example, the `HierarchicalDataTemplate` sets its `ItemsSource` to the `Modules` property of the current object (which is a `Process`). The `Modules` property is a collection of `ProcessModule` objects, each of which is queried for its `ModuleName` and `FileName` properties by the inner `DataTemplate`.

There's more...

Behind the scenes a `TreeView` is composed of `TreeViewItem` objects. A `TreeViewItem` derives from `HeaderedItemsControl`, which means it has a header (typically text and/or image, but can be anything) and can host a collection of other `TreeViewItems`; this nesting can go on as deep as needed. Our data templates create elements that are hosted inside a `TreeViewItem`.

It's worth noting that the `SelectedItem` property of a `TreeView` is read only, and so cannot be data bound for a useful result.

Presenting data in a grid

Some types of data are best shown in a multi row, multi column grid. WPF 4 added support for the `DataGrid` control, which is capable of showing a collection of objects in tabular form, with many customizations possible, out-of-the-box or programmatically.

Getting ready

Make sure Visual Studio is up and running.

How to do it...

We'll create an application that shows some personal information in a grid layout, showing some of the features of the `DataGrid` control.

1. Create a new WPF application named `CH06.DataGridDemo`.
2. Open `MainWindow.xaml`. Add a `DataGrid` to the existing `Grid` and bind it to whatever `DataContext` is available:

   ```
   <DataGrid ItemsSource="{Binding}">
   </DataGrid>
   ```

3. The data we're going to use is a simple personal information record. Add a new class named `PersonInfo`, and implement as follows:

   ```
   enum Gender {
      Unknown,
      Male,
      Female
   }

   class PersonInfo {
      public string FirstName { get; set; }
      public string LastName { get; set; }
      public string Email { get; set; }
      public Gender Gender { get; set; }
      public bool IsEmployed { get; set; }
      public Uri Avatar { get; set; }
   }
   ```

4. Add an `Images` folder to the project.
5. Add some small images to the newly created folder (you can use the ones from the downloadable source, or even a single image that would be used for every person).

6. Open `MainWindow.xaml.cs`. Add the following to the constructor, so that we have some data to work with (correct the image names if necessary):

```
DataContext = new List<PersonInfo> {
   new PersonInfo { FirstName = "Bart", LastName = "Simpson",
      Email = "bart@runaway.com", IsEmployed = false,
      Gender = Gender.Male,
      Avatar = new Uri("Images/sun.png", UriKind.Relative) },
   new PersonInfo { FirstName = "Homer", LastName = "Simpson",
      Email = "homer@springfield.com", IsEmployed = true,
      Gender = Gender.Male, Avatar =
      new Uri("Images/worker.png", UriKind.Relative) },
   new PersonInfo { FirstName = "Marge", LastName = "Simpson",
      Email = "marge@desparatehousewives.com",
      IsEmployed = false, Gender = Gender.Female,
    Avatar = new Uri("Images/violin.png", UriKind.Relative) },
   new PersonInfo { FirstName = "Lisa", LastName = "Simpson",
      Email = "lisa@musiclovers.com", IsEmployed = false,
      Gender = Gender.Female, Avatar = new Uri(
      "Images/woman.png", UriKind.Relative) },
  new PersonInfo { FirstName = "Maggie", LastName = "Simpson",
      IsEmployed = false, Gender = Gender.Female,
      Avatar = new Uri("Images/wine.png", UriKind.Relative) }
};
```

7. Run the application. You should see a grid with all the details. You can also change things such as the first name, last name, e-mail, whether the person is employed, and even his/her gender:

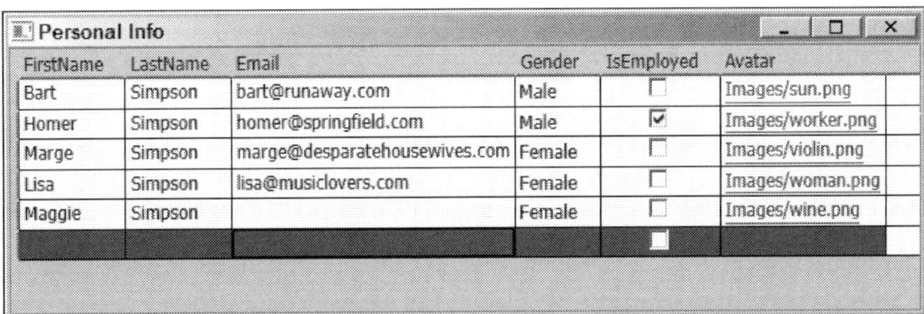

8. Note that the avatar does not show the actual image. Also, the column names are based on the property names and may not be entirely appropriate. All this is because the `AutoGenerateColums` property is set to `true` by default. Let's try to improve things a bit. What about the avatar image? Open `MainWindow.xaml`.

9. Add a `Columns` property to the `DataGrid` with a new template:

```
<DataGrid.Columns>
    <DataGridTemplateColumn Header="Avatar" >
        <DataGridTemplateColumn.CellTemplate>
            <DataTemplate>
                <Image Margin="2" Width="32" Height="32"
                    Source="{Binding Avatar}" />
            </DataTemplate>
        </DataGridTemplateColumn.CellTemplate>
    </DataGridTemplateColumn>
</DataGrid.Columns>
```

10. Run the application. You should see the avatar appearing as the first column.

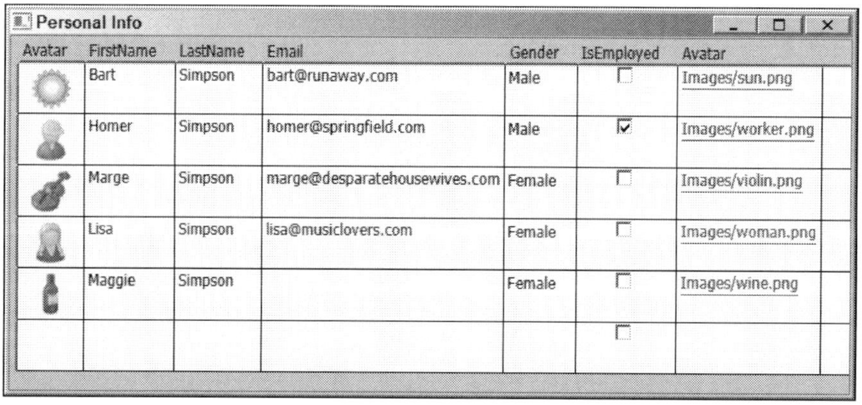

Personal Info

Avatar	FirstName	LastName	Email	Gender	IsEmployed	Avatar
	Bart	Simpson	bart@runaway.com	Male	☐	Images/sun.png
	Homer	Simpson	homer@springfield.com	Male	☑	Images/worker.png
	Marge	Simpson	marge@desparatehousewives.com	Female	☐	Images/violin.png
	Lisa	Simpson	lisa@musiclovers.com	Female	☐	Images/woman.png
	Maggie	Simpson		Female	☐	Images/wine.png
					☐	

11. The `Avatar` column from the auto generating process appears as well (at the end). Let's remove it. Add an event handler on the `DataGrid` for the `AutoGeneratingColumn` event. In the handler, add the following:

```
if(e.PropertyName == "Avatar") {
   e.Cancel = true;
}
```

12. These lines check if the `DataGrid` is currently generating the avatar column, and if so, cancel the operation. Running the application produces the following:

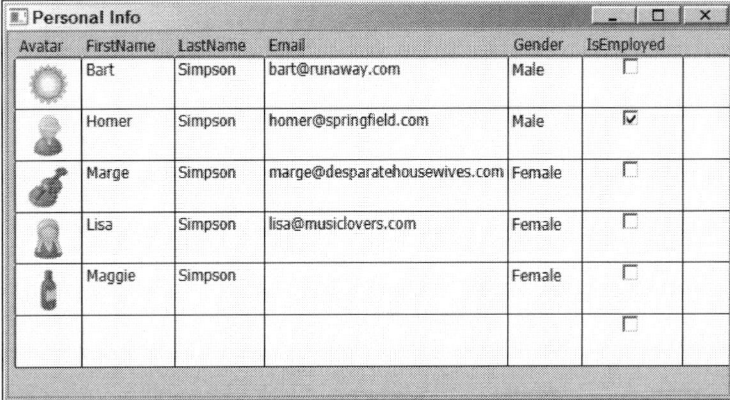

13. The avatar column appears first. What if we wanted to show it last? Add another event handler for the `DataGrid`, `AutoGeneratedColumns`. This handler is called after all columns have been generated. Add the following to the handler:

```
var grid = (DataGrid)sender;
grid.Columns[0].DisplayIndex = 5;
```

14. Run the application. The avatar column should be on the far right:

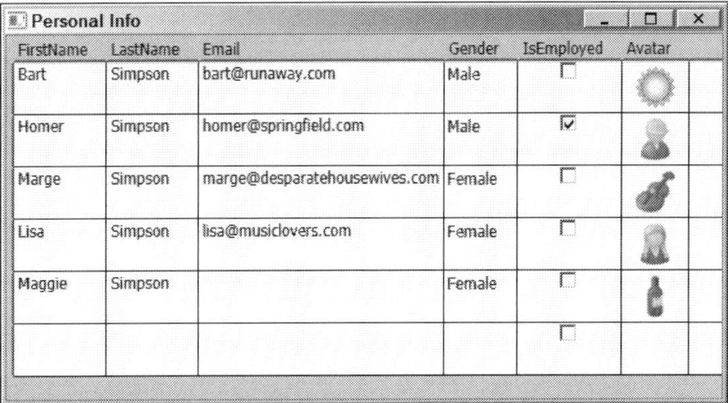

How it works...

The `DataGrid` binds to any collection just like any control derived from `ItemsControl` through the `ItemsSource` property. It actually derives from the more specialized `MultiSelector` class (which itself inherits from `Selector`).

If the AutoGenerateColumns property is true (the default), the DataGrid does all the hard work, creating the columns automatically with appropriate controls (up to a point). In the preceding example, FirstName and LastName were rendered as TextBlock instances, and if double clicked for editing, changed automatically to TextBox instances. The IsEmployed column was rendered as a CheckBox, and the Gender column was rendered as a ComboBox, automatically bound to the enum values. The Email column, on the other hand, was rendered as a simple string (not a clickable URI). The Avatar column was totally misjudged and showed no image, but instead used a Hyperlink (with no click behavior).

As the code demonstrated, it's possible to use the AutoGeneratedColumns, and do some customizations, such as creating a new column to show the avatar image. The DataGrid supports several column types: DataGridTextColumn (for strings), DataGridHyperlinkColumn (strings displayed as URIs with the Hyperlink element), DataGridCheckBoxColumns (for Boolean properties), DataGridComboBoxColumn (for enumerations and other fixed collections of values), and the all-powerful DataGridTemplateColumn, which can be used for anything. In fact, this lets us provide our own DataTemplate. This was exactly what was done with the avatar; we created a DataTemplate that holds an Image element with its Source property bound to the Avatar property.

There's more...

Handling events such as AutoGeneratingColumn is possible, but is very fragile and makes it hard to customize column appearance, especially by a designer. More commonly, the auto generating columns feature is abandoned; this requires more XAML, but less code (or none at all), and makes customizations easy. Here's a revised DataGrid that removes column auto generation and does everything manually. First, the basic markup:

```
<DataGrid ItemsSource="{Binding}" AutoGenerateColumns="False">
    <DataGrid.Columns>
    </DataGrid.Columns>
</DataGrid>
```

The FirstName and LastName columns are straightforward:

```
<DataGridTextColumn Header="First Name"
   Binding="{Binding FirstName}" />
<DataGridTextColumn Header="Last Name"
   Binding="{Binding LastName}" />
```

The Binding property of the DataGridTextColumn object locates the correct property on the data object. The DataGridComboBoxColumn is more challenging, because it needs to bind to a predefined set of values. It's not automatic, because it can bind to any collection of values, not just the values of an enumeration:

```
<DataGridComboBoxColumn Header="Gender"
  SelectedItemBinding="{Binding Gender}"
  ItemsSource="{Binding Source={StaticResource genderEnum}}"/>
```

This can be achieved in a number of ways. In this example, an `ObjectDataProvider` object is used, that can bind to a method on some object. It's created as a `Resource` and binds to the `Enum.GetValues` static method:

```
<ObjectDataProvider x:Key="genderEnum" MethodName="GetValues"
    ObjectType="{x:Type sys:Enum}">
    <ObjectDataProvider.MethodParameters>
        <x:Type Type="local:Gender" />
    </ObjectDataProvider.MethodParameters>
</ObjectDataProvider>
```

This markup declaratively states that the method to call is `Enum.GetValues` with a parameter of `typeof(Gender)` (the `sys` XML prefix is mapped to the `mscorlib` assembly and the `System` namespace).

Next is the e-mail. We may want the e-mail to show as a hyperlink, and clicking on it should launch the default mail client on the system (such as Microsoft Outlook). The `DataGridHyperlinkColumn` is not flexible enough for clicking purposes (it automatically works when the parent is a `NavigationWindow`, for example, which is not that useful). The alternative is a template-based column (the same idea as with the `Avatar` column):

```
<DataGridTemplateColumn Header="Email" >
    <DataGridTemplateColumn.CellTemplate>
        <DataTemplate>
            <TextBlock>
               <Hyperlink NavigateUri="{Binding Email}"
                   Click="OnSendEmail">
                   <Run Text="{Binding Email, Mode=OneWay}" />
               </Hyperlink>
            </TextBlock>
        </DataTemplate>
    </DataGridTemplateColumn.CellTemplate>
</DataGridTemplateColumn>
```

The `Click` event handler for the `Hyperlink` is implemented as follows:

```
void OnSendEmail(object sender, RoutedEventArgs e) {
   var hyperlink = (Hyperlink)sender;
   if(hyperlink.NavigateUri != null)
      Process.Start("mailto: " + hyperlink.NavigateUri);
}
```

The next column on the list is `IsEmployed`. This is the simplest, as we can just use a `DataGridCheckBoxColumn`:

```
<DataGridCheckBoxColumn Header="Employed?"
    Binding="{Binding IsEmployed}" />
```

Again, the `Binding` property points to the actual property to use on the data object. Note the new header text – there's no need to get by with the property name.

The last column, `Avatar`, is implemented the same way as was described in the recipe.

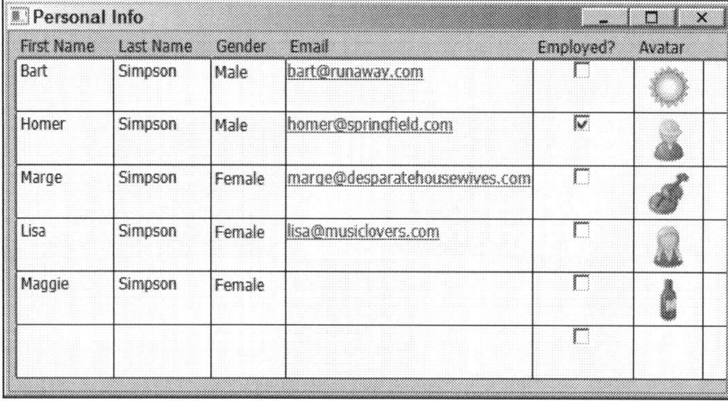

First Name	Last Name	Gender	Email	Employed?	Avatar
Bart	Simpson	Male	bart@runaway.com		
Homer	Simpson	Male	homer@springfield.com	✓	
Marge	Simpson	Female	marge@desparatehousewives.com		
Lisa	Simpson	Female	lisa@musiclovers.com		
Maggie	Simpson	Female			

Editing with a template-based column

Non-template columns, such as `DataGridTextColumn` and `DataGridCheckBoxColumn`, provide automatic editing support (assuming the column property `IsReadOnly` is false). What about `DataGridTemplateColumn`? Trying to edit the `Email` and `Avatar` columns at this time has no effect.

`DataGridTemplateColumn` provides a `CellEditingTemplate` property that can be set to an alternative `DataTemplate` to be used during editing (by double-clicking on the cell). Here's a simple one for changing an e-mail:

```
<DataGridTemplateColumn.CellEditingTemplate>
    <DataTemplate>
        <TextBox Text="{Binding Email}" />
    </DataTemplate>
</DataGridTemplateColumn.CellEditingTemplate>
```

This provides a flexible way to customize editing. As another example, consider a `DateTime` property. It should probably be displayed as a simple string, but for editing purposes it can be replaced with a `DatePicker` control.

The full source of this example is in the `CH06.DataGridDemo2` project, available in the downloadable source for this chapter.

Selecting, resizing, and sorting

The `DataGrid` supports a few ways to do selection. The `SelectionMode` property indicates whether one item can be selected (`Single`) or multiple items (`Extended`, the default). The meaning of "Item" depends on the `SelectionUnit` property. It can be an individual cell (`Cell`), an entire row only (`FullRow`, the default), and a combination of the two (`CellOrRowHeader`). When multi-selection is enabled, the usual *Shift* and *Ctrl* keys can be used for range and non-contiguous selections.

A column or row can be resized by the user by setting `CanUserResizeColumns` and `CanUserResizeRows` properties (both `true` by default). This can be set on a column by column basis if desired (`DataGridColumn.CanUserResize`).

Columns can be reordered if `CanUserReorderColumns` is `true` (the default). Again, this can be customized for particular columns with the `DataGridColumn.CanUserResize` property.

Sorting is supported by clicking on column headers (unless `CanUserSortColumns` is false). For specific columns, use the `DataGridColumn.CanUserSort` property. The `DataGridColumn.SortMemberPath` property can be used to change the default property to sort for, and is a must for template-based columns, as there is no binding expression to indicate how this column is to be sorted.

Other customization options

The `DataGrid` is highly customizable. Almost any aspect of its behavior or look can be changed. Here are some of the possibilities:

- Extra row details: Each row can have extra information set with the `RowDetailsTemplate` (a `DataTemplate`). By default, it's shown only for selected rows, but this can be changed with the `RowDetailsVisibilityMode` property (`VisibileWhenSelected` – the default, `Visible` – shown always, `Collapsed` – never shown).
- Columns can be frozen, meaning they never scroll out of view. These must be leftmost columns only, and cannot be reordered with unfrozen columns. To freeze columns, set the `FrozenColumnCount` to a number greater than zero.
- Many other visual customizations are possible through various styles and templates exposed by the `DataGrid` itself and by columns and rows. For example, a column header does not have to be a string. The `DataGridColumn.HeaderTemplate` can be used to provide a `DataTemplate` that can show anything on a header (an image, for example).

Validating data

Data binding provides automatic updates from a source to a target (and vice versa in a two way binding). Some of these values are provided by some user of the system; consequently, not all values are valid. The binding system should have ways to catch such errors and allow the application to communicate to the user those errors. This is the role of data validation. In this recipe, we'll look at the validation support in data binding scenarios.

Getting ready

Make sure Visual Studio is up and running.

How to do it...

We'll create a simple entry form that validates its inputs according to some application-specific rules.

1. Create a new WPF application named `CH06.ValidatingData`.
2. Add a new class to be used as a data object named `Person`. Implement it as follows:

```
class Person : INotifyPropertyChanged {
   protected virtual void OnPropertyChanged(string propName) {
      var pc = PropertyChanged;
      if(pc != null)
         pc(this, new PropertyChangedEventArgs(propName));
   }

   string _name;
   public string Name {
      get { return _name; }
      set {
         _name = value;
         OnPropertyChanged("Name");
      }
   }

   int _age;
   public int Age {
      get { return _age; }
      set {
         _age = value;
         OnPropertyChanged("Age");
      }
   }

   public event PropertyChangedEventHandler PropertyChanged;
}
```

3. This is a simple class, implementing `INotifyPropertyChanged`, as discussed in the *Binding to a single object* recipe, earlier in this chapter. Open `MainWindow.xaml` and add the following elements to the `Grid`:

```
<Grid TextBlock.FontSize="16">
    <Grid.RowDefinitions>
        <RowDefinition Height="Auto" />
        <RowDefinition Height="Auto" />
    </Grid.RowDefinitions>
    <Grid.ColumnDefinitions>
        <ColumnDefinition Width="Auto" />
        <ColumnDefinition />
    </Grid.ColumnDefinitions>
    <TextBlock Text="Name:" Margin="6"/>
    <TextBox Text="{Binding Name}"
                Grid.Column="1" Margin="6"/>
    <TextBlock Text="Age:" Grid.Row="1" Margin="6"/>
    <TextBox Text="{Binding Age}"
                Grid.Column="1" Grid.Row="1" Margin="6"/>
</Grid>
```

4. Open `MainWindow.xaml.cs`. Add the following to the constructor:

```
DataContext = new Person { Name = "Bart", Age = 10 };
```

5. Run the application. You should be able to change values in the **Name** and **Age** textboxes. However, if you enter incorrect values (say a negative age, or an empty name), nothing happens. Let's change that. Change the property setters of the `Age` and `Name` properties to raise exceptions on incorrect values:

```
public string Name {
   get { return _name; }
   set {
      if(string.IsNullOrWhiteSpace(value))
         throw new ArgumentException(
            "Name cannot be empty");
         _name = value;
         OnPropertyChanged("Name");
   }
}
public int Age {
   get { return _age; }
   set {
      if(value < 1)
         throw new ArgumentException(
           "Age must be a positive integer");
      _age = value;
      OnPropertyChanged("Age");
   }
}
```

6. Run the application now and enter some incorrect values. Nothing happens, because by default WPF swallows the exceptions. We need to set the `Binding.ValidatesOnExceptions` property to `true` (on both textboxes):

```
Text="{Binding Name, ValidatesOnExceptions=True}"
Text="{Binding Age, ValidatesOnExceptions=True}"
```

7. Now run the application and enter some incorrect values. When a `TextBox` loses focus and an exception is thrown by the setter, the offending `TextBox` is highlighted with a thin red border:

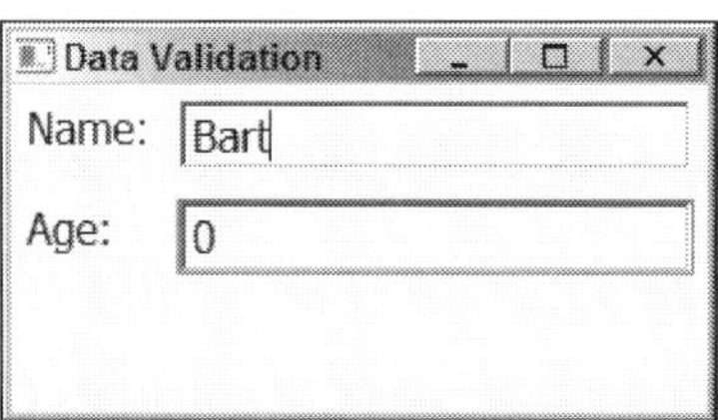

8. Set the `Binding.UpdateSourceTrigger` property of each `TextBox` to `PropertyChanged`. This will call the setter for any character typed, giving an immediate feedback:

```
Text="{Binding Name, ValidatesOnExceptions=True,
   UpdateSourceTrigger=PropertyChanged}"
Text="{Binding Age, ValidatesOnExceptions=True,
   UpdateSourceTrigger=PropertyChanged}"
```

How it works...

Normally, failed setters in data binding, whether caused by an exception thrown in the setter itself, or because of an exception thrown in a value converter, causes WPF to fail the binding. If `Binding.ValidatesOnExceptions` is `false` (the default), nothing else happens. If set to `true`, WPF performs the following actions:

- Sets the attached property `Validation.HasError` to `true` on the bound element (`TextBox` in this example).
- Creates a `ValidationError` object that holds the error details (such as the `Exception` object thrown). This object is added to the collection maintained by the attached property `Validation.Errors` of the bound element.
- If the `Binding.NotifyOnValidationError` is `true`, the `Validation.Error` attached event is raised (a bubbling event).

All binding validation stuff is relevant for a `TwoWay` or `OneWayToSource` binding (from the target to the source) only.

Behind the scenes, the `Binding` object maintains a collection of `ValidationRule` objects (`ValidationRules` property). Setting `ValidatesOnExceptions` to `true` is a shortcut for adding an `ExceptionValidationRule` to this collection.

There's more...

Using property setters for validation is convenient, but not always appropriate. First, raising exceptions may not be ideal; perhaps a temporary incorrect value is acceptable while, for example, objects are populated from some data source. Second, some validations require checking a combination of property values, not just a single one.

An alternative (that can be combined with setter validation) is to implement the `System.ComponentModel.IDataErrorInfo` interface. It has two read only properties: `Error` (which is never called by WPF) and an indexer that provides the property to evaluate. We need to return `null` to indicate no error, or some error string otherwise. Here's a simple implementation for our `Person` class (the implementation of the setters and `INotifyPropertyChanged` is not shown):

```
class Person : INotifyPropertyChanged, IDataErrorInfo {
   // never called by WPF
   public string Error {
      get { return null; }
   }

   public string this[string name] {
      get {
         switch(name) {
            case "Name":
               if (string.IsNullOrWhiteSpace(Name))
                  return "Name cannot be empty";
               break;

            case "Age":
               if (Age < 1)
                  return "Age must be a positive integer";
               break;
         }
         return null;
      }
   }
}
```

To make WPF use this interface, the `Binding.ValidatesOnDataErrors` property must be set to `true` (this adds a `DataErrorValidationRule` to the `ValidationRules` collection). From that point, the same set of actions is taken if the validation fails.

Custom validation rules

A data object may not have all validation required for a particular application. If custom validation is required, a custom validation rule can be created by deriving from the abstract `ValidationRule` class, implementing the only abstract method (`Validate`) and adding that rule to the `ValidationRules` collection. Here's a validation rule class that requires at least some number of characters in a string (exposed at a property):

```
class MinCharsRule : ValidationRule{
   public int MinimumChars { get; set; }

   public override ValidationResult Validate(object value,
      CultureInfo cultureInfo) {
      if(((string)value).Length < MinimumChars)
         return new ValidationResult(false, "Use at least " +
            MinimumChars.ToString() + " characters");
      return new ValidationResult(true, null);
   }
}
```

`Validate` returns a `ValidationResult`, whose constructor accepts a `Boolean` validity flag and an error message (or `null` in the case of validation success).

To apply the rule, we need to add it to the validation rules of the binding:

```
<TextBox.Text>
    <Binding Path="Name" ValidatesOnDataErrors="True"
        UpdateSourceTrigger="PropertyChanged">
        <Binding.ValidationRules>
            <local:MinCharsRule MinimumChars="3" />
        </Binding.ValidationRules>
    </Binding>
</TextBox.Text>
```

This requires using `Binding` with element syntax (rather than markup extension syntax).

Custom error template

When validation fails, the offending control is surrounded by a thin red border. This can be customized to give the user a more meaningful and rich experience. Setting `Validation.ErrorTemplate` to a different control template replaces the default behavior (control templates will be discussed in *Chapter 8, Styles, Triggers, and Custom Templates*, but for now think of it as a variation of a data template). Here's an example template created as a resource (for convenience):

```
<ControlTemplate x:Key="errorTemplate">
    <Border BorderBrush="Red" BorderThickness="2">
        <Grid>
```

```
            <AdornedElementPlaceholder x:Name="_el" />
            <TextBlock Text="{Binding [0].ErrorContent}"
                Foreground="Red" HorizontalAlignment="Right"
                VerticalAlignment="Center" Margin="0,0,6,0"/>
        </Grid>
    </Border>
</ControlTemplate>
```

The interesting part is the `AdornedElementPlaceholder` - this indicates where the real control is. In this case we surround it with a red border and place a `TextBlock` on top of it. The `DataContext` of any binding inside this template is the `Validation.Errors` collection. In this example, we extract the first error's description and show it. You can imagine a scenario where an `ItemsControl` would display all errors (validation rule failures) that occur. An alternative is to use the adorned element's `AdornedElement` property that refers to the actual bound control, and use other properties on the control.

By the way, this template is displayed in the adorner layer of the bound control; this means it's always on top of the control.

To apply the template we set the `Validation.ErrorTemplate` attached property on the bound element (`TextBox` in our example):

```
<TextBox Grid.Column="1" Margin="6"
  Validation.ErrorTemplate="{StaticResource errorTemplate}">
```

Here's the result:

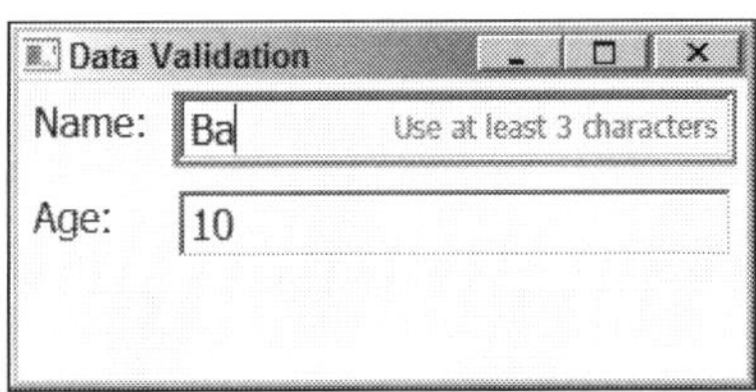

Using data annotations

There is yet another way we can do validation, in a more declarative manner using custom attributes. The `System.ComponentModel.DataAnnotations` namespace (in the `System.ComponentModel.DataAnnotations.Dll` assembly) defines several attributes that can be placed on properties to indicate validation requirements. Once placed, the setter of the property can use methods from the `Validator` static class to force validation based on the specified attributes.

Here's an example for our `Person` class. We'll place some attributes on the `Name` property as follows:

```
[Required(ErrorMessage = "A name is required"), StringLength(
   100, MinimumLength = 3, ErrorMessage =
   "Name must have at least 3 characters")]
public string Name {
   get { return _name; }
   set {
      ValidateProperty(value, "Name");
      _name = value;
      OnPropertyChanged("Name");
   }
}
```

The `Required` attribute indicates the property's value cannot be null or empty, and `StringLength` is pretty self-explanatory.

`ValidateProperty` is a helper method that performs the actual validation using the `Validator.ValidateProperty` static method implemented with the following code:

```
protected void ValidateProperty<T>(T value, string name) {
   Validator.ValidateProperty(value, new ValidationContext(
      this, null, null) { MemberName = name });
}
```

`ValidateProperty` throws an exception if validation fails. This is handled in the same way as a regular setter validation exception. The `Age` property can be similarly decorated:

```
[Range(1, 120,
   ErrorMessage = "Age must be a positive integer")]
public int Age {
   get { return _age; }
   set {
      ValidateProperty(value, "Age");
      _age = value;
      OnPropertyChanged("Age");
   }
}
```

`Range` provides a way to specify a range of acceptable values. The `ErrorMessage` property of all annotation attributes becomes the error content that may be used by the error template. Here's the XAML for the `Name` `TextBox`:

```
<TextBox Grid.Column="1" Margin="6"
   Validation.ErrorTemplate="{StaticResource errorTemplate}"
   Text="{Binding Name, UpdateSourceTrigger=PropertyChanged,
   ValidatesOnExceptions=True}" />
```

The `Age` property `TextBox` is similar. Here's the dialog when both properties fail validation:

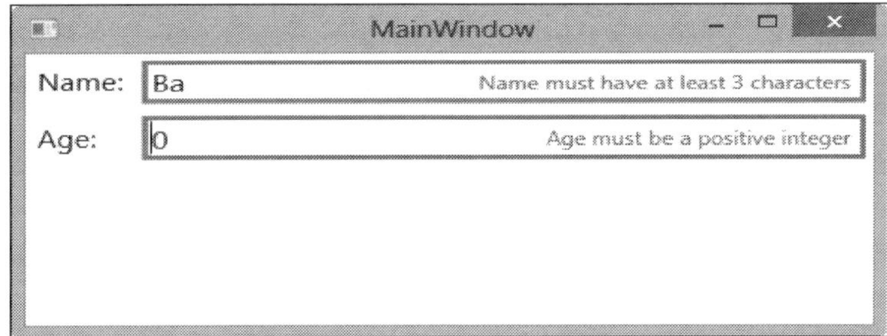

Other attributes that exist include `RegularExpression` that validates a string based on a regular expression (useful for e-mails, phone numbers, and so on) with some new attributes introduced in .NET 4.5 that can provide a shortcut such as `EmailAddress`, `Phone`, and `Url`.

7
Commands and MVVM

In this chapter we will cover the following:

- Using routed commands
- Implementing a basic MVVM application
- Building a simple MVVM framework
- Building a complete MVVM style application
- Creating an undo/redo system

Introduction

The traditional way of connecting a piece of user interface to some logic has been through events. The canonical example is a button – when clicked, some action is undertaken, hopefully accomplishing some goal the user has intended. Although WPF supports this model completely (as other UI frameworks do), it has its drawbacks:

- The event handler is part of the "code behind" where the UI is declared, typically a window or a user control. This makes it difficult to call from other objects that may want to invoke the same logic.
- The aforementioned button may disappear and be replaced by (say) a menu item. This would require the event hooking code to potentially change. What if we wanted both a button and a menu item?
- An action may not be allowed at a certain state – the button (or whatever) needs to be disabled or enabled at the right time. This adds management overhead to the developer – the need to track state and change it for all UI elements that invoke the same functionality.

- An event handler is just a method – there's no easy way to pick it up and save it somewhere, such as for undo/redo purposes.
- It's difficult to test application logic without using actual user interface.

These, and other, more subtle issues, make working with event handlers less than ideal, especially when application logic is involved. If an event is just intended for usability enhancement or for otherwise serving the UI alone, than this is not usually a concern (for example, hovering the mouse cursor over some element causes color changes, enhancing use experience in some way – although even this can be achieved declaratively with triggers – see *Chapter 8, Styles, Triggers, and Control Templates*).

The typical solution to this UI-logic coupling is the concept of commands. This follows the famous "Command design pattern" that abstracts away application logic into distinct objects. Being an object, a command can be invoked from multiple locations, saved in lists (for example, for undo purposes), and so on. It can even indicate whether it's allowable at certain times, freeing other entities to take care of the actual enabling or disabling of controls that may be bound to that command.

WPF provides a basic support for commands with the `ICommand` interface and two built-in implementations, `RoutedCommand` and `RoutedUICommand`. However, the support isn't perfect, which would force us to come up with other implementations of `ICommand`. Still, it's worth understanding where WPF's implementation is good enough and where we need to pave a new path.

Commands are just one aspect of more general patterns for dealing with user interface in non-trivial applications. To that end, a number of UI design patterns appeared, such as Model View Controller (MVC), Model View Presenter (MVP), and Model View View-Model (MVVM). All have something in common: the separation of the actual UI (View) from the application logic (Controller, Presenter, and ViewModel) and the underlying data (Model).

In this chapter, we'll first take a look at commands, and WPF's support in that respect. Then we'll develop a basic framework for MVVM-based applications (what exactly MVVM is and the differences from MVC/MVP will be discussed later in this chapter) and show some common scenarios and the way they are typically handled.

Using routed commands

WPF provides two (similar) implementations for the `ICommand` interface. Commands are invoked (by default) by command sources, implementing the `ICommandSource` interface. These two interfaces comprise the basic abstraction WPF recognizes as far as commands are concerned. In this recipe, we'll examine these interfaces, their out-of-the-box implementations, and how they are typically used.

Getting ready

Make sure Visual Studio is up and running.

How to do it...

We'll create a simple image viewer that provides its functionality via WPF routed commands:

1. Create a new WPF application named `CH07.RoutedCommands`.
2. Open `MainWindow.xaml`. Add the following to the existing `Grid`:

```
<Grid.RowDefinitions>
    <RowDefinition Height="Auto" />
    <RowDefinition />
</Grid.RowDefinitions>
<ToolBar FontSize="14">
</ToolBar>
<ScrollViewer HorizontalScrollBarVisibility="Auto"
    VerticalScrollBarVisibility="Auto" Grid.Row="1">
    <Image Source="{Binding ImagePath}" Stretch="None">
        <Image.LayoutTransform>
            <ScaleTransform ScaleX="{Binding Zoom}"
                            ScaleY="{Binding Zoom}" />
        </Image.LayoutTransform>
    </Image>
</ScrollViewer>
```

3. The `Grid` holds a toolbar (empty at the moment) and a scrollable image. The `Source` property of the `Image` is bound to an `ImagePath` property. It uses a `ScaleTransform`, with its properties bound to a `Zoom` property. All these properties have no source, so let's create one. Add a new class named `ImageData`, defined as follows :

```
class ImageData : INotifyPropertyChanged {
   public string ImagePath { get; private set; }

   public ImageData(string path) {
      ImagePath = path;
   }
   double _zoom = 1.0;

   public double Zoom {
      get { return _zoom; }
      set {
         _zoom = value;
         OnPropertyChanged("Zoom");
      }
   }
```

```
    protected virtual void OnPropertyChanged(string name) {
        var pc = PropertyChanged;
        if (pc != null)
            pc(this, new PropertyChangedEventArgs(name));
    }

    public event PropertyChangedEventHandler PropertyChanged;
}
```

4. The class exposes an `ImagePath` and `Zoom` properties, exactly as expected by the above XAML. Now let's add the following buttons to the `ToolBar`:

```
<Button Content="Open..." Command="Open" Margin="6"/>
<Button Content="Zoom In" Command="IncreaseZoom" Margin="6"/>
<Button Content="Zoom Out" Command="DecreaseZoom" Margin="6"/>
```

5. Note there are no `Click` event handlers; instead the `Command` property of the buttons is set. Running the application at this time shows all buttons as disabled:

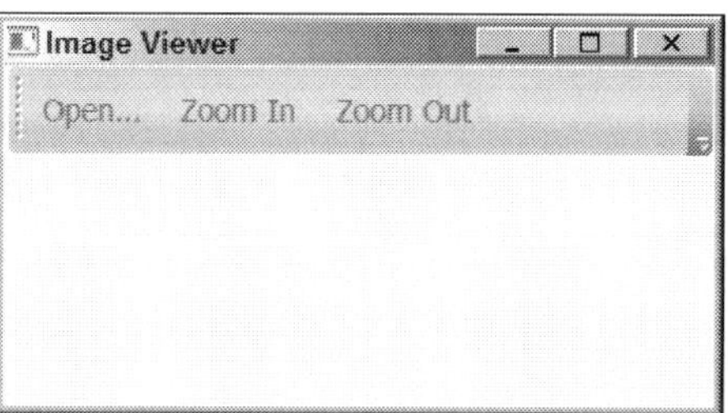

6. We need to add command bindings so that the commands do something useful. Add a `Commandbinding` object to the `Window`'s `CommandBindings` property:

```
<Window.CommandBindings>
    <CommandBinding Command="Open" Executed="OnOpen" />
</Window.CommandBindings>
```

7. Right-click on **OnOpen** and select **Navigate to Event Handler**. Add a private field of type `ImageData` to `MainWindow`:

```
ImageData _image;
```

8. Add the following code for `OnOpen`, allowing the user to select an image file to view:

```
void OnOpen(object sender, ExecutedRoutedEventArgs e) {
    var dlg = new OpenFileDialog {
        Filter = "Image Files|*.jpg;*.png;*.bmp;*.gif"
    };
    if(dlg.ShowDialog() == true) {
        _image = new ImageData(dlg.FileName);
        DataContext = _image;
    }
}
```

9. Run the application. You can now click on **Open** and select an image to view:

10. Now let's take care of the zoom commands. Open `MainWindow.xaml` and add the following command bindings:

```
<CommandBinding Command="IncreaseZoom" Executed="OnZoomIn"
                CanExecute="OnIsImageExist" />
<CommandBinding Command="DecreaseZoom" Executed="OnZoomOut"
                CanExecute="OnIsImageExist" />
```

11. Add a handler for the previous `CanExecute` events:

```
void OnIsImageExist(object s, CanExecuteRoutedEventArgs e) {
   e.CanExecute = _image != null;
}
```

12. The above means that the zoom commands should be disabled when no image is present. Now add the handlers for the `IncreaseZoom` and `DecreaseZoom` commands:

```
void OnZoomOut(object sender, ExecutedRoutedEventArgs e) {
   _image.Zoom /= 1.2;
}

void OnZoomIn(object sender, ExecutedRoutedEventArgs e) {
   _image.Zoom *= 1.2;
}
```

13. Run the application. Notice the zoom buttons are disabled until an image is opened. Now let's create a button that would restore the zoom to 1. First, we need a custom command for that. Add a class named `Commands` and optionally make it static:

```
static class Commands {
}
```

14. Add the following static field and static property to the class:

```
static readonly RoutedUICommand _zoomNormalCommand =
    new RoutedUICommand("Zoom Normal", "Normal",
    typeof(Commands));

public static RoutedUICommand ZoomNormalCommand {
   get { return _zoomNormalCommand; }
}
```

15. Open `MainWindow.xaml` and add an XML namespace mapping to the `CH07.RoutedCommands` namespace.

16. Now add a fourth button to the `ToolBar`:

```
<Button Command="local:Commands.ZoomNormalCommand"
        Content="Normal" Margin="6"/>
```

17. Add a `CommandBinding` to the window's `CommandBindings` collection to handle this command:

```
<CommandBinding Command="local:Commands.ZoomNormalCommand"
   Executed="OnZoomNormal" CanExecute="OnIsImageExist" />
```

18. Implement `OnZoomNormal` as follows:

```
void OnZoomNormal(object sender, ExecutedRoutedEventArgs e) {
   _image.Zoom = 1.0;
}
```

19. Run the application. All buttons should operate as expected: with no image, only the **Open** button is enabled. All buttons are operational when an image is present.

How it works...

The `ICommand` interface is the abstraction of a command. WPF defines it as follows (in the `System.Windows.Input` namespace):

```
public interface ICommand {
   bool CanExecute(object parameter);
   void Execute(object parameter);
   event EventHandler CanExecuteChanged;
}
```

The `Execute` method executes the command. `CanExecute` indicates whether this command is available at this time. If it's not, WPF is smart enough to disable that command source. Both methods accept a parameter that can be anything that affects the way the command is implemented; command sources can set it using the `CommandParameter` property. The remaining event is used to notify WPF when the `CanExecute` method should be called again, because something has changed that may make this method return a different result, and so the enabled/disabled state may need to update.

WPF provides two implementations for the ICommand interface: RoutedCommand and RoutedUICommand. The latter inherits from the former and adds a single Text property that is used automatically with menu items. They implement ICommand explicitly and expose its execution members in a different way:

```
public void Execute(object param, IInputElement target);
public bool CanExecute(object param, IInputElement target);
```

Why is that? The classic command pattern implementation uses a separate class for each command. In this application, we could have had an OpenCommand class, a ZoomInCommand class, and so on, all implementing ICommand. Instead, we use the same type: RoutedUICommand. How can this work?

Routed(UI)Command objects are essentially empty shells. They cannot contain our own implementation, so they hunt for a CommandBinding object up the visual tree from a target element (this is the second argument to the above methods) that indicates it can handle that command. This means that the following line:

```
<CommandBinding Command="IncreaseZoom" Executed="OnZoomIn"
                CanExecute="OnIsImageExist" />
```

Causes the XAML parser to convert the string IncreaseZoom (using a Type Converter) to the static property NavigationCommands.IncreaseZoom (of type RoutedUICommand), the same one used in the button:

```
<Button Content="Zoom In" Command="IncreaseZoom" Margin="6"/>
```

When the button is clicked, Execute (from ICommand) is called on the IncreaseZoom command instance. This explicit implementation inside RoutedUICommand looks for a corresponding CommandBinding, starting from the target element, which is by default the command source itself (the button) and moving up the visual tree until such a command and a handler is found. If not found, the command source is disabled.

Once the CommandBinding is found, its Executed event handler is called - this is where our special implementation is located. Similarly, when WPF calls CanExecute on the RoutedUICommand, the CommandBinding is located in the same way, but this time the CanExecute event handler is called. If it does not exist, but an Executed event does exist, the command source is always enabled (this is the case with our **Open** button). Otherwise, the Boolean property ExecutedRoutedEventArgs.CanExecute indicates whether this command is currently available. In our case, the zoom commands should be available when an image is displayed.

There's more...

WPF provides five classes that contain many static RoutedUICommand properties for commonly used operations: ApplicationCommands (Open, Print, Copy, and many other properties), MediaCommands class (Play, Pause, Stop, and so on), NavigationCommands (BrowseBack, NextPage, Refresh, Search, and so on), ComponentCommands (MoveLeft, MoveDown, ScrollByLine, and so on) and EditingCommands (AlignLeft, Backspace, Delete, TabForward, and so on). Naturally, this list (no matter how comprehensive) cannot possibly fill every application's needs.

We can create custom RoutedUIComamnd objects as was done in the code sample by using the same tactics as WPF: creating a static property in some class of type RoutedUICommand. Again, this is just a shell; a CommandBinding object will supply the actual logic behind the command. A RoutedUICommand can include a name, text, and optional input gestures, such as a keyboard shortcut that should invoke the command. Here's an example that extends the zoom normal command to use a shortcut (*Alt* + *N*):

```
static readonly RoutedUICommand _zoomNormalCommand =
    new RoutedUICommand("Zoom Normal", "Normal",
    typeof(Commands), new InputGestureCollection(new [] {
       new KeyGesture(Key.N, ModifierKeys.Alt)
    }));
```

Many built-in commands have associated gestures, such as *Ctrl* + *N* for ApplicationCommands.New and *Ctrl* + *C* for ApplicationCommands.Copy.

Built-in implementations

It may seem that RoutedUICommands provide very little. After all, they don't actually implement the command logic.

Some controls have their own command bindings, and thus implement some well-known commands. The TextBox control, for example, has command bindings for commands such as Copy, Cut, Paste, and Undo. This means we can create a simple Notepad-like clone by using a TextBox with the right commands. The **Edit** menu for such an implementation is as follows:

```
<MenuItem Header="_Edit">
    <MenuItem Command="Copy" />
    <MenuItem Command="Cut" />
    <MenuItem Command="Paste" />
    <Separator />
    <MenuItem Command="Undo" />
    <MenuItem Command="Redo" />
</MenuItem>
```

This is all that's needed for the `TextBox` to perform these operations. Note that `MenuItem` objects pick up their `Header` from the `Text` property of the `RoutedUICommand` (unless an explicit `Header` is specified).

Similarly, we can hook up buttons in a `ToolBar`:

```
<ToolBar Grid.Row="1">
    <Button Content="Copy" Command="Copy" />
    <Button Content="Cut" Command="Cut" />
    <Button Content="Paste" Command="Paste" />
</ToolBar>
```

The complete source is in the `CH07.SimpleNotepad` project, part of the downloadable source for this chapter.

Command sources

As we've seen, buttons and menu items are capable of invoking commands. This is abstracted by the `ICommandSource` interface, defined as follows:

```
public interface ICommandSource {
   ICommand Command { get; }
   object CommandParameter { get; }
   IInputElement CommandTarget { get; }
}
```

This indicates which command to invoke (`Command`), an optional parameter (`CommandParameter`), and which element is the target from which the lookup for a `CommandBinding` begins (`CommandTarget`). The following elements implement this interface: `MenuItem`, `ButtonBase`, (and thus all buttons) and `Hyperlink`.

What this means is that other controls cannot invoke commands as easily, because they don't implement `ICommandSource`. Furthermore, even controls that do implement `ICommandSource` invoke the command when a specific trigger occurs (such as a click for buttons); but what if we wanted a different trigger to invoke the command? These are things we'll need to address in later recipes, as WPF does not provide solutions to these issues out of the box.

Alternative ICommand implementations

`RoutedUICommand`'s implementation of `ICommand` is fine for some cases, mainly where pure UI is involved. However, if we want to connect a command to some piece of logic that is not part of a `Window`'s code behind, routed commands are problematic. This is because they require `CommandBinding` objects that are part of some visual tree, and use an event handler - this must be tied to a specific `Window`. A more decoupled implementation is preferred, but is not supplied by WPF. We'll see examples in the next recipes.

Implementing a basic MVVM application

The MVC, MVP, and MVVM patterns comprise mostly the same parts: a model, which is the data, a view (or views) that display the data in some meaningful way and provide user interaction, and a third part that is somehow responsible for the logic behind the interactions of view and data. The exact differences between MVC and MVP are not that important (you can find a lot on these topics on the Web). MVVM could be considered a special case of MVP, where data binding is used to connect the View with the ViewModel in a very loose way. This is especially favorable for XAML-based applications, where data binding is both declarative and powerful. In this recipe, we'll move closer to MVVM by taking the previous recipe, *Using routed commands*, and "moving" it towards MVVM.

Getting ready

In Visual Studio, open the `CH07.RoutedCommands` project (from the previous recipe). We'll make changes to this project to make it more MVVM-like.

How to do it...

We'll refactor the image viewer to be more MVVM-like by separating the view from its state and connecting them through data binding:

1. First, we need to get rid of the `RoutedUICommands`. Delete the `Commands.cs` file.
2. Open `ImageData.cs`. Make the property `ImagePath` read/write with a change notification and remove the constructor. The result is as follows:

```
class ImageData : INotifyPropertyChanged {
   string _imagePath;
   double _zoom = 1.0;
   public double Zoom {
      get { return _zoom; }
      set {
         _zoom = value;
         OnPropertyChanged("Zoom");
      }
   }

   public string ImagePath {
      get { return _imagePath; }
      set {
         _imagePath = value;
         OnPropertyChanged("ImagePath");
      }
   }

   protected virtual void OnPropertyChanged(string name) {
```

```
        var pc = PropertyChanged;
        if (pc != null)
            pc(this, new PropertyChangedEventArgs(name));
    }

    public event PropertyChangedEventHandler PropertyChanged;
}
```

3. Add a new project folder named `Commands`.
4. Add a new class to the `Commands` folder called `OpenImageFileCommand`.
5. Make the class implement the `ICommand` interface (add a `using` statement for the `System.Windows.Data.Input` namespace). The skeleton code should look as follows:

```
class OpenImageFileCommand : ICommand {
    public bool CanExecute(object parameter) {
        throw new NotImplementedException();
    }

    public event EventHandler CanExecuteChanged;

    public void Execute(object parameter) {
        throw new NotImplementedException();
    }
}
```

6. Implement `CanExecute` by returning a simple `true`:

```
public bool CanExecute(object parameter) {
    return true;
}
```

7. Implement `Execute` by copying the code from the `MainWindow.OnOpen` method (add a `using` statement for the `Microsoft.Win32` namespace). The code does not compile, as the `_image` and `DataContext` do not exist.
8. Add a constructor for the `OpenImageFileCommand` class that accepts an `ImageData` object and save it in a private field.
9. In the `Execute` method after the dialog is dismissed, set the `ImageData.ImagePath` property to the obtained filename. The entire class is as follows:

```
class OpenImageFileCommand : ICommand {
    ImageData _data;
    public OpenImageFileCommand(ImageData data) {
        _data = data;
    }

    public bool CanExecute(object parameter) {
```

```
            return true;
        }

        public event EventHandler CanExecuteChanged;

        public void Execute(object parameter) {
            var dlg = new OpenFileDialog {
                Filter = "Image Files|*.jpg;*.png;*.bmp;*.gif"
            };
            if(dlg.ShowDialog() == true) {
                _data.ImagePath = dlg.FileName;
            }
        }
    }
```

10. Add another class to the `Commands` folder named `ZoomCommand` that implements `ICommand`. Create a simple `enum` to indicate the required zoom:

    ```
    enum ZoomType {
        ZoomIn,
        ZoomOut,
        ZoomNormal
    }
    ```

11. Add a constructor to `ZoomCommand` that accepts an `ImageData` and save it in a private field.
12. Implement `Execute` as follows:

    ```
    public void Execute(object parameter) {
        var zoomType = (ZoomType)Enum.Parse(typeof(ZoomType),
            (string)parameter, true);
        switch(zoomType) {
            case ZoomType.ZoomIn:
                _data.Zoom *= 1.2;
                break;
            case ZoomType.ZoomOut:
                _data.Zoom /= 1.2;
                break;
            case ZoomType.ZoomNormal:
                _data.Zoom = 1.0;
                break;
        }
    }
    ```

13. The preceding code assumes the parameter of the command holds the zoom type. Implement `CanExecute` with the following code:

```
public bool CanExecute(object parameter) {
   return _data.ImagePath != null;
}
```

14. Let's expose these commands from the `ImageData` class. This turns out to be our View-Model. Open `ImageData.cs`.

15. Add two private fields of type `ICommand` that correspond to the two commands we just created:

```
ICommand _openImageFileCommand, _zoomCommand;
```

16. Create a constructor for `ImageData` and initialize these commands:

```
public ImageData() {
   _openImageFileCommand = new OpenImageFileCommand(this);
   _zoomCommand = new ZoomCommand(this);
}
```

17. Expose the commands as read only properties:

```
public ICommand OpenImageFileCommand {
   get { return _openImageFileCommand; }
}

public ICommand ZoomCommand {
   get { return _zoomCommand; }
}
```

18. Open `MainWindow.xaml`. Remove the command bindings.

19. Replace the command properties of the buttons with simple binding expressions as follows:

```
<Button Command="{Binding OpenImageFileCommand}" Margin="6"
        Content="Open..." />
<Button Content="Zoom In" Command="{Binding ZoomCommand}"
        CommandParameter="ZoomIn" Margin="6"/>
<Button Content="Zoom Out" Command="{Binding ZoomCommand}"
        CommandParameter="ZoomOut" Margin="6"/>
<Button Content="Normal" Command="{Binding ZoomCommand}"
        CommandParameter="ZoomNormal" Margin="6"/>
```

20. Open `MainWindow.xaml.cs`. Remove all methods except the constructor.

21. Add to the constructor code to create an `ImageData` and make it the `DataContext`. The entire code behind should look as follows:

```
public partial class MainWindow : Window {
   public MainWindow() {
      InitializeComponent();
      DataContext = new ImageData();
   }
}
```

22. Run the application. Click on **Open** to load an image. The image shows, but the zoom buttons remain disabled. Open `ZoomCommand.cs` and modify the implementation of the `CanExecuteChanged` event as follows:

```
public event EventHandler CanExecuteChanged {
   add { CommandManager.RequerySuggested += value; }
   remove { CommandManager.RequerySuggested -= value; }
}
```

23. Run the application again. Everything should work as expected.

How it works...

MVVM has three participants. The Model represents the data, or business logic. This may consist of types generated in some way (such as entity classes in Entity Framework or data objects generated by a WCF service metadata). It's typically neutral; that is, it knows nothing of how it's going to be used. It usually implements change notifications for properties (by implementing `INotifyPropertyChanged`).

The View is the actual UI. It should display relevant parts of the model and provide the required interactive functionality. The view should not have a direct knowledge of the model, and this is where data binding comes in. All bindings access a property without explicitly knowing what type of object sits at the other end. This magic is satisfied at runtime by setting the view's `DataContext` to the object providing the data; this is the ViewModel.

The ViewModel is the glue that hands out the required data to the View (based on the Model). The ViewModel is just that – a model for the view. It has several responsibilities:

- Expose properties that allow binding in the view. This may be just by accessing properties on the model, but may be more involved if the model exposes data in another way (such as with methods).
- Expose commands to be invoked by elements in the view.
- Maintain relevant state for the view.

The `ImageData` class in the example code is our ViewModel. It maintains the zoom value for the view to bind to. This zoom has nothing to do with the actual data. It also exposes a set of `ICommand` properties to be invoked by the view. The model has no notion of commands (and it shouldn't).

In the example, there is no separate model, as the application is very simple. We could have taken the `ImagePath` property and put it in a separate class and call that "the model". We'll see a more complex example in the following recipes.

The entire relationship between Model, View, and ViewModel can be summarized with the following diagram:

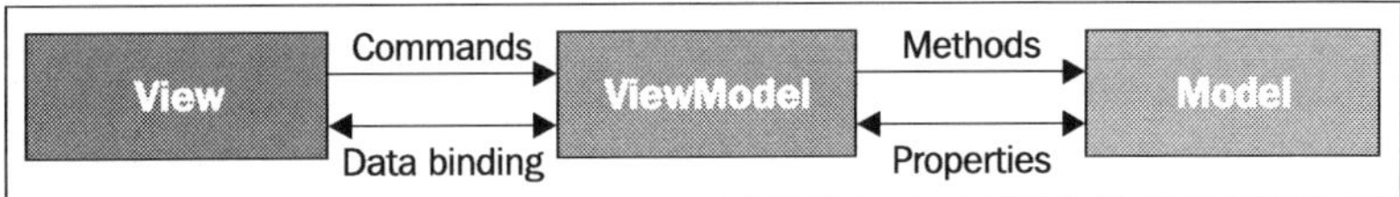

There's more...

The `MainWindow` code behind is practically empty, with just a constructor that after calling `InitializeComponent` creates an instance of `ImageData` (the ViewModel) and sets it as the `DataContext`. This is one way to do this – it's called "View first", as the view (`MainWindow`) is created first and it's responsible for finding its ViewModel (we could do that even in XAML by creating the ViewModel as a resource and making it the value of the View's `DataContext`). The other common way is for another entity to create the ViewModel and the View and "bind" them together. In our example, this could be achieved inside an `Application.OnStartup` override:

```
protected override void OnStartup(StartupEventArgs e) {
   base.OnStartup(e);

   var mainWindow = new MainWindow();
   mainWindow.DataContext = new ImageData();
   mainWindow.Show();
}
```

This assumes that the `Application.StartupUri` property has been removed from `App.xaml`. Now `MainWindow` has virtually no code at all.

Which one is better? This is a matter of taste (and you can find many discussions online), but I prefer the latter approach. This makes things look somewhat "cleaner" as the view remains totally oblivious to the actual ViewModel it binds to. For one, we can change the ViewModel type, and as long as property names remain the same, the view shouldn't know or care.

Implementing ICommand

Clearly, we abandoned WPF's RoutedUICommand objects and instead created our own implementations. A command needs data to work on, and so an ImageData instance is passed to the commands. This keeps the command neutral – it has no idea what controls (if any) would be affected by its execution.

Execute and CanExecute are fairly straightforward to implement. They do what needs to be done, and no more. In our OpenImageFileCommand, CanExecute always returns true, as this command is always valid. ZoomCommand, on the other hand, is only valid if there is an image file (note that the implementation is flawed, as any file path is accepted and never checked if this is in fact a valid image; we'll leave this as an exercise for the reader).

What about the CanExecuteChanged event? In OpenImageFileCommand it's not "implemented" as we don't need to throw this event ever (the command is always valid).

In ZoomCommand, we need to notify WPF when the command validity changes (becomes valid or invalid). How can we do that? In the command we have no way of knowing when the ImagePath changes. Or maybe we do. We can register using INotifyPropertyChanged on ImageData and when that event is raised to raise the CanExecuteChanged event. Although this is possible, there is a simpler approach. WPF raises the CommandManager.RequerySuggested static event when it thinks the execution state of commands may change. This is typically done after some UI actions that may cause something to change in all bound commands. The following implementation causes WPF to call register for its own notification of re-executing CanExecute for all commands that raise the CanExecuteChange event:

```
public event EventHandler CanExecuteChanged {
   add { CommandManager.RequerySuggested += value; }
   remove { CommandManager.RequerySuggested -= value; }
}
```

With this implementation, CanExecute is called more times than it actually should, but since most CanExecute logic is quick, this has no adverse effect.

Blendability

Although we're working mostly with Visual Studio in this book, there is another potentially useful tool for WPF work, Microsoft Expression Blend. This tool is used primarily by designers, and is well beyond the scope of this book. As developers, we may be "forced" to be designers, too, and Blend may be useful in this case, as there are some things that are difficult to create accurately in hand coded XAML (VS 2010's designer is much less powerful than Blend's designer, but VS 2012's designer is on par with Blend's designer), such as animations and other graphic effects. If we're working with a true designer (a person), we may want to give her (or him) a better experience; this is true of Visual Studio's designer as well. If we look at the designer of Visual Studio or Blend with the example application open, we find the following (VS on the left, Blend on the right):

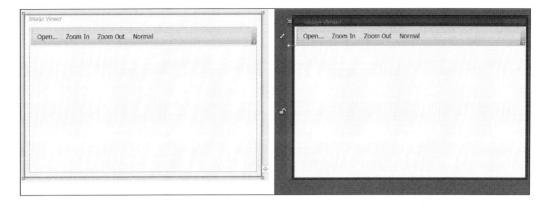

It's more important to note what we don't see: there is no image. A designer (person) may want to know what kind of data the view shows, so she can make the design better - she would like to get a "feel" for the application in design time.

This is sometimes termed "blendability", but it applies equally to Visual Studio's designer. What we want is to create a "default" ViewModel, so that something is shown in design mode, but only in design mode.

Blend includes some XML namespace prefixes that it understands, the most important being the following:

```
xmlns:d=http://schemas.microsoft.com/expression/blend/2008
```

The "d" prefix can now be used to set properties for design time (in this case on the `Window`):

```
d:DataContext="{d:DesignInstance Type=local:ImageData,
    IsDesignTimeCreatable=True}"
```

This instructs the designer to create an instance of `ImageData` (in design time only). The default constructor of `ImageData` does not bind to any default image, so we need to fix it:

```
var prop = DesignerProperties.IsInDesignModeProperty;
bool design = (bool)DependencyPropertyDescriptor.FromProperty(
    prop, typeof(FrameworkElement)).Metadata.DefaultValue;
if(design) {
   ImagePath = Environment.GetFolderPath(
      Environment.SpecialFolder.MyPictures)
      + @"\Sample Pictures\Penguins.jpg";
}
```

The test for design time may look more complicated than it should be – this is required if Visual Studio's designer is to be supported as well as Blend's. After this change, the designers look as follows:

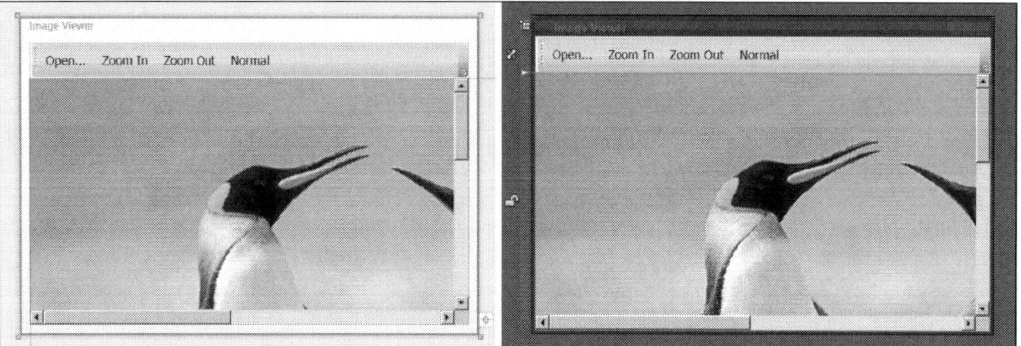

Building a simple MVVM framework

It should be clear at this point that MVVM-based applications have a lot of elements in common, such as change notifications and commands. It would be beneficiary to create a reusable framework that we can simply leverage in many applications. Although there are several good frameworks out there (most are free), building such a framework ourselves will enhance our understanding and may prove easier to extend than other frameworks, which we may be less familiar with.

Getting ready

Make sure Visual Studio is up and running.

How to do it...

We'll create a reusable class library to serve as a basis of a simple MVVM framework and use it (and extend it) in later recipes:

1. Create a new WPF `UserControl` Class Library project named `CH07.CookbookMVVM`. Make sure the checkbox **Create directory for solution** is checked. We don't need any user controls, but this automatically adds WPF assembly references.
2. Delete the file `UserControl1.xaml`.

3. Add the class `ObservableObject` from the recipe *Binding to a single object* in *Chapter 6*. The entire class is as follows (with one small addition):

```
public abstract class ObservableObject : INotifyPropertyChanged {
   public event PropertyChangedEventHandler PropertyChanged;

   protected virtual void OnPropertyChanged(string propName) {
      Debug.Assert(GetType().GetProperty(propName) != null);
      var pc = PropertyChanged;
      if(pc != null)
         pc(this, new PropertyChangedEventArgs(propName));
   }

   protected bool SetProperty<T>(ref T field, T value,
      string propName) {
      if(!EqualityComparer<T>.Default.Equals(field, value)) {
         field = value;
         OnPropertyChanged(propName);
         return true;
      }
      return false;
   }

   protected bool SetProperty<T>(ref T field, T value,
      Expression<Func<T>> expr) {
      if(!EqualityComparer<T>.Default.Equals(field, value)) {
         field = value;
         var lambda = (LambdaExpression)expr;
         MemberExpression memberExpr;
         if(lambda.Body is UnaryExpression) {
            var unaryExpr = (UnaryExpression)lambda.Body;
            memberExpr = (MemberExpression)unaryExpr.Operand;
         }
         else {
            memberExpr = (MemberExpression)lambda.Body;
         }

         OnPropertyChanged(memberExpr.Member.Name);
         return true;
      }
      return false;
   }
}
```

4. For ViewModels, we'll create two abstract base classes that will serve as a basis for any concrete ViewModel. Add a class named `ViewModelBase`, and implement it in a generic and non-generic way as follows:

```
public abstract class ViewModelBase : ObservableObject {
}

public abstract class ViewModelBase<TModel> : ViewModelBase {
   TModel _model;

   public TModel Model {
      get { return _model; }
      set { SetProperty(ref _model, value, () => Model); }
   }

}
```

5. This provides convenient access to the underlying model (if such direct access is needed). Next, we need a generic command implementation class, which should not require us to create new command classes (as in the previous recipe), but just create new instances of it. Add a class named `RelayCommand` and implement it as follows (again, two versions: generic and non-generic). The first is the generic version:

```
public class RelayCommand<T> : ICommand {
   private static bool CanExecute(T parameter) {
      return true;
   }

   readonly Action<T> _execute;
   readonly Func<T, bool> _canExecute;

   public RelayCommand(Action<T> execute,
      Func<T, bool> canExecute = null) {
      if(execute == null)
         throw new ArgumentNullException("execute");
      _execute = execute;
      _canExecute = canExecute ?? CanExecute;
   }

   public bool CanExecute(object parameter) {
      return _canExecute(TranslateParameter(parameter));
   }

   public event EventHandler CanExecuteChanged {
      add {
         if(_canExecute != null)
            CommandManager.RequerySuggested += value;
      }
      remove {
         if(_canExecute != null)
```

```
                CommandManager.RequerySuggested -= value;
            }
        }

        public void Execute(object parameter) {
            _execute(TranslateParameter(parameter));
        }

        private T TranslateParameter(object parameter) {
            T value = default(T);
            if (parameter != null && typeof (T).IsEnum)
                value = (T) Enum.Parse(typeof(T),
                    (string) parameter);
            else
                value = (T) parameter;
            return value;
        }
    }
```

6. The class is based on two delegates; one for executing the command and another for returning the validity of the command. The non-generic version is just a special case for the first, in case the command has no parameter:

   ```
   public class RelayCommand : RelayCommand<object> {
      public RelayCommand(Action execute,
         Func<bool> canExecute = null)
         : base(obj => execute(),
            (canExecute == null ? null :
            new Func<object, bool>(obj => canExecute()))) {
      }
   }
   ```

7. That's it for the basic framework. We'll add some more features in later recipes.

How it works...

The framework currently consists of three classes, and we'll look at them next.

`ObservableObject` implements the class changed notification infrastructure (the `INotifyPropertyChanged` interface), as we've seen already in *Chapter 6*. The only addition is the returning of a `Boolean` value from the `SetProperty<>` methods. This indicates whether the sent value was actually different than the previous one. Most of the time this is unimportant to the caller, but we'll see some scenarios where it is, and so having this information can be beneficial.

The `ViewModelBase` classes simply provide a basis for custom ViewModels. Currently, they have very little - they inherit from `ObservableObject` and the generic `ViewModelBase` can hold its model as a property named `Model`. This is sometimes useful, although it might be dangerous, as the connected view can "bypass" the ViewModel and go straight for the model. The advantage here is that it saves duplicating properties from the model on the ViewModel.

`RelayCommand` is a general purpose command implementation wrapper. In the previous recipe, we created a separate command implementation for each required command (`OpenImageFileCommand`, `ZoomCommand`). Although this is fairly easy to do, it can cause a great number of classes to exist in large applications. The alternative is a single class that encapsulates different business logic using delegates accepted as constructor arguments.

We'll see the usage of these classes in the next recipe, *Building a complete MVVM style application*.

There's more...

There are a number of MVVM frameworks out there; most of them are free and open source, and can be found on Microsoft's CodePlex site (`http://www.codeplex.com`). Here's a list of some of the well-known frameworks:

- MVVM Light Toolkit (`http://mvvmlight.codeplex.com/`): A popular framework supporting both WPF and Silverlight (and now with Windows 8 Store apps as well), written by Laurent Bugnion.
- Simple MVVM Toolkit (`http://simplemvvmtoolkit.codeplex.com/`): Works with WPF, Silverlight, and Windows Phone 7.x. Claims to be more feature rich than MVVM Light Toolkit.
- Caliburn Micro (`http://caliburnmicro.codeplex.com/`): A feature rich framework, closer to Prism in functionality (see next section) that works with WPF, Silverlight, Windows Phone 7.x, and the new Windows 8 Store style applications.

Non-ICommandSource elements and other events

Commands are invoked by elements implementing `ICommandSource`, which exposes the Command and `CommandParameter` properties. What about controls that don't implement that interface? What about using different events to execute commands? For instance, a click of a button causes the bound command to execute. What if we wanted a double click on the button to execute a command?

WPF has no solutions for these issues out of the box. With some creativity, however, this can be solved using attached properties (the general way to extend functionality in WPF) and some clever coding. As the source code is non-trivial, and a large part of it is unrelated directly to WPF (some reflection and dynamic delegate creation), it's not printed here. The complete source is available as part of the `CH07.CookbookMVVM` project.

Here's an example usage: suppose we want a double-click on a `ListBox` to execute some command. The required mark up for this is as follows (the "mvvm" XML prefix is assumed to point to the `CH07.CookbookMVVM` namespace):

```
<ListBox>
    <mvvm:EventsToCommandsMapper.Mapper>
        <mvvm:EventToCommandCollection>
            <mvvm:EventToCommand Event="MouseDoubleClick"
                 Command="{Binding SomeCommand}" />
        </mvvm:EventToCommandCollection>
    </mvvm:EventsToCommandsMapper.Mapper>
</ListBox>
```

This can be used with any element regardless of `ICommandSource`.

What about Prism?

The Prism project (`http://compositewpf.codeplex.com/`) is from Microsoft's Patterns and Practices team. It provides a comprehensive framework for building rich client applications with WPF, Silverlight, and Windows Phone 7.x, by leveraging the MVVM pattern, but also supports Inversion of Control (IoC) containers (it supports Unity and MEF – both are beyond the scope of this book) and more.

It's considered more feature-complete with respect to the toolkits mentioned earlier, but is also more complex. Caliburn Micro is probably the closest one in functionality to Prism.

Building a complete MVVM style application

Now that we have our own (small) framework to assist us with building MVVM applications, it's time to actually build one. Along the way we may find missing features in our framework, but that's ok; it's a normal way for frameworks to evolve.

Getting ready

Run Visual Studio and open the `CH07.CookbookFramework` project. This is a long recipe, but hopefully the end result would be worth it (in terms of understanding, not visually).

How to do it...

We'll create a sample blog viewer application using the simple framework we just built:

1. Add a new WPF project to the current solution, named `CH07.BlogReader`. This will be a fictitious blog reader application with support for adding posts and comments.
2. Add a reference to the `CH07.CookbookMVVM` project.

3. Create three project folders named `Model`, `Views`, and `ViewModels`. The project tree looks as follows:

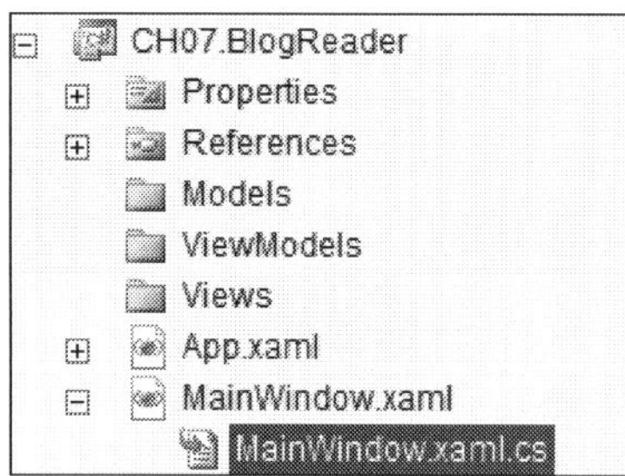

4. We'll start with the models. These will be simple classes that represent some blog properties. Add a class named `BlogComment` to the `Models` folder and implement it as follows:

```
class BlogComment : ObservableObject {
   string _name;
   string _text;
   DateTime _when;

   public string Name {
      get { return _name; }
      set { SetProperty(ref _name, value, () => Name); }
   }

   public string Text {
      get { return _text; }
      set { SetProperty(ref _text, value, () => Text); }
   }

   public DateTime When {
      get { return _when; }
      set { SetProperty(ref _when, value, () => When); }
   }
}
```

5. A `BlogComment` object just holds a few simple properties. Add another class to the `Models` folder called `BlogPost`. Implement it as follows:

```
class BlogPost : ObservableObject {
   string _title;
   string _text;
   DateTime _when;
   ObservableCollection<BlogComment> _comments =
      new ObservableCollection<BlogComment>();
```

```
    public string Title {
        get { return _title; }
        set { SetProperty(ref _title, value, () => Title); }
    }

    public string Text {
        get { return _text; }
        set { SetProperty(ref _text, value, () => Text); }
    }

    public DateTime When {
        get { return _when; }
        set { SetProperty(ref _when, value, () => When); }
    }

    public IList<BlogComment> Comments {
        get { return _comments; }
    }
}
```

6. A `BlogPost` maintains some simple properties and a collection of `BlogComment` objects (`ObservableCollection<T>` is used so that adding or removing objects raises a notification for any bound controls). Add yet another class to the `Models` folder named `Blogger`. This includes some information on a blogger:

```
class Blogger : ObservableObject {
    string _name;
    string _email;
    Stream _picture;

    public string Name {
        get { return _name; }
        set { SetProperty(ref _name, value, () => Name); }
    }

    public string Email {
        get { return _email; }
        set { SetProperty(ref _email, value, () => Email); }
    }

    public Stream Picture {
        get { return _picture; }
        set { SetProperty(ref _picture, value, () => Picture); }
    }
}
```

7. A blogger has a name, an e-mail, and a picture, represented by a neutral `Stream` object. Finally, we'll add a `Blog` class that puts everything together:

```
class Blog : ObservableObject {
   Blogger _blogger;
   ObservableCollection<BlogPost> _posts =
      new ObservableCollection<BlogPost>();
   string _blogTitle;

   public Blogger Blogger {
      get { return _blogger; }
      set { SetProperty(ref _blogger, value, () => Blogger); }
   }

   public IList<BlogPost> Posts {
      get { return _posts; }
   }

   public string BlogTitle {
      get { return _blogTitle; }
      set {
         SetProperty(ref _blogTitle, value, () => BlogTitle);
      }
   }
}
```

8. A blog has a title, a blogger, and a collection of posts. Next, we need to create views and bind them to ViewModels. Assuming some UI design was done, we need to create the actual views. A view can be a `Window`, a `UserControl`, or a data template. As we haven't discussed user controls yet, we'll use data templates and windows.

9. Right-click on the `Views` folder and select **Add Resource Dictionary...**. Name it `BloggerView.xaml`.

10. Add a `DataTemplate` object to the `ResourceDictionary` to indicate how a blogger should be displayed:

```
<DataTemplate x:Key="bloggerTemplate">
    <Grid Background="#c0ffffff">
        <Grid.RowDefinitions>
            <RowDefinition Height="Auto"/>
            <RowDefinition />
        </Grid.RowDefinitions>
        <Grid.ColumnDefinitions>
            <ColumnDefinition  />
            <ColumnDefinition Width="Auto" />
        </Grid.ColumnDefinitions>
```

```
        <TextBlock Text="{Binding Model.Name}"
            FontWeight="Bold" FontSize="16" />
        <TextBlock Grid.Row="1" FontSize="14">
            <Hyperlink>
                <Run Text="{Binding Model.Email}" />
            </Hyperlink>
        </TextBlock>
        <Image Grid.Column="1" Grid.RowSpan="2"
            Source="{Binding Picture}" Width="48" Height="48"
            Stretch="Uniform" Margin="4"/>
    </Grid>
</DataTemplate>
```

11. The bindings assume some ViewModel that is yet to exist. Add a class to the `ViewModels` folder, named `BloggerVM`, and implement it as follows:

```
class BloggerVM : ViewModelBase<Blogger> {
   public ImageSource Picture {
      get {
         if(Model.Picture == null)
            return new BitmapImage(new Uri(
               "/Images/blogger.png",
               UriKind.Relative));
         var bmp = new BitmapImage();
         bmp.BeginInit();
         bmp.StreamSource = Model.Picture;
         bmp.EndInit();
         return bmp;
      }
   }
}
```

12. Add an `Images` folder to the project. Inside add an image and name it `blogger.png` or change the above URI to point to the correct image name.

13. We want a click on the e-mail of the blogger to open the default e-mail client with the blogger's e-mail in the "to" box. Add the following code to the `BloggerVM` class that exposes a `RelayCommand<string>`:

```
ICommand _sendEmailCommand;
public ICommand SendEmailCommand {
   get {
      return _sendEmailCommand ?? (_sendEmailCommand =
         new RelayCommand<string>(email =>
         Process.Start("mailto:" + email)));
   }
}
```

14. This code creates the command the first time it's requested and stores it in a private field. The command must be exposed through a binding. Open `BloggerView.xaml`.
15. Add the following markup to the `Hyperlink` element:

```
Command="{Binding SendEmailCommand}"
CommandParameter="{Binding Model.Email}"
```

16. Let's add more Views and ViewModels. Add another `ResourceDictionary` to the `Views` folder named `BlogView.xaml`.
17. Add a `DataTemplate` object, which should display a blog comment:

```
<DataTemplate x:Key="commentTemplate">
    <Grid Margin="2,8">
        <Grid.RowDefinitions>
            <RowDefinition Height="Auto" />
            <RowDefinition Height="Auto" />
        </Grid.RowDefinitions>
        <StackPanel Orientation="Horizontal">
            <TextBlock Text="{Binding Model.When,
                StringFormat=d}" />
            <TextBlock Margin="10,0,0,0" Text="{Binding Name,
               StringFormat=From: \{0\}}" FontWeight="Bold"/>
        </StackPanel>
        <TextBlock Grid.Row="1" Text="{Binding Text}"
            TextWrapping="Wrap" />
    </Grid>
</DataTemplate>
```

18. This markup shows the date of the comment (`Model.When`), the name of the commenting user (`Name`), and the comment itself (`Text`). The corresponding ViewModel is the `BlogCommentVM` class, added to the `ViewModels` folder:

```
class BlogCommentVM : ViewModelBase<BlogComment> {
   public string Text {
      get { return Model.Text; }
      set {
         Model.Text = value;
         OnPropertyChanged("IsCommentOK");
      }
   }

   public string Name {
      get { return Model.Name; }
      set {
         Model.Name = value;
         OnPropertyChanged("IsCommentOK");
```

```
        }
    }

    public bool IsCommentOK {
        get {
            return !string.IsNullOrWhiteSpace(Model.Name) &&
                !string.IsNullOrWhiteSpace(Model.Text);
        }
    }
}
```

19. The `Name` and `Text` property are reflected off the model because when they change the `IsCommentOK` property is raised. This will be used later to validate a comment.
20. Open `BlogView.xaml`. Let's add another `DataTemplate` for a blog post:

```
<DataTemplate x:Key="blogPostTemplate">
    <Grid Background="#b0dddddd" Margin="2,10">
        <Grid.RowDefinitions>
            <RowDefinition Height="Auto" />
            <RowDefinition Height="Auto" />
            <RowDefinition Height="Auto" />
        </Grid.RowDefinitions>
        <StackPanel Orientation="Horizontal">
            <TextBlock Text="{Binding Title}"
                FontWeight="Bold" />
            <TextBlock Margin="10,0,0,0"
    Text="{Binding Model.When, StringFormat='(\{0\})'}"
    FontStyle="Italic" />
        </StackPanel>
        <TextBlock Grid.Row="1" Text="{Binding Text}"
            Margin="0,10,0,0" TextWrapping="Wrap" />
        <Expander Grid.Row="2" ExpandDirection="Down">
            <Expander.Header>
                <StackPanel Orientation="Horizontal">
                    <TextBlock Text="Comments" />
                    <Button Margin="20,0,0,0"
                      Content="New Comment"
                      Command="{Binding NewCommentCommand}" />
                </StackPanel>
            </Expander.Header>
            <Border BorderBrush="Blue" BorderThickness="2"
                Padding="2" Margin="2">
                <ItemsControl ItemsSource="{Binding Model.
Comments}" ItemTemplate="{StaticResource commentTemplate}" />
            </Border>
        </Expander>
    </Grid>
</DataTemplate>
```

21. This template is more interesting, as it hosts an `ItemsControl` that binds to the `Model.Comments` collection. Also, a **New Comment** button is rendered, its command bound to the `NewCommentCommand` property. All this must be backed up by a proper ViewModel.

22. Before we do that, we need a dialog window that will be used to create a new comment. Add a new `Window` class to the `Views` folder, named `NewCommentWindow.xaml`.

23. Add the following markup to the existing `Grid`:

```
<Grid.RowDefinitions>
    <RowDefinition Height="Auto" />
    <RowDefinition />
    <RowDefinition Height="Auto" />
</Grid.RowDefinitions>
<DockPanel>
    <TextBlock Text="Title:" DockPanel.Dock="Left"
        VerticalAlignment="Center"/>
    <TextBox Margin="10,0,0,0" Text="{Binding Name,
        UpdateSourceTrigger=PropertyChanged}" />
</DockPanel>
<TextBox Margin="4" Grid.Row="1" AcceptsReturn="True"
    Text="{Binding Text, UpdateSourceTrigger=PropertyChanged}"/>
<UniformGrid Rows="1" Columns="2" Grid.Row="2"
   Margin="2,10,2,2">
   <Button HorizontalAlignment="Right" Margin="6,0" Width="50"
      IsEnabled="{Binding IsCommentOK}" Content="OK"
      IsDefault="True" />
    <Button HorizontalAlignment="Left" Margin="6,0" Width="50"
       Content="Cancel" IsCancel="True" />
</UniformGrid>
```

24. The markup consists of a title `TextBox` and a comments `TextBox`, along with an **OK** and **Cancel** button. The properties used are from the `BlogCommentVM` class, which will be provided as the `DataContext` at runtime.

25. Add a **Click** event handler to the **OK** button (yes, we have code in the code behind). The implementation should just dismiss the dialog with a `true` result:

```
private void OnOK(object sender, RoutedEventArgs e) {
   DialogResult = true;
   Close();
}
```

26. Add a class named `BlogPostVM` to the `ViewModels` folder and implement it as follows:

```
class BlogPostVM : ViewModelBase<BlogPost> {
   public string Title {
      get { return Model.Title; }
      set {
         Model.Title = value;
         OnPropertyChanged("IsPostOK");
      }
   }
   public string Text {
      get { return Model.Text; }
      set {
         Model.Text = value;
         OnPropertyChanged("IsPostOK");
      }
   }
   public bool IsPostOK {
      get {
          return !string.IsNullOrWhiteSpace(Model.Title) &&
          !string.IsNullOrWhiteSpace(Model.Text);
      }
   }

   ICommand _newCommentCommand;
   public ICommand NewCommentCommand {
      get {
         return _newCommentCommand ?? (_newCommentCommand =
            new RelayCommand(() => {
               var comment = new BlogComment();
               var dlg = new NewCommentWindow {
                  DataContext =
                     new BlogCommentVM { Model = comment }
               };
               if(dlg.ShowDialog() == true) {
                  comment.When = DateTime.Now;
                  Model.Comments.Add(comment);
               }
         }));
      }
   }
}
```

27. Note the implementation of the command. A `NewCommentWindow` is created (the view) and a `DataContext` is set to an empty `BlogCommentVM`. If closed with **OK**, the comment is added to the model.

28. Next we need a view for an entire blog. Open `BlogView.xaml` and add another `DataTemplate` for a blog (consisting of a title and posts):

```
<DataTemplate x:Key="blogTemplate">
    <Grid Background="LightYellow">
        <Grid.RowDefinitions>
            <RowDefinition Height="Auto" />
            <RowDefinition />
        </Grid.RowDefinitions>
        <StackPanel Orientation="Horizontal">
            <TextBlock Text="{Binding Model.BlogTitle}"
                FontWeight="Bold" />
            <Button Margin="20,0,0,0" Content="New Post"
                Command="{Binding NewPostCommand}" />
        </StackPanel>
        <ScrollViewer Grid.Row="1" Margin="4"
            VerticalScrollBarVisibility="Auto">
            <ItemsControl ItemsSource="{Binding Posts}"
              ItemTemplate="{StaticResource blogPostTemplate}"
                HorizontalContentAlignment="Stretch" />
        </ScrollViewer>
    </Grid>
</DataTemplate>
```

29. This template consists of a title (`Model.BlogTitle`) and a collection of blog posts (`Posts` property). A new post can be added with a button bound to the `NewPostCommand` property (a command). Again, this must be backed up by a proper ViewModel.

30. Once again, we'll first add a `Window` for entering a new blog post. This is similar to the new comment window. You can copy the class definition (`NewPostWindow.xaml/cs`) from the downloadable source for this chapter. Now let's add a ViewModel class for a blog, named `BlogVM`:

```
class BlogVM : ViewModelBase<Blog> {
   public BloggerVM Blogger {
      get { return new BloggerVM { Model = Model.Blogger }; }
   }

   ICommand _newPostCommand;
   public ICommand NewPostCommand {
      get {
```

```
            return _newPostCommand ?? (_newPostCommand =
               new RelayCommand(() => {
               var post = new BlogPostVM {
                  Model = new BlogPost()
               };
               var dlg = new NewPostWindow {
                  DataContext = post
               };
               if(dlg.ShowDialog() == true) {
                  post.Model.When = DateTime.Now;
                  Model.Posts.Add(post.Model);
               OnPropertyChanged("Posts");
               }
            }));
         }
      }

      public IEnumerable<BlogPostVM> Posts {
         get {
            return Model.Posts.Select(post =>
               new BlogPostVM {Model = post});
         }
      }
   }
```

31. The command implementation is similar in concept to `NewCommentCommand`. A `NewPostWindow` is created, the correct `DataContext` is set, and if **OK** is clicked, a new `BlogPost` is added.

32. We want to allow multiple blogs to be managed. We can create another model that is a kind of blog manager that holds a collection of blogs. But in this case, we'll take a shortcut by creating a ViewModel without a separate model class. Add a new class to the `ViewModels` folder called `MainVM` and implement it as follows:

```
class MainVM : ViewModelBase<IEnumerable<Blog>> {
   BlogVM _selectedBlog;

   public IEnumerable<BlogVM> Blogs {
      get { return Model.Select(blog =>
         new BlogVM { Model = blog });
      }
   }

   public BlogVM SelectedBlog {
      get { return _selectedBlog; }
      set {
```

```
            if(SetProperty(ref _selectedBlog, value,
               () => SelectedBlog))
               OnPropertyChanged("IsSelectedBlog");
         }
      }

      public Visibility IsSelectedBlog {
         get {
            return SelectedBlog != null ? Visibility.Visible
               : Visibility.Collapsed;
         }
      }

      public MainVM(IEnumerable<Blog> blogs) {
         Model = new ObservableCollection<Blog>(blogs);
      }
   }
```

33. `MainVM` holds a collection of blogs (provided as via the constructor, or via the `Model` property) and manages the existence of any selected blog (if any, `SelectedBlog` and `IsSelectedBlog`). The corresponding view to `MainVM` is the `MainWindow` itself. Open `MainWindow.xaml`.
34. Add the following markup inside the existing `Grid`:

```
<Grid.RowDefinitions>
    <RowDefinition Height="Auto" />
    <RowDefinition />
</Grid.RowDefinitions>
<StackPanel Orientation="Horizontal" Panel.ZIndex="1000">
    <TextBlock Text="Select blog to read:"
        VerticalAlignment="Center" Margin="2"/>
    <ComboBox ItemsSource="{Binding Blogs}" Margin="10,0,0,0"
        DisplayMemberPath="Model.BlogTitle" Width="170"
        SelectedItem="{Binding SelectedBlog, Mode=TwoWay}">
    </ComboBox>
    <Canvas Visibility="{Binding IsSelectedBlog}" >
        <Expander Margin="10,0,0,0" VerticalAlignment="Center"
            ExpandDirection="Down" Header="Blog Information"
            ContentTemplate="{StaticResource bloggerTemplate}"
            Content="{Binding SelectedBlog.Blogger}">
        </Expander>
    </Canvas>
</StackPanel>
<ContentControl Content="{Binding SelectedBlog}"
     ContentTemplate="{StaticResource blogTemplate}"
     Grid.Row="1" Visibility="{Binding IsSelectedBlog}"
     Margin="2,10,2,2" />
```

35. `MainWindow` consists of a `ComboBox` for selecting a blog to view and a `ContentControl` that uses the blog template – everything else cascades from there.
36. All that's left is to provide some data for the models. Open `App.xaml` and delete the `StartupUri` property.
37. Open `App.xaml.cs` and override the `OnStartup` method as follows:

```
protected override void OnStartup(StartupEventArgs e) {
   base.OnStartup(e);

   // create some dummy blogs
   var blogs = new ObservableCollection<Blog> {
      new Blog {
         Blogger = new Blogger {
            Name = "Bart Simpson",
            Email = "bart@springfield.com",
            Picture = GetResourceStream(new Uri(
            "/Images/bart.png", UriKind.Relative)).Stream
         },
         BlogTitle = "Bart's adventures",
         Posts = {
            new BlogPost {
               When = new DateTime(2000, 8, 12),
               Title = "Post 1",
               Text = "This is the first post of Bart",
               Comments = {
                  new BlogComment {
                     Name = "Homer S.",
                     Text = "Why you little...",
                     When = new DateTime(2000, 8, 13)
                  }
               }
            },
            new BlogPost {
               When = new DateTime(2002, 3, 22),
               Title = "Post 2",
               Text = "This is the the second post",
               Comments = {
                  new BlogComment {
                     Name = "Lisa S.",
                     Text = "Come on bart!",
                     When = new DateTime(2002, 3, 24)
                  },
                  new BlogComment {
```

```
                            Name = "Maggie S.",
                            Text = "Whhhaaa!",
                            When = DateTime.Now
                        }
                    }
                }

            }
        },
    };

    var vm = new MainVM(blogs);
    var win = new MainWindow {
        DataContext = vm
    };
    win.Show();
}
```

38. This code adds a single blog with two posts and some comments. `MainVM` is created with the generated blogs (in a real application these would come from a database, an XML file, a web service, and so on) and makes the `DataContext` of the `MainWindow`.
39. Running the application produces the following (when selecting Bart's blog and expanding the blogger information):

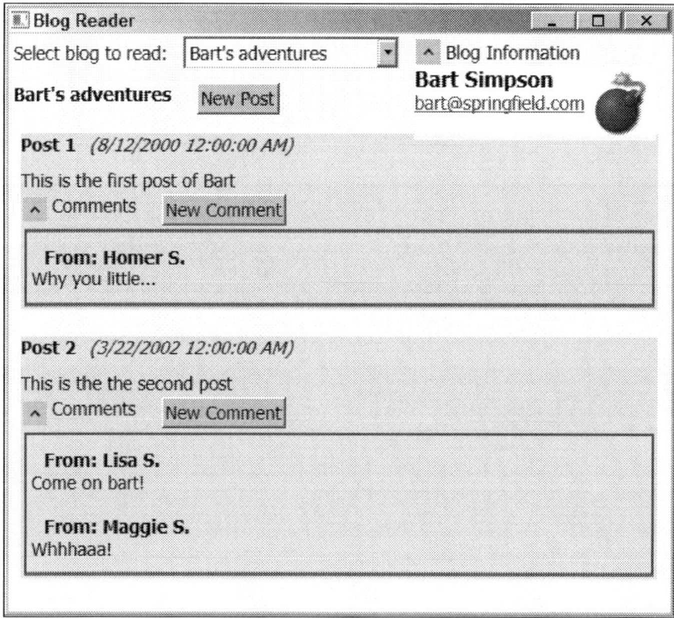

How it works...

A ViewModel is responsible for providing everything a View needs. Data binding is the key to exposing the correct functionality from a ViewModel – mainly properties (for one way or two way communication) and commands (for communication from the View to the ViewModel). There's usually a one to one relationship between a View and a ViewModel, although opinions vary. I think this, at least, provides easy maintenance at the possible cost of some code duplication.

The model should be completely neutral in respect to WPF. That is, it should not use any WPF specific types. In our case, the models inherit from `ObservableObject`, which is part of our little framework, but that's just a convenience for the purpose of the demonstration. The models could have implemented `INotifyPropertyChanged` in any way they choose.

Accessing the model directly by the view through the `Model` property (from `ViewModelBase<TModel>`) is not necessarily ideal, but it can save code duplication that would otherwise be in place to forward relevant property changes to the model. That said, it "feels" a bit lazy, and it means the view knows something about the underlying model, which it ideally should not. This is part of those implementation opinions I mentioned earlier.

There's more...

What about testing? One of the benefits of an MVVM model (that separates the view from the logic behind it) is that we could (at least in theory) test the ViewModels (where the logic lies) without instantiating any views. This is important for automated tests, so that a physical user doesn't have to be present to manipulate an actual UI (which may not even exist yet, or can change).

Currently, this may partially work. For example, we can create a `BlogVM` object, populate the `Model` with a `Blog` object, and start extracting posts, comments, and so on using the existing properties.

However, what about invoking a command? Suppose we want to invoke the `NewPostCommand`. Doing so will pop up the **New Post** window and wait for a physical user to input some blog post information. This is undesirable in a testing environment. A similar issue may arise for commands that need to show any kind of UI, such as a simple Yes/No message box ("Are you sure?" message types). For batch testing, all those message boxes should probably be automatically dismissed with a constant response. How do we deal with this?

The basic idea is to raise the abstraction level. Instead of directly creating a `NewPostWindow` object, we'll abstract that behind an interface. One of the implementations will, in fact, create a dialog. Another implementation could simply pretend there was a dialog and dismiss it. First, we'll create an interface (under our MVVM framework project):

```
public interface IDialogService {
   bool? ShowDialog();
   object ViewModel { get; set; }
}
```

Next, we can provide two implementations. The first shows a real dialog:

```
public sealed class StandardDialogService<TWindow>
   : IDialogService where TWindow : Window, new() {
   public bool? ShowDialog() {
      var win = new TWindow();
      win.DataContext = ViewModel;
      return win.ShowDialog();
   }

   public object ViewModel { get; set; }
}
```

There is also one that fakes a dialog:

```
public sealed class AutoDialogService : IDialogService {
   public bool? DialogResult { get; set; }

   public AutoDialogService() {
      DialogResult = true;
   }

   public bool? ShowDialog() {
      return DialogResult;
   }

   public object ViewModel { get; set; }
}
```

The dialog service should be exposed as a property on the `BlogVM` class:

```
public IDialogService NewPostDialogService { get; set; }
```

The `NewPostCommand` would be implemented as follows (we leverage the command parameter to provide an existing blog post if needed):

```
ICommand _newPostCommand;
public ICommand NewPostCommand {
   get {
      if(NewPostDialogService == null)
         NewPostDialogService = new
            StandardDialogService<NewPostWindow>();
      return _newPostCommand ?? (_newPostCommand =
         new RelayCommand<BlogPost>(post => {
         if(post == null)
            post = new BlogPost();
         var vm = new BlogPostVM { Model = post };
         var dlg = NewPostDialogService;
         dlg.ViewModel = vm;
         if(dlg.ShowDialog() == true) {
            post.When = DateTime.Now;
            Model.Posts.Add(post);
            OnPropertyChanged("Posts");
         }
      }));
   }
}
```

The default dialog service uses the UI, while an external client (such as a unit test client) would fill the property with an `AutoDialogService` instance beforehand.

If no post is provided, this means the command is invoked from the regular UI, so a new blank post is created. Otherwise, the provided blog post is used as is. The dialog is invoked through the `IDialogService` interface only. Here's how a unit test client would invoke the command (this is in a Visual Studio Test project):

```
[TestMethod]
public void TestAddPost() {
   var post = new BlogPost {
      Title = "Some title",
      Text = "Some text"
   };
   var vm = new BlogVM { Model = _blog };
   vm.NewPostDialogService = new AutoDialogService() {
      ViewModel = post
   };
   vm.NewPostCommand.Execute(post);
   Assert.IsTrue(_blog.Posts.Count == 3);
}
```

This allows batch execution of a multitude of commands without any UI popping up unnecessarily. The full source code is available with the downloadable source for this chapter.

MVVM implementations

It's important to remember that MVVM is a design pattern - it constitutes an idea; it says nothing about the actual implementation. Whenever something seems to be too "hard coded", it should be abstracted away using interfaces, providing a kind of "plugin" model.

Creating an undo/redo system

Up until now we have been executing commands by using the `RelayCommand` helper class. This allows us to separate the command implementation (in the ViewModel) from the view without creating a separate class for each command. Many applications need to not only execute commands, but also to undo already executed commands; the canonical case may be a text editor, but it can be anything. Let's see one way to build an undo/redo system that integrates with the commands infrastructure we've seen so far.

Getting ready

We'll use two projects we've already created. The first is `CH07.CookbookMVVM`, our MVVM framework (which we'll expand), and there is also `CH07.BlogReader` to demonstrate adding undo/redo capabilities.

How to do it...

We'll add undo/redo capabilities to the blog reader application, both at the MVVM framework level and application level:

1. Add a new interface to the `CH07.CookbookMVVM` project and name it `IUndoCommand`. Define it as follows:

   ```
   public interface IUndoCommand : ICommand {
      void Undo();
   }
   ```

2. This interface extends `ICommand` to allow a command to be undone. Add a new class to the `CH07.CookbookMVVM` project named `UndoManager`.
3. Add some fields to the class—two lists to hold commands to undo/redo and an optional undo limit:

   ```
   readonly List<IUndoCommand> _undoList, _redoList;
   public int UndoLimit { get; private set; }
   ```

4. Next, add a constructor to initialize the lists and undo limit:

```
public UndoManager(int limit = 0) {
   if(limit < 0) throw new ArgumentException(
      "undo limit must be a positive integer", "limit");
   UndoLimit = limit;
   _undoList = new List<IUndoCommand>(limit > 0 ? limit : 16);
   _redoList = new List<IUndoCommand>(limit > 0 ? limit : 16);
}
```

5. The undo functionality should have an `Undo` method and a property indicating whether anything can be undone:

```
public virtual bool CanUndo {
   get { return _undoList.Count > 0; }
}

public virtual void Undo() {
   if (!CanUndo)
      throw new InvalidOperationException("can't undo");
   int index = _undoList.Count - 1;
   _undoList[index].Undo();
   _redoList.Add(_undoList[index]);
   _undoList.RemoveAt(index);
}
```

6. Calling `Undo` gets the last command in the undo list and undoes it, removes it from the undo list, and adds it to the redo list. The redo functionality is similarly implemented:

```
public virtual bool CanRedo {
   get { return _redoList.Count > 0; }
}

public virtual void Redo() {
   if(!CanRedo)
      throw new InvalidOperationException("Can't redo");
   var cmd = _redoList[_redoList.Count - 1];
   cmd.Execute(null);
   _redoList.RemoveAt(_redoList.Count - 1);
   _undoList.Add(cmd);
}
```

7. To get commands into the lists, we'll add the following method:

```
public void AddCommand(IUndoCommand cmd) {
   _undoList.Add(cmd);
   _redoList.Clear();
   if(UndoLimit > 0 && _undoList.Count > UndoLimit)
      _undoList.RemoveAt(0);
}
```

8. This adds a command to the undo list (and removes the oldest command if an undo limit has been set and was reached).

9. To somewhat automate the use of undoable commands we'll add a helper command. Add a class to the same project named `ReversibleCommand` that implements `ICommand` as follows:

```
public sealed class ReversibleCommand : ICommand {
   readonly IUndoCommand _command;
   readonly UndoManager _mgr;
 public ReversibleCommand(UndoManager mgr, IUndoCommand cmd) {
      _mgr = mgr;
      _command = cmd;
   }

   public bool CanExecute(object parameter) {
      return _command.CanExecute(parameter);
   }
   public event EventHandler CanExecuteChanged {
      add { _command.CanExecuteChanged += value; }
      remove { _command.CanExecuteChanged -= value; }
   }

   public void Execute(object parameter) {
      _command.Execute(parameter);
      _mgr.AddCommand(_command);
   }
}
```

10. This class executes the actual command (passed to the constructor) in its `Execute` method and adds it to the `UndoManager` object for possible undoing.

11. Now let's move to the `CH07.BlogReader` project. First, we need to add buttons for undo and redo. Open `MainWindow.xaml`.

12. Add two buttons inside the `StackPanel` between the `ComboBox` and the `Canvas` for invoking undo or redo:

```
<Button Content="Undo" Command="{Binding UndoCommand}"
        Margin="6,2,2,2"/>
<Button Content="Redo" Command="{Binding RedoCommand}"
        Margin="2"/>
```

13. The commands themselves should be exposed from the main ViewModel. Open `MainVM.cs` and add the following inside the `MainVM` class:

```
ICommand _undoCommand, _redoCommand;

public ICommand UndoCommand {
   get {
     return _undoCommand ?? (_undoCommand =
         new RelayCommand(() => UndoManager.Undo(),
         () => UndoManager.CanUndo));
   }
}

public ICommand RedoCommand {
   get {
      return _redoCommand ?? (_redoCommand =
         new RelayCommand(() => UndoManager.Redo(),
         () => UndoManager.CanRedo));
   }
}
```

14. Add an automatic property to hold an `UndoManager` and create an instance in the constructor:

```
public UndoManager UndoManager { get; private set; }

public MainVM(IEnumerable<Blog> blogs) {
   Model = new ObservableCollection<Blog>(blogs);
   UndoManager = new UndoManager();
}
```

15. Undo/redo operations typically span multiple ViewModels. We'll add the ability to link ViewModels in a parent-child relationship, if needed. Open `ViewModelBase.cs` and add a new generic class named `ViewModelBase` with two generic arguments as follows:

```
public abstract class ViewModelBase<TModel, TParentVM>
   : ViewModelBase<TModel> {
   public ViewModelBase(TModel model = default(TModel),
      TParentVM parentVM = default(TParentVM)) {
      Model = model;
      Parent = parentVM;
   }

   public TParentVM Parent { get; set; }
}
```

16. We'll make adding a blog post an undoable command. `RelayCommand` alone is not enough here, as we need to maintain a state. First, we'll add a bit more infrastructure; add a new class named `CommandBase` to the `CH07.CookbookMVVM` project and implement it as follows:

```
public abstract class CommandBase : IUndoCommand {
   public virtual bool CanExecute(object parameter) {
      return true;
   }

   public event EventHandler CanExecuteChanged {
      add { CommandManager.RequerySuggested += value; }
      remove { CommandManager.RequerySuggested -= value; }
   }

   public abstract void Execute(object parameter);
   public abstract void Undo();
}
```

17. `CommandBase` is a helper for implementing reversible commands. Add a project folder named `Commands` to the `CH07.BlogReader` project.

18. Add a class to the `Commands` folder named `NewBlogPostCommand` and implement it as follows:

```
class NewBlogPostCommand : CommandBase {
   Blog _blog;
   BlogPost _post;
   public NewBlogPostCommand(Blog blog) {
      _blog = blog;
   }

   public override void Execute(object parameter) {
      if(_post == null) _post = (BlogPost)parameter;
      _blog.Posts.Add(_post);
   }

   public override void Undo() {
      _blog.Posts.Remove(_post);
   }
}
```

19. The command needs the blog in question and the post. To use it, we'll change the way the new post command is exposed through the blog ViewModel. Open `BlogVM.cs`.

20. Make the `BlogVM` class use the enhanced `ViewModelBase` that has a link to its parent ViewModel:

```
public class BlogVM : ViewModelBase<Blog, MainVM> {
   public BlogVM(Blog blog, MainVM parent)
      : base(blog, parent) {
      var notify = (INotifyCollectionChanged)blog.Posts;
      if(notify != null) {
         notify.CollectionChanged += delegate {
            OnPropertyChanged("Posts");
         };
      }
   }
```

21. The additions in the constructor allow the ViewModel to be notified when something interesting has changed in the model, so it can appropriately update itself.

22. Change the implementation of the `NewPostCommand` read only property to use a `ReversibleCommand` as follows:

```
public ICommand NewPostCommand {
   get {
      if(NewPostDialogService == null)
         NewPostDialogService =
            new StandardDialogService<NewPostWindow>();
      return _newPostCommand ?? (_newPostCommand =
         new RelayCommand<BlogPost>(post => {
         if(post == null)
            post = new BlogPost();
         var vm = new BlogPostVM { Model = post };
         var dlg = NewPostDialogService;
         dlg.ViewModel = vm;
         if(dlg.ShowDialog() == true) {
            post.When = DateTime.Now;
            var cmd = new ReversibleCommand(
               Parent.UndoManager,
               new NewBlogPostCommand(Model));
            cmd.Execute(post);
         }
      }));
   }
}
```

23. A `ReversibleCommand` is created, wrapping the "real" `NewBlogPostCommand` object. When executed, it places the wrapped command in the undo list of the `UndoManager`.

24. Run the application and select a blog to view. The **Undo** and **Redo** buttons are grayed out:

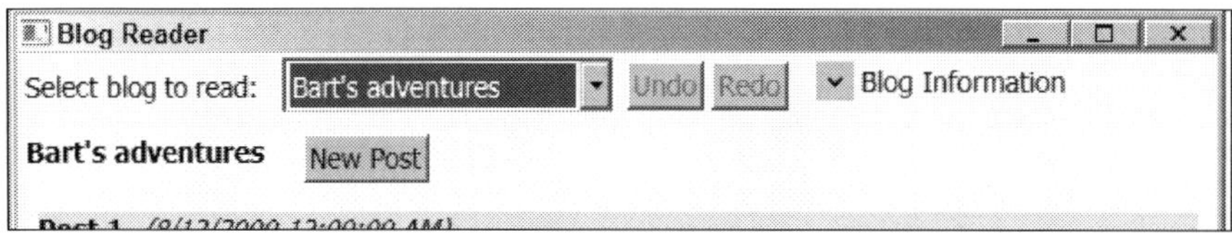

25. Click on **New Post** and type a title and some text for the post; then click on **OK**:

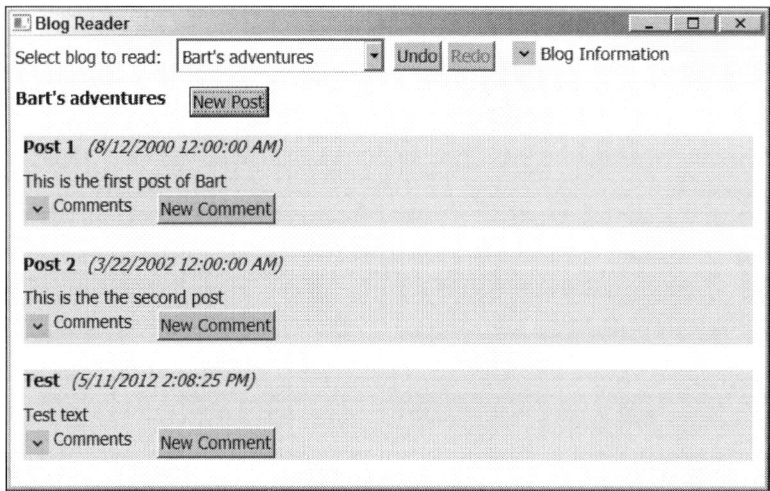

26. The **Undo** button is enabled. Click on **Undo** and watch the post disappear. Click on **Redo** and the post returns.

How it works...

WPF does not provide any out-of-the-box functionality as it is related to undo/redo. The `ICommand` interface is not enough – this is why we created the `IUndoCommand` that adds an `Undo` method. The regular `Execute` is the "Redo" method, as it naturally complements `Undo`.

The classic "command pattern" is typically implemented using a class for each unique command. We used the `RelayCommand` class to implement a command generically by supplying delegates as implementations for `Execute` and `CanExecute`. This works up to a point. When dealing with undo/redo, a state must be maintained, so using `RelayCommand` is not enough in most cases.

The `NewBlogPostCommand` class created in step 18 is a standalone command, which has all the information it needs to do its job and to undo it. It holds the relevant blog and the blog post to add or remove, provided (one time only) by the command parameter, and saved by the command for later invocations of `Undo` or `Execute` (Redo).

Managing commands in undo/redo lists is the responsibility of the `UndoManager` class. It holds an undo list and a redo list, managing their dependencies as commands are added, undone, or redone. Notice how easy it is to create an undo limit, which may be required if objects are large and memory footprint should be constrained; for small objects, leaving the undo limit as unbounded is probably acceptable.

The placement of an `UndoManager` instance is important. In our example, it was placed in `MainVM` and used by sub-ViewModels, such as `BlogVM`; this means that switching blogs and clicking on **Undo** would undo the last operation in the blog where that post was created. If, however, each `BlogVM` had its own `UndoManager`, then switching between blogs would not allow undoing commands executed within another blog. This is something that needs consideration when using an undo/redo system – the operations' scope.

`ReversibleCommand` is a helper class that communicates with the passed in `UndoManager` and adds the command to the undo list (by calling `UndoManager.AddCommand`).

8
Styles, Triggers, and Control Templates

In this chapter we will cover the following:

- Creating and using styles
- Applying a style automatically
- Creating a property trigger
- Using data triggers
- Creating an event trigger
- Creating a multi trigger
- Using behaviors
- Replacing the control template of a progress bar
- Replacing the control template of a scroll bar
- Customizing selection in a Selector control

Introduction

Consistency in a user interface is an important trait; there are many facets of consistency, one of which is the consistent look and feel of controls. For example, all buttons should look roughly the same – similar colors, the same margins, and so on.

Styles are objects that hold property setters to provide a way to apply a bunch of settings as a group to elements and controls. Control templates provide the ultimate control customization power, allowing the complete replacing of a control's look and feel without affecting its behavior. This is one of the most famous of WPF's traits, very different from the old Win32/WinForms model where looks and behavior were tightly bundled; any customization required code that subclassed/inherited from the base control and provides the appropriate painting logic. In the WPF world, a control template is created entirely in XAML with no code required; designer oriented tools such as Expression Blend make this even easier – and more productive in the hands of true designers.

In this chapter, we'll take a look at styles, triggers, control templates, their relationships, and typical scenarios where they are applied.

Creating and using styles

Styles provide a convenient way to group a set of properties (and triggers) under a single object, and then selectively (or automatically as we'll see later) apply it to elements. In this recipe, we'll create some styles and apply them to elements to show how useful these are in any application.

Getting ready

Make sure Visual Studio is up and running.

How to do it...

We'll create a calculator-like user interface and use styles to change its look:

1. Create a new WPF Application named `CH08.StyledCalculator`.
2. Open `MainWindow.xaml` and change the following `Window` properties:

   ```
   Title="Styled Calculator" SizeToContent="WidthAndHeight"
   ResizeMode="CanMinimize"
   ```

3. Add four columns and five rows to the existing `Grid`, all with auto sizing:

   ```
   <Grid.ColumnDefinitions>
       <ColumnDefinition Width="Auto" />
       <ColumnDefinition Width="Auto" />
       <ColumnDefinition Width="Auto" />
       <ColumnDefinition Width="Auto" />
   </Grid.ColumnDefinitions>
   <Grid.RowDefinitions>
       <RowDefinition Height="Auto" />
       <RowDefinition Height="Auto" />
   ```

```
        <RowDefinition Height="Auto" />
        <RowDefinition Height="Auto" />
        <RowDefinition Height="Auto" />
    </Grid.RowDefinitions>
```

4. Add the following controls to the `Grid`:

```
<TextBox Background="Cyan" IsReadOnly="True"
    Grid.ColumnSpan="4"/>
<Button Content="7" Grid.Row="1"/>
<Button Content="8" Grid.Row="1" Grid.Column="1"/>
<Button Content="9" Grid.Row="1" Grid.Column="2"/>
<Button Content="4" Grid.Row="2"/>
<Button Content="5" Grid.Row="2" Grid.Column="1"/>
<Button Content="6" Grid.Row="2" Grid.Column="2"/>
<Button Content="1" Grid.Row="3"/>
<Button Content="2" Grid.Row="3" Grid.Column="1"/>
<Button Content="3" Grid.Row="3" Grid.Column="2"/>
<Button Content="0" Grid.Row="4"/>
<Button Content="=" Grid.Row="4" Grid.Column="1"
    Grid.ColumnSpan="2"/>
<Button Content="+" Grid.Row="4" Grid.Column="3"/>
<Button Content="-" Grid.Row="3" Grid.Column="3"/>
<Button Content="X" Grid.Row="2" Grid.Column="3"/>
<Button Content="/" Grid.Row="1" Grid.Column="3"/>
```

5. Looking at the XAML designer, the calculator UI looks something like the following screenshot:

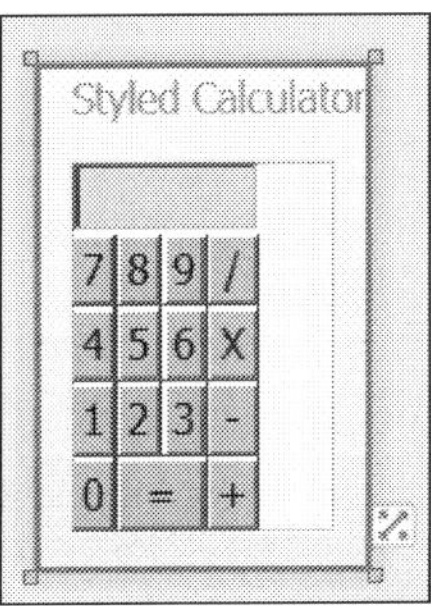

6. We'd like to get some margins for the buttons, change fonts, and so on. Let's create a style to be used for the "numeric" buttons. Add a `Style` object in the `Resources` property of the `Window` and set its `TargetType` property and give it a name:

```
<Window.Resources>
   <Style TargetType="Button" x:Key="numericStyle">
   </Style>
</Window.Resources>
```

7. Inside the `Style`, add the following `Setter` objects:

```
<Setter Property="FontSize" Value="20" />
<Setter Property="Margin" Value="4" />
<Setter Property="Padding" Value="6" />
<Setter Property="Effect">
    <Setter.Value>
        <DropShadowEffect Color="Blue"/>
    </Setter.Value>
</Setter>
```

8. This sets up some properties common to all buttons. To apply the style, we'll change the `Style` property for all numeric buttons. The following is an example of one such button:

```
<Button Content="7" Grid.Row="1"
    Style="{StaticResource numericStyle}"/>
```

9. Let's create another style that inherits from the first, to be used by operator buttons:

```
<Style TargetType="Button" x:Key="operatorStyle"
    BasedOn="{StaticResource numericStyle}">
    <Setter Property="FontWeight" Value="ExtraBold" />
    <Setter Property="Effect">
        <Setter.Value>
            <DropShadowEffect Color="Red" />
        </Setter.Value>
    </Setter>
</Style>
```

10. Let's apply this style to the operator buttons. Here's one of them:

```
<Button Content="+" Grid.Row="4" Grid.Column="3"
    Style="{StaticResource operatorStyle}"/>
```

11. Change the font size of the `TextBox` to `20`. The following screenshot shows how this looks in the designer right now:

12. We want the "=" operator to have a different drop shadow color, so we can change it for that button only. The complete markup is as follows:

```
<Button Content="=" Grid.Row="4" Grid.Column="1"
   Grid.ColumnSpan="2" Style="{StaticResource operatorStyle}">
   <Button.Effect>
      <DropShadowEffect Color="Green" />
   </Button.Effect>
</Button>
```

How it works...

A `Style` is a container for a bunch of `Setter` objects (and triggers, as we'll see later). Each setter indicates which property should have which value; the property must be a dependency property. The `FrameworkElement` class exposes a `Style` property that can be set to such a `Style` object. Styles are always built as resources, as any other way defeats the purpose of a style - that is, bundling a set of properties that can be applied to more than one element.

The `TargetType` property of a `Style` is typically set, which makes the `Style` applicable to that particular type (this can be any type, even a type of a custom control) and any derived types. In this example, these styles work on `Button` objects (and anything that inherits from `Button`). Trying to apply such `Style` to some other element type causes a runtime exception to be thrown.

An element that uses a style can change a property that is set explicitly by a `Style` (a local value), and this is stronger than a `Style` property setter. This is exactly what we did for the "=" operator; although it should have had a red drop shadow that was placed there by the `Style` it uses, it "overrides" the `Effect` property to have a different value (this is due to the dependency property priority system described in *Chapter 1, Foundations*).

There's more...

The `TargetType` property is not mandatory. The first `Style` could have been written as follows to get the same result:

```
<Style x:Key="numericStyle">
    <Setter Property="Button.FontSize" Value="20" />
    <Setter Property="Button.Margin" Value="4" />
    <Setter Property="Button.Padding" Value="6" />
    <Setter Property="Button.MinWidth" Value="40" />
    <Setter Property="Button.Effect">
        <Setter.Value>
            <DropShadowEffect Color="Blue"/>
        </Setter.Value>
    </Setter>
</Style>
```

The difference is the full property qualifications. Why would that be useful? With this `Style` defined, it can be used with any element, such as a `TextBox`. However, the `Style` would not have any effect on a `TextBox`, unless we write `Setter`(s) a bit differently. For example:

```
<Setter Property="Control.Effect">
    <Setter.Value>
        <DropShadowEffect Color="Blue"/>
    </Setter.Value>
</Setter>
```

This setting will work on anything deriving from `Control`, such as a `TextBox`. If the element does not support such a property, no exception is thrown. Practically speaking, using this capability is not recommended, as it's difficult to maintain these settings in complex styles. For example, we may want to change some property on a `TextBox` specifically and this would require adding a specific setting for a `TextBox` to the same style, but this could affect other `TextBox` controls in an unintended way. So, in practice, `TargetType` is always specified, even if this causes some `Setter` duplication. The up side is that if a change is needed for some specific element type, no other element type would be affected.

Style inheritance

Styles support the notion of inheritance, somewhat similar to the same concept in object orientation. This is done using the `BasedOn` property that must point to another `Style` to inherit from. If a `TargetType` is specified in the base `Style`, it must be specified by the derived `Style` as well (with the same type or a more derived type).

An inherited style can add `Setter` objects for new properties to set, or it can provide a different value for a property that was set by the base `Style`. In the code example, the second style (for operators) inherits from the first, adds a `FontWeight` setting, and changes the `Effect` property setting.

Style inheritance may seem very useful, but should be used with caution. It suffers from the same issues as object oriented inheritance in a deep inheritance hierarchy: a change in a base style up in the hierarchy can affect a lot of styles, being somewhat unpredictable, leading to a maintenance nightmare. Thus, a good rule of thumb to use is to have no more than two inheritance levels. Any more than that may cause things to get out of hand.

Other places to set styles

The example shows styles applied to the `FrameworkElement.Style` property, but this is not the only property that can accept a `Style`. Other examples include the following:

- `FrameworkElement.FocusVisualStyle` property: Accepts a `Style` that affects the way the focus indicator is rendered when that element has the keyboard focus.
- `ItemsControl.ItemContainerStyle` property: Accepts a `Style` that affects the container element of each data item (for example, `ListBoxItem` for a `ListBox`).

- DataGrid.CellStyle: Accepts a Style that affects the way a cell is rendered. Similar properties exposed by the DataGrid include ColumnHeaderStyle, DragIndicatorStyle, DropLocationIndicatorStyle, RowHeaderStyle, and RowStyle.

Some style keys are exposed by specific controls that use a Style with a specific key, which can be replaced seamlessly. For example, the MenuItem.SeparatorStyleKey static property is a resource key that if used, will be applied to separators in that MenuItem. Another example is the ToolBar, with static properties such as ButtonStyleKey, CheckBoxStyleKey, RadioButtonStyleKey, and MenuStyleKey.

Applying a style automatically

The previous recipe showed how to create styles that have a name (x:Key) and how to apply them. Sometimes, however, we would like a style to be applied automatically to all elements of a certain type, to give the application a consistent look. For example, we may want all buttons to have a font size of 14 by default (unless a specific button chooses a different value). This makes creating new buttons easier, as the developer/designer doesn't have to know what style to apply (if any) – if an automatic style has been configured it will be used automatically. Let's see how this is done.

Getting ready

Open the project CH08.StyledCalculator from the previous recipe. We'll modify it to use automatic styles. Alternatively, you can copy the project with a new folder and project name, so as not to disturb the previous project.

How to do it...

We'll modify the calculator to use automatic styles where possible, only using named styles where necessary:

1. We'd like to make the numeric button style the default for all buttons unless otherwise specified. Open MainWindow.xaml.
2. Remove all references to the numericStyle style in the buttons. For example, the 8 button's markup should look as follows:

   ```
   <Button Content="8" Grid.Row="1" Grid.Column="1" />
   ```

3. Cut the numericStyle Style and paste it in the resources section of App.xaml and remove its x:Key attribute. This applies the Style automatically to all buttons (I added a MinWidth setting):

   ```
   <Application.Resources>
       <Style TargetType="Button">
   ```

```
            <Setter Property="FontSize" Value="20" />
            <Setter Property="Margin" Value="4" />
            <Setter Property="Padding" Value="6" />
            <Setter Property="MinWidth" Value="40" />
            <Setter Property="Effect">
                <Setter.Value>
                    <DropShadowEffect Color="Blue"/>
                </Setter.Value>
            </Setter>
        </Style>
    </Application.Resources>
```

4. Open `MainWindow.xaml`. The `operatorStyle` now fails to find its base `Style`. Change the `BasedOn` property to point to the automatic style in `App.xaml`:

```
<Style TargetType="Button" x:Key="operatorStyle"
    BasedOn="{StaticResource {x:Type Button}}">
```

5. Run the application. The calculator UI should look as it did before:

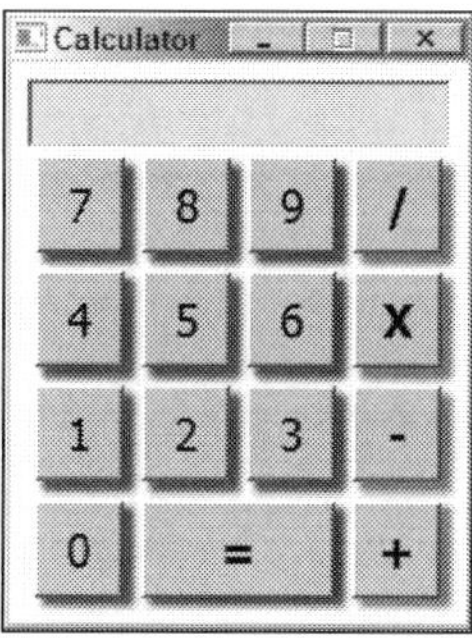

How it works...

Automatic styles are created as resources without a key. This does not mean there is no key, because it's still a dictionary. The key becomes the actual type to apply the style to defined by the `TargetType` property (this also means `TargetType` is mandatory with automatic styles). We've seen a similar approach with `DataTemplate`s that have a `DataType` property and no key.

This is typically set in the application's resources so it can affect all windows in the application. The `Style` is applied to all elements of the target type, but not derived types. Any element that does not set its style explicitly obtains that style automatically. If an element wishes to revert to its default style, it can set its `Style` property to `null` (`{x:Null}` in XAML) or set its `Style` to another named style.

The `operatorStyle` in the example derives from the automatic style and this is specified by looking up a resource with the key of `typeof(Button)`, expressed in XAML as `{x:Type Button}`.

There's more...

Automatic styles are a great way to create a consistent look and feel without burdening the developer (or the designer) with the details of the various visual properties. It can also be used as a quick way to implement skinning.

A classic example of skinning (sometimes referred to as theming, although themes usually mean the look and feel provided by the operating system as opposed to an application) is Microsoft Word 2007 and up, which support a "Color Scheme" setting in the screenshot:

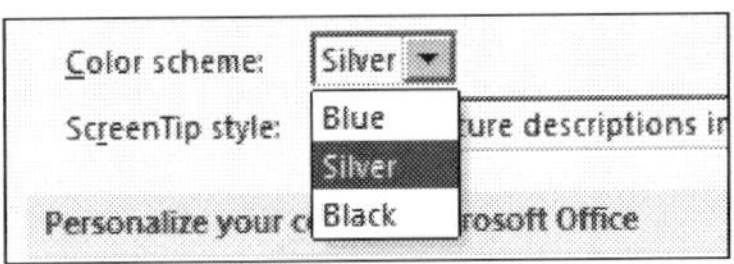

Selecting a scheme changes the look immediately. We can do the same in WPF by defining separate resource dictionaries with automatic styles for all the controls we're interested in. For example, here's a simple `ResourceDictionary` that sets some styles for `TextBox` and `Button` controls (the default XML namespace mappings are omitted for brevity):

```
<ResourceDictionary
    <Style TargetType="TextBox">
        <Setter Property="Background" Value="LightBlue" />
        <Setter Property="Foreground" Value="Black" />
        <Setter Property="BorderThickness" Value="2" />
        <Setter Property="BorderBrush" Value="DarkBlue" />
        <Style.Triggers>
            <Trigger Property="IsReadOnly" Value="True">
                <Setter Property="Background" Value="Blue" />
            </Trigger>
        </Style.Triggers>
    </Style>
    <Style TargetType="Button">
        <Setter Property="Background" Value="Cyan" />
    </Style>
</ResourceDictionary>
```

This markup includes a simple trigger (discussed in later recipes) that provides an alternative background brush for read-only `TextBox` controls.

We can create several of those ("skins") with different settings. The following simple application uses three different skins:

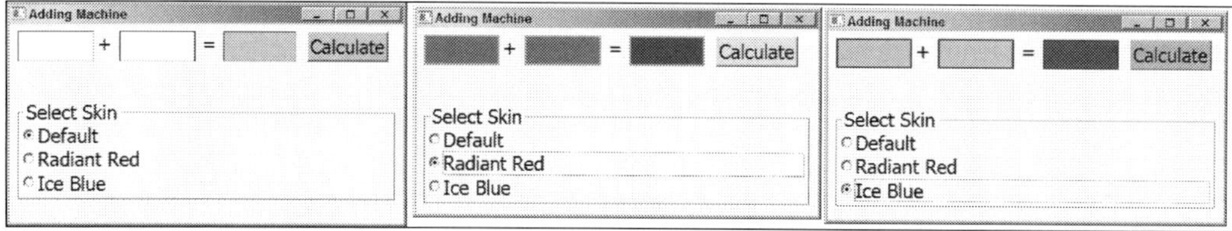

The different skins were placed in a project folder, but their **Build Action** property setting was set to **Content** and **Copy to Output Directory** set to **Copy if newer**:

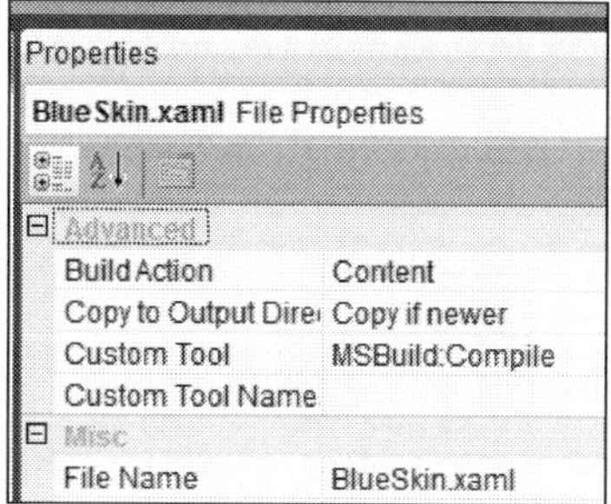

These settings prevent the default compilation to BAML and also provide the flexibility to change the skins without recompilation. To do the actual switch, a helper method is used:

```
void ChangeSkin(string skinRelativeUri) {
   var si = Application.GetContentStream(new Uri(
      skinRelativeUri, UriKind.Relative));
   var rd = (ResourceDictionary)XamlReader.Load(si.Stream);
   Application.Current.Resources.MergedDictionaries.Clear();
   Application.Current.Resources.MergedDictionaries.Add(rd);
}
```

This method extracts the specified skin, loads its XAML, clears all application's `MergedDictionaries` collection, and adds the newly loaded one. Of course, clearing the collection may be too disruptive (there may be other general purpose dictionaries lurking inside), so we can just replace the specific dictionary index. The complete source is available in the `CH08.SkinningDemo` project.

Creating a property trigger

So far we've used styles that have a collection of setters. A `Style` also has a `Triggers` collection property that provides a declarative way to make some property changes without a need for actual code. As such triggers are part of a style, they are naturally applied to more than one element. There are three types of triggers supported by WPF, and in this recipe we'll examine the simplest one - the property trigger.

Getting ready

Open the `CH08.StyledCalculator` project.

How to do it...

We'll add an effect when clicking a button in the calculator project using a property trigger:

1. We want to add a trigger to one of the styles we created in an earlier recipe. Open `MainWindow.xaml` and look for the style with the key `numericStyle`.
2. Add a `Triggers` property inside the style:

```
<Style.Triggers>
</Style.Triggers>
```

3. Add a property trigger inside the style (after the setters, before the closing style tag). The trigger will be invoked when the `IsPressed` property is changed to `true`:

```
<Trigger Property="IsPressed" Value="True">
</Trigger>
```

4. If the button is clicked, we want some of its properties changed. This is done with setters, placed inside the trigger:

```
<Setter Property="Effect" Value="{x:Null}" />
<Setter Property="RenderTransform">
    <Setter.Value>
        <TranslateTransform X="4" Y="4" />
    </Setter.Value>
</Setter>
```

5. We remove the effect and move the button slightly to the right and down, if the button is clicked.

6. Run the application and press some buttons. Notice the change in appearance (the digit **6** in the following screenshot):

How it works...

A trigger contains a condition to be checked and a set of actions to execute if that condition is satisfied. The trigger in this example is the poorly named `Trigger` class, which is a property trigger, meaning it compares a dependency property to a specific value; if they are equal, a set of actions can execute. In the code sample, these are `Setter` objects (the same ones used by a `Style`), which change properties on the styled element.

When the condition becomes false, the setters are logically removed, reverting the properties to their previous values. This means that it's unnecessary to provide an "opposite" trigger (and problematic in the general case because only the "equals" operator is supported by triggers).

There's more...

Another set of actions available for triggers involve animations. These are provided by the `EnterActions` and `ExitActions` properties of triggers (inherited from the base `TriggerBase` class).

Suppose we want to create some animation for the operator buttons of the calculator when the mouse pointer hovers over such a button. We can add a property trigger to the operator button `Style`. First, we'll add some default setters. The following is the basic `Style`:

```
<Style TargetType="Button" x:Key="operatorStyle"
    BasedOn="{StaticResource numericStyle}"  >
    <Setter Property="FontWeight" Value="ExtraBold" />
    <Setter Property="Effect">
        <Setter.Value>
            <DropShadowEffect Color="Red" />
        </Setter.Value>
```

```
    </Setter>
    <Setter Property="RenderTransformOrigin" Value=".5,.5" />
    <Setter Property="RenderTransform">
        <Setter.Value>
            <ScaleTransform ScaleX="1" ScaleY="1"/>
        </Setter.Value>
    </Setter>
```

Now let's add the property trigger itself. When it's triggered, we'll set the `Panel.ZIndex` property to a large value to make sure the button is on top of all others:

```
<Style.Triggers>
    <Trigger Property="IsMouseOver" Value="True">
        <Setter Property="Panel.ZIndex" Value="100" />
```

Next, we'll start animations when the trigger fires via the `EnterActions` property:

```
<Trigger.EnterActions>
   <BeginStoryboard>
      <Storyboard >
         <DoubleAnimation To="1.3" Duration="0:0:0.3"
       Storyboard.TargetProperty="RenderTransform.ScaleX" />
         <DoubleAnimation To="1.3" Duration="0:0:0.3"
       Storyboard.TargetProperty="RenderTransform.ScaleY" />
      </Storyboard>
   </BeginStoryboard>
</Trigger.EnterActions>
```

We'll discuss animations in the next chapter; in essence, an action that starts an animation (`BeginAnimation`) is used to start an animation timeline (`Stroyboard`) containing two property based animations, each working on the `ScaleTransform` object within the `RenderTransform` property of the button, going to 1.3 over 300 milliseconds.

When the mouse leaves the button, we want to reverse the animation by using the `ExitActions` property:

```
<Trigger.ExitActions>
   <BeginStoryboard>
      <Storyboard >
         <DoubleAnimation Duration="0:0:0.1"
      Storyboard.TargetProperty="RenderTransform.ScaleX" />
         <DoubleAnimation Duration="0:0:0.1"
      Storyboard.TargetProperty="RenderTransform.ScaleY" />
      </Storyboard>
   </BeginStoryboard>
</Trigger.ExitActions>
```

The following screenshot shows how it looks when the mouse hovers over the multiplication operator:

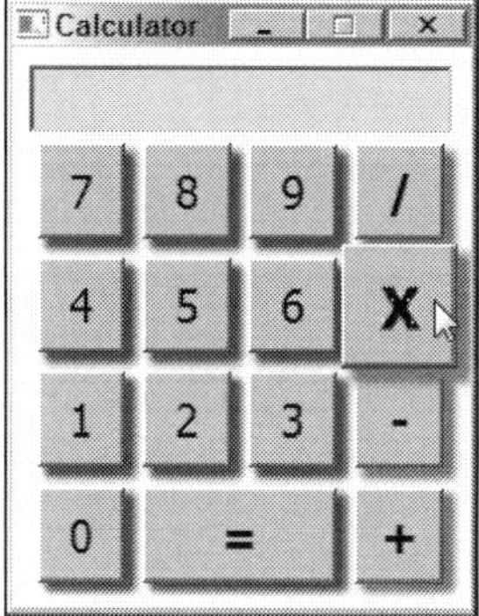

Trigger limitations

Property triggers and data triggers (discussed in the next recipe) suffer from one serious limitation: the comparison of the property to the value is an equality comparison only. There is no way to check for (for example) greater than, less than, not equal, and so on.

Furthermore, all triggers suffer from two other limitations:

- Custom triggers cannot be created. At first, it may seem that to create a custom trigger type, you just need to derive a class from `TriggerBase` and override a method. However, this doesn't work, because the constructor of `TriggerBase` is declared as internal, so cannot be used outside the declaring WPF assembly.
- Custom actions cannot be created either; again, the obvious thing to do is inherit from `TriggerAction`, the base class of all existing actions (such as `BeginStoryboard`), but this cannot be done because its constructor is internal, and it has two abstract methods (named `Invoke`) that are internal as well, so cannot be overridden outside the declaring assembly.

These last two points mean that the trigger mechanism of WPF cannot be extended directly – not with new triggers and not with new actions. This is certainly a shame, and led to other triggers and actions being defined by the Expression Blend tool (technically, it's SDK) that can be used instead, or in conjunction with the native WPF trigger. We'll see how to use those in the *Using behaviors* recipe later in this chapter.

When to use triggers

It's important to note that triggers are useful for changing appearance in various ways; they are not meant to be used as part of an application's logic. In ideal scenarios, a developer should not know anything about triggers that may or may not be used. This is the job of the UI designer (typically working with a designer oriented tool, such as Expression Blend).

Other locations of triggers

A `Style` is not the only object that contains a `Triggers` property. There are three other such properties found in WPF:

- `DataTemplate.Triggers`: A `DataTemplate` can have triggers, as is demonstrated in the next recipe, *Using data triggers* (these can be any triggers, not just data triggers).
- `ControlTemplate.Triggers`: A `ControlTemplate` can have triggers as well, as we'll see in the recipe *Replacing the control template of a progress bar*, later in this chapter.
- `FrameworkElement.Triggers`: An element can host triggers as well, but these are limited to `EventTrigger` objects only. This limitation is a bit artificial, but in practice, using triggers on some specific element is rare. It's much more common to use triggers to tweak the behavior of many elements, through a `Style`, `DataTemplate`, or `ControlTemplate`.

Trigger priorities

Several triggers may be present within a style (or a template), which may overlap. For example, two property triggers may want to set the background of an element to different brushes; both triggers may be triggered (they check different properties). In such cases, the later appearing trigger (in the markup) wins out.

This means that the order of triggers may be important. For example, styling a button may involve checking if it's being hovered over by the mouse, and if so, making a change to its background brush. If, however, the button is disabled (`IsEnabled = false`), it should have a different background, regardless of the hovering state. This means that the `IsEnabled` trigger should be placed after the `IsMouseOver` trigger, so it could win in case both triggers fire.

See also

For discussion of data triggers, see the next recipe, *Using data triggers*. For discussion of other trigger actions, see the recipe *Creating an event trigger*, later in this chapter.

Using data triggers

Property triggers work with dependency properties only, but what about regular properties? This is where data triggers come in. They are able to inspect any property, but their usefulness lies within data templates that naturally bind to data objects (which utilize non-dependency properties). Let's see how to set that up.

Getting ready

Make sure Visual Studio is up and running.

How to do it...

We'll create a simple application to show books with a `DataTemplate` that is customized with data triggers to show some books a bit differently:

1. Create a new WPF application named `CH08.DataTriggerDemo`.
2. Add a new class to the project named `Book` and implement it as follows:

```
class Book {
   public string BookName { get; set; }
   public string AuthorName { get; set; }
   public bool IsFree { get; set; }
}
```

3. Open `MainWindow.xaml`. Add a `ListBox` to the existing `Grid` and set a few properties:

```
<ListBox HorizontalContentAlignment="Stretch"
    ItemsSource="{Binding}">
```

4. We'll create a `DataTemplate` that shows a `Book` instance. Set a `DataTemplate` to the `ListBox.ItemTemplate` property with some markup that binds to the properties of a `Book`:

```
<DataTemplate>
    <Border Margin="2" BorderBrush="Blue" BorderThickness="1"
        Padding="2" x:Name="_border">
        <Grid>
            <Grid.RowDefinitions>
                <RowDefinition Height="Auto" />
                <RowDefinition Height="Auto" />
            </Grid.RowDefinitions>
            <TextBlock Text="{Binding BookName}" FontSize="20"
                 FontWeight="Bold" />
           <TextBlock Grid.Row="1" Text="{Binding AuthorName}"
                 FontSize="16" Foreground="Blue" />
            <TextBlock Opacity=".5" FontWeight="Bold"
                FontStyle="Italic" Foreground="Red"
                TextAlignment="Right" Grid.RowSpan="2"
               VerticalAlignment="Center" Visibility="Hidden"
                x:Name="_free" Text="Free!"
```

```
                Margin="4" FontSize="25"/>
        </Grid>
    </Border>
</DataTemplate>
```

5. Note that the last `TextBlock` is not visible. We'll show it when a trigger fires later on.
6. Open `MainWindow.xaml.cs`. In the constructor, create a few books and set them as the `DataContext`:

```
DataContext = new List<Book> {
   new Book { BookName = "Windows Internals",
       AuthorName = "Mark Russinovich", IsFree = false },
   new Book { BookName = "AJAX Introduction",
       AuthorName = "Bhanwar Gupta", IsFree = true },
   new Book { BookName = "Essential COM",
       AuthorName = "Don Box", IsFree = false },
   new Book {
       BookName = "Blueprint for a Successful Presentation",
       AuthorName = "Biswajit Tripathy", IsFree = true }
};
```

7. Run the application. You should see the books displayed with the supplied data template:

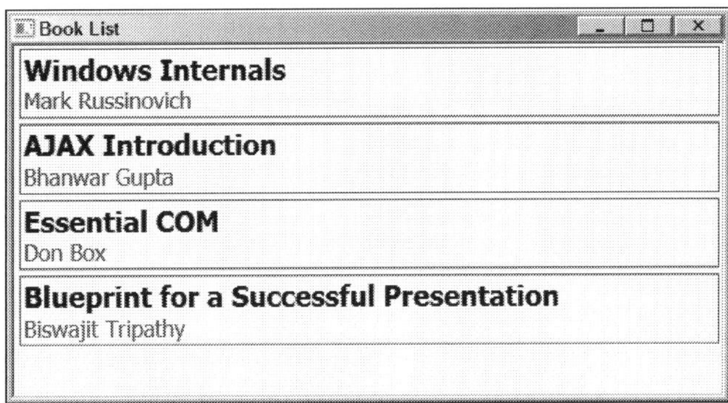

8. We want the display of a book to change if that book is free. Add a `Triggers` property to `DataTemplate`:

```
<DataTemplate.Triggers>
</DataTemplate.Triggers>
```

9. Add a `DataTrigger` object that fires when `Book.IsFree` is `true`, making the hidden `TextBlock` appear and changing the background brush of the `Border` element:

```
<DataTrigger Binding="{Binding IsFree}" Value="True">
    <Setter Property="Background" TargetName="_border"
        Value="Yellow" />
    <Setter Property="Visibility" Value="Visible"
        TargetName="_free" />

</DataTrigger>
```

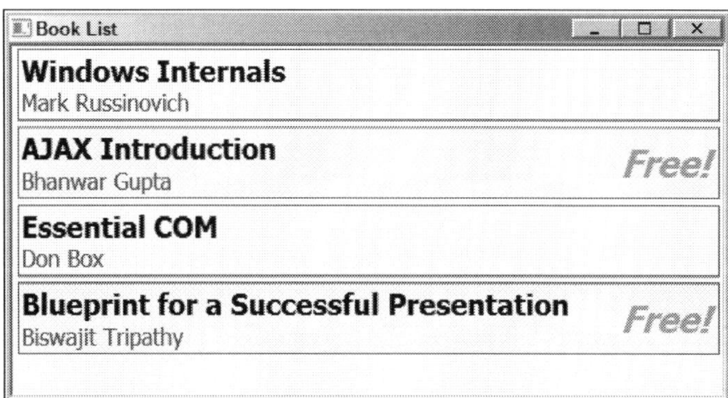

How it works...

Data triggers find their property via the `Binding` property, which should be a binding expression. In our case, it's bound to the `IsFree` property of the current `Book`. Similar to a property trigger, it tests equality with a value (`true`, in this case) and if equal, executes a bunch of actions, based on `Setter` objects (it can also use the `EnterActions` and `ExitActions` properties to manipulate animations).

Notice that the setters can use the `TargetName` property (which cannot be used in a style trigger) to change a property on a particular element in the data template's markup.

Creating an event trigger

We've seen property triggers and data triggers. Both triggers are based on comparing a property to a value. The third type of supported trigger is an event trigger. This trigger type fires when a routed event occurs, executing animation-related actions. Let's see how to configure an event trigger.

Getting ready

Open the `CH08.StyledCalculator` project.

How to do it...

We'll continue with the calculator sample by making the UI come into view with an animation set up by an event trigger:

1. We want the calculator UI to start from a zero size and reach its full size using an animation when the application starts. Open `MainWindow.xaml`.
2. Add a starting point for the animation with a transformation properties to the main `Grid` as follows:

```
<Grid Margin="8" RenderTransformOrigin=".5,.5">
    <Grid.RenderTransform>
        <ScaleTransform ScaleX="0" ScaleY="0" />
    </Grid.RenderTransform>
```

3. We'll use an event trigger to start the animation when the grid loads (the `Loaded` routed event):

```
<Grid.Triggers>
    <EventTrigger RoutedEvent="Loaded">
        <BeginStoryboard>
            <Storyboard>
                <DoubleAnimation To="1" Duration="0:0:.8"
        Storyboard.TargetProperty="RenderTransform.ScaleX" />
                <DoubleAnimation To="1" Duration="0:0:.8"
        Storyboard.TargetProperty="RenderTransform.ScaleY" />
            </Storyboard>
        </BeginStoryboard>
    </EventTrigger>
</Grid.Triggers>
```

4. The code starts two simultaneous animations that scale the `Grid` from 0 to 1 (normal size). Run the application and watch the calculator pop into view.

How it works...

An event trigger can be used with routed events only, providing a set of actions that execute when that event occurs. These actions inherit from the `TriggerAction` abstract base class with several concrete implementations, most of them targeting a `Storyboard` object (representing an animation time line), as in the code example (`BeginStoryboard` action). Apart from animations, there is a `System.Windows.Controls.SoundPlayerAction` class used to play WAV audio files (by setting its `Source` property).

As mentioned previously, `TriggerAction` has internal constructors only, so the list of supported actions cannot be extended. A possible solution is to use behaviors, as discussed in a later recipe, *Using behaviors*.

There's more...

There seems to be an overlap of the functionality provided by property triggers and event triggers. For example, the `IsMouseOver` property seems to add no real value that is gained by using the `MouseEnter` and `MouseLeave` routed events.

The problem is that event triggers can only execute actions based on `TriggerAction` objects – they cannot use setters to change property values. Property triggers, on the other hand, support using setters, and can also use `TriggerActions` with the `EnterActions` and `ExitActions` properties. This means that a property trigger that seemingly gives out the same information as a routed event is actually opening up the possibility of using setters, something that's not possible with `TriggerActions` objects.

Creating a multi trigger

An active trigger can execute actions, but sometimes a trigger needs to be composed of multiple conditions that activate the entire trigger if all conditions are met. This is exactly what the `MultiTrigger` and `MultiDataTrigger` types are capable of. Let's see how to create a `MultiTrigger`.

Getting ready

Make sure Visual Studio is up and running.

How to do it...

We'll create a simple application that changes the way a button appears by using multiple properties set up inside a `MultiTrigger`:

1. Create a new WPF application named `CH08.MultiTriggerDemo`.
2. Open `MainWindow.xaml`. Replace the existing `Grid` with a `StackPanel`.
3. Add the following controls inside the `StackPanel`:

```
<Button Content="Move mouse over me" FontSize="20"
    HorizontalAlignment="Center" Margin="20" Padding="6"
    x:Name="theButton" />
<CheckBox Content="Default button" Margin="10"
    IsChecked="{Binding IsDefault, ElementName=theButton,
       Mode=TwoWay}" FontSize="15"/>
```

4. Add a `Resources` property to the `Window`.
5. Add a `Style` object targeting buttons with a key of `hoverStyle`.
6. Add the following trigger to the `Triggers` collection of the `Style`:

```
<MultiTrigger>
    <MultiTrigger.Conditions>
        <Condition Property="IsMouseOver" Value="True" />
        <Condition Property="IsDefault" Value="True" />
    </MultiTrigger.Conditions>
    <Setter Property="Background" Value="Cyan" />
    <Setter Property="Effect">
        <Setter.Value>
            <DropShadowEffect />
        </Setter.Value>
    </Setter>
</MultiTrigger>
```

7. Run the application. Hover with the mouse over the button when the checkbox is unchecked; nothing should happen. Now check the checkbox (making the button the default button) and hover over the button again. It should change background and have a drop shadow:

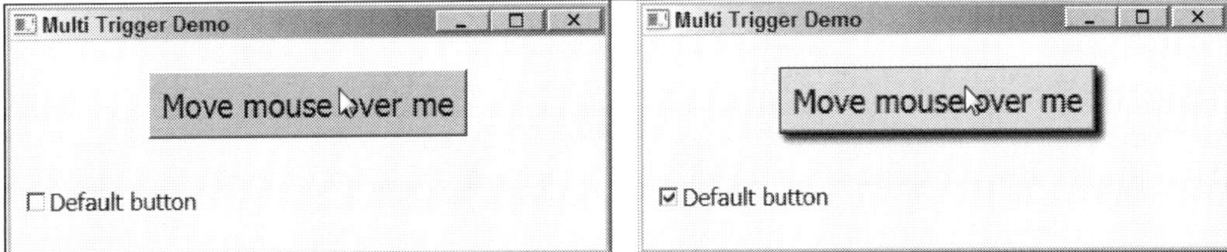

How it works...

A `MultiTrigger` object hosts a collection of `Condition` objects (in its `Conditions` property), each of which indicates the (dependency) `Property` and `Value` to check for. If all conditions are satisfied, the entire trigger fires - any `Setters` execute (`EnterActions` and `ExitActions` exist as well, as they do for a regular property trigger).

In the code sample, the `Button`'s `IsDefault` and `IsMouseOver` properties are used as conditions. Only when both are true, does the trigger fire.

There's more...

Similarly to a `MultiTrigger`, a `MultiDataTrigger` class exists, hosting multiple `DataTrigger` objects exposed as a collection of `Condition` objects (the same as for `MultiTrigger`), but this time the `Binding` property must be set (using a binding expression as used by a `DataTrigger`) as well as the `Value` property to compare with.

Curiously enough, these types of multi triggers cannot be combined. That is, a `MultiTrigger` can only contain property triggers, and a `MultiDataTrigger` can only contain data triggers. Event triggers are unsupported as multiple triggers go.

What about an OR style operator (instead of AND)? There's no explicit support for that; we can, however, create separate triggers with the same set of actions to execute to simulate an OR type multi trigger.

Using behaviors

Triggers have inherent limitations; new trigger types cannot be created, nor new trigger actions. These decisions made by the WPF designers are somewhat arbitrary, as there may be useful triggers and actions that could have been created by developers. It may be somewhat justified, however, preventing abuse of this feature that may degrade performance (for heavy duty triggers or actions). Still, abuse is possible almost everywhere that software exists.

Whether this decision is justified or not is a matter of opinion; it is a fact nonetheless.

A possible solution to the extensibility problem is to write a similar open-ended mechanism and expose it through attached properties. This is exactly what was done by the Expression Blend team that wanted to expose new trigger and action types to be provided as a reusable library. They created a trigger/action mechanism that is packaged as two assemblies, one of which provides the core capabilities, and the other providing a set of built-in triggers and actions. A trigger and a set of actions can be logically grouped together, known as behaviors.

In this recipe, we'll see how to use Expression Blend's support for behaviors from within Expression Blend and from Visual Studio, leading to new opportunities for XAML use and reuse.

Getting ready

Make sure Visual Studio and Expression Blend are up and running.

How to do it...

We'll create a simple circle that may be moved across a `Canvas` without using event handling code; instead we'll use a behavior:

1. Switch Visual Studio. Create a new WPF application named `CH08.MovingCircle`.
2. Open `MainWindow.xaml`. Change the existing `Grid` to a `Canvas`.
3. Add the following `Ellipse` to the `Canvas`:

```
<Ellipse Width="50" Height="50" Fill="Red" Stroke="Black"
    StrokeThickness="2" />
```

4. Switch to Expression Blend. Open the existing project (or solution) using the **File | Open Project/Solution** menu item:

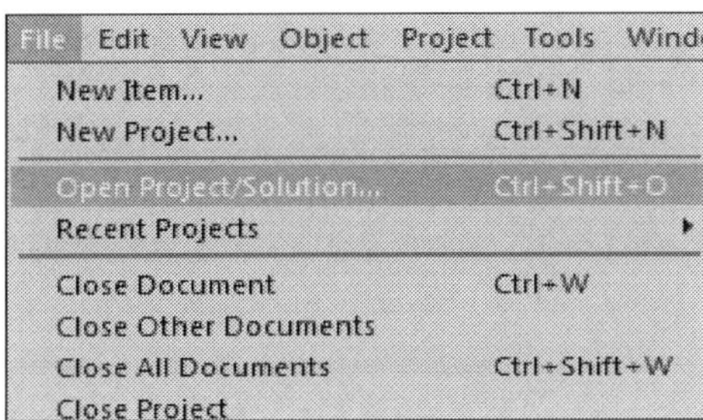

5. Make sure the **Projects** tab is selected. Open `MainWindow.xaml`. The file should be shown within the main (designer) view of Blend.
6. Select the **Assets** tab and click on **Behaviors**:

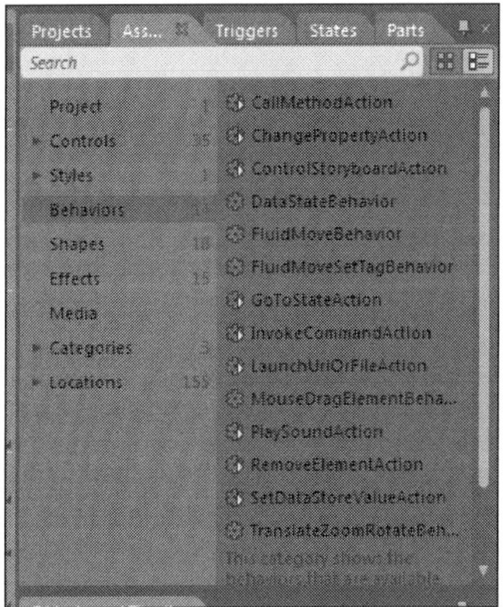

7. Hold and drag the **MouseDragElementBehavior** behavior over the circle in the designer:

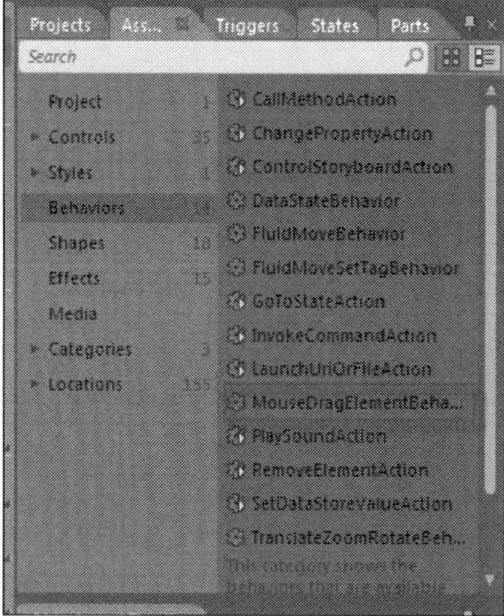

8. Press *F5* to build and run the application from within Blend. You can now drag the circle around.
9. Switch back to Visual Studio and accept its offer to reload changes.

How it works...

Dragging the behavior in Blend did several things. First, it added two references to the Blend SDK assemblies that provide the generic support (`System.Windows.Interactivity`) and the behaviors library (`Microsoft.Expression.Interactions`).

Second, it mapped two XAML namespaces pointing at those two assemblies (look at `MainWindow.xaml`):

```
xmlns:i="http://schemas.microsoft.com/expression/2010/interactivity"
xmlns:ei="http://schemas.microsoft.com/expression/2010/interactions"
```

Third, it added the actual behavior to the required element (within an `Interaction.Behaviors` attached property):

```
<Ellipse Width="50" Height="50" Fill="Red" Stroke="Black"
    StrokeThickness="2">
    <i:Interaction.Behaviors>
        <ei:MouseDragElementBehavior/>
    </i:Interaction.Behaviors>
</Ellipse>
```

Other behaviors can be added to the same element in a similar manner.

There's more...

Expression Blend itself is not required to get the support for behaviors, as the two required assemblies are part of the Blend SDK, and can be downloaded from Microsoft independently of Blend. Using the actual Blend tool simplifies adding the assembly references themselves and the XAML mappings; these can be added in the usual way from within Visual Studio (albeit without the drag-and-drop experience).

Custom behaviors

Behaviors are classes that inherit from `Behavior<T>`, where `T` is the minimal element type that can be used as a target for the behavior. The `AssociatedObject` property provides the actual object on which the behavior operates. The `OnAttached` and `OnDetaching` methods should be overridden to provide a way to connect to the object in question so that the behavior can actually do something. The following is an example of a simple behavior that opens a process when the element is clicked:

```
class RunProcessBehavior : Behavior<FrameworkElement> {
   public string Program { get; set; }
   public string Arguments { get; set; }
   protected override void OnAttached() {
      AssociatedObject.MouseLeftButtonUp += OnMouseClick;
   }

   void OnMouseClick(object sender, RoutedEventArgs e) {
      Process.Start(Program, Arguments);
   }

   protected override void OnDetaching() {
      AssociatedObject.MouseLeftButtonUp -= OnMouseClick;
   }
}
```

`OnAttached` is used to register for the appropriate event and `OnDetaching` unregisters to keep things clean and avoid leaks. Two custom properties have been added so that the behavior can be customized. The following is an an example usage of an `Rectangle` object:

```
<Rectangle Fill="Yellow" Width="100" Height="50"
    Canvas.Top="100" Stroke="Black">
    <i:Interaction.Behaviors>
        <local:RunProcessBehavior Program="Notepad" />
    </i:Interaction.Behaviors>
</Rectangle>
```

Clicking the `Rectangle` (in this example) launches `notepad.exe`.

The `Program` and `Arguments` properties can be turned into dependency properties, so that they can be targets for data binding, which is very useful in practice.

Replacing the control template of a progress bar

WPF prides itself on separating appearance from behavior. This is more evident with control templates than anything else. A control template is just that: a template for a control's appearance, which does not affect its behavior. In this recipe, we'll take a look at the basics of writing a control template by creating a custom template for a `ProgressBar` control. In later recipes we'll discuss other, more complex control templates.

Getting ready

Make sure Visual Studio is up and running.

How to do it...

We'll create an alternative control template for a `ProgressBar` to demonstrate the basics of control template authoring:

1. Create a new WPF application named `CH08.CustomProgressBar`.
2. Open `App.xaml`. Add a new resource of type `ControlTemplate` as follows:

```
<ControlTemplate TargetType="ProgressBar" x:Key="pt1">
</ControlTemplate>
```

3. Inside the `ControlTemplate` add the following markup:

```
<Grid>
    <Rectangle x:Name="PART_Track">
        <Rectangle.Fill>
            <LinearGradientBrush EndPoint="1,0">
                <GradientStop Color="DarkBlue" Offset="0" />
                <GradientStop Color="LightBlue" Offset="1" />
            </LinearGradientBrush>
        </Rectangle.Fill>
    </Rectangle>
    <Rectangle x:Name="PART_Indicator" Fill="Orange"
        Stroke="Black" StrokeThickness="1"
        HorizontalAlignment="Left" />
</Grid>
```

4. Open `MainWindow.xaml`. Change the existing `Grid` into a `StackPanel`.
5. Add a `ProgressBar` control to the `StackPanel` that uses the previous template:

```
<ProgressBar Height="30" Value="60" Margin="20"
    Template="{StaticResource pt1}" x:Name="pb1" />
```

6. Add another `ProgressBar` that does not use the new template:

```
<ProgressBar Height="30" Value="60" Margin="20" />
```

7. Run the application and note the differences between the new look and the default look (the default look depends on the current Windows theme):

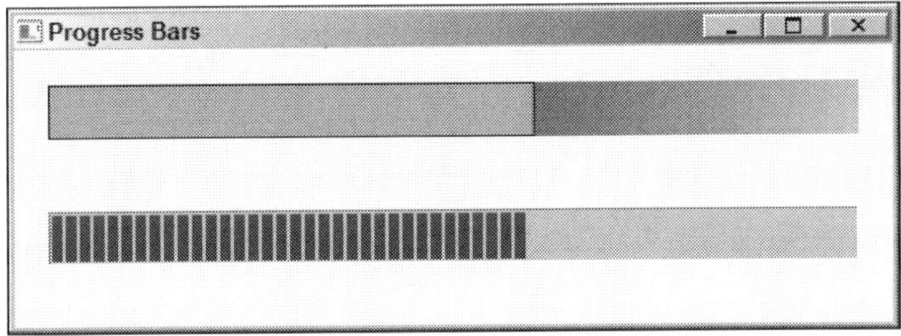

8. Open `MainWindow.xaml`. Add a checkbox that binds to the `IsIntermediate` property of the first progress bar:

```
<CheckBox Content="Indeterminate" FontSize="16" Margin="4"
    IsChecked="{Binding IsIndeterminate, ElementName=pb1}" />
```

9. Run the application and check the checkbox. The progress bar doesn't look too interesting. Let's add a trigger to make it a bit more interesting. Open `App.xaml`.
10. Add a `Triggers` property to the `ControlTemplate` with a property trigger for the `IsIndeterminate` property:

```
<ControlTemplate.Triggers>
    <Trigger Property="IsIndeterminate" Value="True">
        <Setter Property="Fill" TargetName="PART_Indicator">
            <Setter.Value>
                <LinearGradientBrush EndPoint=".1,1"
                    SpreadMethod="Repeat">
                    <GradientStop Offset="0" Color="Orange" />
                    <GradientStop Offset="1" Color="Red" />
                </LinearGradientBrush>
            </Setter.Value>
        </Setter>
    </Trigger>
</ControlTemplate.Triggers>
```

11. Run the application and check the checkbox:

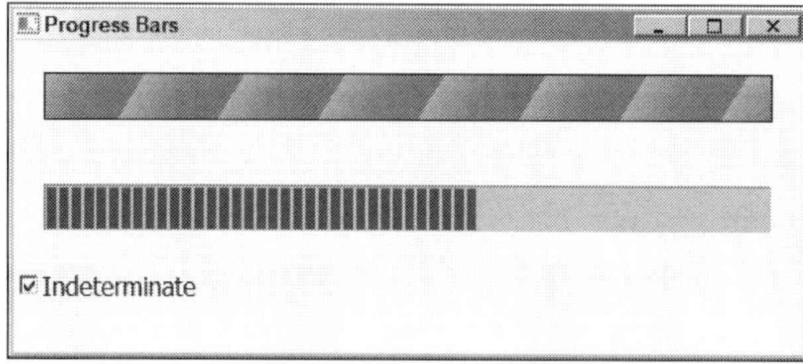

How it works...

Every control (deriving from `Control`) has a `Template` property that points to a `ControlTemplate` object that holds the visual appearance of the control. Every control provides a default control template (that may be different depending on the current Windows theme), but that template can be changed without harming the control's functionality.

The `ProgressBar` is one of the simplest controls to template because it's not interactive – the user can't click it, drag it, or anything like that. The example template uses two rectangles placed on top of each other. It seems that the second rectangle changes its width in correct relation to the progress bar's `Value` property. But how does that happen? There is no binding expression for the `Width` property of that rectangle.

The secret lies in the name of the rectangle (`PART_Indicator` in this case). This "part" is looked up by the progress bar control, and if found, it changes its `Width` appropriately without us needing to intervene. How did I know this particular name would work? This is published by attributes on the control's class. If we take a look at the `ProgressBar` class (with Visual Studio for example), this is what we'll find:

```
[TemplatePart(Name="PART_Indicator",
    Type=typeof(FrameworkElement))]
[TemplatePart(Name="PART_Track",
    Type=typeof(FrameworkElement)))]
[TemplatePart(Name="PART_GlowRect",
    Type=typeof(FrameworkElement))]
public class ProgressBar : RangeBase
```

The `ProgressBar` control "advertises" the named parts it knows about, which we can use. Each part indicates the minimal element type that can be used. In this case, it's `FrameworkElement`, which means it can be anything.

There's more...

Many controls have internal states that influence the way a control looks (and sometimes behaves). For example, a button can be clicked or not, enabled or disabled, and so on. A progress bar can be in the indeterminate state, meaning the application can't tell when that long operation finishes or how it's coming along.

These "states" can be handled by triggers. In the code example, a property trigger is used with the `IsIndeterminate` property, changing some aspect of the template so it would be obvious that the progress bar is not displaying a real progress indicator. An animation would be more appropriate here, hopefully to be accomplished by a designer.

What about the control's properties?

The above template is pretty static in the sense that changing the progress bar properties makes little difference. For example, changing properties such as `Background` or `Foreground` will have no effect. That's because the template doesn't bind to any of the progress bar properties. Sometimes it's not appropriate to do that, especially if that would change the look and feel that the template tries to convey. However, sometimes that's very relevant.

Suppose we want to add some text on top of the progress indicator displaying the `Value` property with a per cent sign. This would require tapping into the `Value` property and perhaps some other properties. Here's how to do it:

```
<TextBlock Text="{Binding Value, RelativeSource={RelativeSource
TemplatedParent}, StringFormat=\{0\}%}"
    Foreground="{TemplateBinding Foreground}"
    VerticalAlignment="Center" HorizontalAlignment="Center"/>
```

There are a couple of points here. The first is the use of the `TemplateBinding` markup extension. This extension does a one way binding to a property on the templated control. This is the preferred way of binding to a control's property from within its control template as it's very concise. The second point involves using the `RelativeSource` markup extension with the `TemplatedParent` mode to bind to a control's property from its control template in all other cases (such as a two way binding, or in this case, because a `StringFormat` is needed, which unfortunately does not exist on a `TemplateBinding`).

Binding to a control's own properties makes the template more flexible, which is a good thing most of the time.

Combining a control template with a style

A control template cannot be applied automatically on its own. Typically, the template would be combined with a style, that can be applied automatically as we've already see in the recipe *Applying a style automatically* in this chapter.

Even if an automatic style is not used, the style can still be used to set default properties, one of which is the `Template` property, just like any other. Here's a skeletal example (the complete source code is available with the downloadable code for this chapter):

```
<Style TargetType="ProgressBar">
    <Setter Property="Template">
        <Setter.Value>
            <ControlTemplate TargetType="ProgressBar" >
...
            </ControlTemplate>
        </Setter.Value>
    </Setter>
    <Setter Property="Background">
        <Setter.Value>
            <LinearGradientBrush EndPoint="1,0">
                <GradientStop Color="DarkBlue" Offset="0" />
                <GradientStop Color="LightBlue" Offset="1" />
            </LinearGradientBrush>
        </Setter.Value>
    </Setter>
    <Setter Property="Foreground" Value="Black" />
</Style>
```

Extending a template with attached properties

Binding to a control's template is certainly useful. However, what happens if there is no appropriate property to bind to? In the progress bar's template, a `TextBlock` is used to show the current value of the progress bar. What if we wanted to provide the option to hide that text? We would have wanted to have a Boolean property on the progress bar that we can bind to. Although we may be able to find a Boolean property and "hijack" it for this purpose, this rarely sits well and is usually unintuitive.

A better solution is to create attached properties and bind to those. For the progress bar we can create the following simple class:

```
public static class ProgressBarAttributes {
   public static bool GetShowText(DependencyObject obj) {
      return (bool)obj.GetValue(ShowTextProperty);
   }

   public static void SetShowText(DependencyObject obj,
      bool value) {
      obj.SetValue(ShowTextProperty, value);
   }
```

```
    public static readonly DependencyProperty ShowTextProperty
        = DependencyProperty.RegisterAttached("ShowText",
        typeof(bool), typeof(ProgressBarAttributes),
        new UIPropertyMetadata(true));
}
```

Given this `ShowText` property we can set the `Visibility` of the `TextBlock` as follows:

```
Visibility="{TemplateBinding  local:ProgressBarAttributes.ShowText,
Converter={StaticResource bool2vis}}"
```

The `bool2vis` resource points to the `System.Windows.Controls.BooleanToVisibilityConverter` class provided by WPF, which allows quick conversions between a simple Boolean and the `Visibility` enumeration:

```
<BooleanToVisibilityConverter x:Key="bool2vis" />
```

Can we replace just part of a template?

Creating a full control template is a lot of work. Wouldn't it be better if we could replace just part of a control's template - and leave the rest of it as is? Unfortunately, that's not directly supported. The control template is an all or nothing proposition. The best we can do is start with some existing template and then tweak or extend it.

One way to get a control's default template to be used as a starting point is by leveraging Expression Blend. In Blend, we can drag the required control on the design surface, right-click on it, and select **Edit Template | Edit a Copy...**.

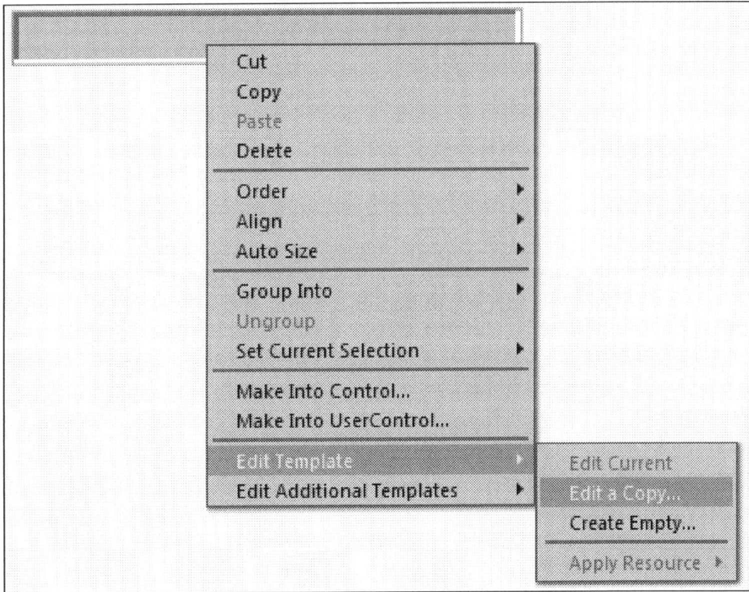

This can also give us some ideas for implementing the template. This is especially important if complex triggers are involved (because of non-trivial state management inside the control).

This is also possible directly from within Visual Studio 2012, which shares the same designer with Blend.

Another option (often a better one) is to use the "SimpleStyles" sample available in the MSDN docs and through Blend:

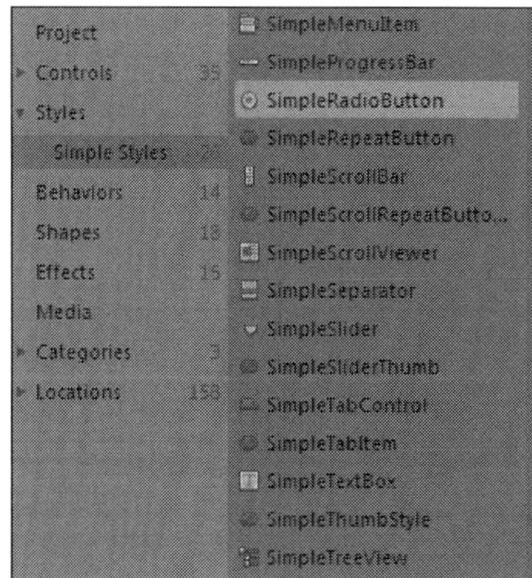

"SimpleStyles" provides relatively simple control templates for most controls; these can be used as a starting point for our own templates. The "real" templates are often very complex and contain various (usually unnecessary) decorators and other adornments that most custom templates don't need or want.

What about the Visual State Manager?

Silverlight, WPF's little brother, doesn't have the support WPF has for triggers (in fact, only the `Loaded` event trigger is supported). Instead, Silverlight introduced something known as the Visual State Manager (VSM) that provides an alternative means for controlling state changes in controls. A typical control template in Silverlight defines state transitions and other related ingredients, based on the control's advertisement of its supported states (using attributes, similar to named parts).

WPF added support for the Visual State Manager starting from version 4. However, these cannot actually be used for authoring control templates, because the current control implementation uses triggers and not the VSM. That means the control does not change states via the VSM, so any template that relies on such behavior is doomed to fail.

The VSM can still be used in WPF when authoring custom controls, but because the built-in controls are already implemented, it's not possible to add support for the VSM unless Microsoft changes the way the built-in controls operate.

Replacing the control template of a scroll bar

The `ScrollBar` control is rarely used on its own. This is hinted by the fact that it's located in the `System.Windows.Controls.Primitives` namespace. It is, however, an important building block for many elements, such as `ScrollViewer` and `ListBox`. Instead of trying to customize the template for a `ScrollViewer` or a `ListBox` to get a different look for the scroll bars, it's better to customize the `ScrollBar` itself (usually with an automatic style), causing all `ScrollBar` controls to appear the same way no matter which other, higher-level controls, use them. Let's see what it takes to replace a scroll bar's control template.

Getting ready

Make sure Visual Studio is up and running.

How to do it...

We'll create a simple application that uses a custom ScrollBar template, showing the ingredients of such a template:

1. Create a new WPF application named `CH08.CustomScrollBars`.
2. Open `App.xaml`. First, we need to create some helper templates for `RepeatButton` controls and for a `Thumb` control.
3. Add the following inside the application resources:

```
<ControlTemplate TargetType="RepeatButton"
    x:Key="repeatTransTemplate">
    <Rectangle Fill="Transparent" />
</ControlTemplate>
<ControlTemplate TargetType="RepeatButton"
    x:Key="plainTemplate">
    <Grid>
       <ContentPresenter Margin="{TemplateBinding Padding}" />
    </Grid>
</ControlTemplate>
<ControlTemplate TargetType="Thumb" x:Key="vthumbTemplate">
    <Rectangle RadiusX="5" RadiusY="10"
        Stroke="{TemplateBinding BorderBrush}"
```

```
        StrokeThickness="{TemplateBinding BorderThickness}"
        Fill="{TemplateBinding Background}" />
</ControlTemplate>
```

4. Add the basic `ControlTemplate` for a vertical `ScrollBar`:

```
<ControlTemplate TargetType="ScrollBar"
    x:Key="verticalScrollBarTemplate">
</ControlTemplate>
```

5. The template will be composed of three parts, laid out with a `Grid`. Add the following inside the template:

```
<Grid>
    <Grid.RowDefinitions>
        <RowDefinition Height="Auto" />
        <RowDefinition />
        <RowDefinition Height="Auto" />
    </Grid.RowDefinitions>
```

6. The most important part (the middle) should contain a `Track` control (a named part) that the `ScrollBar` is looking for:

```
<Border BorderBrush="DarkBlue" BorderThickness="1"
    Background="LightBlue" Grid.Row="1">
    <Track x:Name="PART_Track" IsDirectionReversed="True">
    </Track>
</Border>
```

7. The `Track` contains two `RepeatButton`s that serve as "page up" and "page down" for scrolling (connected through commands):

```
<Track.DecreaseRepeatButton>
    <RepeatButton Command="ScrollBar.PageUpCommand"
       Template="{StaticResource repeatTransTemplate}" />
</Track.DecreaseRepeatButton>
<Track.IncreaseRepeatButton>
    <RepeatButton Command="ScrollBar.PageDownCommand"
        Template="{StaticResource repeatTransTemplate}" />
</Track.IncreaseRepeatButton>
```

8. The moving part of the `Track` is a `Thumb`, set using the `Track.Thumb` property:

```
<Track.Thumb>
    <Thumb Template="{StaticResource vthumbTemplate}"
        BorderBrush="Black" BorderThickness="1">
        <Thumb.Background>
            <LinearGradientBrush EndPoint="0,1">
                <GradientStop Offset="0" Color="DarkGreen" />
                <GradientStop Offset="1" Color="LightGreen" />
```

```
            </LinearGradientBrush>
        </Thumb.Background>
    </Thumb>
</Track.Thumb>
```

9. We want to add an element to the first row of the `Grid` to be used for smooth scrolling up (insert right after the closing `Border` tag):

```
<Viewbox>
    <RepeatButton Command="{x:Static ScrollBar.LineUpCommand}"
Template="{StaticResource plainTemplate}">
        <Path Data="M 25,0 L 50,50 L 0,50 Z" Fill="Blue" />
    </RepeatButton>
</Viewbox>
```

10. Similarly, the third row should include an element to scroll smoothly down:

```
<Viewbox Grid.Row="2">
  <RepeatButton Command="{x:Static ScrollBar.LineDownCommand}"
Template="{StaticResource plainTemplate}">
      <Path Data="M 25,50 L 0,0 L 50,0 Z" Fill="Blue" />
  </RepeatButton>
</Viewbox>
```

11. A similar `ControlTemplate` is built for a horizontal scroll bar:

```
<ControlTemplate TargetType="ScrollBar"
    x:Key="horizontalScrollBarTemplate">
</ControlTemplate>
```

12. The complete source can be found with the downloadable code for this chapter. The template is largely the same; changes reflect the horizontal orientation (`Grid` contains columns, not rows, brush gradient slanted horizontally, and so on). Finally, an automatic `Style` selects the correct template based on the `ScrollBar` orientation:

```
<Style TargetType="ScrollBar">
    <Style.Triggers>
        <Trigger Property="Orientation" Value="Vertical">
            <Setter Property="Template"
     Value="{StaticResource verticalScrollBarTemplate}" />
        </Trigger>
        <Trigger Property="Orientation" Value="Horizontal">
            <Setter Property="Template"
     Value="{StaticResource horizontalScrollBarTemplate}" />
        </Trigger>

    </Style.Triggers>
</Style>
```

13. To test this, open `MainWindow.xaml`. Add an existing large image to the project (such as `penguin.jpg` from the `Sample Pictures` folder).
14. Add the following markup to the existing `Grid`:

```
<ScrollViewer VerticalScrollBarVisibility="Auto"
    HorizontalScrollBarVisibility="Auto">
    <Image Source="penguins.jpg" Stretch="None" />
</ScrollViewer>
```

15. Run the application and make sure the window is small enough so that the scroll bars will be forced to display:

How it works...

A `ScrollBar` control template contains only one named part, `PART_Track`, of type `Track`. This element expects two `RepeatButton` controls (`Track.DecreaseRepeatButton` and `Track.IncreaseRepeatButton`) and a `Thumb` control (`Track.Thumb` property) - the rest is taken care of by the `ScrollBar`. The `RepeatButton`s are typically used to do page level scrolling, connected as such with the `Command` property of those buttons. The line (small step) based scrolling is not an essential part of the `ScrollBar` and need not be supplied. In the demoed template, two extra `RepeatButton`s are provided and connected using commands to the line scrolling functionality. The `ScrollBar` control is built as follows:

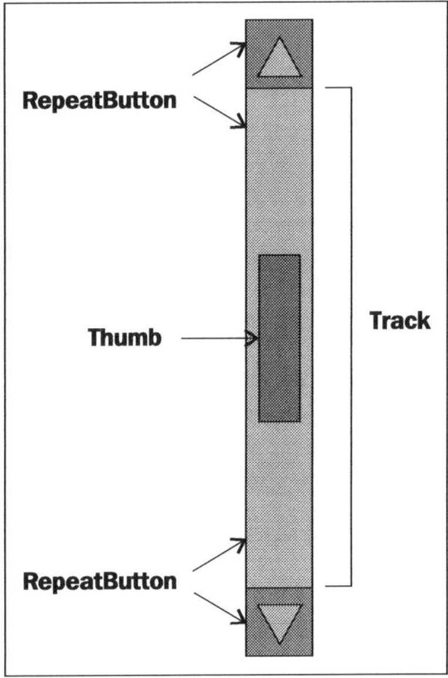

The middle RepeatButtons (part of the Track) are themselves templated as empty rectangles filled with a transparent brush. It's important this is transparent and not null, otherwise no clicks would be registered on these buttons.

The top and bottom little arrows are RepeatButtons themselves templated as simple content containers. This is achieved using a ContentPresenter, which is an element that is roughly equivalent to a ContentControl whose Content property binds to the button's Content property. The actual content of these buttons is composed of a ViewBox (that provides automatic scaling) containing a Path element that is shaped like a little triangular arrow.

The Style for the ScrollBar selects (using a property trigger) the correct template (vertical or horizontal) based on the Orientation property.

Customizing selection in a Selector control

Controls deriving from Selector such as ListBox and CombobBox have rich template support with the ItemTemplate property. There is no direct support, however, for customizing the way a selected item is rendered. At first, this seems easily fixable with a property trigger for the Selector.IsSelected property; however, due to the way the default ListBoxItem/ ComboBoxItem control template is designed, the result is suboptimal. Let's see how to customize selection rendering despite this inconvenience.

Getting ready

Run Visual Studio and open the `CH08.DataTriggerDemo` project.

How to do it...

We'll customize the appearance of selection in the `ListBox` used to show books with a fancy `DataTemplate`:

1. Run the application as is. Click an item; it's back-filled with a blue color (the exact color depends on the Windows theme and any personalization that may have been made), causing a not-so-nice effect (for example, the author name becomes invisible for non-free books).
2. Open `MainWindow.xaml`. Add the following property to the `ListBox`:

```
<ListBox.ItemContainerStyle>
   <Style TargetType="ListBoxItem">
   </Style>
</ListBox.ItemContainerStyle>
```

3. Add a setter for a new `ControlTemplate` for the `ListBoxItem`:

```
<Setter Property="Template">
   <Setter.Value>
      <ControlTemplate TargetType="ListBoxItem">
          <Border BorderBrush="{TemplateBinding BorderBrush}"
                  Background="{TemplateBinding Background}"
                  Margin="{TemplateBinding Padding}"
        BorderThickness="{TemplateBinding BorderThickness}">
             <ContentPresenter HorizontalAlignment="{TemplateBindi
ng HorizontalContentAlignment}"
                               VerticalAlignment="{TemplateBinding
VerticalContentAlignment}" />
            </Border>
        </ControlTemplate>
    </Setter.Value>
</Setter>
```

4. This sets an alternative template that we can control. Let's add some more setters as default values:

```
<Setter Property="Background" Value="Transparent" />
<Setter Property="BorderThickness" Value="2" />
<Setter Property="BorderBrush" Value="Transparent" />
```

5. To change the way selection looks, we'll add a property trigger:

```
<Style.Triggers>
    <Trigger Property="IsSelected" Value="True">
        <Setter Property="BorderBrush" Value="Red" />
    </Trigger>
</Style.Triggers>
```

6. Run the application and select an item. A red border marks the selection:

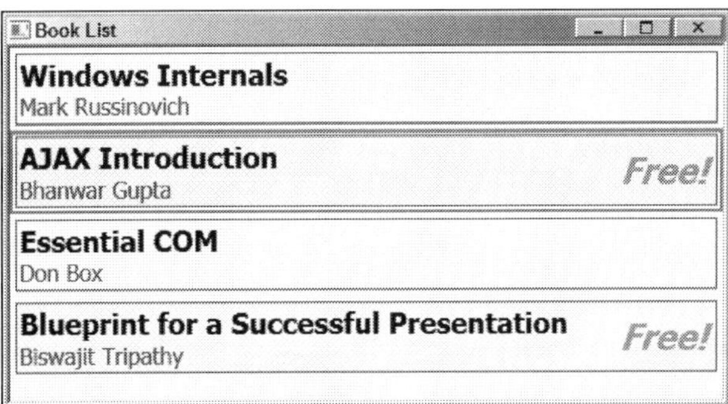

How it works...

The container of each item in a `ListBox` is a `ListBoxItem` (a `ContentControl`); similarly, `ComboBoxItem` objects wrap the content in a `ComboBox`. The container item style can be changed (for every `ItemsControl`-derived type) using the `ItemContainerStyle` property. In this case, the `Template` property needs to change, because the default template uses the current selection color (configured through the **Personalization** applet in **Control Panel**) in an internal element that we cannot reach from a simple style.

Our only reasonable alternative is to replace the entire control template of that `ListBoxItem`, which is not difficult to do – a `ContentPresenter` (to show the actual data template associated with each item) inside something like a `Border` (we can use something more complex if desired). The rest is just a regular property trigger to get the required effect.

`ContentPresenter` is an element used mostly in control templates, which renders the `Content` of the templated control based on the usual rules of the `Content` property (meaning it uses a `DataTemplate` if provided, and so on). It can technically bind to another property (of type `Object`) by setting the `ContentSource` property to the base property name; for example, for `HeaderedContentControl` template, a `ContentPresenter` would set `ContentSource` to "Header", so that it looks at `Header` and `HeaderTemplate` as appropriate.

A similar element, `ItemsPresenter` is used for the `ItemsControl`-derived templates to show a collection of objects.

There's more...

ItemsControl-derived types have another interesting template customization hook: the ItemsPanel property (of type ItemsPanelTemplate). This changes the way items are arranged in the ItemsControl-derived control. ListBox, for instance, uses a vertical VirtualizingStackPanel by default – that's why items are placed one below the other. A VirtualizingStackPanel is similar to a regular StackPanel, but items that are out of view are not created until actually needed – this increases responsiveness if the ListBox holds many items. ItemsControl uses a vertical StackPanel; StatusBar uses a DockPanel; MenuItem uses a WrapPanel.

What can we place instead of the default items panel? One option is to continue to use a (Virtualizing)StackPanel, but make it horizontal.

Another useful possibility is to use a WrapPanel; this has a similar effect to the "icon" style views seen in Windows Explorer.

Yet another interesting idea is to use a UniformGrid, setting an appropriate number of Rows and Columns. This places items in a tabular grid, while still maintaining all the characteristics of a ListBox.

Here are some examples of arranging a bunch of circles in a ListBox with various panels:

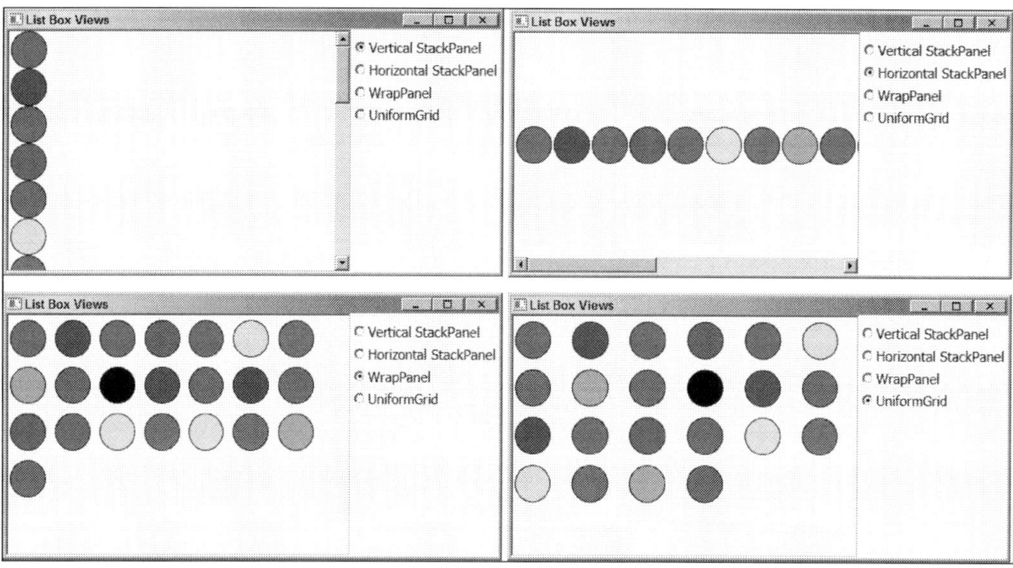

The complete source is located in the CH08.CustomLItemsPanel project available with the downloadable source for this chapter.

9

Graphics and Animation

In this chapter we will cover the following:

- Creating a custom shape
- Applying transforms on elements
- Manipulating a bitmap programmatically
- Creating adorners
- Creating property-based animations
- Creating path-based animations
- Creating custom animations
- Adding animation easing to animations
- Using custom effects with pixel shaders

Introduction

WPF has a very impressive graphic stack. That's one of the obvious selling points of the technology, as it's very visual and immediately recognizable. WPF's graphic capabilities range from simple 2D to arbitrarily complex 3D, with the typical integration we come to expect from WPF; everything can be interacted with anything – a 3D scene can be animating inside a button and that button still behaves like a button.

WPF also provides a powerful, declarative, animation engine. This makes using animations easy, removing the need to use timers, do refresh updates, and other low level tasks that are typical with other graphic frameworks.

This chapter explores some of WPF's graphic and animation capabilities. Missing from the chapter is discussion of WPF's 3D graphic support; this is simply beyond the scope of this book, as it must maintain a reasonable number of pages. 3D is a complex topic in itself; WPF makes using 3D relatively easy. Other sources have discussions on 3D in general and WPF in particular. The interested reader can do a simple web search to find relevant information. 2D however, is not as easy as it may sound – WPF has a variety of ways of creating 2D graphics. This chapter has recipes that show ways to effectively use WPF's capabilities.

Creating a custom shape

Shapes are (mostly) simple elements deriving from the `Shape` abstract base class, which derives directly from `FrameworkElement`; shapes providing an inherent graphical representation that can easily be filled, stroked and stretched. Shapes are not controls – they have no template associated with them. They are, however, full elements, providing support for the full range of capabilities, including participation in layout, hit testing, and the multitude of properties and events that make working with these entities as easy as any control.

We can create new shapes by deriving from `Shape`, providing a new graphical representation, and taking advantage of the functionality provided by the base `Shape` class.

Getting ready

Make sure Visual Studio is up and running.

How to do it...

We'll create a ring shape element, demonstrating the steps necessary to create custom `Shape` classes that fit naturally with the rest of WPF, just as the built-in shapes do:

1. Create a new WPF application named `CH09.CustomShape`.
2. We're going to create a ring shape that should function like any of the built in shapes. Add a new class to the project named `RingShape`.
3. Add using statements for `System.Windows`, `System.Windows.Media`, and `System.Windows.Shapes`.
4. Make `RingShape` derive from `Shape`:

   ```
   public class RingShape : Shape {
   }
   ```

5. Add a private field of type `Rect` that we'll use to manage the bounds of a shape:

   ```
   Rect _rect;
   ```

6. We'd like to provide a property to customize the width of the ring. Add a dependency property named `RingWidth` of type `double`:

```
public double RingWidth {
   get { return (double)GetValue(RingWidthProperty); }
   set { SetValue(RingWidthProperty, value); }
}

public static readonly DependencyProperty RingWidthProperty =
   DependencyProperty.Register("RingWidth", typeof(double),
   typeof(RingShape), new FrameworkPropertyMetadata(
   .1, FrameworkPropertyMetadataOptions.AffectsRender));
```

7. `RingWidth` will be a percentage fraction of the width/height of the shape (for example, 0.2=20% of width/height). A custom shape must override the `DefiningGeometry` protected property and return a `Geometry` representing the shape. Override the property as follows:

```
protected override Geometry DefiningGeometry {
   get {
      if(_rect.IsEmpty)
         return Geometry.Empty;

      var rc = _rect;
      rc.Inflate(-RingWidth * _rect.Width,
         -RingWidth * _rect.Height);
      return new CombinedGeometry(GeometryCombineMode.Exclude,
         new EllipseGeometry(_rect), new EllipseGeometry(rc));
   }
}
```

8. The `_rect` field must be updated if the size of the shape is queried. For this purpose, we'll override the `MeasureOverride` method (commonly overridden by panels) and compute `_rect` based on the current `Stretch` property value:

```
protected override Size MeasureOverride(Size constraint) {
   if(double.IsInfinity(constraint.Width) ||
      double.IsInfinity(constraint.Height)) {
      _rect = Rect.Empty;
      return Size.Empty;
   }

   double size;
   switch(Stretch) {
      case Stretch.Fill:
         _rect = new Rect(constraint);
         break;
      case Stretch.Uniform:
         size = Math.Min(constraint.Width, constraint.Height);
         _rect = new Rect(new Size(size, size));
         break;
```

```
        case Stretch.UniformToFill:
            size = Math.Max(constraint.Width, constraint.Height);
            _rect = new Rect(new Size(size, size));
            break;

        case Stretch.None:
            _rect = double.IsNaN(Width) || double.IsNaN(Height)
                ? Rect.Empty : new Rect(new Size(Width, Height));
            break;
    }
    return _rect.Size;
}
```

9. Finally, the default value of the `Stretch` property (inherited from `Shape`) is `None`. This would cause the `RingShape` to have zero size. Let's change the default in the static constructor:

```
static RingShape() {
    StretchProperty.OverrideMetadata(typeof(RingShape),
        new FrameworkPropertyMetadata(Stretch.Uniform,
        FrameworkPropertyMetadataOptions.AffectsMeasure |
        FrameworkPropertyMetadataOptions.AffectsRender));
}
```

10. We need to test this. Open `MainWindow.xaml`.
11. Map an XML namespace to the `CH09.CustomShape` namespace:

```
xmlns:local="clr-namespace:CH09.CustomShape"
```

12. Add a `RingShape` inside the existing `Grid`:

```
<local:RingShape Fill="Red" Stroke="Black" StrokeThickness="4"
                 RingWidth=".15"/>
```

13. Run the application:

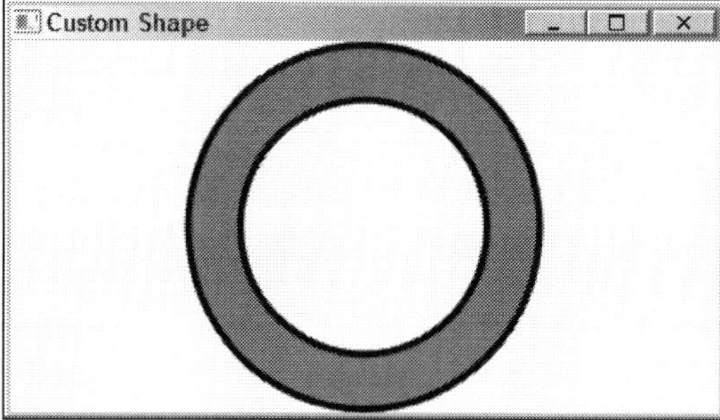

14. You can change the `Stretch` property value, or set an explicit `Width`/`Height` to see the effects.

How it works...

The Shape abstract class defines one abstract member, the DefiningGeometry property. This property must be overridden and return a Geometry (see *There's more...* section for more information on geometries) that defines the shape's shape. Everything else is taken care of by the base Shape class.

The actual size of the shape should be calculated based on the Stretch inherited property (that's the reason MeasureOverride is needed). Strictly speaking, we could have removed MeasureOverride entirely and just initialized the _rect field to some non-empty rectangle. This would cause a Stretch value of None to just use the default rectangle-initialized size. This is acceptable, but using a zero size shape when Stretch is None is consistent with the way the built in shapes operate.

The geometry provided by the RingShape consists of a small ellipse (EllipseGeometry) subtracted from a larger ellipse (using a CombinedGeometry object combined with mode of Exclude).

There's more...

The Shape class does the actual drawing of the geometry by overriding the UIElement.OnRender method. This method accepts a DrawingContext, which is an abstraction of a painting capable object (similar in concept to a GDI+ Graphics object or Win32 device context).

Overriding OnRender provides the ability to add other graphical effects outside the Geometry provided by the DefiningGeometry property. However, if this method is overridden, the base class implementation must be called; otherwise DefiningGeometry will have no effect. Here's a proper implementation skeleton:

```
protected override void OnRender(DrawingContext dc) {
   base.OnRender(dc);
   // do custom drawing
}
```

Geometries

Geometry is a mathematical abstraction that defines some 2D construct. Geometry is an abstract base class that defines some basic functionality common to all geometries. The Bounds property returns the minimal axis-aligned bounding rectangle (Rect struct) that encapsulates the geometry. The Transform property allows transformations to be applied on the geometry (see the *Applying transforms on elements* recipe later in this chapter for a discussion of transforms). The GetArea method calculates the area occupied by the geometry and FillContains can be used to check if a given point or another geometry is contained within the given geometry (with a rich set of overloads). There are other interesting methods on the base Geometry class that make geometries useful in other scenarios.

> Some of the interesting `Geometry` methods are as follows: `GetArea` calculates the area of the `Geometry` (no matter how complex); `FillContains` indicates whether the `Geometry` contains the specified `Point` or another `Geometry`; `GetRenderBounds` returns a rectangle that contains the `Geometry` painted with a specified `Pen`; `GetFlattenedGeometry` returns a `PathGeometry` that is a polygonal approximation of the `Geometry`; the static `Combine` method combines two `Geometry` objects based on a `GeometryCombineMode` value (`Exclude`, `Union`, `Xor`, or `Intersect`) with an optional `Transform` applied.

`Geometry` derives from `Animatable` (itself deriving from `Freezable`), thus supports all `Freezable` features, such as cloning, becoming read only, and easy sharing through resources.

The simple geometries are `LineGeometry`, `EllipseGeometry`, and `RectangleGeometry`, all pretty self-explanatory. The more complex geometries include:

- `GeometryGroup`: Can host any number of geometries as a single unit. Adds a `FillRule` property to indicate the way intersections are handled in the geometry (similar to `FillRule` of the `Polygon` and `Polyline` shapes).
- `CombinedGeometry`: Combines two geometries (`Geometry1` and `Geometry2` properties) with a set operator (`GeometryCombineMode` property), resulting in a new geometry. Possible values are `Intersect`, `Exclude`, `Union`, and `Xor`. The following illustration shows the various modes in action:

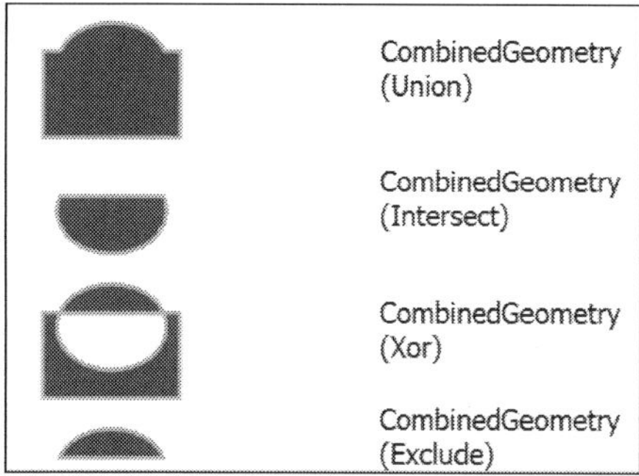

- `PathGeometry`: The most complex geometry that can replace all others and do much more. It contains a collection of `PathFigure` objects (`Figures` property). Each `PathFigure` represents a connected series of lines and curves, represented as a collection of `PathSegment` objects (`Segments` property). `PathSegment` is an abstract class – its derivatives provide concrete lines or curves. These include simple segments (`LineSegment`, `PolyLineSegment`), an arc (`ArgSegment`), and an assortment of Bezier curves (`BezierSegment`, `PolyBezierSegment`, `QuadraticBezierSegment`, and `PolyQuadraticBezierSegment`).

Building a complex `PathGeometry` may take a lot of XAML (or code). To mitigate that from a practical perspective, a "geometry mini language" has been created that allows creating figures and segments using a string in XAML that's converted (using a `GeometryConverter` type converter) into a `PathGeometry`. For example, the following XAML is a long way to create a triangle geometry:

```
<PathGeometry>
    <PathFigure IsClosed="True" StartPoint="10,100">
        <LineSegment Point="100,100" />
        <LineSegment Point="100,50" />
    </PathFigure>
</PathGeometry>
```

The short version is as follows:

```
<Geometry>M 10,100 L 100,100 L 100,50 Z</Geometry>
```

- Here's a quick rundown of this string: M starts a new figure followed by the starting point of that figure. L means line, followed by the end point of the line (there are two lines) and finally Z means the figure is done and closed (which creates the third triangle line). All possible segment types are included in the mini language.

  For complex shapes, this "mini language" shortens markup considerably. The resulting object is actually a `StreamGeometry`, not a `PathGeometry` (`StreamGeometry` is discussed in the next bullet). To create an actual `PathGeometry`, the markup needs to change a bit:

  ```
  <PathGeometry Figures="M 10,100 L 100,100 L 100,50 Z" />
  ```

- `StreamGeometry`: Similar to a `PathGeometry` in terms of its contents – contains figures, each of which contains segments; however, these are not exposed as properties. Instead, we must call the `Open` method on the `StreamGeometry`, getting back a `StreamGeometryContext` that exposes the ability to create figures (`BeginFigure` and `Close` methods) and add segments (`LineTo`, `ArcTo`, `BezierTo`, `PolyBezierTo`, `QuadraticBezierTo`, and `PolyQuadraticBezierTo` methods).

  A `StreamGeometry` is a lightweight version of `PathGeometry`. It does not support data binding, animations, or modifications.

As geometries are abstract entities (in the mathematical sense, not the object oriented sense), they appear in other objects. Examples include path-based animations that use a `PathGeometry` (see the recipe *Creating custom animations* later in this chapter), the `UIElement.Clip` property that accepts any geometry, and some `Drawing`-derived types (`GeometryDrawing.Geometry` and `DrawingGroup.ClipGeometry`).

Built-in shapes

WPF provides six built-in shapes. The simplest shapes are `Line`, `Ellipse`, and `Rectangle`. The more complex shapes are `Polygon` and `Polyline`, which are very similar and contain a collection of points (the `Points` property). The only difference between them is that a `Polygon` adds a line from the last point to the first automatically, whereas `Polyline` does not (both are filled in the exact same way - a `Polyline` is assumed to be closed for this purpose, as if it were a `Polygon`).

The most complex shape (by far) is the `Path`, which can replace all other shapes. It renders a `Geometry` (set with the `Data` property), which means it can render anything.

Expression Blend provides more custom shapes through its **Assets** | **Shapes** window (implemented in the `Microsoft.Expression.Drawing.dll` assembly), such as arrows and callouts:

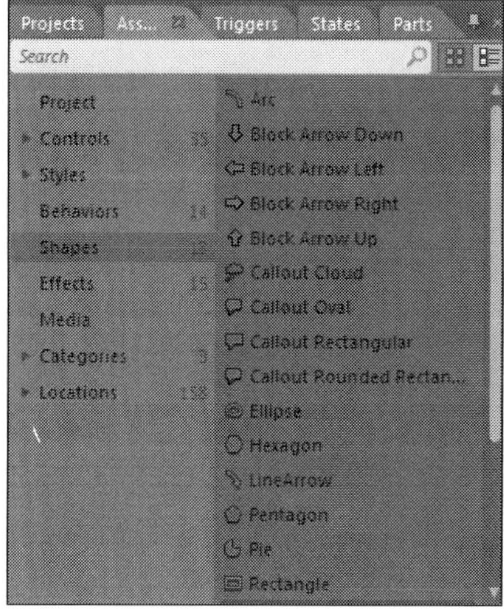

Shapes versus geometries

Sometimes there is some confusion between shapes and geometries; they seem similar, such as `Rectangle` and `RectangleGeometry`, `Path` and `PathGeometry`.

There is a fundamental difference, however: shapes are elements - they are visual objects, can be placed somewhere in the visual tree and are part of the layout phase within a panel, and so on.

Geometries, on the other hand, are mathematical abstractions. They cannot be placed in the visual tree and cannot draw themselves.

Applying transforms on elements

Transforms allow manipulating an entity's coordinates in various ways, the most common being translating (moving), scaling, and rotating. This ability provides a lot of flexibility in the way elements (and other objects) present themselves. Combined with animations and some creativity, transforms are even more powerful. In this recipe, we'll examine the ways to use transforms and discuss the available transform types.

Getting ready

Make sure Visual Studio is up and running.

How to do it...

We'll create some images and apply a rotation transform to some, showing the common properties that accept transforms:

1. Create a new WPF application named `CH09.Transforms`.
2. Add an existing image to the project, such as `"penguins.jpg"` from the `Sample Pictures` folder.
3. Open `MainWindow.xaml`. Add the following properties to the `Window`:

   ```
   SizeToContent="WidthAndHeight" FontSize="16"
       ResizeMode="CanMinimize"
   ```

4. Remove the `Width` and `Height` property settings of the `Window`.
5. Add three columns to the existing `Grid`:

   ```
   <Grid.ColumnDefinitions>
       <ColumnDefinition />
       <ColumnDefinition Width="40"/>
       <ColumnDefinition />
   </Grid.ColumnDefinitions>
   ```

6. Add a `StackPanel` in the first column that contains three images, the middle being rotated 45 degrees using a `RotateTransform`:

   ```
   <StackPanel>
       <Image Source="Penguins.jpg" Height="100" Margin="5" />
       <Image Source="Penguins.jpg" Height="100" Margin="5">
           <Image.LayoutTransform>
               <RotateTransform Angle="45" />
           </Image.LayoutTransform>
       </Image>
       <Image Source="Penguins.jpg" Height="100" Margin="5" />
   </StackPanel>
   ```

7. Add another `StackPanel` with three images to the third column of the `Grid`, this time rotating the second image with the `RenderTransform` property:

```
<StackPanel Grid.Column="2">
    <Image Source="Penguins.jpg" Height="100" Margin="5" />
    <Image Source="Penguins.jpg" Height="100" Margin="5"
        RenderTransformOrigin=".5,.5">
        <Image.RenderTransform>
            <RotateTransform Angle="45" />
        </Image.RenderTransform>
    </Image>
    <Image Source="Penguins.jpg" Height="100" Margin="5" />
</StackPanel>
```

8. Run the application and observe the results:

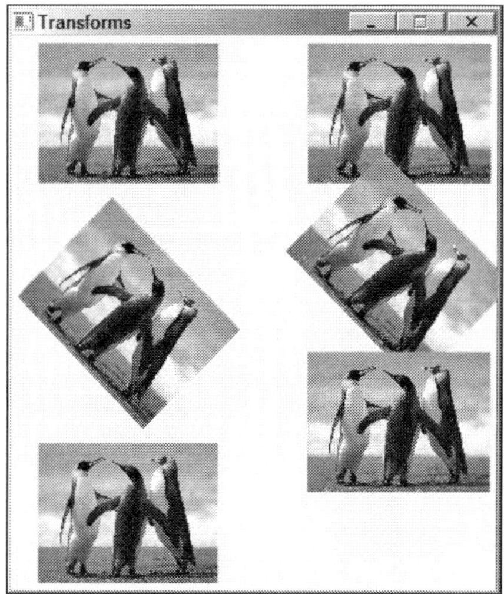

How it works...

Transforms are based around the abstract `Transform` class. A transform is inherently represented by a 3 x 3 matrix (`Matrix` struct). In fact, we can specify the exact matrix element using one of the derivatives of `Transform`, `MatrixTransform` (although that is uncommon).

The example code creates a `RotateTransform` object with an `Angle` of 45 degrees (angles are not expressed in radians, as they are with the `Math` class methods). That transform is applied to an element using the `UIElement.RenderTransform` or `FrameworkElement.LayoutTransform` properties. The former makes the transformation after the layout pass is over, while the latter takes the transform changes into consideration as part of the layout phase.

This means that `RenderTransform` does not take into account the new size requirements (either bigger or smaller) for layout purposes, so the element may overlap other elements (depending on the particular transform). The middle right image overlaps the first and third images because its new space requirements were not taken into account. The middle left image, on the other hand, using `LayoutTransform`, received the extra space it needs because of the actual transform.

As `RenderTransform` happens after the layout phase, it is important to the anchor point where transform begins. This can be changed using the `RenderTransformOrigin` property (of type `Point`), (0,0) being the default – meaning the top left corner of the affected element. The value is relative to the size of the element, so (0.5,0.5) means the element center and (1,1) means the bottom right corner of the element's bounding rectangle. Technically, the value may be outside the (0,0)-(1,1) range if desirable.

Here's an example of the effect `RenderTransformOrigin` has when rotation is used:

The middle left image has `RenderTransformOrigin` equal to (.5,.5). The middle right image maintains the default value of (0,0). Notice the rotation is happening around the top-left corner of the image.

Using `RenderTransform` is more light weight than using `LayoutTransform`, especially when animations are involved. Try to use `RenderTransform` whenever possible in lieu of `LayoutTransform`.

There's more...

The common `Transform` derivatives to use are `TranslateTransform` (translations being set with the `X` and `Y` properties), `ScaleTransform` (resizing with the `ScaleX` and `ScaleY` properties, as well as the center point around which scaling happens with the `CenterX` and `CenterY` properties), and `RotateTransform` (rotating by the angle specified with the `Angle` property as well setting an alternate center of rotation with the `CenterX` and `CenterY` properties).

`ScaleTransform` can be used to flip the coordinate system by specifying negative values for `ScaleX` and/or `ScaleY` (effecting flipping the affected objects). Note that their default value is 1.0, that is maintain original size. A value larger than 1 increases size while a value between 0 and 1 decreases size.

The last useful transform is `TransformGroup`. This simply allows combining transforms to create a new transform. Behind the scenes this means multiplying matrices to get a result matrix. The important thing to note is that matrix multiplication is not commutative - meaning that in general the order of transforms matters.

The last transform type is `SkewTransform`, the weirdest of them all. This transform can be simply explained as turning a rectangle into a parallelogram. The `AngleX` and `AngleY` properties are used to set the skew angle and the `CenterX` and `CenterY` properties may be used to change the reference point of skewing.

Other uses for transforms

Transforms are powerful tools, not just because of their direct capabilities, but also because they are animatable - every property can be independently animated to produce effects only limited by creativity and imagination.

Transforms are not used just for elements. Geometries can be arbitrarily transformed using the `Geometry.Transform` property. Brushes can be transformed as well using the `Brush.Transform` property. Both properties, coupled with possible animation, are a powerful tool in the WPF graphics arsenal.

Manipulating a bitmap programmatically

Bitmaps are used in one form or another mainly to display existing images. These typically are placed as a source of an `Image` element. When a static image is added to a project and set to the `Image.Source` property, a `BitmapImage` is created behind the scenes. This simple class provides a read-only view to the bitmap's bits.

Sometime it's desirable to manipulate a bitmap's bit values dynamically based on a runtime algorithm. WPF provides the `WriteableBitmap` that allows us to do just that. Let's look at how to use this capability.

Getting ready

Make sure Visual Studio is up and running.

How to do it...

We'll create an application that displays the famous Mandelbrot set, requiring calculating colors for each pixel in the resulting image. This will show a typical usage of `WriteableBitmap`.

1. Create a new WPF application named `CH09.MandelbrotSet`.
2. Open `MainWindow.xaml`. Add the following `Image` element inside the existing `Grid`:

   ```
   <Image Width="600" Height="600" x:Name="_image" />
   ```

3. Set the following properties on the `Window` itself:

   ```
   Title="Mandelbrot Set" SizeToContent="WidthAndHeight"
       ResizeMode="CanMinimize"
   ```

4. Remove the `Width` and `Height` property settings of the `Window`.
5. Open `MainWindow.xaml.cs`. Add a private field of type `WriteableBitmap`:

   ```
   WriteableBitmap _bmp;
   ```

6. In the constructor, after the call to `InitializeComponent`, we'll create a `WriteableBitmap` object (having a potential grayscale image) and connect it to the `Image` element:

   ```
   _bmp = new WriteableBitmap(600, 600, 0, 0, PixelFormats.Gray8,
      null);
   _image.Source = _bmp;
   ```

7. Add a reference to the `System.Numeric` assembly. This is required to get the support for the Complex value type.
8. Add a `using` statement for the `System.Numeric` namespace for the same reason.
9. The application calculates something known as the Mandelbrot Set. Add a private method named `MandelbrotColor` that calculates the color of a given point expressed as a complex number:

   ```
   int MandelbrotColor(Complex c) {
      int color = 256;
      Complex z = Complex.Zero;
      while(z.Real + z.Imaginary < 4 && color > 0) {
         z = z * z + c;
         color--;
      }
      return color;
   }
   ```

10. Add a private method named `CalcMandelbrotSet`:

```
void CalcMandelbrotSet() {
}
```

11. Let's implement its body. First, we'll set up the boundaries for calculations:

```
var from = new Complex(-1.5, -1);
var to = new Complex(1, 1);
double deltax = (to.Real - from.Real) / _bmp.Width;
double deltay = (to.Imaginary - from.Imaginary) / _bmp.Height;
```

12. Next, we'll allocate an array of bytes that would hold color values for an entire row:

```
byte[] pixels = new byte[_bmp.PixelWidth];
```

13. Now we should create a double loop to walk through all pixels in the bitmap (600 x 600) and calculate the color values for each row:

```
for(int y = 0; y < _bmp.PixelHeight; y++) {
   for (int x = 0; x < _bmp.PixelWidth; x++)
      pixels[x] = (byte)MandelbrotColor(from + new Complex(
          x * deltax, y * deltay));
```

14. After the `x` loop is done, we'll update that particular line in the actual bitmap:

```
_bmp.WritePixels(new Int32Rect(0, y, _bmp.PixelWidth, 1),
  pixels, _bmp.BackBufferStride, 0);
```

15. Close the outer loop and the method itself.
16. Add a call to `CalcMandelbrot` as the last operation in the constructor.
17. Run the application. You should see output similar to this:

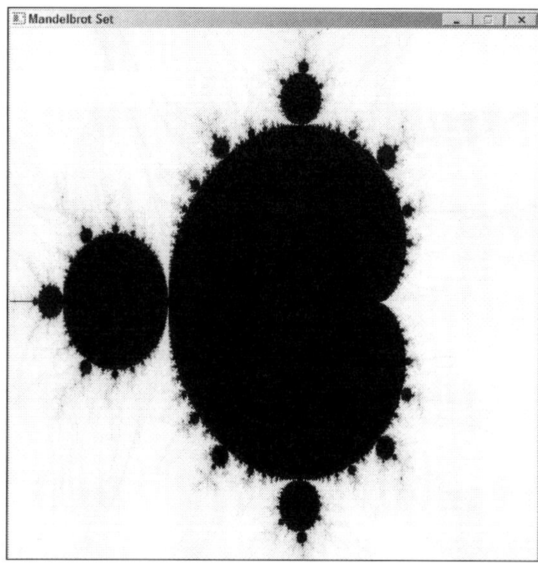

How it works...

`WriteableBitmap` inherits from the abstract `BitmapSource` class, which itself derives from `ImageSource`. This means `WriteableBitmap` is accepted as any other `ImageSource`, such as with the `Image.Source` property.

Creating a `WriteableBitmap` involves selecting the bitmap width and height and its format. The preceding code uses `PixelFormats.Gray8`, which means one byte per pixel consisting of gray levels only. `PixelFormats` is a static class, consisting of many predefined pixel formats, such as Bgr24, Gray2, Rgb24, and bgra32. The format is important when changing actual pixels.

To change the actual pixels, the code uses the `WritePixels` method, which accepts an appropriate array with the values that need to be set (in this case, byte values representing gray levels) and a Rect specifying the region to change. The stride parameter indicates the byte difference between two consecutive lines in the bitmap. This may seem obvious - the pixel width of the bitmap multiplied by the number of bytes per pixel. This is not always the case (because of alignment issues), so it's always a good idea to get that information from the bitmap itself (using the `BackBufferStride` property).

There's more...

An alternative method for changing the contents of a `WriteableBitmap` is to call the `Lock` method and then retrieve a direct pointer to the underlying bitmap bits using the `BackBuffer` property (of type `IntPtr`). Lock causes WPF not to update whoever is holding that bitmap until the `Unlock` method has been called.

This returned pointer may be handed off to native code, or manipulated in C# inside an unsafe context. This allows many updates to happen without bothering WPF with updates. Before calling `Unlock`, the `AddDirtyRect` should be called to give WPF a hint to location of the changed bits.

`WritePixels` conceptually calls `Lock`, writes the pixels, calls `AddDirtyRect`, and calls `Unlock`. It does, however, make a lot of parameter and other checks, which makes it slower compared to directly calling Lock/Unlock and manipulating the bits.

How about higher-level access to WriteableBitmap?

`WriteableBitmap` is really a bare-bones object. It provides the most primitive type of access to the bitmap bits. Calling `WritePixels` or using the `BackBuffer` property is too low level for some scenarios. There are no methods to draw 2D constructs such as lines, ellipses, or rectangles; no easy way to copy parts of images to a given `WriteableBitmap`; no transforms on the existing bits.

Codeplex, Microsoft's open source community, has a project named `WriteableBitmapEx`, that provides an impressive set of extension methods that fill this gap (`http://writeablebitmapex.codeplex.com/`). The library is available not just for WPF, but for Silverlight, Windows Phone, and Windows Runtime (Windows 8 runtime for Metro style applications).

See also

For more information on the Mandelbrot Set, check out Wikipedia at `http://en.wikipedia.org/wiki/Mandelbrot_set`.

Creating adorners

Adorners are elements that exist in a distinct adorner layer, not part of the normal visual tree. All adorners in a particular layer always sit on top (higher Z index) of the element they adorn. This characteristic of adorners makes them an excellent choice for things such as selection handles, popup elements, and other special tasks where bothering with the normal visual tree is impossible or complicated at best.

In this recipe, we'll take a look at creating and using adorners to indicate selection.

Getting ready

Make sure Visual Studio is up and running.

How to do it...

We'll create an application that draws a bunch of circles that can be dragged with the mouse. The currently selected circle will be marked with an adorner.

1. Create a new WPF application named `CH09.AdornerDemo`.
2. Open `MainWindow.xaml`. Replace the existing `Grid` with a `Canvas` as follows:

   ```
   <Canvas x:Name="_canvas" Background="White">
   </Canvas>
   ```

3. Open `MainWindow.xaml.cs`. We want to create a bunch of random circles that can be dragged with the mouse.
4. Create a private method named `CreateCircles` and implement as follows:

   ```
   void CreateCircles() {
      var rnd = new Random();
      int start = rnd.Next(30);
      for(int i = 0; i < 10; i++) {
   ```

```
        var circle = new Ellipse {
           Stroke = Brushes.Black,
           StrokeThickness = 1,
           Width = 50,
           Height = 50
        };
        var fill = typeof(Brushes).GetProperties(
           BindingFlags.Static | BindingFlags.Public)[start]
           .GetValue(null, null) as Brush;
        circle.Fill = fill;
        Canvas.SetLeft(circle, rnd.NextDouble() * ActualWidth);
        Canvas.SetTop(circle, rnd.NextDouble() * ActualHeight);
        _canvas.Children.Add(circle);
        start += 2;
     }
  }
```

5. This method creates 10 randomly colored, randomly positioned circles. Add to the constructor a call to this method when the `Loaded` event fires (important so that `ActualWidth` and `ActualHeight` are updated):

```
Loaded += delegate {
   CreateCircles();
};
```

6. An adorner type must be created. Add a new class named `SelectionAdorner`.
7. Add using statements for the `System.Windows`, `System.Windows.Media`, and `System.Windows.Documents` namespaces.
8. Make the `SelectionAdorner` inherit from `Adorner` and implement a constructor that accepts an element and calls the base constructor:

```
class SelectionAdorner : Adorner {
public SelectionAdorner(UIElement element)
      : base(element) {
   }
```

9. An adorner needs to override `OnRender` and provide its visual appearance. Add the following static helper graphic objects to the `SelectionAdorner` class:

```
static readonly Pen _pen = new Pen(Brushes.Black, 1) {
   DashStyle = DashStyles.Dash };
static readonly Brush _rectFill = new SolidColorBrush(
   Color.FromArgb(30, 0, 0, 255));
static readonly Brush _circleFill = new SolidColorBrush(
   Color.FromArgb(60, 255, 0, 0));
const double _circleRadius = 6;
```

10. Override `OnRender` as follows:

```
protected override void OnRender(DrawingContext dc) {
   dc.DrawRectangle(_rectFill, _pen, new Rect(
      AdornedElement.DesiredSize));
   dc.DrawEllipse(_circleFill, null, new Point(0, 0),
      _circleRadius, _circleRadius);
   dc.DrawEllipse(_circleFill, null, new Point(
      AdornedElement.DesiredSize.Width, 0),
   _circleRadius, _circleRadius);
   dc.DrawEllipse(_circleFill, null, new Point(
      AdornedElement.DesiredSize.Width,
      AdornedElement.DesiredSize.Height),
      _circleRadius, _circleRadius);
   dc.DrawEllipse(_circleFill, null, new Point(
      0, AdornedElement.DesiredSize.Height),
     _circleRadius, _circleRadius);
}
```

11. Open `MainWindow.xaml`. Add event handlers to the `Canvas` for the `MouseLeftButtonDown`, `MouseLeftButtonUp`, and `MouseMove` events.

12. Open `MainWindow.xaml.cs`. Add the following private fields that will help manage the state in the `Window`:

```
Point _current;
FrameworkElement _currentShape;
bool _moving;
Adorner _adorner;
```

13. We'll now implement the `MouseLeftButtonDown` event handler. First, we'll remove any previous adorner if it exists:

```
var layer = AdornerLayer.GetAdornerLayer(_canvas);
if(_adorner != null) {
   layer.Remove(_adorner);
   _adorner = null;
}
```

14. Next, we'll check if a circle was clicked or an empty space. If it's a circle, we'll save some state and add an adorner for that circle:

```
var shape = e.Source as Shape;
if(shape != null) {
   _moving = true;
   _current = e.GetPosition(_canvas);
   _currentShape = shape;

   // draw adorner
```

```
        _adorner = new SelectionAdorner(shape);
        layer.Add(_adorner);

        _canvas.CaptureMouse();
    }
```

15. Now we'll implement the `MouseMove` event handler. In the case we're dragging a circle, we need to change its position accordingly:

```
    if(_moving) {
        var pt = e.GetPosition(_canvas);
        Canvas.SetLeft(_currentShape, Canvas.GetLeft(_currentShape)
            + pt.X - _current.X);
        Canvas.SetTop(_currentShape, Canvas.GetTop(_currentShape)
            + pt.Y - _current.Y);
        _current = pt;
    }
```

16. In the `MouseLeftButtonUp` event handler, we simply do some cleanup:

```
    if(_moving) {
        _moving = false;
        _canvas.ReleaseMouseCapture();
    }
```

17. Run the application and drag some circles. Notice the adorner on the currently selected circle. If you click an empty space, the adorner is removed.

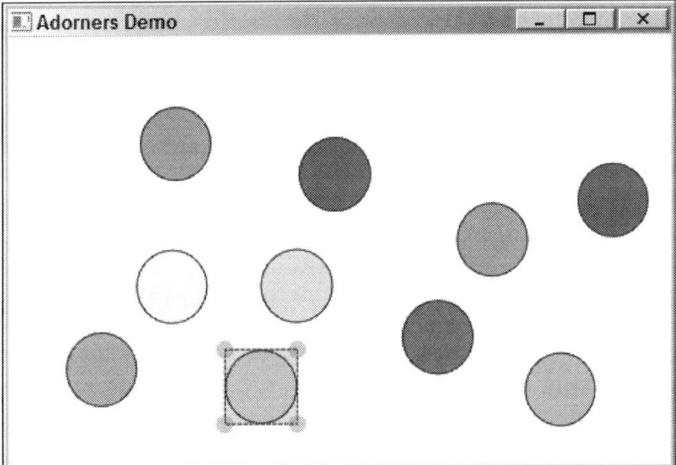

How it works...

Adorners are placed in their own layer, away from the accessible visual tree. This layer can be accessed only programmatically via the static `AdornerLayer.GetAdornerLayer` method. Given that `AdornerLayer`, adorners can be added with `Add` and removed with `Remove`.

An adorner must inherit from the abstract `Adorner` class and provide some visual representation by overriding the `OnRender` method. The `AdornedElement` property inherited from `Adorner` provides the information necessary to create the required graphical representation, such as the size of an element.

There's more...

The adorner layer itself is hosted in an `AdornerDecorator` (a `Decorator`). This can be viewed using the WPF Visualizer with the debugger. Here's a screenshot with an application running and an existing adorner:

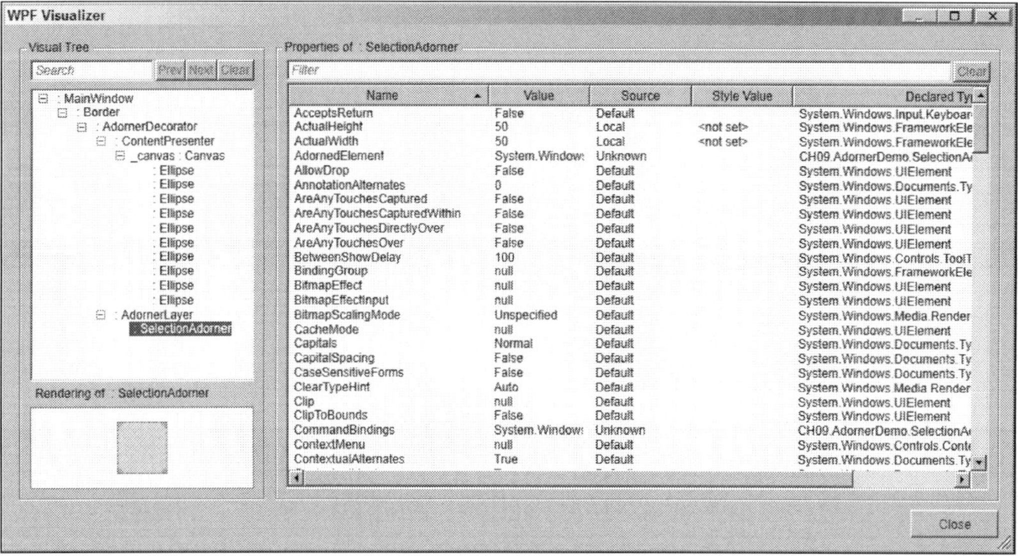

Creating property-based animations

WPF includes a sophisticated and elegant animation engine that takes animations to the declarative level. Instead of dealing with timers and graphic updates, an animation object holds all the required information for the animation to commence. WPF does the rest.
In this recipe, we'll take a look at property-based animations – the simplest and most often used kind.

Getting ready

Make sure Visual Studio is up and running.

How to do it...

We'll create some property-based animations on some shapes inside a Canvas, showing the basic steps involved in creating animations:

1. Create a new WPF application named `CH09.SimpleAnimation`.
2. Open `MainWindow.xaml`. Add the following two rows to the existing `Grid`:

```
<Grid.RowDefinitions>
    <RowDefinition Height="Auto" />
    <RowDefinition />
</Grid.RowDefinitions>
```

3. Add a `Canvas` to the second row with a bunch of elements:

```
<Canvas Grid.Row="1">
    <Rectangle Canvas.Left="60" Canvas.Top="40" Width="40"
        Height="40" x:Name="r1" Fill="Red" Stroke="Black"
        StrokeThickness="2">
        <Rectangle.RenderTransform>
            <RotateTransform x:Name="rot1" />
        </Rectangle.RenderTransform>
    </Rectangle>
    <Ellipse Canvas.Left="20" Canvas.Top="100" Width="40"
        Height="40" x:Name="e1" Fill="Blue" Stroke="Black"
        StrokeThickness="2"/>
    <Rectangle Canvas.Left="20" Canvas.Top="160" Width="350"
        Height="60" x:Name="r2" Stroke="Black"
        StrokeThickness="2">
        <Rectangle.Fill>
            <LinearGradientBrush EndPoint="1,0">
                <GradientStop Offset="0" Color="Yellow" />
                <GradientStop Offset="1" Color="Black"
                              x:Name="g1" />
            </LinearGradientBrush>
        </Rectangle.Fill>
    </Rectangle>
</Canvas>
```

4. Add a horizontal `StackPanel` in the first row of the `Grid`.

5. Add a button to the `StackPanel` as follows:

```
<Button Content="Rotate rectangle" Margin="4" />
```

6. Add a `Click` event handler for this button. In the first example, we'll create the animation in code to rotate the first rectangle within the `Canvas`.
7. Add the following to the `Click` event handler:

```
var animation = new DoubleAnimation(360,
    TimeSpan.FromSeconds(2), FillBehavior.Stop);
Storyboard.SetTarget(animation, rot1);
rot1.BeginAnimation(RotateTransform.AngleProperty, animation);
```

8. Run the application and click the button. The `Rectangle` should rotate 360 degrees around its top-left corner.
9. Open `MainWindow.xaml`. The next animation should move the ellipse to the right (and back) – this time entirely in XAML.
10. Add a button to the `StackPanel` with an event trigger:

```
<Button Content="Move Circle" Margin="4">
    <Button.Triggers>
        <EventTrigger RoutedEvent="Button.Click">
            <BeginStoryboard>
                <Storyboard>
                    <DoubleAnimation
                     Storyboard.TargetName="e1"
                     Storyboard.TargetProperty="(Canvas.Left)"
                     To="400" Duration="0:0:3"
                     AutoReverse="True"/>
                </Storyboard>
            </BeginStoryboard>
        </EventTrigger>
    </Button.Triggers>
</Button>
```

11. Run the application and click this button. The ellipse should move to the right and then reverse its motion back to the starting point.
12. The next animation will be of a color. Add another button to the `StackPanel` and set up an event trigger as follows:

```
<Button Content="Animate Color" Margin="4">
    <Button.Triggers>
        <EventTrigger RoutedEvent="Button.Click">
            <BeginStoryboard>
                <Storyboard>
                    <ColorAnimation To="Red" Duration="0:0:4"
                        Storyboard.TargetName="g1"
```

```
                    Storyboard.TargetProperty="Color"
                    AutoReverse="True" />
            </Storyboard>
        </BeginStoryboard>
    </EventTrigger>
</Button.Triggers>
</Button>
```

13. Run the application and click the third button – watch one of the gradients change from black to red and then reverse. Click more than one button – you should see multiple animations running at the same time. Here's a snapshot:

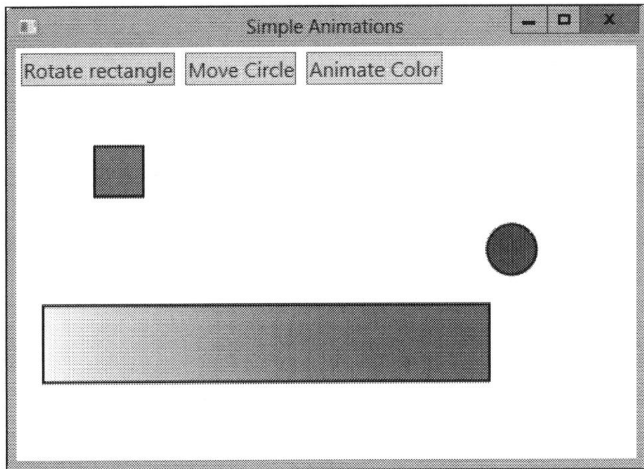

How it works...

Property-based animations are based on a single idea: changing a dependency property from one value to another in a specified amount of time. Various animation classes exist, based on the type of property being animated, such as `DoubleAnimation`, `ColorAnimation`, and `PointAnimation` (all in the `System.Windows.Media.Animation` namespace). All animation types inherit from the abstract `Timeline` class that provides most of the common properties to all animation types.

Animations may be created manually by constructing the appropriate animation type, specifying properties and then calling `BeginAnimation` on the element to animate, providing the dependency property to animate and the animation object. This is illustrated in step 7: a `DoubleAnimation` object is created to animate the `Angle` property (a double) of a `RotateTransform` object. Various constructors exist – and there's always a way to use simple properties – in this case the `To` value is set, the duration (a `Duration` object, convertible from a `TimeSpan`) and a `FillBehavior` (what to do when the animation ends – see more in the next section). Then `BeginAnimation` is called on the rectangle object to animate with the dependency property field and the just created animation object.

Although animations in code are sometimes useful when the animation parameters are highly dynamic, more often than not animations are created in XAML.

The most useful object to use is a Storyboard, which is a kind of `Timeline` (a `ParallelTimeline` to be exact), that can contain multiple animations that are guaranteed to be synchronized (start at the same time); there can even be other `Storyboard` objects if needed. The other advantage of a `Storyboard` is its ability to be manipulated by `TriggerAction` objects related to animations (such as `BeginStoryboard`) available with event triggers and property triggers.

To set up an animation with a `Storyboard`, child animation objects are created (such as `DoubleAnimation`) with the relevant properties. Two attached properties defined on `Storyboard` should be used, `TargetProperty` and `TargetName` (or `Target` if more convenient). In the ellipse example, `TargetName` is "e1" (the ellipse name) and `TargetProperty` is `"(Canvas.Left)"`. Note the parenthesis – these are required when animating an attached property.

The `Storyboard` class defines several `Begin` methods that can be used to run a `Storyboard` programmatically. A `BeginStoryboard` object is typically used in XAML to start a `Storyboard`.

The third example uses a `ColorAnimation`, to demonstrate how similar the various animation types are – they mainly differ in the type, but the same concepts apply.

There's more...

The following common properties are available on most animation types (partial list):

- `From`: Indicates the starting value for animation. If omitted, uses the current value.
- `To`: It is the target value of the animation. If omitted, it means the property value without the animation effect.
- `By`: Sometimes more convenient to use instead of the `To` property. Not all animation types support it – for example, for `ColorAnimation` there is no meaning to `By`.
- `Duration`: The duration of animation and is similar (and convertible from) to a `TimeSpan`. Adds two special values, `Duration.Automatic` (one second for true animation types such as `DoubleAnimation`, end of child animations for container `Timeline`s) and `Duration.Forever` (infinite length). Mostly specified in XAML using the format "hrs:min:sec.msec".
- `FillBehavior`: Indicates the animation's behavior when it ends. `FillEnd` (the default) means the last animation value is kept; the previous value (before the animation) will have no effect. The other value, `Stop`, destroys the animation, and reverts the property to its value without the animation present.
- `BeginTime`: Sets a delay before the animation really begins. Can be used to synchronize follow-ups in `Storyboard`s.

- `AutoReverse`: Indicates if the animation should reverse automatically. If `true`, the total animation duration is effectively doubled.
- `SpeedRatio`: Allows speeding up or slowing down the timeline (effectively changing the duration).
- `RepeatBehavior`: Specifies how many times, or the total time, to repeat the animation; can be `RepeatBehavior.Forever` to repeat the animation for eternity (mostly useful when `AutoReverse` is `true`).

Alternative way to specify the animation property

Sometimes the property we want to animate is not available on an easily named object. For example, the following `LinearGradientBrush` is used in the code example:

```
<LinearGradientBrush EndPoint="1,0">
    <GradientStop Offset="0" Color="Yellow" />
    <GradientStop Offset="1" Color="Black" x:Name="g1" />
</LinearGradientBrush>
```

We want to animate the color of the second `GradientStop` and that's conveniently named `"g1"`. However, if that brush is the result of (for example) data binding, the second gradient will not be named. Still we can get to it in a slightly longer way starting from the actual element itself (the `Rectangle`, named `"r2"`) as follows:

```
Storyboard.TargetName="r2" Storyboard.TargetProperty=
    "Fill.(LinearGradientBrush.GradientStops)[1].Color"
```

The parentheses are required. This indicates that the property `Fill` is in fact of type `LinearGradientBrush` (and not a generic `Brush`) and that the interesting property is `GradientStops`; then we use the required index because that property has an indexer.

More on storyboards

`Storyboard` objects can be started with the `BeginStoryboard` action, but there are other actions that can be used to otherwise control an animation, including `StopStoryboard`, `PauseStoryboard`, `ResumeStoryboard`, `SeekStoryboard`, `SkipStoryboardToFill`, `SetStoryboardSpeedRatio`, and `RemoveStoryboard`. These are less commonly used, but it's good to know they're there if needed.

`Storyboard` (and other `Timeline` based types) supports a bunch of events (all regular .NET events, not routed events), of which the most useful is `Completed` that notifies when a `Timeline` completes. This can be used to remove the `Storyboard`, set some properties, or anything else that requires special logic when an animation is done.

Animations with Expression Blend

Although simple animations are possible to do with direct XAML coding, more complex animations that require precision are usually done using Expression Blend (preferably by a graphic designer). Blend has a timeline view accessible from the **Objects and Timeline** window that allows dragging to a specific time stamp and then changing properties to their values at that time stamp. This can go on as needed – the correct XAML will be generated by Blend (although usually more verbose than would be created by careful XAML manipulation). Working with Expression Blend is beyond the scope of this book, but some experimentation can go a long way.

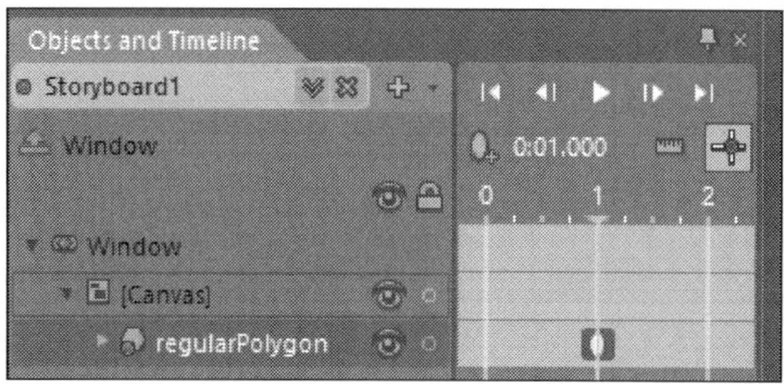

Should I always use animations?

Some applications benefit directly from animations, such as graphic-heavy applications, data visualization, and games .

For other, more "traditional" applications, it may seem that animations may not be very important – even something to be avoided. Out of place animations that exist just for their own sake is certainly something to avoid. However, done right, animations can enhance the user experience in a subtle and unforgettable way. Small animations that may not be noticeable at all can have an impact that is only realized when those animations are removed.

Creating path-based animations

Property-based animations are certainly the most common animations to use. WPF supports another form of animation – path-based animation; that is, an animation that runs along a `PathGeometry`. Let's see how to achieve that.

Getting ready

Make sure Visual Studio is up and running.

How to do it...

We'll create a circle that moves along a path laid out by a `PathGeometry` object:

1. Create a new WPF application named `CH09.PathBasedAnimation`.
2. Open `MainWindow.xaml`. Add a `PathGeometry` object to the `Resources` property of `Window` that describes a rectangular path:

```
<Window.Resources>
    <PathGeometry x:Key="rg">
        <PathFigure IsClosed="True" StartPoint="20,20">
            <PolyLineSegment
                Points="300,20 300,200 20,200 20,200" />
        </PathFigure>
    </PathGeometry>
</Window.Resources>
```

3. Add two rows to the existing `Grid` as follows:

```
<Grid.RowDefinitions>
  <RowDefinition Height="Auto" />
  <RowDefinition />
</Grid.RowDefinitions>
```

4. Add a `Canvas` to the second row of the `Grid` that holds an `Ellipse` that would be animated to move along the path defined by the geometry:

```
<Canvas Grid.Row="1">
   <Ellipse Fill="Red" Stroke="Black" StrokeThickness="2"
       Width="40" Height="40" x:Name="e1"
       Canvas.Left="20" Canvas.Top="20"/>
</Canvas>
```

5. Add a button to the first row, with an event trigger for the `Click` event:

```
<Button Content="Start Animation" FontSize="16" Margin="8">
   <Button.Triggers>
      <EventTrigger RoutedEvent="Button.Click">
      </EventTrigger>
   </Button.Triggers>
</Button>
```

6. When that event hits, we want to start a `Storyboard` to animate the `Canvas.Left` and `Canvas.Top` properties (at the same time) based on the defined `PathGeometry`. Add the following inside the `EventTrigger`:

```
<BeginStoryboard>
    <Storyboard RepeatBehavior="Forever">
        <DoubleAnimationUsingPath Duration="0:0:3"
```

```
                    Storyboard.TargetName="e1"
                    Storyboard.TargetProperty="(Canvas.Left)"
                    PathGeometry="{StaticResource rg}" Source="X" />
               <DoubleAnimationUsingPath Duration="0:0:3"
                    Storyboard.TargetName="e1"
                    Storyboard.TargetProperty="(Canvas.Top)"
                    PathGeometry="{StaticResource rg}" Source="Y"/>
          </Storyboard>
     </BeginStoryboard>
```

7. Run the application and click the button. The circle should move in a rectangular fashion (repeating its path indefinitely).

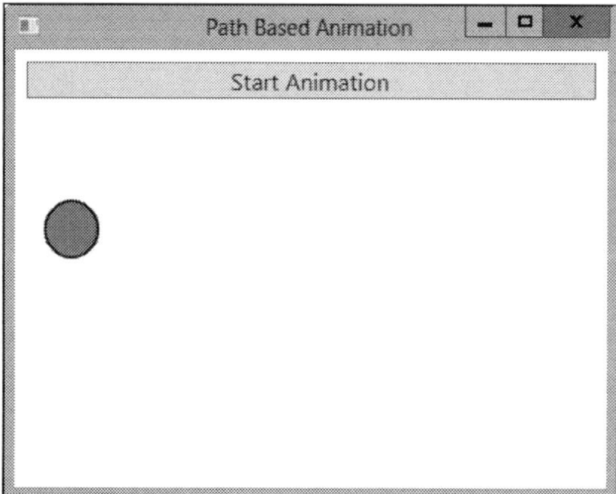

How it works...

Path based animations use a `PathGeometry` (see the *Creating a custom shape* recipe for more information on a `PathGeometry`) as a path (composed of the figures making up the `PathGeometry`). As `PathGeometry` is a 2D representation of a path, it can be provided directly to a `Point` based animation (`PointAnimationUsingPath`), but in this case, where `Canvas.Left` and `Canvas.Top` are the target properties to be animated, we use the `DoubleAnimationUsingPath.Source` property to indicate which coordinate we want to use for a "regular" double value (X or Y):

```
<DoubleAnimationUsingPath … PathGeometry="{StaticResource rg}"
                            Source="X" />
```

There's more...

There is another type of animation supported by WPF – key frame animations. These animations work with "key frames" – specific values along an animation, where WPF interpolates between points in one of several ways (such as linear or Bezier).

Here's a simple example that animates a property of type `double` (the `Offset` of `GradientStop`) in linear piecewise steps:

```
<Storyboard>
    <DoubleAnimationUsingKeyFrames Storyboard.TargetName="gs"
        Storyboard.TargetProperty="Offset" AutoReverse="True"
        RepeatBehavior="Forever">
        <LinearDoubleKeyFrame Value="0" KeyTime="0:0:0" />
        <LinearDoubleKeyFrame Value=".3" KeyTime="0:0:2" />
        <LinearDoubleKeyFrame Value=".8" KeyTime="0:0:5" />
        <LinearDoubleKeyFrame Value="1" KeyTime="0:0:7" />
        <LinearDoubleKeyFrame Value="1.5" KeyTime="0:0:8" />
    </DoubleAnimationUsingKeyFrames>
</Storyboard>
```

Animation performance

Complex or multiple animations may take their toll on application performance. Although WPF works by leveraging DirectX, this is not "raw" DirectX, and in any case may depend on graphic hardware capabilities. Potentially, resource hogging animations should be optional – there should be a way for the user to turn them off, or at least remove some of them to keep the application from consuming too many resources.

Here are some tips on animation performance:

- Animating font sizes is typically slow – avoid these.
- If opacity animation is required, try to animate a brush opacity (`Brush.Opacity`) instead of element opacity (`UIElement.Opacity`).
- Decrease the frame rate for slow changing animations; there's no need for WPF to refresh more times than necessary. To set the desired frame rate, set the attached `Timeline.DesiredFrameRate` property on a top-level `Storyboard` object. The opposite may also be desired – increase the frame rate for fast changing animations to reduce tearing effects.
- Stop running animations when the application is deactivated (the user has switched to another application; use the `Application.Deactivated` event).

Creating custom animations

The three types of animations provided by WPF (property, path, and key frame) are declarative in nature, which is in large part what makes them easy to use. There's no need to handle timers, change positions manually, or anything like that.

Occasionally, dynamic changes are required which cannot be represented using the built-in animations. Examples include movements that use complex formulas and changes based on user interaction. In such scenarios, it's possible to perform the changes manually with some help from WPF.

Getting ready

Make sure Visual Studio is up and running.

How to do it...

We'll create a bouncing ball application that uses complex movements and optional user interaction to control the ball:

1. Create a new WPF application named `CH09.CustomAnimation`.
2. Add a new class named `Ball`. Add using statements to the `System.ComponentModel` and `System.Windows` namespaces.
3. Implement the `INotifyPropertyChanged` interface with the event declaration and a simple `OnPropertyChanged` method:

   ```
   class Ball : INotifyPropertyChanged {
      public event PropertyChangedEventHandler PropertyChanged;

      void OnPropertyChanged(string propName) {
         var pc = PropertyChanged;
         if (pc != null)
            pc(this, new PropertyChangedEventArgs(propName));
      }
   ```

4. Add some fields and properties controlling the position, size, and speed of the ball:

   ```
   Point _position, _velocity;
   public double X {
      get { return _position.X; }
      set {
         _position.X = value;
         OnPropertyChanged("X");
      }
   }
   ```

```
public double Y {
   get { return _position.Y; }
   set {
      _position.Y = value;
      OnPropertyChanged("Y");
   }
}

public double Width { get; set; }
public double Height { get; set; }
public Point Velocity {
   get { return _velocity; }
   set {
      _velocity = value;
      OnPropertyChanged("Velocity");
   }
}
```

5. Add a new class named `Environment` that adds some realism to the bouncing ball simulation. Implement with the following code:

```
class Environment : INotifyPropertyChanged {
   public static double Traction = .95;
   double _gravity;
   public double Gravity {
      get { return _gravity; }
      set {
         _gravity = value;
         OnPropertyChanged("Gravity");
      }
   }
   public event PropertyChangedEventHandler PropertyChanged;

   void OnPropertyChanged(string propName) {
      var pc = PropertyChanged;
      if(pc != null)
         pc(this, new PropertyChangedEventArgs(propName));
   }
}
```

6. The `Traction` value will be used to slow down the ball when impacting a wall; the `Gravity` property is pretty self-evident.

7. Open `Ball.cs`. Add a property and a constructor for the `Environment` type:

```
public Environment Environment { get; private set; }

public Ball(Environment env) {
   Environment = env;
}
```

8. We need to set up a method that moves the ball in the current direction (`Velocity` property) and flips the direction if it collides with the bounds of the environment. Add a method to the `Ball` class implemented with the following code:

```
public void Move(Rect bounds) {
   _velocity.Y += Environment.Gravity;
   X += Velocity.X;
   Y += Velocity.Y;
   bool xhit = false, yhit = false;
   if(X < bounds.Left) {
      X = bounds.Left;
      xhit = true;
   }
   else if(X > bounds.Right - Width) {
      X = bounds.Right - Width;
      xhit = true;
   }
   if(Y < bounds.Top) {
      Y = bounds.Top;
      yhit = true;
   }
   else if(Y > bounds.Bottom - Height) {
      Y = bounds.Bottom - Height;
      yhit = true;
   }

   if(xhit) {
      _velocity.X = -_velocity.X;
      _velocity.X *= Environment.Traction;
   }
   if(yhit) {
      _velocity.Y = -_velocity.Y;
      _velocity.Y *= Environment.Traction;
   }
}
```

9. Open `MainWindow.xaml`. Add two rows to the exiting `Grid`:

```
<Grid.RowDefinitions>
    <RowDefinition Height="Auto" />
    <RowDefinition />
</Grid.RowDefinitions>
```

10. Add a `StackPanel` to the first row with a `Slider` bound to the `Gravity` property:

```
<StackPanel Orientation="Horizontal" Margin="8">
    <TextBlock Text="Gravity:" VerticalAlignment="Center"
               FontSize="15" />
    <Slider Minimum="0" Maximum="3" Margin="10,0,0,0"
            Value="{Binding Environment.Gravity}"
            Width="100"/>
</StackPanel>
```

11. Add a `Canvas` to the second row holding an `Ellipse`, to serve as the ball:

```
<Canvas x:Name="_canvas" Grid.Row="1">
    <Ellipse Fill="Red" Stroke="Black" StrokeThickness="2"
        Cursor="Hand" Width="{Binding Width, Mode=TwoWay}"
        Height="{Binding Height, Mode=TwoWay}"
        Canvas.Left="{Binding X}" Canvas.Top="{Binding Y}" />
</Canvas>
```

12. Open `MainWindow.xaml.cs`. Add some private fields to the `MainWindow` class:

```
Ball _ball;
bool _grabbing;
private Point _mousePos, _lastDelta;
const double MaxSpeed = 20;
```

13. Add the following lines to the constructor (after the call to `InitializeComponent`) to create a `Ball` object, initialize it, and register for the `CompositionTarget.Rendering` static event, which is the key to custom animations:

```
var env = new Environment { Gravity = .8 };
_ball = new Ball(env) { Width = 40, Height = 40,
   Velocity = new Point(3, 1) };
DataContext = _ball;

CompositionTarget.Rendering += CompositionTarget_Rendering;
```

14. Implement the static event with the following code:

```
void CompositionTarget_Rendering(object sender, EventArgs e) {
   if(!_grabbing)
      _ball.Move(new Rect(new Point(0, 0), _canvas.RenderSize));
}
```

15. Open `MainWindow.xaml`. Add an event handler or the `MouseLeftButtonDown`, `MouseMove`, and `MouseLeftButtonUp` events on the `Ellipse`, so that the user can grab it and send it hurling in some direction:

```
MouseLeftButtonDown="OnGrabObject" MouseMove="OnMouseMove"
    MouseLeftButtonUp="OnReleaseObject"
```

16. Implement `OnGrabObject` with the following code:

```
void OnGrabObject(object sender, MouseButtonEventArgs e) {
   _grabbing = true;
   _mousePos = e.GetPosition(_canvas);
   e.Handled = true;
   var element = sender as FrameworkElement;
   element.CaptureMouse();
}
```

17. Implement `OnMouseMove` with the following code:

```
void OnMouseMove(object sender, MouseEventArgs e) {
   if(_grabbing) {
      Point pt = e.GetPosition(_canvas);
      _lastDelta = new Point(pt.X - _mousePos.X,
         pt.Y - _mousePos.Y);
      _ball.X += _lastDelta.X; _ball.Y += _lastDelta.Y;
      _mousePos = pt;
   }
}
```

18. Implement `OnReleaseObject` with the following code:

```
void OnReleaseObject(object sender, MouseButtonEventArgs e) {
   if(_grabbing) {
      _grabbing = false;
      e.Handled = true;
      ((FrameworkElement)sender).ReleaseMouseCapture();
      if(Math.Abs(_lastDelta.X) > MaxSpeed)
         _lastDelta.X = MaxSpeed * Math.Sign(_lastDelta.X);
      if(Math.Abs(_lastDelta.Y) > MaxSpeed)
         _lastDelta.Y = MaxSpeed * Math.Sign(_lastDelta.Y);
      _ball.Velocity = _lastDelta;
   }
}
```

19. Run the application. Move the slider to change the gravity factor. Grab the ball with the mouse and drag it in some direction.

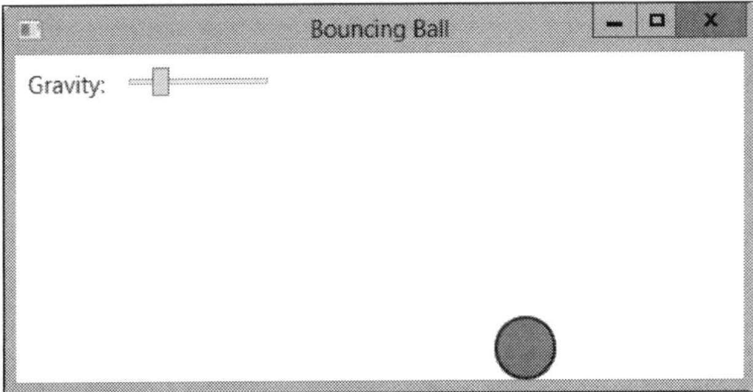

How it works...

The static `CompositionTarget.Rendering` event is fired before every frame is rendered by WPF – the last chance to change things before they are handed off to the rendering layer. The ball (ellipse) is moved in a way that is too complex, or at least unpredictable, for declarative animations.

Every frame the `Ball.Move` method is called is to change the ball's position, which is bound to the `Canvas.Left` and `Canvas.Top` properties of the `Ellipse` element, representing the ball. The `Move` method also checks if the ball is out of bounds; if it is, it reverses direction and the speed of the ball decreases a bit (based on the `Environment.Traction` field). The vertical speed is also changed by the amount of gravity to provide more realistic movement (if gravity is greater than zero).

The mouse event handlers in `MainWindow` allow the user to "grab" the ball (if she's quick enough) and drag it, sending it flying in that particular direction.

Adding animation easing to animations

Property-based animations are linear – they progress at a constant rate. This is fine for many scenarios, but for some scenarios this feels too mechanical. Key frame animations can use Bezier-based interpolations (which are certainly not linear), but it's not easy to configure or guess their effects.

Animation easing (introduced in WPF 4) provides a viable alternative that can turn a (maybe boring) linear animation into a non-linear one.

Getting ready

Make sure Visual Studio is up and running.

How to do it...

We'll create a linear animation and another same animation mutated with animation easing:

1. Create a new WPF application named `CH09.AnimationEasing`.
2. Open `MainWindow.xaml`. Add two rows to the existing `Grid`:

```
<Grid.RowDefinitions>
    <RowDefinition Height="Auto" />
    <RowDefinition />
</Grid.RowDefinitions>
```

3. Add a `StackPanel` to the first row of the `Grid`. Place two buttons inside similar to the following:

```
<StackPanel Orientation="Horizontal">
    <Button Content="Linear Animation" Margin="8"
        FontSize="16" />
    <Button Content="Animation with Easing" Margin="8"
        FontSize="16" />
</StackPanel>
```

4. Add a `Canvas` to the second row of the `Grid`. Add an `Ellipse` to the `Canvas` to be used for animation purposes:

```
<Canvas Grid.Row="1">
   <Ellipse Fill="Red" Stroke="Black" StrokeThickness="2"
      Width="40" Height="40" Canvas.Left="20"
      Canvas.Top="30" x:Name="e1"/>
</Canvas>
```

5. Let's set the animations using an event trigger. Add the following `Triggers` property for the first button that uses a regular linear animation:

```
<Button.Triggers>
    <EventTrigger RoutedEvent="Button.Click">
        <BeginStoryboard>
            <Storyboard>
                <DoubleAnimation To="400" From="20"
          Storyboard.TargetName="e1"
          Storyboard.TargetProperty="(Canvas.Left)"
          Duration="0:0:3" />
            </Storyboard>
        </BeginStoryboard>
    </EventTrigger>
</Button.Triggers>
```

6. The animation moves the circle across the window in 3 seconds. Add a similar `Triggers` property to the second button, but this time set up animation easing for the `DoubleAnimation` object:

```
<Button.Triggers>
    <EventTrigger RoutedEvent="Button.Click">
        <BeginStoryboard>
            <Storyboard>
                <DoubleAnimation To="400" From="20"
          Storyboard.TargetName="e1"
          Storyboard.TargetProperty="(Canvas.Left)"
          Duration="0:0:3" >
                    <DoubleAnimation.EasingFunction>
                        <CircleEase />
                    </DoubleAnimation.EasingFunction>
                </DoubleAnimation>
            </Storyboard>
        </BeginStoryboard>
    </EventTrigger>
</Button.Triggers>
```

7. Run the application. Click the first button – a regular linear animation runs. Click the second button, and the result is certainly noticeably different (unfortunately, no image can convey this; you'll need to actually run this to see the effects).

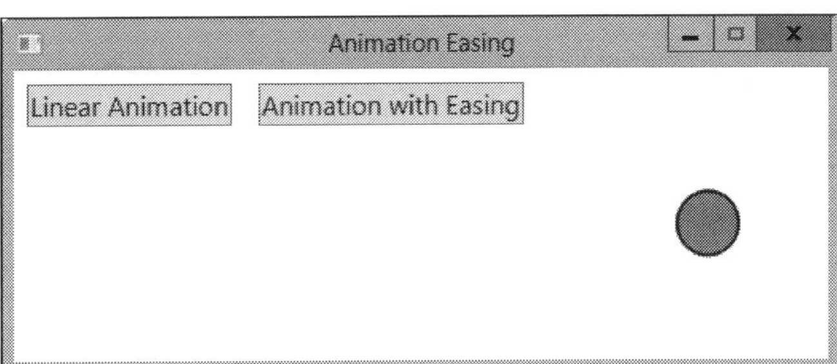

How it works...

Animation easing applies a function to the animation value, altering it from its normally linear value (the value changes uniformly with time). There are 11 built-in easing functions in WPF 4.5, all deriving from the abstract `EasingFunctionBase` class. `EasingFunctionBase` implements the `IEasingFunction` interface (having just one method: `Ease`) and adds the `EasingMode` property that indicates whether the "easing" function should be applied at the start of the animation (`EaseIn`), the end of the animation (`EaseOut`), or both (`EaseInOut`).

The example uses the `CircleEase` function. As the `EasingMode` property was not modified, it uses its default value of `EaseOut`. The exact function used can be found in the documentation. `CircleEase` does not add any properties to customize its behavior, but many do. For example, the `ElasticEase` class (providing a spring-like behavior) adds two properties, `Oscillations` and `Springiness`, allowing fine tuning of its effects.

There's more...

The built-in easing functions should suffice for most needs. Special needs, however, may require creating a new easing function. To do that, we need to derive a class from `EasingFunctionBase` and implement two abstract methods: `EaseInCore` (which `EasingFunctionBase` defines) and `CreateInstanceCore` (required by `Freezable`, the base class of `EasingFunctionBase`). Here's a simple implementation that reverses the animation and slows it down at the start and/or end (depending on the `EasingMode` property):

```
class CustomEaseFunction : EasingFunctionBase {
   protected override double EaseInCore(double time) {
      return 1 - time * time;
   }

   protected override Freezable CreateInstanceCore() {
      return new CustomEaseFunction();
   }
}
```

The relevant function is `EaseInCore`. It accepts a normalized time argument, between 0 and 1, and should return a new normalized value. In the trivial case, we can return the same value we get, and that is a regular linear animation.

We should return something different, typically based on some formula. However, it's important to make sure the formula provides values in the 0 to 1 range, otherwise the animation will move out of its from/to values (which may be ok in some cases). Creating a good function is not an easy task. The preceding function, for instance, behaves ok in `EaseIn` and `EaseOut` modes, but becomes weird in `EaseInOut` mode. Getting the function just right may not be easy.

Thankfully, with `EasingFunctionBase`, there's no need to tackle the `EaseOut` or `EaseInOut` easing modes, as these are computed automatically (by using a symmetric approach).

Using custom effects with pixel shaders

WPF 4 includes two special effect classes, `BlurEffect` and `DropShadowEffect`. These are built internally using pixel shaders, which are little programs that run on the graphics processing unit (GPU) as one of the final parts of rendering. These shaders originate from DirectX (WPF's lowest level rendering engine), so other effects can be used with the proper setup. Let's take a look at using a custom pixel shader to get special effects, otherwise very difficult or slow to achieve.

Getting ready

To compile shader files, you'll need the DirectX SDK, which can be downloaded from the DirectX portal at `http://msdn.microsoft.com/en-US/directx`. Click on **Get the latest DirectX SDK**, download the installer, and install the SDK.

How to do it...

We'll create a simple shader effect and make it available to WPF:

1. Create a new WPF application named `CH09.CustomEffect`.
2. Add a folder to the project named `Effects`.
3. Add a new text file to the newly created folder and name it `red.fx`. This is the pixel shader code.
4. Add the following High Level Shader Language (HLSL) code to the newly created file:

```
sampler2D input : register(s0);

float4 main(float2 uv : TEXCOORD) : COLOR {
   float4 src = tex2D(input, uv);
   float4 dst = src;
   dst.gb = 0;

   return dst;
}
```

5. This code strips the green and blue components of every pixel color. Save the file.
6. We need to compile the HLSL file to its binary format by using the `fxc.exe` compiler (the effects compiler), part of the DirectX SDK. Open the DirectX command prompt by clicking the **Start** button, going to **Programs** | **DirectX SDK** | **DirectX SDK Command Prompt** (in Windows 8 go to the Start screen and type **DirectX**, and locate the **DirectX SDK Command Prompt** result).

7. In the command prompt, navigate to the `Effects` folder that was created and type in the following command:

   `fxc /T ps_2_0 /E main /Fo red.ps red.fx`

8. If everything goes well, a success message should be displayed:

```
C:\Users\Pavel\Documents\WPFBook\Chapter09\CH09\CH09.CustomEffect\Effects>fxc /T ps_2_0 /E
 main /Fo red.ps red.fx
Microsoft (R) Direct3D Shader Compiler 9.29.952.3111
Copyright (C) Microsoft Corporation 2002-2009. All rights reserved.

compilation succeeded; see C:\Users\Pavel\Documents\WPFBook\Chapter09\CH09\CH09.CustomEffe
ct\Effects\red.ps
```

9. If the compiler complains about a bad character at position (1,1), make sure you save the `red.fx` file with an ASCII based code page. To do this, select from the menu **File | Advanced Save Options...** and then select the **Western European** encoding as shown here:

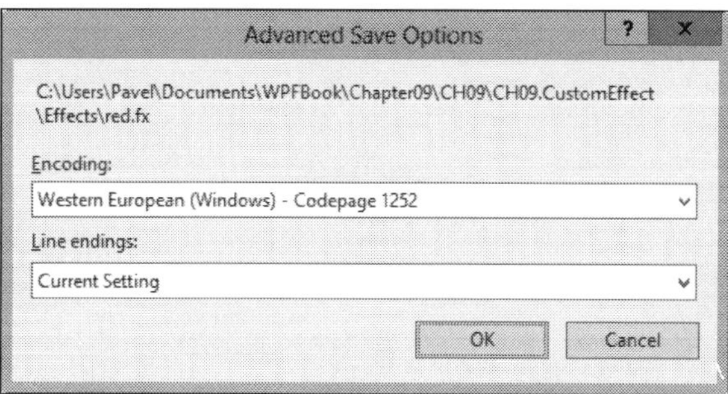

10. The resulting file is `red.ps`, which is what we want. Add the file to `Effects` folder and change its **Build Action** to **Resource**.
11. Now we need to create a custom effect class to wrap the effect. Add a new class to the project, named `RedEffect`.
12. Derive the class from `ShaderEffect` (in the `System.Windows.Media.Effects` namespace).
13. Add a special dependency property to the class to represent the implicit input to the shader using the following code inside the class:

```
public static readonly DependencyProperty InputProperty =
    RegisterPixelShaderSamplerProperty("Input",
    typeof(RedEffect), 0);

public Brush Input {
   get { return (Brush)GetValue(InputProperty); }
   set { SetValue(InputProperty, value); }
}
```

14. Add a public constructor to the class that loads the correct compiled shader, as shown in the following code snippet:

```
public RedEffect() {
   PixelShader = new PixelShader();
   PixelShader.UriSource = new Uri("/Effects/red.ps",
      UriKind.Relative);
   UpdateShaderValue(InputProperty);
}
```

15. We're now ready to test the effect. Open `MainWindow.xaml` and add two equal sized columns to the existing `Grid`:

```
<Grid.ColumnDefinitions>
   <ColumnDefinition />
   <ColumnDefinition />
</Grid.ColumnDefinitions>
```

16. Add an image file to the project, such as the `Penguins.jpg` from the `Sample Images` folder.
17. Add an XML namespace mapping to the local namespace:

```
xmlns:local="clr-namespace:CH09.CustomEffect"
```

18. Add two images of penguins to each cell of the `Grid`, with the second image with the created effect applied on it:

```
<Image Source="Penguins.jpg" />
<Image Source="Penguins.jpg" Grid.Column="1">
    <Image.Effect>
        <local:RedEffect />
    </Image.Effect>
</Image>
```

19. The designer view should already be a clue as to how this would look at runtime. Run the application anyway:

How it works...

A pixel shader is practically the last stage of graphic processing (known as the rendering pipeline) done by the graphic card before the final pixel color is rendered to the frame buffer. This is the last chance to make changes to the resulting pixel color coming from previous processing stages.

To make actual changes, we need to execute code in the context of the GPU – that's the job of the little program typically written in High Level Shader Language (HLSL). HLSL is beyond the scope of this book, as it has nothing special to do with WPF – it originates in DirectX – but briefly, HLSL is a C-like language with relevant extensions, able to receive a pixel (in the case of pixel shaders) and transform its color in any way desired. In our case, the pixel color was stripped of its B (blue) and G (green) components, maintaining the R (red) and A (alpha) from the original color:

```
float4 dst = src;
dst.gb = 0;
```

The syntax may be somewhat weird, but that's just a part of HLSL. Once the effect file is compiled with the `FXC.exe` compiler, it's added as a resource (the original source file is not needed), and a custom class is created to host the effect, loading it in the constructor.

The compilation line:

```
fxc /T ps_2_0 /E main /Fo red.ps red.fx
```

Roughly means: compile with pixel shader version 2.0 (guaranteed to work in WPF), with `main` being the entry function, send the output to the `red.ps` file and the input file (last argument) is `red.fx`.

The static `PixelShader.RegisterPixelShaderSamplerProperty` method connects a dependency property (in this case named `Input`) to the pixel input provided to the shader. This is the minimum requirement so that the shader class can interact with the actual shader. The rest is handled by `PixelShader` itself.

The effect object is applied to the `UIElement.Effect` property (of type `System.Windows.Media.Effects.Effect`) – this means it can be used on anything, not just an image.

There's more...

Naturally, writing shaders is not easy, except for very simple effects. A large list of shaders ready to be plugged into WPF (and Silverlight) can be found at a CodePlex project named `wpffx` (`http://wpffx.codeplex.com/`).

Another useful tool called Shazzam Shader Editor (by Walt Ritschter) is available free of charge from `http://shazzam-tool.com`. This tool provides a graphic way to visualize shaders, tweak their parameters with immediate feedback, and even get the C# (or VB) source code required to use them in a WPF (or Silverlight) application. A side benefit of the tool is that the DirectX SDK is not needed, as it compiles the shaders on its own by calling DirectX shader compilation functions directly using P/Invoke.

Using the built-in effects

Two built in effects exist - `BlurEffect` and `DropShadowEffect`, and both are used like any other effect. Here's an example of two buttons using these effects:

```
<StackPanel>
    <Button Content="Blurred Button" FontSize="25" Margin="10">
        <Button.Effect>
            <BlurEffect Radius="6" />
        </Button.Effect>
    </Button>
    <Button Content="Drop Shadow Button" FontSize="25"
            Margin="10">
        <Button.Effect>
            <DropShadowEffect BlurRadius="10" Color="Black"
                              Opacity=".7" />
        </Button.Effect>
    </Button>
</StackPanel>
```

Here's the result:

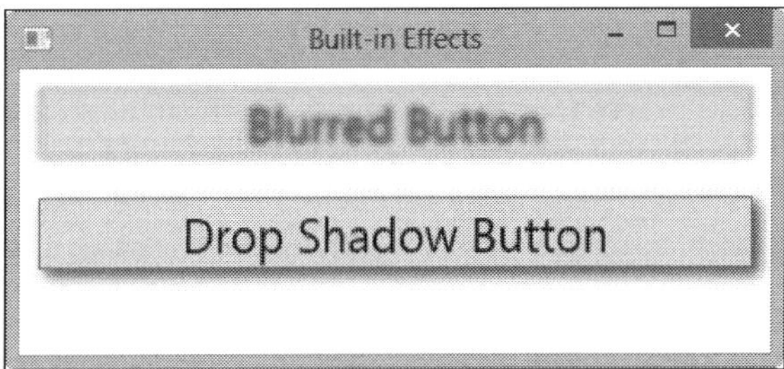

Other shader types

Direct3D supports other type of shaders, namely vertex shaders and geometry shaders. Using these shaders is unsupported in WPF, as these are too low level, and only make sense in a lower-level DirectX application or game. WPF does all vertex and geometry setup on its own and there's no way to customize that. Only pixel shaders are supported, as they don't interfere with WPF's work.

What about the BitmapEffect class and its derivatives?

The first version of WPF provided a set of six built-in graphic effects, deriving from `BitmapEffect` and applied using the `UIElement.BitmapEffect` property (and similar properties on other objects). These effects are obsolete starting from WPF 4 – they simply don't work anymore.

One problem these effects faced was the fact that they were never hardware-accelerated, meaning they always executed on the CPU, never on the GPU; performance suffered, especially for large affected elements. Starting with WPF 4 they have no effect if used; the alternative is using the effects discussed in this recipe, as these execute on the GPU whenever possible.

10
Custom Elements

In this chapter we will cover the following:

- Creating a user control
- Handling standard commands in a user control
- Creating a custom (templated) control
- Customizing a custom control's default template
- Creating a custom panel
- Creating a lightweight custom element

Introduction

WPF provides several ways to customize elements, from simple property changes, through content changes of content controls with data templates, up to using an entirely new control template.

All these options change the way an element appears, but its functionality is unchanged. If a new functionality is desired, a custom element is needed.

In this chapter, we'll take a look at a number of ways of creating custom elements and controls. Some are simple, but lack flexibility, while others are extremely flexible, but require more work.

Creating a user control

A user control is typically used to group related elements and controls together, for the purpose of reuse. Appropriate properties and events are exposed from this control, providing easy access to its functionality. As an added bonus, the Visual Studio designer supports user control design, just as it does for a window.

In WPF, user controls derive from the `UserControl` class (in itself a `ContentControl`). The UI design is effectively the `Content` property of the control, just like any other content control. The `UserControl` class just changes some property values (with respect to its base `ContentControl` class), and has a control template that provides a border that can be used to alter the basic outlook of the user control.

In this recipe, we'll build a user control with all the typical features.

Getting ready

Make sure Visual Studio is up and running.

How to do it...

We'll create a color picker user control that we will be able to reuse where needed. Here's a preview of the control in action:

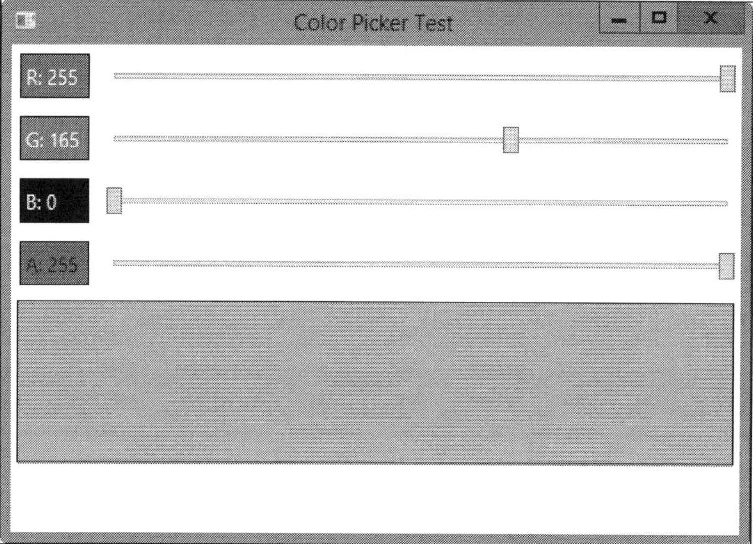

1. Create a new WPF User Control Library named `CH10.UserControls`.

2. A default `UserControl1.xaml` and associated C# files are created. Delete the `UserControl1.xaml` file using the **Solution Explorer**.
3. Right-click on the project node in **Solution Explorer** and select **Add | User Control**.
4. Type **ColorPicker** in the **Name** textbox and click on **Add**.
5. First, we'll add dependency properties for our control. In this case, just one: **SelectedColor**. Open `ColorPicker.xaml.cs`. Add a dependency property to the `ColorPicker` class (you can use the `propdp` code snippet):

```
public static readonly DependencyProperty
   SelectedColorProperty = DependencyProperty.Register(
   "SelectedColor", typeof(Color), typeof(ColorPicker),
   new UIPropertyMetadata(Colors.Black,
   OnSelectedColorChanged));

public Color SelectedColor {
   get { return (Color)GetValue(SelectedColorProperty); }
   set { SetValue(SelectedColorProperty, value); }
}
```

6. `OnSelectedColorChanged` will be used to fire an event signifying a color change. For this purpose, let's define a routed event, `SelectedColorChanged`, to be fired whenever the selected color changes (using the UI or programmatically). There is no code snippet for that, so we have to type things manually:

```
public static RoutedEvent SelectedColorChangedEvent =
   EventManager.RegisterRoutedEvent("SelectedColorChanged",
   RoutingStrategy.Bubble,
   typeof(RoutedPropertyChangedEventHandler<Color>),
   typeof(ColorPicker));

public event RoutedPropertyChangedEventHandler<Color>
   SelectedColorChanged {
   add { AddHandler(SelectedColorChangedEvent, value); }
   remove { RemoveHandler(SelectedColorChangedEvent, value); }
}
```

7. `RoutedPropertyChangedEventHandler<T>` is a convenient delegate that uses a `RoutedPropertyChangedEventArgs<T>` to convey a property change with the `OldValue` and `NewValue` properties. To raise the actual event, we need to know when the selected color changes. Implement the `OnSelectedColorChanged` method with the following code:

```
static void OnSelectedColorChanged(DependencyObject obj,
   DependencyPropertyChangedEventArgs e) {
   var cp = (ColorPicker)obj;
cp.RaiseEvent(new RoutedPropertyChangedEventArgs<Color>(
```

```
            (Color)e.OldValue, (Color)e.NewValue,
            SelectedColorChangedEvent));
    }
}
```

8. Let's switch to building the actual color picker UI. We're aiming for the following layout (seen in design view):

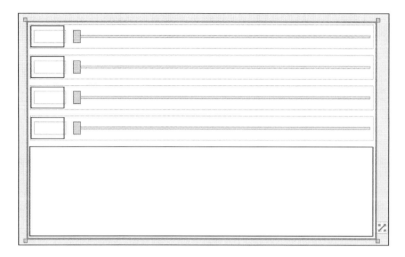

9. Open `ColorPicker.xaml`. Add 4 rows to the existing `Grid` like the following:

```
<Grid.RowDefinitions>
    <RowDefinition Height="Auto" />
    <RowDefinition Height="Auto" />
    <RowDefinition Height="Auto" />
    <RowDefinition Height="Auto" />
    <RowDefinition />
</Grid.RowDefinitions>
```

10. We're going to need some `TextBlock` elements as well as `Rectangle` elements and `Slider` elements. Let's add styles for those to encapsulate common properties:

```
<UserControl.Resources>
    <Style TargetType="Rectangle">
        <Setter Property="Margin" Value="2" />
        <Setter Property="Width" Value="50" />
        <Setter Property="Height" Value="30" />
        <Setter Property="Stroke" Value="Black" />
        <Setter Property="StrokeThickness" Value="1" />
    </Style>
    <Style TargetType="TextBlock">
        <Setter Property="Margin" Value="6,0,0,0" />
```

```
        <Setter Property="Foreground" Value="White" />
        <Setter Property="VerticalAlignment" Value="Center" />
        <Setter Property="FontSize" Value="14" />
    </Style>
    <Style TargetType="Slider">
        <Setter Property="Maximum" Value="255" />
        <Setter Property="VerticalAlignment" Value="Center" />
        <Setter Property="Margin" Value="10,0,0,0" />
        <Setter Property="LargeChange" Value="10" />
    </Style>
</UserControl.Resources>
```

11. Give the user control a name, for data binding purposes:

```
x:Name="uc"
```

12. The big `Rectangle` is the easiest to add, as its fill color can be bound directly to the `SelectedColor` property:

```
<Rectangle Grid.Row="4" Margin="4" Style="{x:Null}"
    StrokeThickness="1" Stroke="Black">
    <Rectangle.Fill>
        <SolidColorBrush Color="{Binding SelectedColor,
            ElementName=uc}" />
    </Rectangle.Fill>
</Rectangle>
```

13. The sliders and other rectangles are more challenging. First, we need to bind a `Value` of the `slider` to a color component (red, green, blue, or alpha) in both directions. As a `Color` cannot be mapped automatically to a `double` (and vice versa), we need a converter. Add a class named `ColorToDoubleConverter` to serve as a converter.
14. Add `using` statements to the `System.Windows.Input`, `System.Windows.Media`, `System.Globalization`, and `System.Windows` namespaces.
15. Implement the `IValueConverter` interface:

```
class ColorToDoubleConverter : IValueConverter {
```

16. The conversion should be both ways: a change in a slider affects the selected color, and a change in the selected color should affect the slider. First, let's convert a `Color` to a `double`; for that, we need to use a parameter to indicate which component of the color to return:

```
public object Convert(object value, Type targetType,
   object parameter, CultureInfo culture) {
   var color = (Color)value;
   switch((string)parameter) {
      case "r": return color.R;
```

```
        case "g": return color.G;
        case "b": return color.B;
        case "a": return color.A;
    }
    return Binding.DoNothing;
}
```

17. Going in the other direction is a little more complex. We need to take a `double` and change the intensity of the component specified by the converter parameter, while leaving all other components intact. This requires the converter to keep track of the last used color. Add a private field to the converter to keep that information:

    ```
    private Color _lastColor;
    ```

18. Given this definition, we can implement `ConvertBack` with the following code:

    ```
    public object ConvertBack(object value, Type targetType,
       object parameter, CultureInfo culture) {
       Color color = _lastColor;
       var intensity = (byte)(double)value;
       switch((string)parameter) {
          case "r":
             color.R = intensity;
             break;
          case "g":
             color.G = intensity;
             break;
          case "b":
             color.B = intensity;
             break;
          case "a":
             color.A = intensity;
             break;
       }
       _lastColor = color;
       return color;
    }
    ```

19. The currently selected color will simply get updated by the `Convert` method. These are the first two lines of `Convert` (the second line is new):

    ```
    var color = (Color)value;
    _lastColor = color;
    ```

20. To fill the remaining rectangles correctly we require another converter from the selected color to a brush, with a single color component. Add a new class named `ColorToBrushConverter` that implements `IValueConverter`.

21. Add four private fields representing the four distinct brushes we need, one for each color component:

```
SolidColorBrush _red = new SolidColorBrush(),
    _green = new SolidColorBrush(),
    _blue = new SolidColorBrush(),
    _alpha = new SolidColorBrush();
```

22. Implement the `Convert` method using the following code:

```
public object Convert(object value, Type targetType,
   object parameter, CultureInfo culture) {
   var color = (Color)value;
   switch((string)parameter) {
      case "r":
         _red.Color = Color.FromRgb(color.R, 0, 0);
         return _red;
      case "g":
         _green.Color = Color.FromRgb(0, color.G, 0);
         return _green;
      case "b":
         _blue.Color = Color.FromRgb(0, 0, color.B);
         return _blue;
      case "a":
         _alpha.Color = Color.FromArgb(color.A,
           128, 128, 128);
         return _alpha;
   }
   return Binding.DoNothing;
}
```

23. Open `ColorPicker.xaml`. Add instances for these converters to the user control's resources (also add an XML namespace mapping named `local` to the `CH10.UserControls` namespace):

```
<local:ColorToBrushConverter x:Key="color2brush" />
<local:ColorToDoubleConverter x:Key="color2double" />
```

24. Here's the markup for the first (red) component, consisting of a `Rectangle`, a `TextBlock` and a `Slider` (all wrapped in a `Grid`), that use the preceding converters:

```
<Grid Margin="4">
    <Grid.ColumnDefinitions>
        <ColumnDefinition Width="Auto" />
        <ColumnDefinition />
    </Grid.ColumnDefinitions>
```

```
        <Rectangle Fill="{Binding SelectedColor, ElementName=uc,
         Converter={StaticResource color2brush},
         ConverterParameter=r}" />
        <Slider Grid.Column="1" Value="{Binding SelectedColor,
         ElementName=uc, Converter={StaticResource color2double},
         ConverterParameter=r}" />
        <TextBlock Text="{Binding SelectedColor, ElementName=uc,
         Converter={StaticResource color2double},
         ConverterParameter=r, StringFormat=R: {0}}" />
    </Grid>
```

25. Repeat the same idea for the green, blue, and alpha components, changing the converter parameter and the grid row:

```
<Grid Margin="4" Grid.Row="1">
    <Grid.ColumnDefinitions>
        <ColumnDefinition Width="Auto" />
        <ColumnDefinition />
    </Grid.ColumnDefinitions>
    <Rectangle Fill="{Binding SelectedColor, ElementName=uc,
     Converter={StaticResource color2brush},
     ConverterParameter=g}"  />
    <Slider Grid.Column="1" Value="{Binding SelectedColor,
     ElementName=uc, Converter={StaticResource color2double},
     ConverterParameter=g}" />
    <TextBlock Text="{Binding SelectedColor, ElementName=uc,
     Converter={StaticResource color2double},
     ConverterParameter=g, StringFormat=G: {0}}" />
</Grid>
<Grid Margin="4" Grid.Row="2">
    <Grid.ColumnDefinitions>
        <ColumnDefinition Width="Auto" />
        <ColumnDefinition />
    </Grid.ColumnDefinitions>
    <Rectangle Fill="{Binding SelectedColor, ElementName=uc,
     Converter={StaticResource color2brush},
     ConverterParameter=b}"  />
    <Slider Grid.Column="1" Value="{Binding SelectedColor,
     ElementName=uc, Converter={StaticResource color2double},
     ConverterParameter=b}" />
    <TextBlock Text="{Binding SelectedColor, ElementName=uc,
     Converter={StaticResource color2double},
     ConverterParameter=b, StringFormat=B: {0}}" />
</Grid>
<Grid Margin="4" Grid.Row="3">
```

```
        <Grid.ColumnDefinitions>
            <ColumnDefinition Width="Auto" />
            <ColumnDefinition />
        </Grid.ColumnDefinitions>
        <Rectangle Fill="{Binding SelectedColor, ElementName=uc,
         Converter={StaticResource color2brush},
         ConverterParameter=a}" />
        <Slider Grid.Column="1" Value="{Binding SelectedColor,
         ElementName=uc, Converter={StaticResource color2double},
         ConverterParameter=a}" />
        <TextBlock Foreground="Black"
         Text="{Binding SelectedColor, ElementName=uc,
         Converter={StaticResource color2double},
         ConverterParameter=a, StringFormat=A: {0}}" />
    </Grid>
```

26. The control is done. To test it, add a new WPF application project to the solution named `CH10.TestUserControls`.

27. Add an assembly reference to the `CH10.UserControls` project.

28. Open `MainWindow.xaml`. Add an XML namespace mapping to the user control library:

```
xmlns:ctls="clr-namespace:CH10.UserControls;assembly=Ch10.
UserControls"
```

29. Add the following markup to the existing `Grid`:

```
<Grid.RowDefinitions>
    <RowDefinition />
    <RowDefinition Height="Auto" />
</Grid.RowDefinitions>
<ctls:ColorPicker SelectedColorChanged="OnColorChanged" />
<TextBlock x:Name="_tbColor" FontSize="20"
           Grid.Row="1" Margin="8"/>
```

30. Notice the event handler for the `SelectedColorChanged` event. Implement the handler using the following code:

```
void OnColorChanged(object sender,
    RoutedPropertyChangedEventArgs<Color> e) {
   if(_tbColor != null)
      _tbColor.Text = string.Format("Selected Color: {0}",
          e.NewValue);
   }
```

31. Run the application and adjust the sliders to your favorite color.

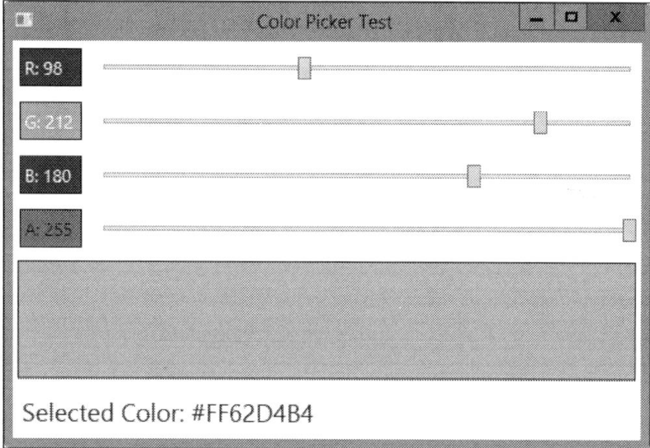

How it works...

A user control wraps a piece of UI with appropriate properties and events for reuse. With the color picker, we expose a new property, `SelectedColor` (step 5); it should always be a dependency property, as we want the control's user to benefit from all that the dependency properties can provide: data binding as targets, animations, and so on. Similarly, we're defining a routed event (with the Bubble routing strategy, step 6). Again, we don't want a regular .NET event, but a routed one. Raising the event is done when the `SelectedColor` property changes (step 7); notice that we don't raise the event as a regular .NET event, because that would not get us the "bubbling" behavior (firing the event on elements up the visual tree, as explained in *Chapter 1, Foundations*). Instead, we call `UIElement.RaiseEvent` which does the right thing.

A user control can have any content, and this is exactly what we build with XAML in the usual way. Note the data bindings; they use `ElementName` to get to the user control itself (and the `SelectedColor` property). A more elegant way would be to use `RelativeSource` with a `Mode` of `FindAncestor`, but `ElementName` is simply easier to use.

The converters are required for this example, but simpler controls may not need them.

Using the control is simply a matter of referencing its assembly (step 28) and creating it (typically in XAML, step 29) just like any other control.

There's more...

The main advantage of a user control is its ease of use. Creating many instances of a user control is easy, and there is full design time support in Visual Studio. Its main disadvantage is the difficulty of customization. For example, suppose we didn't want the user to select an alpha level for the color. There's no easy way to remove that. If we, as the control's authors consider that in advance, we could add a Boolean property just for this:

```
public bool ShowAlphaChannel {
   get { return (bool)GetValue(ShowAlphaChannelProperty); }
   set { SetValue(ShowAlphaChannelProperty, value); }
}
public static readonly DependencyProperty
   ShowAlphaChannelProperty = DependencyProperty.Register(
   "ShowAlphaChannel", typeof(bool), typeof(ColorPicker),
   new UIPropertyMetadata(true));
```

And use the property with the `Visibility` of the `Grid` holding the alpha channel UI:

```
Visibility="{Binding ShowAlphaChannel, ElementName=uc,
  Converter={StaticResource bool2vis}}"
```

The code assumes the `bool2vis` resource name is of type `BooleanToVisibilityConverter`, provided by WPF for mapping Boolean values (`true`/`false`) to `Visibility` values (`Visible`/`Collapsed`), and vice versa.

Other customizations may be more subtle. For example, suppose the control user wants to change the rectangle showing the final color to an ellipse? Or perhaps make the sliders vertical? Or place the big rectangle on the right side (instead of at the bottom)? Although it's possible to provide properties for these configurations, there's no way we can anticipate every possible customization option.

This leads to the conclusion that user controls are great when customization requirements are limited, such as a piece of UI that needs to repeat in various windows in the same application and should look basically the same. Further customizations require changing a control's template, and for that we should build the control differently, as we'll see in the recipe *Creating a custom (templated) control* in this chapter.

Optimizing converters

You may be wondering why the `ColorToBrushConverter` defines four `SolidColorBrush` objects and then returns the appropriate one based on the converter parameter. Wouldn't it be easier to simply change a single `SolidColorBrush` object and return that? Take a look at an alternative:

```
var color = (Color)value;
var brush = new SolidColorBrush();
```

```
switch((string)parameter) {
   case "r":
      brush.Color = Color.FromRgb(color.R, 0, 0);
      break;
   case "g":
      brush.Color = Color.FromRgb(0, color.G, 0);
      break;
   case "b":
      brush.Color = Color.FromRgb(0, 0, color.B);
      break;
   case "a":
      brush.Color = Color.FromArgb(color.A, 128, 128, 128);
      break;
}
return brush;
```

Although this code works, it's inefficient. We construct a new `SolidColorBrush` every time `Convert` is called, which may be many times – each time any slider moves. This causes a lot of objects to be created and then deemed garbage as we're not holding on to any of them except the four currently in use by the four color channel rectangles. This is wasteful and will increase memory consumption and the frequency of garbage collection.

A better approach would be to reuse the same four objects throughout the lifetime of the converter, thus creating no new brushes whatsoever. This keeps memory consumption to a minimum and does not promote garbage collection.

Adding a tunneling event

The `SelectedColorChanged` event we used is of the bubbling routing strategy. Suppose we wanted to provide its tunneling counterpart, `PreviewSelectedColorChanged`, similar to the existing pairs in WPF, such as `MouseDown`/`PreviewMouseDown` and `KeyUp`/`PreviewKeyUp`.

First, we declare the event with the `Tunnel RoutingStrategy`:

```
public static RoutedEvent PreviewSelectedColorChangedEvent =
   EventManager.RegisterRoutedEvent(
   "PreviewSelectedColorChanged", RoutingStrategy.Tunnel,
   typeof(RoutedPropertyChangedEventHandler<Color>),
   typeof(ColorPicker));
public event RoutedPropertyChangedEventHandler<Color>
   PreviewSelectedColorChanged {
   add {
      AddHandler(PreviewSelectedColorChangedEvent, value);
   }
   remove {
      RemoveHandler(PreviewSelectedColorChangedEvent, value);
   }
}
```

When the selected color changes, we need to raise the `preview` event first, and if it wasn't handled, raise its bubbling buddy:

```
static void OnSelectedColorChanged(DependencyObject obj,
   DependencyPropertyChangedEventArgs e) {
   var cp = (ColorPicker)obj;
   var args = new RoutedPropertyChangedEventArgs<Color>(
      (Color)e.OldValue, (Color)e.NewValue,
      PreviewSelectedColorChangedEvent);
   cp.RaiseEvent(args);
   if(!args.Handled)
      cp.RaiseEvent(new RoutedPropertyChangedEventArgs<Color>(
         (Color)e.OldValue, (Color)e.NewValue,
         SelectedColorChangedEvent));
}
```

The `Handled` property needs to be checked manually, and only if it's unset, the bubbling event is raised.

Handling standard commands in a user control

A typical user control exposes properties and events, but it can also handle commands. These can be standard commands (`RoutedUICommand`s defined by WPF) or custom commands exposed as properties and invoked by the control. In this recipe, we'll see how to add command handling to a user control.

Getting ready

We'll use the projects we created in the previous recipe, *Creating a user control*, so make sure the solution is open.

How to do it...

We'll add handling for the standard `MediaCommands.ChannelUp` and `MediaCommands.ChannelDown` commands. `ChannelUp` will increase each of the RGB values and `ChannelDown` will decrease them.

1. Open `ColorPicker.xaml.cs`. Add a static constructor to the class that registers for command handling:

```
static ColorPicker() {
   CommandManager.RegisterClassCommandBinding(
      typeof(ColorPicker), new CommandBinding(
```

```
        MediaCommands.ChannelUp,
        ChannelUpExecute, ChannelUpCanExecute));
    CommandManager.RegisterClassCommandBinding(
        typeof(ColorPicker), new CommandBinding(
        MediaCommands.ChannelDown,
        ChannelDownExecute, ChannelDownCanExecute));
}
```

2. To make this work, we need to implement the preceding methods. First, let's implement `ChannelUpExecute`:

```
static void ChannelUpExecute(object sender,
   ExecutedRoutedEventArgs e) {
   var cp = (ColorPicker)sender;
   var color = cp.SelectedColor;
   if(color.R < 255) color.R++;
   if(color.G < 255) color.G++;
   if(color.B < 255) color.B++;
   cp.SelectedColor = color;
}
```

3. The code simply increments the red, green, and blue of the selected color (if possible). This should be enabled if any of the channels has not yet reached 255:

```
static void ChannelUpCanExecute(object sender,
   CanExecuteRoutedEventArgs e) {
   var color = ((ColorPicker)sender).SelectedColor;
   e.CanExecute = color.R < 255 || color.G < 255
      || color.B < 255;
}
```

4. The code for handling the `ChannelDown` command is very similar:

```
static void ChannelDownExecute(object sender,
   ExecutedRoutedEventArgs e) {
   var cp = (ColorPicker)sender;
   var color = cp.SelectedColor;
   if(color.R > 0) color.R--;
   if(color.G > 0) color.G--;
   if(color.B > 0) color.B--;
   cp.SelectedColor = color;
}
static void ChannelDownCanExecute(object sender,
   CanExecuteRoutedEventArgs e) {
   var color = ((ColorPicker)sender).SelectedColor;
   e.CanExecute = color.R > 0 || color.G > 0 || color.B > 0;
}
```

5. To test this, open `MainWindow.xaml` from the `CH10.TestUserControls` project, and add a third row to the `Grid`:

```
<RowDefinition Height="Auto" />
```

6. Name the `ColorPicker` **picker** (`x:Name`).
7. Add a `UniformGrid` for the third row, hosting two `RepeatButton` objects that execute the required commands on the color picker:

```
<UniformGrid Grid.Row="2" Columns="2">
   <RepeatButton Content="&lt;&lt;" FontSize="30"
      Command="ChannelDown" Margin="4"
      CommandTarget="{Binding ElementName=picker}" />
   <RepeatButton Content="&gt;&gt;" FontSize="30"
      Command="ChannelUp" Margin="4"
      CommandTarget="{Binding ElementName=picker}" />
</UniformGrid>
```

8. Run the application. Click the repeat buttons and watch the RGB sliders move:

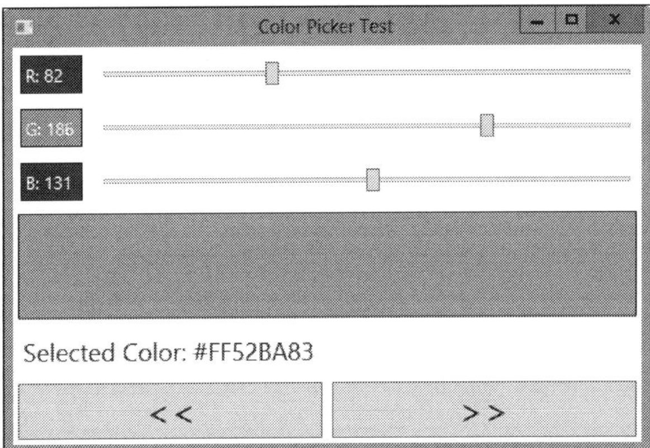

How it works...

The control registers itself for command handling using the static `CommandManager.RegisterClassCommandBinding`, specifying a `CommandBinding` that connects to the requested command. As this is called in the static constructor, the handlers must be static methods. Otherwise, they're handled in a pretty standard way, as discussed in *Chapter 7*.

It's also possible to register commands to the current instance using the property of `Commandbinding` inherited from `UIElement`, but that's a bit wasteful, as it's called for each `ColorPicker` instance as opposed to a single call from the static constructor.

The `CommandTarget` property value bound to the `ColorPicker` is necessary in this case because without it the `RepeatButton` itself becomes the target – going up the visual tree we will not find the command bindings attached to the color picker, as the color picker is not a parent of those buttons.

There's more...

An alternative to implementing standard commands is to implement the `ICommandSource` interface (just like buttons do), thus providing the `Command` (`ICommand`), `CommandParameter` (`object`), and `CommandTarget` (`IInputElement`) properties that a client can set. The control, in turn, will invoke the command if appropriate.

Creating a custom (templated) control

User controls are great for encapsulating a piece of UI functionality that can be easily reused. Their potential disadvantage is the lack of deep customization. In case such customization is required (or at least anticipated), a custom control should be built. This is a class deriving from `Control`, that provides a default look (through a control template), but that template can be changed if needed, without harming the control's functionality. In fact, this is how all WPF controls work – they provide some default template (look), but we can replace that template while preserving the control's behavior, as we've seen in *Chapter 8, Styles, Triggers, and Control Templates*.

In this recipe, we'll take a look at creating a custom control, and highlight the differences with respect to a user control.

Getting ready

Open the `CH10.UserControls` project from the *Creating a user control* recipe. We'll use that as a reference and even copy some things that don't need to change with a custom control. Open a second Visual Studio instance for creating the custom control.

How to do it...

We'll create an alternative color picker control (as a custom control), so that its look can be changed by replacing its control template.

1. Create a new **WPF Custom Control Library** project named `CH10.CustomControls`. Technically, you can use a **User Control Library** as well.
2. A default control file named `CustomControl1.cs` is created. Delete that file using **Solution Explorer**.

3. A `Generic.xaml` file was created by Visual Studio and placed in a project folder named `Themes`. Open this file and delete the `Style` inside to get rid of the last remains of that default custom control.

4. Right-click on the project in **Solution Explorer** and select **Add | New Item...** and then select **Custom Control** under the **WPF** folder. Type the name **ColorPicker** in the **Name** box and click on **Add**.

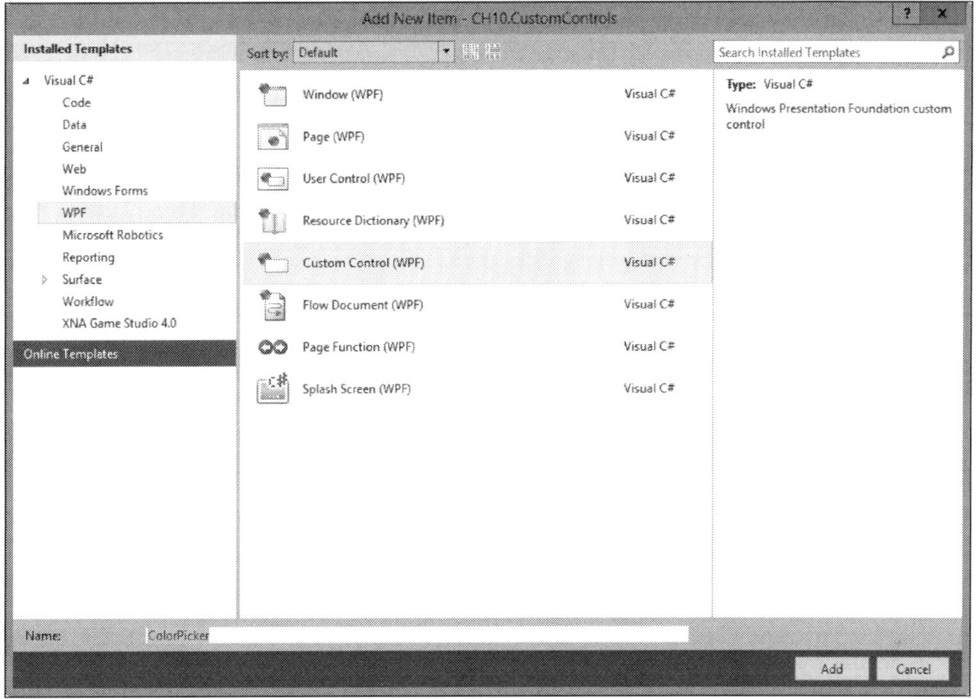

5. Open `ColorPicker.cs`. Copy the `SelectedColor` dependency property definition (including the `OnSelectedColorChanged` method) and the `SelectedColorChanged` routed event definitions from the `ColorPicker.xaml.cs` file in the `CH10.UserControls` project. This code does not need to change at all.

6. Build the project and make sure it is successful. If not, check the code you copied to make sure nothing was left behind. This is the entire code of `ColorPicker.cs`:

```
public class ColorPicker : Control {
   static ColorPicker() {
      DefaultStyleKeyProperty.OverrideMetadata(
         typeof(ColorPicker), new FrameworkPropertyMetadata(
         typeof(ColorPicker)));
   }
```

```
        public static readonly DependencyProperty
           SelectedColorProperty =
           DependencyProperty.Register("SelectedColor",
           typeof(Color), typeof(ColorPicker),
           new UIPropertyMetadata(Colors.Black,
           OnSelectedColorChanged));

        public Color SelectedColor {
           get { return (Color)GetValue(SelectedColorProperty); }
           set { SetValue(SelectedColorProperty, value); }
        }

        public static RoutedEvent SelectedColorChangedEvent =
           EventManager.RegisterRoutedEvent(
             "SelectedColorChanged", RoutingStrategy.Bubble,
           typeof(RoutedPropertyChangedEventHandler<Color>),
           typeof(ColorPicker));


        public event RoutedPropertyChangedEventHandler<Color>
           SelectedColorChanged {
           add { AddHandler(SelectedColorChangedEvent, value); }
           remove {
              RemoveHandler(SelectedColorChangedEvent, value);
           }
        }

        static void OnSelectedColorChanged(DependencyObject obj,
           DependencyPropertyChangedEventArgs e) {
           var cp = (ColorPicker)obj;
             cp.RaiseEvent(
              new RoutedPropertyChangedEventArgs<Color>(
              (Color)e.OldValue, (Color)e.NewValue,
              SelectedColorChangedEvent));
        }
    }
```

7. Now let's turn our attention to the user interface. We need to create a default template for the control (otherwise, it won't have a default look). Open `Generic.xaml`. An automatic style was placed there by Visual Studio. It has a setting for the `Template` property (a `ControlTemplate`) that has a border. Copy the XAML from `ColorPicker.xaml` (in the `CH10.UserControls` project), starting from the outermost `Grid` into the existing `Border`.

8. We'll have to do some work for this XAML do the right thing. First, copy the `ColorToBrushConverter.cs` and `ColorToDoubleConverter.cs` files from the `CH10.UserControls` project to the current one. You can do that by selecting the files from **Solution Explorer**, right-clicking on it and selecting **Copy** and then right-clicking on the target project and selecting **Paste**:

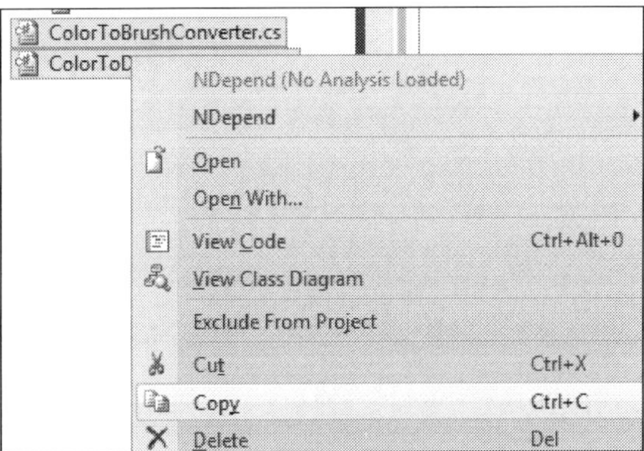

9. Next, open the new `ColorToBrushConverter.cs` and `ColorToDoubleConverter.cs` files and rename the namespaces from `CH10.UserControls` to `CH10.CustomControls`, so that the namespace is consistent across all files in the project.

10. Copy the `UserControls.Resources` section from `ColorPicker.xaml` (in the `CH10.UserControls` project) to the `Generic.Xaml` file, under the `ControlTemplate`.

11. Replace the `UserControl` occurrences with `ControlTemplate`. The entire `Resources` collection should look like this:

```
<ControlTemplate.Resources>
    <Style TargetType="Rectangle">
        <Setter Property="Margin" Value="2" />
        <Setter Property="Width" Value="50" />
        <Setter Property="Height" Value="30" />
        <Setter Property="Stroke" Value="Black" />
        <Setter Property="StrokeThickness" Value="1" />
    </Style>
    <Style TargetType="TextBlock">
        <Setter Property="Margin" Value="6,0,0,0" />
        <Setter Property="Foreground" Value="White" />
        <Setter Property="VerticalAlignment" Value="Center" />
        <Setter Property="FontSize" Value="14" />
    </Style>
    <Style TargetType="Slider">
        <Setter Property="Maximum" Value="255" />
```

```
            <Setter Property="VerticalAlignment" Value="Center" />
            <Setter Property="Margin" Value="10,0,0,0" />
            <Setter Property="LargeChange" Value="10" />
        </Style>
        <local:ColorToBrushConverter x:Key="color2brush" />
        <local:ColorToDoubleConverter x:Key="color2double" />
    </ControlTemplate.Resources>
```

12. Make sure the project is built successfully.
13. All data binding expressions use the `ElementName=uc` property. This works fine for a user control, but we have no control to name when writing a template, so the bindings need to change. However, we'll do something else – we'll create the bindings in code. The exact reason will become apparent in the next steps (with a detailed explanation in the *How it works...* section). Remove all bindings from the XAML; that means removing any property whose value is set with a binding expression.
14. To find elements from code, we need to name them. Each element or control that may be replaced by a custom template should have a name. Add names to certain elements as shown below, after the bindings have been deleted. This is the new, simplified, control template with named parts:

```
<Border Background="{TemplateBinding Background}"
        BorderBrush="{TemplateBinding BorderBrush}"
        BorderThickness="{TemplateBinding BorderThickness}">
    <Grid>
      <Grid.RowDefinitions>
          <RowDefinition Height="Auto" />
          <RowDefinition Height="Auto" />
          <RowDefinition Height="Auto" />
          <RowDefinition Height="Auto" />
          <RowDefinition />
      </Grid.RowDefinitions>
      <Grid Margin="4">
          <Grid.ColumnDefinitions>
              <ColumnDefinition Width="Auto" />
              <ColumnDefinition />
          </Grid.ColumnDefinitions>
          <Rectangle x:Name="PART_RedShape"/>
          <Slider Grid.Column="1" x:Name="PART_RedSlider"/>
          <TextBlock x:Name="PART_RedText"/>
      </Grid>
      <Grid Margin="4" Grid.Row="1">
          <Grid.ColumnDefinitions>
              <ColumnDefinition Width="Auto" />
              <ColumnDefinition />
          </Grid.ColumnDefinitions>
```

```
            <Rectangle x:Name="PART_GreenShape"/>
            <Slider Grid.Column="1" x:Name="PART_GreenSlider" />
            <TextBlock x:Name="PART_GreenText"/>
        </Grid>
        <Grid Margin="4" Grid.Row="2">
            <Grid.ColumnDefinitions>
               <ColumnDefinition Width="Auto" />
                <ColumnDefinition />
            </Grid.ColumnDefinitions>
            <Rectangle x:Name="PART_BlueShape" />
            <Slider Grid.Column="1" x:Name="PART_BlueSlider" />
            <TextBlock x:Name="PART_BlueText" />
        </Grid>
        <Grid Margin="4" Grid.Row="3" >
            <Grid.ColumnDefinitions>
                <ColumnDefinition Width="Auto" />
                <ColumnDefinition />
            </Grid.ColumnDefinitions>
            <Rectangle x:Name="PART_AlphaShape" />
            <Slider Grid.Column="1" x:Name="PART_AlphaSlider" />
            <TextBlock Foreground="Black"
                       x:Name="PART_AlphaText"/>
        </Grid>
        <Rectangle Grid.Row="4" Margin="4" Style="{x:Null}"
                   StrokeThickness="1" Stroke="Black">
            <Rectangle.Fill>
                <SolidColorBrush x:Name="PART_SelectedColor" />
            </Rectangle.Fill>
        </Rectangle>
      </Grid>
</Border>
```

15. Remove all the converter creation in the XAML resources; we won't need them in XAML as we don't have any bindings in XAML.
16. We need to create the bindings in code if we want to have any functionality. Open `ColorPicker.cs` and add an override to the virtual `OnApplyTemplate` method:

```
public override void OnApplyTemplate() {
   base.OnApplyTemplate();
}
```

17. This method is called whenever a new control template is applied to the control. We'll create some helper methods first, and then call them from `OnApplyTemplate`. Add two private fields to the `ColorPicker` class to hold the converters we'll need:

```
ColorToBrushConverter _color2brush =
   new ColorToBrushConverter();
ColorToDoubleConverter _color2double =
   new ColorToDoubleConverter();
```

18. Add a private method named `BindShape` that's used to bind shapes (rectangles in our default template), implemented with the following code:

```
void BindShape(string partName, string parameter) {
   var shape = GetTemplateChild(partName) as Shape;
   if(shape == null) return;

   var binding = new Binding("SelectedColor");
   binding.Source = this;
   binding.Converter = _color2brush;
   binding.ConverterParameter = parameter;
   shape.SetBinding(Shape.FillProperty, binding);
}
```

19. `GetTemplateChild` returns the named part, and if it exists, binds it using the same logic as in the user control case, but all done programmatically. Note that we look for any `Shape`-derived type, not necessarily a `Rectangle`. This provides more flexibility with custom templates, and is good enough because we're interested in the `Fill` property, which is defined by the base `Shape` class. Add another private method named `BindSlider`, to provide bindings to the sliders in a similar manner:

```
void BindSlider(string partName, string parameter) {
   var slider = GetTemplateChild(partName) as RangeBase;
   if(slider == null) return;

   var binding = new Binding("SelectedColor");
   binding.Source = this;
   binding.Converter = _color2double;
   binding.ConverterParameter = parameter;
   binding.Mode = BindingMode.TwoWay;
   slider.SetBinding(RangeBase.ValueProperty, binding);
}
```

20. Notice that we look for a type derived from `RangeBase` – similar to the preceding `Shape` example. Add yet another private method named `BindText`, used to bind the `TextBlock` instances, with the following implementation:

```
void BindText(string partName, string parameter,
   string format) {
```

```
    var tb = GetTemplateChild(partName) as TextBlock;
    if(tb == null) return;
    var binding = new Binding("SelectedColor");
    binding.Source = this;
    binding.Converter = _color2double;
    binding.ConverterParameter = parameter;
    binding.StringFormat = format;
    tb.SetBinding(TextBlock.TextProperty, binding);
}
```

21. Now it's time to implement `OnApplyTemplate`, and bind to the main selected color, using the following code:

```
public override void OnApplyTemplate() {
    // bind component shapes
    BindShape("PART_RedShape", "r");
    BindShape("PART_GreenShape", "g");
    BindShape("PART_BlueShape", "b");
    BindShape("PART_AlphaShape", "a");
    // bind sliders
    BindSlider("PART_RedSlider", "r");
    BindSlider("PART_GreenSlider", "g");
    BindSlider("PART_BlueSlider", "b");
    BindSlider("PART_AlphaSlider", "a");
    // bind text blocks
    BindText("PART_RedText", "r", "R: {0}");
    BindText("PART_GreenText", "g", "G: {0}");
    BindText("PART_BlueText", "b", "B: {0}");
    BindText("PART_AlphaText", "a", "A: {0}");
    // bind main color
    var solidBrush = GetTemplateChild("PART_SelectedColor")
        as SolidColorBrush;
    if(solidBrush != null) {
        var binding = new Binding("SelectedColor");
        binding.Source = this;
        BindingOperations.SetBinding(solidBrush,
            SolidColorBrush.ColorProperty, binding);
    }
}
```

22. That should be enough to test the control. Add a new WPF application project named `CH10.TestCustomControls`.

23. Add a reference to the `CH10.CustomControls` project.

24. Open `MainWindow.xaml`. Add an XML namespace mapping to the `CH10.CustomControls` library:

```
xmlns:ctls="clr-namespace:CH10.CustomControls;assembly=CH10.
CustomControls"
```

25. Add an instance of the color picker control to the existing `Grid`:

```
<ctls:ColorPicker />
```

26. Run the application. You should find the color picker custom control looks and behaves in much the same way as the color picker that was built as a user control.

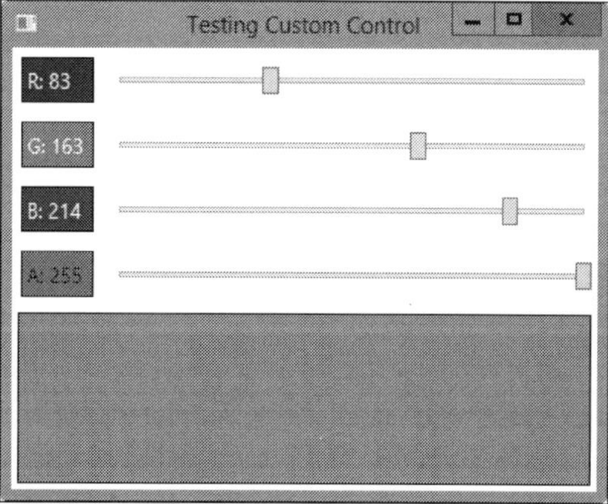

How it works...

A custom control derives from `Control`, and exposes properties and events, just like a user control. In fact, we used the exact same code copied from the color picker user control. The difference is the way the user interface is built.

The control provides an automatic style that has a `Template` property setting that provides a default control template (look) for the control. Much of the XAML was copied from the user control version; there are, however, some important changes. The most striking is the removal of all binding expressions and setting them up in code. Why? Couldn't we just change the `ElementName=uc` to something else that worked?

We could. The way to do that is to use the `TemplateBinding` markup extension (for one way binding) or `RelativeSource` markup extension (with a `Mode` of `TemplatedParent`) for two way bindings (and when something like `StringFormat` needs to be set because `TemplateBinding` does not support it). For example, the red rectangle `Fill` property binding could change to this:

```
Fill="{TemplateBinding SelectedColor, Converter={StaticResource
color2brush}, ConverterParameter=r}"
```

And it would have worked just fine. So why didn't we do that?

The problem is that if a custom control template is provided, the provider would have to construct such bindings manually, which is difficult at best (and impossible at times if the required converters are not publicly available). We want to make it easy to change templates, so the control author takes upon himself the task of setting the bindings correctly in code, so that a custom control template becomes easier to write, as it requires no bindings.

This poses a problem, though: how would we know which control we should bind to if we don't know which template is actually used and how those controls are located within it? The solution is to look for the parts with specific names (such as `PART_RedSlider`) and bind to those (if they exist). This means a custom template just needs to name the appropriate elements with the correct names, and the rest is taken care of by the control (in `OnApplyTemplate`). We'll see an example of changing the control template in the next recipe.

Creating bindings in code is not super-fun, but it's not difficult either. A `Binding` instance is created with an optional constructor accepting the source property path to bind to (the alternative is to use the `Path` property explicitly). Other properties are set as appropriate (`Converter`, `Mode`, `Source`, and so on) and finally, the `FrameworkElement.SetBinding` method is called, or the static `BindingOperations.SetBinding` method (this was used in the `SolidColorBrush` case, as it does not derive from `FrameworkElement`), connecting the target object, target property, and the `Binding` object together.

The code that looks for named parts is tolerant of non-existing parts – if parts are not found, no exception is thrown. We don't want to force certain parts to exist. For example, a custom template may not require a slider for the alpha component. The control should not mind, but simply disregard that part and move on. This maintains template flexibility, as we can't know in advance how the custom control would be used in all scenarios.

There's more...

How would a custom control user know which named parts are searched for by the control? One obvious way is to read conventional documentation. The other is to document the possible parts and their types by the control author via the `TemplatePart` custom attribute. In the color picker case, this should look like the following:

```
[TemplatePart(Name = "PART_RedShape", Type = typeof(Shape))]
[TemplatePart(Name = "PART_GreenShape", Type = typeof(Shape))]
[TemplatePart(Name = "PART_BlueShape", Type = typeof(Shape))]
[TemplatePart(Name = "PART_AlphaShape", Type = typeof(Shape))]
[TemplatePart(Name = "PART_RedSlider",
   Type = typeof(RangeBase))]
[TemplatePart(Name = "PART_GreenSlider",
   Type = typeof(RangeBase))]
[TemplatePart(Name = "PART_BlueSlider",
   Type = typeof(RangeBase))]
```

```
[TemplatePart(Name = "PART_AlphaSlider",
   Type = typeof(RangeBase))]
[TemplatePart(Name = "PART_RedText",
   Type = typeof(TextBlock))]
[TemplatePart(Name = "PART_GreenText",
   Type = typeof(TextBlock))]
[TemplatePart(Name = "PART_BlueText",
   Type = typeof(TextBlock))]
[TemplatePart(Name = "PART_AlphaText",
   Type = typeof(TextBlock))]
[TemplatePart(Name = "PART_SelectedColor",
   Type = typeof(SolidColorBrush))]
public class ColorPicker : Control {
```

Part names start with `PART_` by convention, but technically any name can be set.

This "documentation" can not only be used by us humans, but also by tools such as Expression Blend.

It's best to use the most common element type possible so as to maintain as much flexibility as possible, for example, using Shape instead of Rectangle. In the case of the `TextBlock` and `SolidColorBrush`, which these are very specific (in fact, nothing in WPF inherits from those); this limits flexibility. A possible solution is to provide alternative parts (such as a `Run` object as well as `TextBlock`).

Other things to set in code

The main issue that needs to be dealt with in `OnApplyTemplate` is bindings but there may be others. Some properties may need to be set to get correct behavior. For example, the sliders in the color picker need to have a maximum of 255. Currently, this is set via a `Style` within the default template, but that becomes problematic if the control template is replaced. It's best to make that change in code (in `ColorPicker.BindSlider`):

```
slider.Maximum = 255;
slider.Minimum = 0;
```

Another thing that may be needed is the handling of certain events for elements within the template. This is not required in the color picker example, but may be required elsewhere. For instance, the `Click` event of a `Button` may need to be handled to trigger some desired behavior. Again, doing so in XAML is impractical - it must be done in code. The common thread for all of this is simple: make replacing the default control template easy, leaving the hard stuff to the control's author.

What is that Generic.xaml?

The automatic style is placed in a file called `Generic.xaml` in a project folder named `Themes`. Why?

A default control template can technically be built differently for different Windows themes. Perhaps we want the control to look one way in the Windows 7 Aero theme, but look different in the Classic theme. In such cases, several templates can be built and placed in appropriate files under the `Themes` folder (the file name must be something like `Aero.NormalColor.xaml`). We won't delve into that too much because it's not that useful in practice. It's something Microsoft uses to make the WPF controls look consistent with the currently selected Windows theme.

Custom controls typically don't care about the Windows theme (and in any case, there are many possible themes), and so `Generic.xaml` acts as a fallback for any non-theme specific style.

Refactoring of Generic.xaml

Because of the reasons just discussed, all custom controls' styles in the project end up in `Generic.xaml`. This is less than ideal, as that file grows larger all the time, making maintenance difficult; also, from a practical perspective, that single file may be required by several developers at the same time (working on different controls), and that would require multiple check-outs from a source control repository and then merging the changes adding to the maintenance hassle.

The solution is to segregate the controls' style into different files and to reference them from `Generic.xaml`. For example, we'll create a `ColorPicker.xaml` resource dictionary file inside the `Themes` folder, and place the style inside:

```
<ResourceDictionary xmlns=http://schemas.microsoft.com/winfx/2006/
xaml/presentation
    xmlns:x=http://schemas.microsoft.com/winfx/2006/xaml
    xmlns:local="clr-namespace:CH10.CustomControls">
    <Style TargetType="{x:Type local:ColorPicker}">
...
    <Style>
```

In `Generic.xaml`, we reference `ColorPicker.xaml` with the `ResourceDictionary.MergedDictionaries` collection:

```
<ResourceDictionary.MergedDictionaries>
     <ResourceDictionary Source="pack://application:,,,/CH10.
CustomControls;component/Themes/ColorPicker.xaml" />
</ResourceDictionary.MergedDictionaries>
```

In this way, each control has its own file; `Generic.xaml` simply aggregates the files.

Customizing a default template of custom control

Custom controls provide default control templates so that they have some look if used as is. However, the real power of custom controls is the ability to change the template without harming any functionality. In this recipe, we'll change the template for our color picker control to get a different look with the same functionality without writing any code – just a different control template.

Getting ready

Open the `CH10.TestCustomControls` project. We'll use that project to create the new template and compare it to the default one.

How to do it...

We'll create a different control template that utilizes just some of the capabilities of the color picker control and makes sure the control is tolerant of missing pieces.

1. Open `App.xaml`.
2. Add a `ControlTemplate` resource that builds an alternative look for a color picker. Notice the part names:

```
<ControlTemplate x:Key="cpTemplate">
    <Grid>
        <Grid.ColumnDefinitions>
            <ColumnDefinition Width="Auto" />
            <ColumnDefinition Width="Auto" />
            <ColumnDefinition Width="Auto" />
            <ColumnDefinition />
        </Grid.ColumnDefinitions>
        <Slider x:Name="PART_RedSlider" Margin="5"
           Orientation="Vertical" />
        <Slider x:Name="PART_GreenSlider" Margin="5"
           Orientation="Vertical" Grid.Column="1" />
        <Slider x:Name="PART_BlueSlider" Margin="5"
           Orientation="Vertical" Grid.Column="2" />
        <Grid Grid.Column="3">
            <Rectangle RadiusX="20" RadiusY="20" Margin="5"
               Stroke="Black" StrokeThickness="1">
               <Rectangle.Fill>
                  <SolidColorBrush x:Name="PART_SelectedColor"
/>
```

```
                    </Rectangle.Fill>
                </Rectangle>
                <StackPanel VerticalAlignment="Center"
                    TextBlock.FontSize="16">
                     <TextBlock x:Name="PART_RedText"
      Foreground="White" HorizontalAlignment="Center"/>
                     <TextBlock x:Name="PART_GreenText"
      Foreground="White" HorizontalAlignment="Center"/>
                     <TextBlock x:Name="PART_BlueText"
      Foreground="White" HorizontalAlignment="Center"/>
                </StackPanel>
            </Grid>
        </Grid>
</ControlTemplate>
```

3. Open `MainWindow.xaml`. and create two columns for the existing `Grid`:

```
<Grid.ColumnDefinitions>
    <ColumnDefinition />
    <ColumnDefinition />
</Grid.ColumnDefinitions>
```

4. One color picker is already in that `Grid`. Add another `ColorPicker` control that uses the newly created control template:

```
<ctls:ColorPicker Template="{StaticResource cpTemplate}"
    Grid.Column="1"/>
```

5. Run the application. Two color pickers are shown, both of the same type, both behave in the same way, but they look quite different:

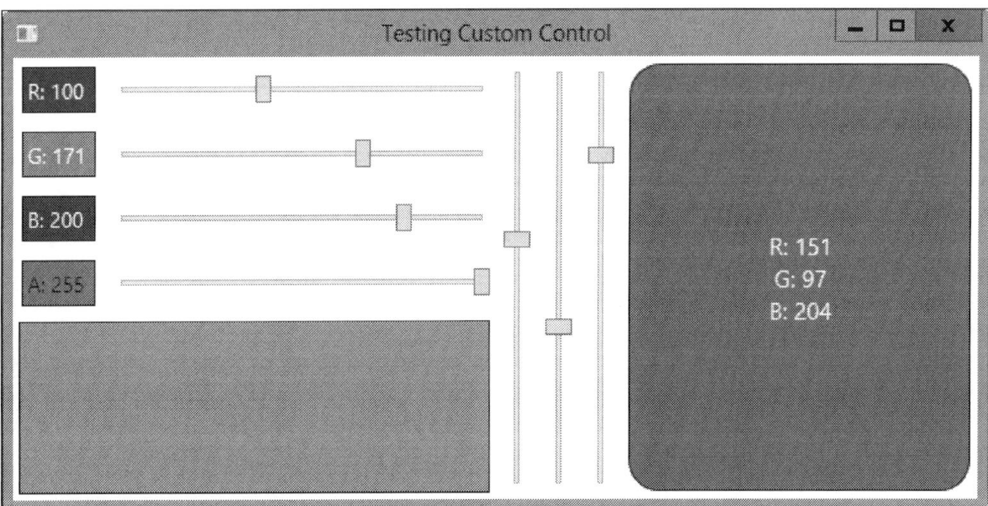

How it works...

Replacing the control template of our custom `ColorPicker` is no different than replacing any other WPF control's template – we just set the `Template` property and we're done.

The simple requirement for this magic to work is to provide the correct named parts, such as `PART_RedSlider`. The rest is taken care of by the control itself. This is exactly what makes custom controls so powerful.

Creating a custom panel

WPF panels are layout containers. Each `Panel` provides its own layout logic; combining them in various ways allows the creation of a complex yet flexible user interface. The built-in panels, such as `Grid`, `StackPanel`, and `Canvas` seem to provide everything we need to create a conceivable user interface. Sometimes, however, there is a need to go beyond the built-in panels, to create some other unique way to lay out elements. Although everything is possible using transforms, using a custom panel has its benefits, one of which is ease of use. Other benefits include the ability to use the panel in an unorthodox way, such as with the `ItemsPanel` property of an `ItemsControl` and its derivatives.

In this recipe, we'll create a custom panel, showing a typical way of implementing such functionality.

Getting ready

Make sure Visual Studio is up and running.

How to do it...

We'll create a radial panel that arranges its children along the circumference of an ellipse.

1. Create a new WPF application named `CH10.CustomPanel`.
2. Add a new class to the project named `RadialPanel` and derive it from `Panel` (add a `using` statement for `System.Windows.Controls`):

   ```
   class RadialPanel : Panel {
   }
   ```

3. Add a using namespace for `System.Windows`.
4. First we need to override the `MeasureOverride` method, and ask every child element its desired size. We'll also keep track of the largest element.

   ```
   protected override Size MeasureOverride(Size availableSize) {
      Size maxSize = Size.Empty;
      foreach(UIElement child in Children) {
   ```

```
        child.Measure(availableSize);
        maxSize = new Size(
            Math.Max(maxSize.Width, child.DesiredSize.Width),
            Math.Max(maxSize.Height, child.DesiredSize.Height));
    }
```

5. The last thing to do is to return the desired size of the `RadialPanel` itself. We should never return the available size passed to this method, as it may contain an infinite size in one or both directions (`double.PositiveInfinity`). In this case, we'll return the available size if possible, or the largest element multiplied by a factor otherwise:

```
return new Size(double.IsPositiveInfinity(availableSize.Width) ?
maxSize.Width * 2 : availableSize.Width,
    double.IsPositiveInfinity(availableSize.Height) ?
    maxSize.Height * 2 : availableSize.Height);
```

6. The `RadialPanel` should arrange its child elements along the circumference of an ellipse. Each element would be evenly spaced (angle-wise), starting from angle zero. To make the panel more customizable, we'll add a dependency property for a different starting angle:

```
public double StartAngle {
    get { return (double)GetValue(StartAngleProperty); }
    set { SetValue(StartAngleProperty, value); }
}

public static readonly DependencyProperty StartAngleProperty =
    DependencyProperty.Register("StartAngle", typeof(double),
    typeof(RadialPanel), new FrameworkPropertyMetadata(
    0.0, FrameworkPropertyMetadataOptions.AffectsRender));
```

7. The next, and more complex step, is to override the `ArrangeOverride` method. Here we need to tell each child element its exact position and size; that's what makes our panel unique. Add an override for that method:

```
protected override Size ArrangeOverride(Size finalSize) {
    return base.ArrangeOverride(finalSize);
}
```

8. We'll implement the method by placing the elements across the entire 360 degree circle, taking into consideration the starting angle. This requires some trigonometry:

```
var count = Children.Count;
if(count > 0) {
    Point center = new Point(finalSize.Width / 2,
        finalSize.Height / 2);
    double step = 360 / count;
    int index = 0;
```

```
        foreach(UIElement element in Children) {
            double angle = StartAngle + step * index++;
            // reverse default angle increment, shift and
            // convert to radians
            angle = (90 - angle) * Math.PI / 180;
            Rect rc = new Rect(new Point(
                center.X - element.DesiredSize.Width / 2 +
                (center.X - element.DesiredSize.Width / 2) *
                Math.Cos(angle),
                center.Y - element.DesiredSize.Height / 2 -
                (center.Y - element.DesiredSize.Height / 2) *
                Math.Sin(angle)), element.DesiredSize);
            element.Arrange(rc);
        }
    }
    return finalSize;
```

9. Let's test the panel. Open `MainWindow.xaml` and map an XML namespace to the `CH10.CustomPanel` namespace:

```
xmlns:local="clr-namespace:CH10.CustomPanel"
```

10. Add two rows to the existing `Grid`:

```
<Grid.RowDefinitions>
    <RowDefinition />
    <RowDefinition Height="Auto" />
</Grid.RowDefinitions>
```

11. Add a `Slider` to the second row of the grid, to be used for manipulating the panel's starting angle:

```
<Slider Margin="4" Maximum="360" x:Name="_startAngle"
   Grid.Row="1" />
```

12. Add a `RadialPanel` to the first row of the grid with some elements:

```
<local:RadialPanel
   StartAngle="{Binding Value, ElementName=_startAngle}">
    <Ellipse Fill="Red" Stroke="Black" StrokeThickness="2"
       Width="40" Height="40"  />
    <Ellipse Fill="Green" Stroke="Black" StrokeThickness="2"
       Width="40" Height="40" />
    <Ellipse Fill="Blue" Stroke="Black" StrokeThickness="2"
       Width="40" Height="40"/>
    <Ellipse Fill="Red" Stroke="Black" StrokeThickness="2"
       Width="40" Height="40" />
```

```
    <Ellipse Fill="Yellow" Stroke="Black" StrokeThickness="2"
      Width="40" Height="40" />
    <Ellipse Fill="Brown" Stroke="Black" StrokeThickness="2"
      Width="40" Height="40"/>
    <Ellipse Fill="Orange" Stroke="Black" StrokeThickness="2"
      Width="40" Height="40"/>
    <Ellipse Fill="Red" Stroke="Black" StrokeThickness="2"
      Width="40" Height="40"/>
    <Ellipse Fill="LightBlue" Stroke="Black"
      StrokeThickness="2" Width="40" Height="40"/>
    <Ellipse Fill="Red" Stroke="Black" StrokeThickness="2"
      Width="40" Height="40"/>
    <Ellipse Fill="Cyan" Stroke="Black" StrokeThickness="2"
      Width="40" Height="40"/>
    <Ellipse Fill="Red" Stroke="Black" StrokeThickness="2"
      Width="40" Height="40"/>
</local:RadialPanel>
```

13. Run the application. Move the slider and watch the elements rotate.

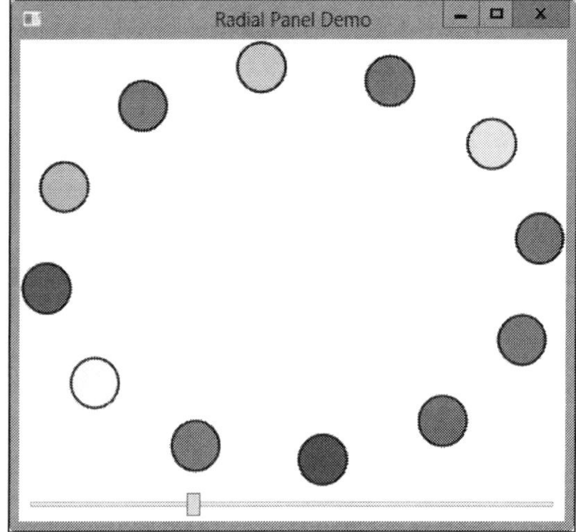

How it works...

The layout process is a two-step process: measure and arrange. This is modeled precisely by the panel's need to override two methods for this exact purpose, `MeasureOverride` and `ArrangeOverride`.

MeasureOverride asks the panel (or any element that overrides it, for that matter) what size it requires. For a panel, the main concern is the requirements of its child elements. The call to UIElement.Measure is mandatory and causes the MeasureOverride method of element to be called (and this may go on if that child is a panel, or acts like a panel, in itself).

The panel needs to decide what size it requires based on its children's requirements and the layout logic it wants to employ. The parameter sent to MeasureOverride is the available size provided by that panel's container. This can be double.PositiveInfinity in either or both dimensions (for example, a ScrollViewer indicates it has infinite space in directions where scrolling is available). It's important to return a finite size; otherwise WPF has no way of knowing how much space to leave for the panel and throws an exception. In our example, if the input is infinite, the returned size is based on twice the size of the largest element (however, any size can be arbitrarily selected).

ArrangeOverride is the more interesting method that actually implements that special layout logic, for which the panel was created. In this case, the implementation calculates the position and size of the elements along the circumference of an imaginary ellipse stretched over the entire size the panel was given by its parent (through the input size argument). Each element receives a call to UIElement.Arrange that forces that element to be placed within a specific rectangle. Note that this doesn't mean the element is actually rectangular – it can be any shape; the rectangle is the bounds to which its layout is confined.

The mathematics involved may seem complicated or not, based on your trigonometric prowess. The generally interesting part is the UIElement.DesiredSize property, which indicates the size of a particular child. In this case, this is used to attach the element to the outer boundary of the panel.

The StartAngle dependency property is used in the calculations, and affects rendering, indicated with the FrameworkPropertyMetadataOptions.AffectsRender flag. This is a hint to WPF to redraw the panel if that property changes. In the test window, the Value property of Slider is bound to StartAngle, demonstrating nicely its effect on the final result.

There's more...

This and other panels can be extended in a multitude of ways. One such way is to define attached properties that children can use to affect their layout strategy (this is exactly the case with properties such as Canvas.Left and Grid.Row). For example, we may want to allow an element to be placed in a specific angle, regardless of other elements. Here's one way to do it. First, define the attached property:

```
[AttachedPropertyBrowsableForChildren]
public static double GetAngle(DependencyObject obj) {
   return (double)obj.GetValue(AngleProperty);
}
```

```
[AttachedPropertyBrowsableForChildren]
public static void SetAngle(DependencyObject obj, double value) {
   obj.SetValue(AngleProperty, value);
}

public static readonly DependencyProperty AngleProperty =
   DependencyProperty.RegisterAttached("Angle",
   typeof(double), typeof(RadialPanel),
   new FrameworkPropertyMetadata(double.NaN,
      FrameworkPropertyMetadataOptions.AffectsRender));
```

The `AttachedPropertyBrowsableForChildren` custom attributes is a hint to the XAML intellisense engine that suggests this property automatically on elements placed inside a `RadialPanel`; it has no other effect.

The default value for this property is set to `double.NaN`, as an indicator that it wasn't set. We now need to modify `ArrangeOverride` to take this property into consideration:

```
double angle = StartAngle + step * index++;
double pangle = RadialPanel.GetAngle(element);
if(!double.IsNaN(pangle))
   angle = pangle;
```

The last 3 lines are new. We can apply this property on elements, such as the following:

```
<Ellipse Fill="Red" Stroke="Black" StrokeThickness="2"
   Width="40" Height="40" local:RadialPanel.Angle="30"/>
```

Running the test application with two elements set with angles equal to 30 and 170 degrees yields the following while dragging the slider:

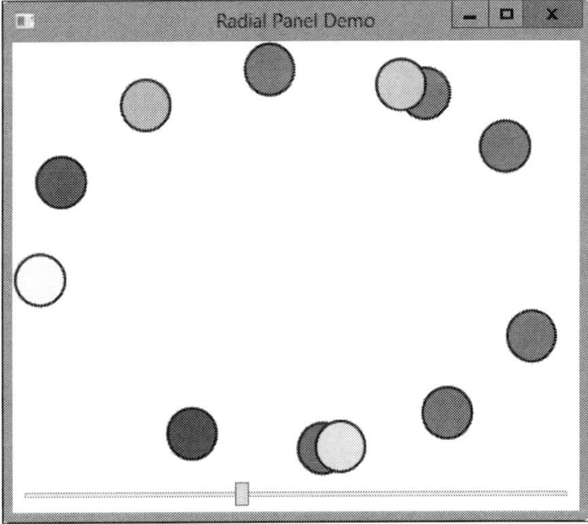

The downloadable source for this chapter has some more customizations for the `RadialPanel`, such as the ability to specify an angle increment between elements, thus not necessarily filling an entire 360 dial (or filling more than 360 degrees).

Where are custom panels used?

A custom panel can be used just like any other panel. First, it's an element, which means it can be anywhere in the visual tree. Second, as a panel it can be used as a host for types derived from `ItemsControl` through the `ItemsPanel` property. This is a very interesting capability, that coupled with data binding, can be used to create interesting effects. For example, a solar system simulation can hold the planets in some collection and bind them to a `ListBox` that uses a `RadialPanel` as its `ItemsPanel` (through the `ItemsPanelTemplate` object). Binding the attached `RadialPanel.Angle` property to similar information on a planet object can be used to easily move or animate the planet around its sun.

Creating a lightweight custom element

Custom controls provide a way to create a user interface based on XAML elements. Sometimes, however, a more complex UI is required, that cannot be easily achieved by XAML alone, or where low level control is desired. In such cases, we can create a lightweight element, deriving from `FrameworkElement` that does its own drawing without creating any particular element. This makes the control consume less memory and WPF layout logic does not need to consider many elements.

In this recipe, we'll take a look at the way to implement such lightweight elements.

Getting ready

Make sure Visual Studio is up and running.

How to do it...

We'll create a simple bar graph control to demonstrate the ability to draw in a more "manual" fashion.

1. Create a new WPF application project named `CH10.CustomRendering`.
2. Add a new class named `BarGraph` that derives from `FrameworkElement`. This class will hold an array of values to show as a bar graph.
3. Add a dependency property named `Values` to the `BarGraph` class to hold the data to display:

```
public static readonly DependencyProperty ValuesProperty =
   DependencyProperty.Register("Values", typeof(double[]),
```

```
    typeof(BarGraph), new FrameworkPropertyMetadata(null,
    FrameworkPropertyMetadataOptions.AffectsRender));
public double[] Values {
    get { return (double[])GetValue(ValuesProperty); }
    set { SetValue(ValuesProperty, value); }
}
```

4. Let's add some more properties that allow some control over the rendering aspects:

```
public static readonly DependencyProperty FillProperty =
    Shape.FillProperty.AddOwner(typeof(BarGraph),
    new FrameworkPropertyMetadata(Brushes.White,
    FrameworkPropertyMetadataOptions.AffectsRender));
public static readonly DependencyProperty StrokeProperty =
    Shape.StrokeProperty.AddOwner(typeof(BarGraph),
    new FrameworkPropertyMetadata(Brushes.Black,
    FrameworkPropertyMetadataOptions.AffectsRender));
public static readonly DependencyProperty
    StrokeThicknessProperty = Shape.StrokeThicknessProperty.
    AddOwner(typeof(BarGraph), new FrameworkPropertyMetadata(
    1.0, FrameworkPropertyMetadataOptions.AffectsRender));

public Brush Fill {
    get { return (Brush)GetValue(FillProperty); }
    set { SetValue(FillProperty, value); }
}

public Brush Stroke {
    get { return (Brush)GetValue(StrokeProperty); }
    set { SetValue(StrokeProperty, value); }
}

public double StrokeThickness {
    get { return (double)GetValue(StrokeThicknessProperty); }
    set { SetValue(StrokeThicknessProperty, value); }
}
```

5. Finally, let's add a property that allows the drawing of an average line for the values in question:

```
public bool ShowAverage {
    get { return (bool)GetValue(ShowAverageProperty); }
    set { SetValue(ShowAverageProperty, value); }
}
public static readonly DependencyProperty
    ShowAverageProperty = DependencyProperty.Register(
```

```
    "ShowAverage", typeof(bool), typeof(BarGraph),
    new FrameworkPropertyMetadata(false,
    FrameworkPropertyMetadataOptions.AffectsRender));
```

6. The element has no XAML associated with it. Its entire rendering is based on overriding the `OnRender` method. Add a using statement for the `System.Windows.Media` namespace.
7. Override the `OnRender` method with the following code:

```
protected override void OnRender(DrawingContext dc) {
   if(Values == null || Values.Length == 0) return;

   double max = Values.Max();
   var pen = new Pen(Stroke, StrokeThickness);
   var barSize = ActualWidth / Values.Length;
   for(int i = 0; i < Values.Length; i++) {
      dc.DrawRectangle(Fill, pen, new Rect(
      new Point(i * barSize, ActualHeight -
      Values[i] * ActualHeight / max),
      new Point((i + 1) * barSize, ActualHeight)));
   }
   if(ShowAverage) {
      var avg = ActualHeight - Values.Average()
         * ActualHeight / max;
      dc.DrawLine(pen, new Point(0, avg),
       new Point(ActualWidth, avg));
   }
}
```

8. The code uses a `DrawingContext` to do all the required drawing. Let's set up a bar graph with some data. Open `MainWindow.xaml` and add an XAML namespace, mapping to the `CH10.CustomRendering` namespace:

```
xmlns:local="clr-namespace:CH10.CustomRendering"
```

9. Create a `BarGraph` element inside the existing `Grid` with the following markup:

```
<local:BarGraph x:Name="_graph" ShowAverage="True">
    <local:BarGraph.Fill>
        <LinearGradientBrush EndPoint="0,1">
            <GradientStop Color="LightBlue" Offset="0" />
            <GradientStop Color="Blue" Offset="1" />
        </LinearGradientBrush>
    </local:BarGraph.Fill>
</local:BarGraph>
```

10. Open `MainWindow.xaml.cs` and add the following code inside the constructor after the call to `InitalizeComponent`:

```
double[] values = { 45, 22, 104, 77, 18, 56, 39, 120 };
_graph.Values = values;
```

11. Run the application. You should see a simple bar graph with an average line:

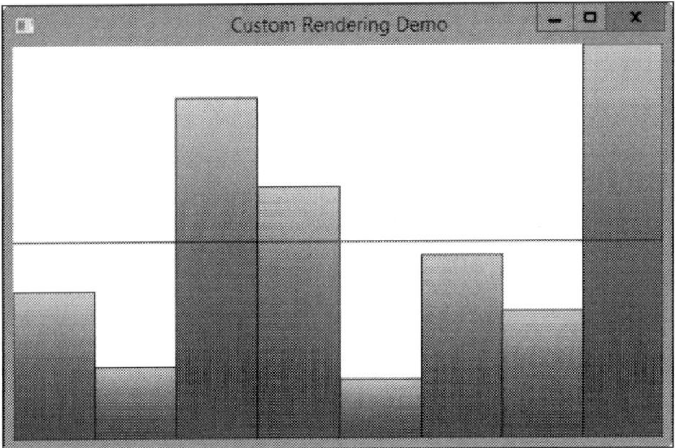

How it works...

The `UIElement.OnRender` method is used to render the entire UI of the custom element. It accepts a `DrawingContext` object, which is an abstraction over some drawing tools. It's similar in concept to the `System.Drawing.Graphics` GDI+ class (used by WinForms) or to the Win32 device context. There is an important difference, however, that goes beyond the fact that WPF works through DirectX. WPF has a retained mode graphics system, meaning the "drawing" done with `DrawingContext` as opposed to (say) `Graphics`. `DrawingContext` is a kind of cache for graphic operations. For example, `OnRender` is not called when minimizing and restoring the window. WPF remembers the commands to use and redraws automatically. On the other hand, in GDI+ it's necessary to invoke the drawing code explicitly from a `Paint` event – otherwise the drawing would disappear if the window is minimized and restored, for instance; this is known as an immediate mode rendering system.

`DrawingContext` contains a bunch of methods, such as `DrawRectangle`, `DrawLine`, and `DrawText`. In the bar graph, `DrawRectangle` and `DrawLine` are used with a `Pen` and a `Brush` (a `Pen` encapsulates a `Brush` with line-related properties such as thickness and dashes).

There's more...

Using `UIElement.OnRender` is also possible for "regular" custom controls that derive from control. This method is called as part of the rendering cycle, thus providing a way to use XAML for the basic control and a `DrawingContext` for other, more complex drawing operations.

Dependency property ownership

The `Stroke`, `StrokeThickness`, and `Fill` dependency properties were not defined from scratch using `DependencyProperty.Register`. As some form of these exists elsewhere in WPF, and the required meaning for this control is practically the same, it's cheaper to add the control as an owner to an existing property, rather than defining it from scratch. The `DependencyProperty.AddOwner` provides a way to do that, optionally changing the property metadata (as was used here so that the default brushes are not null).

More DrawingContext

Apart from the obvious methods, a `DrawingContext` has some other interesting methods:

- `DrawGeometry` provides a way to draw any `Geometry`-derived object
- `DrawDrawing` draws a object derived from `Drawing` (a lightweight object representing a 2D drawing).
- `DrawVideo` draws a `MediaPlayer` object inside a rectangle, essentially showing a running movie
- `Push` methods that allow changing the state of the `DrawingContext`, such as `PushOpacity` and `PushTransform`, until a `Pop` method is called, restoring the state before the last `Push` call
- Most methods have overloads that accept an `AnimationClock` object, which provides animation control capabilities for the drawn element

11
Threading

In this chapter we will cover:

- Updating the UI from a non-UI thread
- Adding cancelation support
- Using the BackgroundWorker component
- Adding cancelation and progress with BackgroundWorker
- Using a timer to do periodic updates
- Using C# 5.0 to perform asynchronous operations

Introduction

The computer world is going through a revolution in terms of the way code is written. From (mostly) single CPU systems, current computers have multi-core processors, capable of performing concurrent operations. The shift is mostly due to hardware limitations that don't allow current technology to increase CPU clock frequency by much (if at all). The solution: create more cores.

But, more cores means the "free lunch is over" (as Herb Sutter put it nicely). If we continue writing single threaded code, no amount of cores can help us speed things up. A lot of effort is now going in to getting back "the free lunch". One such effort is the Task Parallel Library introduced in .NET 4.

The UI world remains mainly single threaded. What concerns a UI framework, such as WPF, is keeping the UI responsive, which means offloading any significant work or significant wait to some background thread in some way so that the UI thread can keep pumping messages, keeping the application responsive. One problem that arises, however, is that a background operation cannot touch the user interface on a non-UI thread. WPF has to provide some facility to marshal the required call to the UI thread for processing.

In this chapter, we'll take a look at WPF's (and .NET's) support for working with asynchronous operations, including cancelation and reporting progress. We won't discuss actual threading techniques in depth as this is not specific to WPF; still, we'll see some typical examples that use the thread pool and the Task Parallel Library.

Updating the UI from a non-UI thread

User interface in WPF (as with WinForms) is managed by a single thread. More accurately, a thread that creates windows is the owner of those windows; it means that thread must process UI messages, a process usually known as message pumping. This message pumping activity is provided by the framework (in WPF it's in the `Dispatcher.Run` static method; in WinForms it's `Application.Run`, but the idea is the same). If the UI thread is doing a lot of work or enters a wait state (by doing some I/O, for example), it won't be able to process UI messages, causing the UI to freeze, also known as "not responding". This is very bad from a user experience standpoint, and should be avoided at all costs. The simple rule is that if some operation may be long, offload it to another thread in some way, keeping the UI thread responsive.

Sounds simple, doesn't it? Sometimes it is simple, sometimes not so much. One of the common issues is the need to update something in the user interface from a non-UI thread. The direct approach causes an exception to be thrown. In this recipe, we'll see one way to circumvent that exception and update the user interface correctly.

Getting ready

Make sure Visual Studio is up and running.

How to do it...

We'll create a simple application that counts prime numbers on a non-UI thread and updates the UI when the result is available.

1. Create a new WPF Application named `CH11.AsyncCalc`.
2. Open `MainWindow.xaml`. Set the following `Window` properties:

```
Title="Prime Counter" SizeToContent="WidthAndHeight"
ResizeMode="CanMinimize"
```

3. Build the following simple user interface starting with the existing `Grid`:

```
<Grid TextBlock.FontSize="16">
    <Grid.RowDefinitions>
        <RowDefinition Height="Auto"/>
        <RowDefinition Height="Auto" />
        <RowDefinition Height="Auto" />
```

```
        <RowDefinition Height="Auto" />
    </Grid.RowDefinitions>
    <StackPanel Orientation="Horizontal" Margin="6">
        <TextBlock Text="From:" />
        <TextBox Margin="10,2,2,2" Width="120"
                 MaxLength="10" x:Name="_from"/>
        <TextBlock Text="To:" Margin="20,0,0,0"/>
        <TextBox Margin="10,2,2,2" Width="120"
                 MaxLength="10" x:Name="_to"/>
    </StackPanel>
    <StackPanel Orientation="Horizontal" Grid.Row="1"
                Margin="6">
        <Button Content="Calculate" Padding="4" />
    </StackPanel>
    <TextBlock x:Name="_result" Grid.Row="3" FontSize="20"
                Margin="6" HorizontalAlignment="Center" />
</Grid>
```

4. Open `MainWindow.xaml.cs`. We'll create a general method that counts the number of prime numbers in a given range. Add a static method named `CountPrimes` and implement with the following code:

```
static int CountPrimes(int from, int to) {
   int total = 0;
   for(int i = from; i <= to; i++) {
      bool isPrime = true;
      int limit = (int)Math.Sqrt(i);
      for(int j = 2; j <= limit; j++)
         if(i % j == 0) {
            isPrime = false;
            break;
         }
      if(isPrime)
         total++;
   }
   return total;
}
```

5. The method searches for prime numbers (not with the most efficient way, but that's unimportant for our purposes). Now we need to invoke it at the right time. Add a `Click` event handler for the button.

6. The first thing to do in the event handler is to get the range of numbers to look for primes and disable the button until the calculation is done:

```
int first = int.Parse(_from.Text), last = int.Parse(_to.Text);
var button = (Button)sender;
button.IsEnabled = false;
```

7. Note that there is no proper error handling in the preceding code (`int.Parse` may throw an exception); that's not the focus here. As identifying prime numbers can be time consuming for a large set of numbers, it's best to set the operation in motion in another thread so that the UI thread is kept responding. There are a few ways to do an operation on a different thread (explicitly creating a thread, using the thread pool, using a task - to name the common ways); here we'll use the thread pool by calling `ThreadPool.QueueUserWorkItem`:

```
ThreadPool.QueueUserWorkItem(_ => {
   int total = CountPrimes(first, last);
```

8. `CountPrimes` runs on a thread pool thread. When the call returns we want to show results by accessing the `TextBlock.Text` property. Direct access would cause an exception (`InvalidOperationException`). One way to "return" to the UI thread is to use the `Dispatcher` on any UI element like the following code demonstrates:

```
Dispatcher.BeginInvoke(new Action(() => {
      _result.Text = "Total Primes: " + total.ToString();
      button.IsEnabled = true;
   }));
});
```

9. `Dispatcher.BeginInvoke` causes the specified delegate to be scheduled to execute on the UI thread as soon as possible (it actually depends on a `DispatcherPriority` and the actual work the UI thread is doing).
10. Run the application. Enter `3` for **From** and `10000000` for **To** and click the button. During the calculation the UI is responsive – you can drag the window around. Eventually, the result should be displayed (664578 prime numbers in that range).

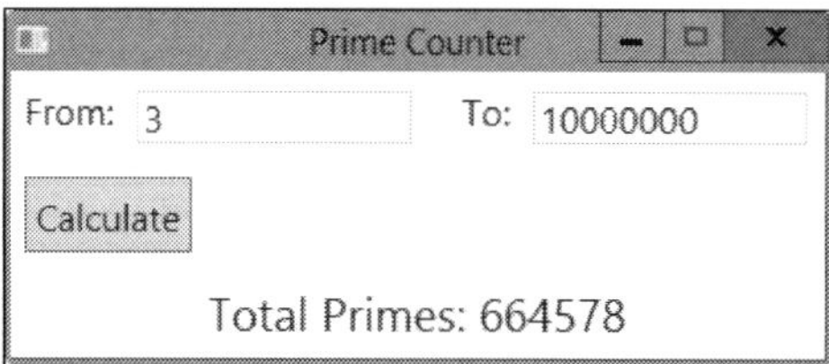

How it works...

All WPF elements inherit from `DispatcherObject` (which only inherits from `object`), which means an element is always associated with a `System.Windows.Threading.Dispatcher`, or to be more precise, a UI thread is associated with a `Dispatcher`. This `Dispatcher` can be accessed at any time using the `DispatcherObject.Dispatcher` property inherited by all WPF elements.

Calling `Dispatcher.Invoke` or `Dispatcher.BeginInvoke` schedules a delegate (of whatever kind) to execute on the thread associated with that dispatcher. The dispatcher is also accessible from the UI thread using the `Dispatcher.CurrentDispatcher` static property (this may be useful when non-UI aware code is running on the UI thread).

The call to `ThreadPool.QueueUserWorkItem` (step 7) causes a delegate to execute as soon as possible on the CLR's thread pool (one thread pool in a process). This means the passed in delegate never executes on the UI thread. When the operation completes and the UI needs to be updated, it must be done on the UI thread. This is where the `Dispatcher` comes in. The call to `Dispatcher.BeginInvoke` causes a delegate to run on the UI thread, making accessing the UI possible.

There's more...

The `Dispatcher` supports two ways of invocation: `Invoke` and `BeginInvoke`. `Invoke` does not return until the operation runs on the UI thread, whereas `BeginInvoke` returns immediately to do other work while the delegate to run on UI thread is scheduled for execution. The choice doesn't matter most of the time, but `BeginInvoke` is preferred unless there is a specific reason to wait for the UI operation to complete, such as when a result is expected.

The `Dispatcher` maintains queues of requests that need to be processed on the UI thread. There are several priorities available, `DispatcherPriority.Normal` being the default.

Some overloads for `Invoke` and `BeginInvoke` accept a `DispatcherPriority` as well as the delegate to execute. Here are the existing priority levels (from lowest to highest):

- `Inactive`: Operations are not processed
- `SystemIdle`: Processed when the system is idle
- `ApplicationIdle`: Processed when the application is idle
- `ContextIdle`: Processed after background operations are complete
- `Background`: Processed after all non-idle operations are complete
- `Input`: Processed in the same priority as input
- `Loaded`: Processed after layout and render have finished (this is when the `Loaded` event fires)
- `Render`: Processed at the same priority as render
- `DataBind`: Processed at same priority as data binding operations
- `Normal`: Processed at normal application priority (the default)
- `Send`: Highest priority level, processed before any asynchronous operations

The default value of `Normal` would suffice in most cases, but for frequent updates we may choose a lower priority level, making sure important operations such as data binding occur first.

Dispatcher alternative

Using the dispatcher is not the only way to schedule something on the UI thread. Another, more agnostic way is to use a `SynchronizationContext`. A `SynchronizationContext` can be obtained by calling the static `SynchronizationContext.Current` property. For a UI thread, the synchronization context represents the affinity with that thread. For non-UI threads, the context may be different or even `null` (which it is on a thread pool thread).

The way to use the `SynchronizationContext` is to "capture" it on the UI thread, and later call its `Post` or `Send` methods to schedule a delegate to run on a thread represented by that context (always a single thread in the UI case). Here's an alternative event handler that does essentially the same thing (steps 6 to 8):

```
int first = int.Parse(_from.Text), last = int.Parse(_to.Text);
var button = (Button)sender;
button.IsEnabled = false;
var sc = SynchronizationContext.Current;
ThreadPool.QueueUserWorkItem(_ => {
   int total = CountPrimes(first, last);
   sc.Post(delegate {
      _result.Text = "Total Primes: " + total.ToString();
      button.IsEnabled = true;
   }, null);
});
```

`SynchronizationContext.Post` is an asynchronous call (non-blocking), similar to `Dispatcher.BeginInvoke`, while `SynchronizationContext.Send` is similar to `Dispatcher.Invoke`.

What's the advantage of using a `SynchronizationContext`? Although it's less flexible than `Dispatcher`, it's technology-agnostic. This means the same code works in WPF, WinForms, Silverlight, and even Windows Phone 7.x.

The secret to its operation is the returned object from `SynchronizationContext.Current`. It's a different one in WPF (`System.Windows.Threading.DispatcherSynchronizationContext`) than in WinForms (`System.Windows.Forms.WindowsFormsSynchronizationContext`) - each provides a different implementation to Send and Post (WPF uses its `Dispatcher`, WinForms uses its `ISynchronizeInvoke` interface implementation on `System.Windows.Forms.Control`). Because of its neutrality, it can be used without specifically referencing WPF or WinForms assemblies.

Dispatcher enhancements in WPF 4.5

The `Dispatcher` that's available with WPF 4.5 has some enhancements worth noting:

- The `Invoke` method has more overloads. Some accept an `Action` delegate (instead of the base `Delegate` class), which simplifies coding. A generic `Invoke<T>` exists that returns a `T` as a result from the synchronous call.
- The `InvokeAsync` method (with overloads) was added that allows using the C# `await` keyword to wait for the operation to complete without blocking. We'll see an example of the C# 5.0 `await` keyword in a later recipe.

More Dispatcher

Some extension methods exist for `Dispatcher` from the `System.Windows.Threading.DispatcherExtension` class for `Invoke` and `BeginInvoke` that accept an `Action` instead of any `Delegate`. Strangely, this class resides in the `System.Windows.Presentation` assembly, which is not added by Visual Studio by default.

WPF uses `Dispatcher.VerifyAccess` in many code paths to make sure the call happens on the UI thread. If not, `VerifyAccess` throws an `InvalidOperationException`. Alternatively, it's possible to call `Dispatcher.CheckAccess` that returns `true` if called on the correct (UI) thread and `false` otherwise. This could help in certain scenarios, where the `Dispatcher` may be circumvented if the call happens to be on the UI thread.

What about data binding?

In a more realistic code, data binding would be used. In such a case, if a property is changed from a non-UI thread, what would happen if that property is data bound by some element? It turns out this works ok for simple properties.

Collections, however, cannot be modified from a non-UI thread if that collection is data bound; that would generate an exception. In WPF 4 or earlier, such an operation would have to be marshaled to the UI thread with the aid of the `Dispatcher` or `SynchronizationContext`.

Starting from WPF 4.5, collections (such as `ObservableCollection<T>`) can be modified from non-UI threads, provided they are registered correctly using the `BindingOperations.EnableCollectionSynchronization` static method. Here's an example for a list of simple integers:

```
public partial class MainWindow : Window {
   ObservableCollection<int> _numbers =
      new ObservableCollection<int>();
   object _lock = new object();

   public MainWindow() {
      InitializeComponent();
```

```
            _list.ItemsSource = _numbers;
            BindingOperations.EnableCollectionSynchronization(
                _numbers, _lock);

            ThreadPool.QueueUserWorkItem(_ => {
                var rnd = new Random();
                for(; ;) {
                    lock(_lock) {
                        _numbers.Add(rnd.Next(1000));
                    }
                    Thread.Sleep(1000);
                }
            });
        }
    }
```

`_list` is a `ListBox` reference, bound to the `ObservableCollection<int>`. The `BindingOperations.EnableCollectionSynchronization` accepts the collection for which to allow modifications, and a lock object. That's the same idea behind the C# `lock` keyword (`Monitor.Enter/Exit` of the framework), which means it can be any reference type, but the actual object is unimportant. This lock object is required so that the collection can be synchronized when accessed from a non-UI thread or accessed on the UI thread for binding purposes.

It's important to note that this still means that our code needs to use locking with the same lock object to make sure the collection is not corrupted in any way.

Adding cancelation support

Long running operations are typically performed on a different thread, which keeps the UI responsive, but that may not be enough. Applications may want to provide a way to cancel a long-running operation. Prior to .NET 4, developers used various ways to orchestrate cancelations. Starting from .NET 4 there is a standard way to convey cancelation requests.

In this recipe, we'll see how to use this cancelation mechanism.

Getting ready

Open the `CH11.AsyncCalc` project. We'll enhance it with cancelation support.

How to do it...

We'll add the option to cancel the prime calculation operation.

1. Open `MainWindow.xaml`. Add another button to the second `StackPanel` with the following markup:

   ```
   <Button Content="Cancel" Padding="4" Margin="10,0,0,0"
           IsEnabled="False" x:Name="_cancelButton" />
   ```

2. Name the **Calculate** button `_calcButton`.

3. Open `MainWindow.xaml.cs`. Change the `CountPrimes` method to accept a `CancellationToken`:

   ```
   static int CountPrimes(int from, int to,
      CancellationToken ct) {
   ```

4. Modify `CountPrimes` to check whether `CancellationToken.IsCancellationRequested` is `true`, and if so, return immediately. This is how the loop should look:

   ```
   for(int i = from; i <= to; i++) {
      if(ct.IsCancellationRequested)
         return -1;
      bool isPrime = true;
      int limit = (int)Math.Sqrt(i);
      for(int j = 2; j <= limit; j++)
         if(i % j == 0) {
            isPrime = false;
            break;
         }
      if(isPrime)
         total++;
   }
   ```

5. To make this work, we need to create a `CancellationTokenSource`, which is the provider of `CancellationToken` objects. Add a private field of type `CancellationTokenSource` to the `MainWindow` class:

   ```
   public partial class MainWindow : Window {
      CancellationTokenSource _cts;
   ```

6. Change the **Calculate** button event handler to create a `CancellationTokenSource` and use it to provide a `CancellationToken` to `CountPrimes`, and act upon the result:

   ```
   int first = int.Parse(_from.Text), last = int.Parse(_to.Text);
   _calcButton.IsEnabled = false;
   _cancelButton.IsEnabled = true;
   _cts = new CancellationTokenSource();
   ThreadPool.QueueUserWorkItem(_ => {
      int total = CountPrimes(first, last, _cts.Token);
      Dispatcher.BeginInvoke(new Action(() => {
   ```

```
            _result.Text = total < 0 ? "Cancelled!" :
               "Total Primes: " + total.ToString();
            _cancelButton.IsEnabled = false;
            _calcButton.IsEnabled = true;
         }));
      });
```

7. To set all this in motion, add a `Click` event handler for the **Cancel** button. Implement it with the following code:

```
if(_cts != null) {
   _cts.Cancel();
   _cts = null;
}
```

8. Run the application. Start a long calculation and cancel it midway; alternatively, let it run all the way through. The UI should remain responsive at all times.

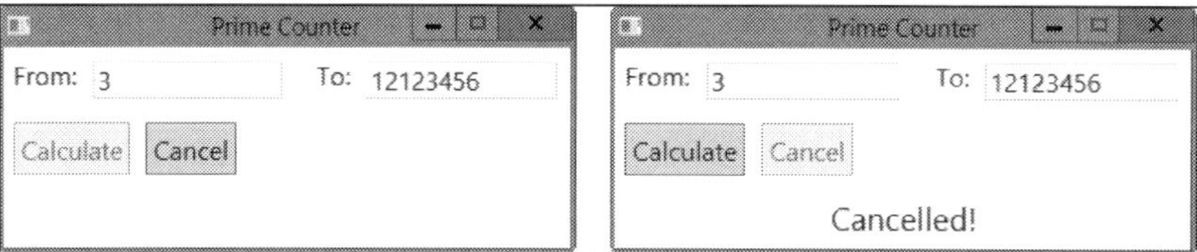

How it works...

A `CancellationTokenSource` represents a logical operation that may be canceled. That source provides `CancellationToken` objects through its `Token` property to individual objects or methods that provide part of that logical operation. In the simplest case (as it is in the above code), only one such token is distributed, meaning a single entity (a method in this case) does all the work.

Whenever the `Cancel` method is called on a `CancellationTokenSource` instance, all distributed tokens from that source have their `IsCancellationRequested` property set to true. Hopefully, the code holding on to a `CancellationToken` is able to poll that property in sufficiently small intervals, and if true, make an effort to bail out early. In our example, the loop simply returns with a special value (-1) indicating cancellation.

There's more...

It's important to realize that the `CancellationTokenSource` and `CancellationToken` types have no abilities of their own in terms of actually canceling anything. They provide a piece of logic for cooperative cancellation. Calling `CancellationTokenSource.Cancel` does not guarantee cancellation – it's merely a request to cancel, that can hopefully be carried out by entities holding `CancellationToken` objects obtained from that source.

Never cancel by aborting a thread

Sometimes developers try to abort asynchronous operations by aborting the thread that carries the operation. This is almost always a bad idea. There are several reasons for this, one of which is the difficulty in knowing what that thread has done and what it had yet to do before being terminated. The application may be left in an inconsistent state as a result of an abrupt thread termination.

It's much better to facilitate termination with some piece of logic involving synchronization objects, such as `AutoResetEvent` or `ManualResetEvent(Slim)`. Using these objects is beyond the scope of this book as these have nothing special to do with WPF.

Using the BackgroundWorker component

The asynchronous operation we used in the previous examples used the thread pool explicitly to do the long running work on another thread. Updating the UI required marshaling code to the UI thread from another thread, to keep the rule of updating the UI from the UI thread intact. All this required some manually managed code.

An alternative is using the `BackgroundWorker` class that provides automatic management and marshaling for the purpose of performing a long running operation on a background thread.

In this recipe, we'll use the `BackgroundWorker` to do asynchronous operations without blocking the UI thread and understand its pros and cons.

Getting ready

We'll duplicate most of the UI from the `CH11.AsyncCalc` project, so keep it open while we create the new project.

How to do it...

We'll count prime numbers (as before) on a different thread, but we'll let the `BackgroundWorker` take care of all the gory details.

1. Create a new WPF Application named `CH11.AsyncCalcWithBackgroundWorker`.
2. Copy the XAML from `MainWindow.xaml` from the `CH11.AsyncCalc` project to this project's `MainWindow.xaml`. Remove the cancel button markup for now. Also remove the `Click` event setting from the calculate button's markup. This is the resulting XAML (without the `x:Class` and default XAML namespace mappings):

```
<Window Title="Primes Counter" ResizeMode="CanMinimize"
    SizeToContent="WidthAndHeight">
    <Grid TextBlock.FontSize="16">
```

```
        <Grid.RowDefinitions>
            <RowDefinition Height="Auto"/>
            <RowDefinition Height="Auto" />
            <RowDefinition Height="Auto" />
            <RowDefinition Height="Auto" />
        </Grid.RowDefinitions>
        <StackPanel Orientation="Horizontal" Margin="6">
            <TextBlock Text="From:" />
            <TextBox Margin="10,2,2,2" Width="120"
                MaxLength="10" x:Name="_from"/>
            <TextBlock Text="To:" Margin="20,0,0,0"/>
            <TextBox Margin="10,2,2,2" Width="120"
            MaxLength="10" x:Name="_to"/>
        </StackPanel>
        <StackPanel Orientation="Horizontal" Grid.Row="1"
            Margin="6">
            <Button Content="Calculate" Padding="4"
                    x:Name="_calcButton"/>
        </StackPanel>
        <TextBlock x:Name="_result" Grid.Row="3" Margin="6"
              HorizontalAlignment="Center" FontSize="20" />
    </Grid>
</Window>
```

3. Open `MainWindow.xaml.cs`. Add a private field to the `MainWindow` class of type `BackgroundWorker`:

```
BackgroundWorker _worker;
```

4. Add a `Click` event handler to the **Calculate** button named `OnCalculate`. The first thing to do in the event handler is to set up the `BackgroundWorker`. This is done by wiring up two events, `DoWork` and `RunWorkerCompleted` (you can press *Tab* twice to let Visual Studio create the actual event handlers):

```
_worker = new BackgroundWorker();
_worker.DoWork += _worker_DoWork;
_worker.RunWorkerCompleted += _worker_RunWorkerCompleted;
```

5. Next, we want to disable the **Calculate** button to prevent another operation from starting and then kick off the operation. First, we'll create a small class to hold the information that needs to be passed to the `DoWork` event handler. Add a class named `PrimeInputData` defined with the following simple code:

```
class PrimeInputData {
   public int First { get; set; }
   public int Last { get; set; }
}
```

6. Continuing in the `Click` handler of a button, add the following code that sets up the data to work with and initiates the work asynchronously:

```
_calcButton.IsEnabled = false;
_result.Text = "Calculating...";

var data = new PrimeInputData {
   First = int.Parse(_from.Text),
   Last = int.Parse(_to.Text)
};
_worker.RunWorkerAsync(data);
```

7. `RunWorkerAsync` causes the `DoWork` event handler to be called on a thread pool thread. Implement the `DoWork` event handler with the following code:

```
void _worker_DoWork(object sender, DoWorkEventArgs e) {
   var data = (PrimeInputData)e.Argument;
   int count = 0;
   for(int i = data.First; i <= data.Last; i++) {
      int limit = (int)Math.Sqrt(i);
      bool isPrime = true;
      for(int j = 2; j <= limit; j++)
         if(i % j == 0) {
            isPrime = false;
            break;
         }
      if(isPrime)
         count++;
   }
   e.Result = count;
}
```

8. When the `DoWork` event handler is done, the `RunWorkerCompleted` event is fired on the UI thread (automatically). Implement the handler as follows:

```
void _worker_RunWorkerCompleted(object sender,
   RunWorkerCompletedEventArgs e) {
   _result.Text = string.Format("Total Primes: {0}",
      e.Result);
   _calcButton.IsEnabled = true;
}
```

9. Run the application. Enter some numbers and click on **Calculate**. Make sure the window is responsive throughout the calculation.

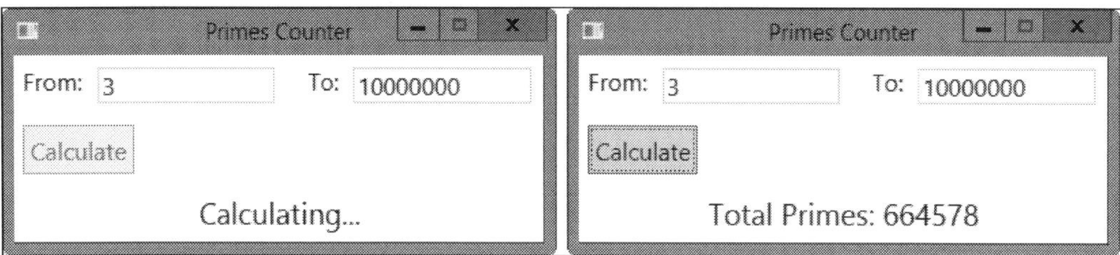

How it works...

The `BackgroundWorker` class uses events to coordinate the work. The `DoWork` event is raised on a thread pool thread when the `RunWorkerAsync` method is called. The `DoWork` event handler is where the long running code is used. An optional argument can be passed to `RunWorkerAsync` which is passed to the `DoWork` handlers in the `DoWorkEventArgs.Argument` property. This is used here to pass information about the prime numbers to be counted (step 6). Any result can be stored in the `DoWorkEventArgs.Result` property.

When the `DoWork` event handler completes, the `BackgroundWorker` raises the `RunWorkerCompleted` event, always on the UI thread, which is convenient as we probably want to update the UI when the work is done. Any result passed from the `DoWork` handler is received in the `RunWorkerCompletedEventArgs.Result` property. Here it's the count of prime numbers (step 8).

The `BackgroundWorker` is easy to use as we didn't create any threads, used the thread pool, or marshaled calls to the UI thread.

There's more...

The `BackgroundWorker` was introduced in .NET 2.0, and one of its curious attributes is that it works in all UI technologies in .NET: WPF, WinForms, Silverlight, and Windows Phone 7.x. It may seem like a kind of magic, as WPF (for example) was created after the `BackgroundWorker` was.

The secret to its work is that it uses the `SynchronizationContext` class we met already. This makes it agnostic to the actual technology used because the correct `SynchronizationContext` would be created by the relevant technology when `SynchronizationContext.Current` is called by the `BackgroundWorker`.

Did we really have to pass the argument to RunWorkerAsync?

The DoWork event handler is part of the MainWindow class, so why did we pass the information to the handler via the Argument property? Wouldn't it be simpler to just call int.Parse in the DoWork event handler for both TextBox objects?

We must remember that this code is called by a thread pool thread, meaning accessing any UI element would cause an exception. This is why we first got values on the UI thread before invoking the BackgroundWorker. The DoWork event handler is too late to access UI elements.

What about the Task Parallel Library?

.NET 4 introduced the Task Parallel Library (TPL) for working more conveniently and efficiently with concurrent operations. These can be used in cases where it's possible to run things faster by using multiple CPU cores. For example, our prime counting code is single threaded. We could change it to the following parallel code that would use the available cores on the machine to count primes faster with Parallel.For:

```
Parallel.For(data.First, data.Last + 1, i => {
   int limit = (int)Math.Sqrt(i);
   bool isPrime = true;
   for(int j = 2; j <= limit; j++)
      if(i % j == 0) {
         isPrime = false;
         break;
      }
   if(isPrime)
      Interlocked.Increment(ref count);
});
```

The TPL is beyond the scope of this book as it's not specific to WPF. You can find a lot of information online (you can start at http://msdn.microsoft.com/concurrency).

Adding cancellation and progress with BackgroundWorker

The BackgroundWorker supports two extra features: cancellation and progress. We already looked at cooperative cancellation with the CancellationTokenSource and CancellationToken types, but the BackgroundWorker defines its own mechanism (it was created long before the latter types were).

In this recipe, we'll take a look at adding cancelation to the primes counting endeavor. Also, in a long running operation it's nice to indicate to the user how things are progressing. The BackgroundWorker has good support for that, too.

Getting ready

We'll continue with the `CH11.AsyncCalcWithBackgroundWorker` project. Alternatively, you can make a copy of it and work on that.

How to do it...

We'll add a **Cancel** button and a `ProgressBar` and use the support of `BackgroundWorker` for these features.

1. Open `MainWindow.xaml`. Add a **Cancel** button to the second `StackPanel`, right after the **Calculate** button:

```
<Button Content="Cancel" Padding="4" x:Name="_cancelButton"
        IsEnabled="False" Margin="10,0,0,0" />
```

2. Add a `ProgressBar` to the third row of the `Grid` like so:

```
<ProgressBar x:Name="_progress" Grid.Row="2" Height="30"
             Margin="4"/>
```

3. Open `MainWindow.xaml.cs`. To set up cancellation, we first need to enable it for the `BackgroundWorker`. In the **Calculate** button's `Click` event handler, after the `BackgroundWorker` creation, add the following code:

```
_worker.WorkerSupportsCancellation = true;
```

4. After the **Calculate** button is disabled, enable the **Cancel** button:

```
_cancelButton.IsEnabled = true;
```

5. Add a `Click` event handler to the **Cancel** button. Implement the handler as follows:

```
private void OnCancel(object sender, RoutedEventArgs e) {
   _worker.CancelAsync();
}
```

6. Cancellation support is cooperative. The long running operation needs to check the `BackgroundWorker.CancellationPending` property periodically, and if it returns `true`, this means a cancellation is requested. We'll modify the `DoWork` event handler to check for this property with every iteration:

```
for(int i = data.First; i <= data.Last; i++) {
   if(_worker.CancellationPending) {
      e.Cancel = true;
      break;
   }
```

7. Setting `DoWorkEventArgs.Cancelled` to `true` indicates that the operation was in fact canceled. When the `RunWorkerCompleted` event handler fires, we need to check the `RunWorkerCompletedEventArgs.Cancelled` property, and if true, do something different. Replace the `RunWorkerCompleted` event handler with the following code:

```
_result.Text = e.Cancelled ? "Operation Cancelled" :
   string.Format("Total Primes: {0}", e.Result);
_calcButton.IsEnabled = true;
_cancelButton.IsEnabled = false;
```

8. Run the application. Enter some numbers and click on **Calculate**. Click on **Cancel** mid operation and watch the cancellation result.

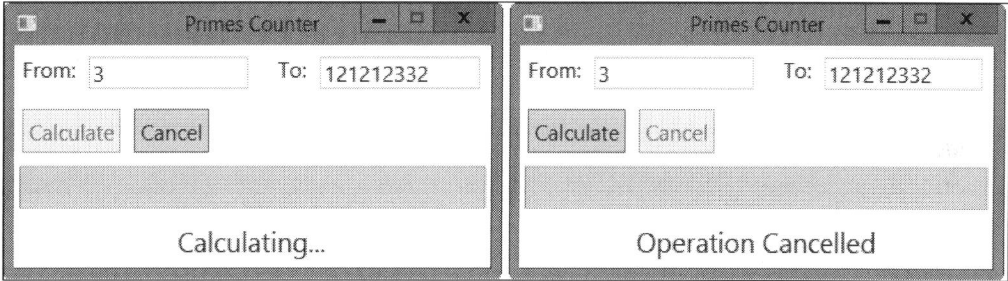

9. Now we want to indicate progress. First, we need to enable support for progress reporting in the `BackgroundWorker`. Add the following line after the `BackgroundWorker` creation in the `Click` event handler of the **Calculate** button:

```
_worker.WorkerReportsProgress = true;
```

10. Next, we need to register for another event the `BackgroundWorker` supports, `ProgressChanged`. This event is fired on the UI thread whenever the long running operation reports a progress change. Add the following line after the `RunWorkerCompleted` event registration (you can press *Tab* twice to get Visual Studio's auto completion):

```
_worker.ProgressChanged += _worker_ProgressChanged;
```

11. In the created handler, add the following code:

```
_progress.Value = e.ProgressPercentage;
```

12. This sets the `Value` property of `Progress` bar based on the `ProgressChangedEventArgs.ProgressPercentage` property. Who is providing that value? That's part of the `DoWork` event handler. Modify the `DoWork` event handler to incorporate progress related code. Here's the complete implementation:

```
var data = (PrimeInputData)e.Argument;
int count = 0;
_worker.ReportProgress(0);
```

```
int range = data.Last - data.First + 1, progressCount = 0;
for(int i = data.First; i <= data.Last; i++) {
   if(_worker.CancellationPending) {
      e.Cancel = true;
      break;
   }
   int limit = (int)Math.Sqrt(i);
   bool isPrime = true;
   for(int j = 2; j <= limit; j++)
      if(i % j == 0) {
         isPrime = false;
         break;
      }
   if(isPrime)
      count++;
   if(++progressCount % 100 == 0)
      _worker.ReportProgress(progressCount * 100 / range);
}
if(!e.Cancel) {
   _worker.ReportProgress(100);
   e.Result = count;
}
```

13. Run the application. Enter numbers to work with, click on **Calculate** and watch the progress change.

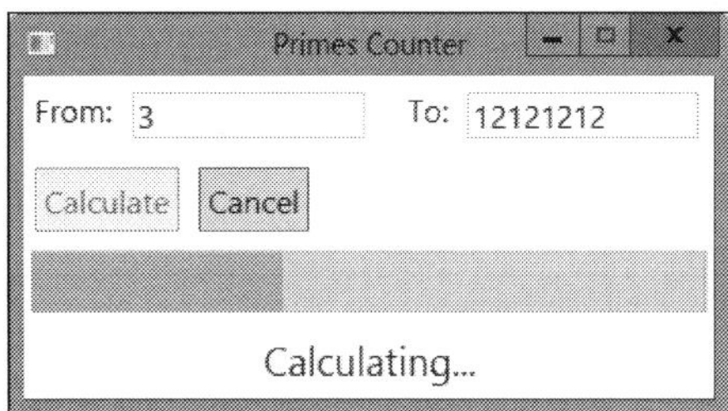

How it works...

Cancellation initiation with the `BackgroundWorker` works by calling the `CancelAsync` method. This sets the `CancellationPending` property to `true`, that (hopefully) the `DoWork` event handler inspects from time to time. This is, just like `CancellationToken(Source)`, cooperative cancellation. In our case, if the flag is set, the `DoEventArgs.Cancel` property is explicitly set to true, indicating the operation has actually been canceled. The `RunWorkerCompletedEventArgs.Cancelled` conveys that information, allowing the correct result to be presented.

Reporting progress is a matter of calling `BackgroundWorker.ReportProgress` method with some number indicating progress. Note that the number doesn't have to be between zero and 100, but can be anything that makes sense for the application. In the preceding code, for every 100 numbers the progress is reported. Reporting the progress causes the `ProgressChanged` event to be fired on the UI thread where some UI can be modified - the `Value` of `ProgressBar` in this case.

There's more...

It may be tempting to report progress after each and every number, but that would stress the UI thread too much and cause the dreaded "not responding" result, defeating the very purpose the `BackgroundWorker` was designed for. This is why the progress should be reported in reasonable intervals, so that the UI thread is busy only momentarily.

What about Parallel.For?

If we use the `Parallel.For` to parallelize the computation to make better use of the available cores, how do we cancel the operation? Using the following code does not compile:

```
if(_worker.CancellationPending) {
   e.Cancel = true;
   break;
}
```

Why? The break instruction fails to compile because there is no loop here - it's just a delegate that's passed in to `Parallel.For`. How can we handle that? Fortunately, `Parallel.For` can accept an alternative delegate, `Action<int, ParallelLoopState>` (instead of `Action<int>`) that can be used for such matters. The entire `Parallel.For` call should be changed to this:

```
Parallel.For(data.First, data.Last + 1, (i, state) => {
   if(_worker.CancellationPending) {
      e.Cancel = true;
      state.Stop();
   }
   int limit = (int)Math.Sqrt(i);
   bool isPrime = true;
   for(int j = 2; j <= limit; j++)
      if(i % j == 0) {
         isPrime = false;
         break;
      }
   if(isPrime)
      Interlocked.Increment(ref count);
});
```

Calling `ParallelLoopState.Stop` breaks out of the entire parallel loop as soon as possible; this is exactly what we want.

Implementing progress correctly with `Parallel.For` is left as an exercise for the reader.

Using a timer to do periodic updates

It is sometimes useful to update parts of the user interface periodically. For example, an application may need to display the current time in some part of the UI. Or some color changes need to be made on a regular basis based on some runtime criteria. Although it's possible to create a thread that sleeps for a certain amount of time and then does the updates, this has two flaws: the first is that most of the time the thread sleeps. Threads are supposed to do useful work and not sleep most of the time – the very fact the thread exists requires it to have its stack space (1MB by default), which may be wasteful in such a case. The second flaw is that we would have to marshal the UI update call using some mechanism we've already seen (`Dispatcher`, `SynchronizationContext`, and so on), which makes the code cumbersome.

A timer can be used instead if such updates are required, without the need to create additional threads. In this recipe, we'll use the `DispatcherTimer` class to implement a timer that can be used easily to update the UI, as its `Tick` event always fires on the UI thread.

Getting ready

Make sure Visual Studio is up and running.

How to do it...

We'll create a simple demo that changes some text and a brush in regular time intervals.

1. Create a new WPF application named `CH11.PeriodicUpdates`.
2. Open `MainWindow.xaml`. We'll create a `TextBlock` and an `Ellipse` to be modified by a timer. Add the following markup to the existing `Grid`:

```
<Grid.RowDefinitions>
    <RowDefinition Height="Auto" />
    <RowDefinition />
</Grid.RowDefinitions>
<TextBlock x:Name="_time" HorizontalAlignment="Center"
           FontSize="20" Margin="8"/>
<Ellipse Margin="10" Stroke="Black" StrokeThickness="2"
         x:Name="_el" Grid.Row="1" />
```

3. Open `MainWindow.xaml.cs`. Add `using` statements for the `System.Reflection` and `System.Windows.Threading` namespaces.

4. Add the following private fields to the `MainWindow` class:

```
DispatcherTimer _timer = new DispatcherTimer();
int _counter;
Random _rnd = new Random();
```

5. Add the following code to set up the timer and handle its `Tick` event in the constructor, after the call to `InitializeComponent`:

```
_timer.Interval = TimeSpan.FromSeconds(.5);
_timer.Tick += delegate {
   _time.Text = DateTime.Now.ToLongTimeString();
   if(++_counter == 3) {
      var brushes = typeof(Brushes).GetProperties(
      BindingFlags.Public | BindingFlags.Static);
      _e1.Fill = (Brush)brushes[_rnd.Next(brushes.Length)].
         GetValue(null, null);
      _counter = 0;
   }
};
_timer.Start();
```

6. Run the application. You should see the time being updated, while the `Ellipse Fill Brush` changes every 1.5 seconds.

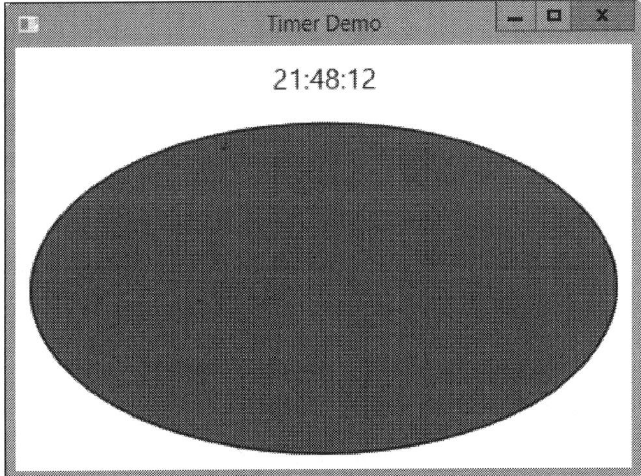

How it works...

The `System.Windows.Threading.DispatcherTimer` class represents a timer that is bound to the UI thread. The `Interval` property indicates the period of the timer; the `Tick` event is raised every such interval on the UI thread. The timer can be started by calling the `Start` method or setting the `IsEnabled` property to `true` (same effect).

Similarly, stopping the timer can be done with the `Stop` method or by setting `IsEnabled` to `false`.

As the `Tick` event is raised on the UI thread, we should make sure the work being done is not a lengthy one. If it is, the UI may become unresponsive; in such a case, offload the work to another thread.

There's more...

.NET defines no less than four timers. One such timer is WinForm's equivalent to `DispatcherTimer`, namely `System.Windows.Forms.Timer`.

The `System.Threading.Timer` is a general purpose timer that invokes a delegate (`TimerCallback`, provided in the constructor) on a thread pool thread. This means that if a UI update is required, marshaling must be used to do the UI update. On the other hand, long running work is possible without blocking the UI thread.

The `System.Timers.Timer` derives from `System.ComponentModel.Component`, which means it has designer-friendly features, and was mostly used in the WinForms world. Its `Elapsed` event can be raised in the UI thread if its `SynchronizationObject` property is set to an object that implements the `ISynchronizeInvoke` interface (which all WinForms controls do), otherwise it's raised on a thread pool thread.

I recommend using `System.Threading.Timer` for things that don't require UI updates.

Using C# 5.0 to perform asynchronous operations

Using synchronous operations is really easy. Just call some operation, wait for it to return, and use the result. As we've seen, the problem is that slow operations block the calling (UI) thread or that thread does some hard CPU bound work; in both cases, the UI may become unresponsive. We have seen several ways to deal with that. These require running the long operation on a different thread, and when the results are finally available, marshal some code to update the UI.

The net result is code complexity, which grows quickly with more and more asynchronous operations happening. And if we consider more than one operation at a time, potential cancellations, adding timeouts, handling exceptions conveniently – code complexity climbs quickly.

C# 5.0 has a new feature related to calling operations running asynchronously and waiting efficiently for the result without all the required marshaling and code complexity. In this recipe, we'll take a brief look at using this feature to make asynchronous calls look very similar to synchronous ones, but still maintain responsive UI.

Getting ready

We'll need Visual Studio 2012 or later for this recipe. Make sure it's up and running.

How to do it...

We'll use the same prime counting example, but convert that to a C# 5.0 version, along with cancellation and progress.

1. Create a new WPF application named `CH11.AsyncCalcWithCS5`.
2. Open `MainWindow.xaml`. Add the following properties to the `Window` (remove the `Width` and `Height` properties):

```
Title="Async Calc with C# 5.0" ResizeMode="CanMinimize"
SizeToContent="WidthAndHeight"
```

3. Add the following inside the existing `Grid` (this is pretty much the same UI as the other prime counting samples):

```
<Grid.RowDefinitions>
    <RowDefinition Height="Auto"/>
    <RowDefinition Height="Auto" />
    <RowDefinition Height="Auto" />
    <RowDefinition Height="Auto" />
</Grid.RowDefinitions>
<StackPanel Orientation="Horizontal" Margin="6">
    <TextBlock Text="From:" />
    <TextBox Margin="10,2,2,2" Width="120"
             MaxLength="10" x:Name="_from"/>
    <TextBlock Text="To:" Margin="20,0,0,0"/>
    <TextBox Margin="10,2,2,2" Width="120" MaxLength="10"
             x:Name="_to"/>
</StackPanel>
<StackPanel Orientation="Horizontal" Grid.Row="1" Margin="6">
    <Button Content="Calculate" Padding="4"
            x:Name="_calcButton" Margin="4"/>
```

```
    <Button Content="Cancel" Padding="4" Margin="4"
            x:Name="_cancelButton" IsEnabled="False"/>
</StackPanel>
<ProgressBar x:Name="_progress" Grid.Row="2" Margin="4"
             Height="30" />
<TextBlock x:Name="_result" Grid.Row="3" Margin="6"
           HorizontalAlignment="Center" FontSize="20" />
```

4. Open `MainWindow.xaml.cs`. Add using statement for the `System.Threading` and `System.Threading.Tasks` namespaces.
5. Add a method that would count prime numbers asynchronously with the following implementation:

```
async Task<int> CountPrimesAsync(int first, int last,
   CancellationToken ct, IProgress<double> progress) {
   var task = Task.Run(() => {
      int total = 0;
      int range = last - first + 1;
      int pcount = 0;
      for(int i = first; i <= last; i++) {
         ct.ThrowIfCancellationRequested();
         bool isPrime = true;
         int limit = (int)Math.Sqrt(i);
         for(int j = 2; j <= limit; j++)
            if(i % j == 0) {
               isPrime = false;
               break;
            }
         if(isPrime)
            total++;
         if(++pcount % 1000 == 0)
            progress.Report(pcount * 100.0 / range);
      }
      return total;
   });
   return await task;
}
```

6. The `async` and `await` keywords are new in C# 5.0. A detailed explanation of the way this method works follows in the *How it works...* section. Add a private field to the `MainWindow` class of type `CancellationTokenSource`:

```
CancellationTokenSource _cts;
```

7. Add a `Click` event handler for the **Calculate** button. Implement the handler as follows (note the `async` keyword must be added to the event handler for this method to compile successfully):

```
async void OnCalculate(object sender, RoutedEventArgs e) {
   int first = int.Parse(_from.Text),
      last = int.Parse(_to.Text);
   _cts = new CancellationTokenSource();
   _calcButton.IsEnabled = false;
   _cancelButton.IsEnabled = true;
   _result.Text = "Calculating...";
   var progress = new Progress<double>(
      value => _progress.Value = value);

   try {
      int count = await CountPrimesAsync(first, last,
         _cts.Token, progress);
      _result.Text = "Total Primes: " + count;
   }
   catch(OperationCanceledException ex) {
      _result.Text = "Operation cancelled";
   }
   finally {
      _cts.Dispose();
      _calcButton.IsEnabled = true;
      _cancelButton.IsEnabled = false;
   }
}
```

8. `CountPrimesAsync` returns a `Task<int>` but we just "await" the actual result and use it very naturally, just as if it was a synchronous call (and it's not). Add a `Click` event handler for the **Cancel** button and implement with the following code:

```
void OnCancel(object sender, RoutedEventArgs e) {
   _cts.Cancel();
}
```

9. That's it. Run the application and try counting some primes. Try the **Cancel** button as well.

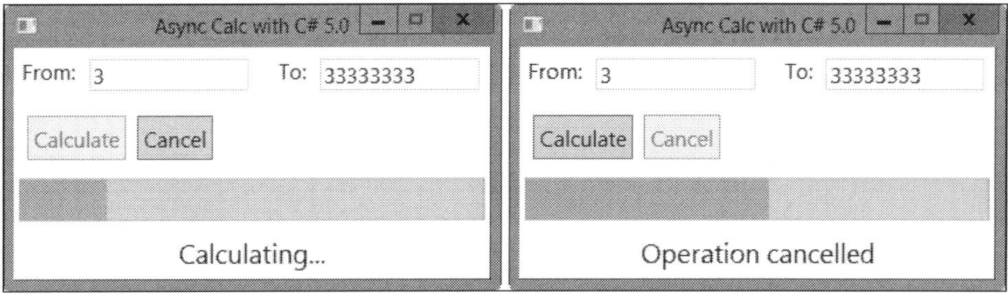

How it works...

C# 5.0 adds two keywords related to asynchronous programming: `async` and `await`. The `await` keyword can be used on anything that is "awaitable", which means following a certain pattern the compiler looks for in that particular object. Most of the time `await` is used on `Task` or `Task<T>`, which are the most common built-in "awaitables". The result of awaiting `Task<T>` is `T`. As `CountPrimesAsync` returns a `Task<int>`, awaiting that task yields an `int` (which is the required result).

Clearly, `await` must return only when the awaited `Task` is done. What does the thread do until that time? It returns to its caller. In our case, it simply returns to processing UI messages, which keeps the UI responsive. This is *not* the same as calling `Task<T>.Result` or `Task.Wait` - these methods may block the calling thread, and since it's the UI thread, the UI will become unresponsive; and that's a very big difference.

You may wonder how all this works. The full details are beyond the scope of this recipe, but here's the gist of it: the compiler splits the method into two parts: before the call to `await`, and everything after that. The latter is invoked as a continuation when the task is complete (on the same `SynchronizationContext`). You can open a tool, such as Reflector, and view the generated code; it's not pretty, but it works.

All this means that the following line waits asynchronously for the returned `Task` to complete and harvests the result:

```
int count = await CountPrimesAsync(first, last, _cts.Token,
   progress);
```

The calling thread literally returns from the call at the await point and somehow returns to the call after `await` is done and the result is available. If we were to write a synchronous version of this code it would look something like this:

```
int count = CountPrimes(first, last, _cts.Token, progress);
```

Note the high degree of similarity - this is the power of C# 5.0 - of asynchronous code looking like synchronous code; and this is just the tip of the iceberg.

What's the purpose of the `async` keyword? On a purely syntactic level, a method that uses `await` must be marked with `async`. This method can only return `void`, `Task`, or `Task<T>`. In the case of a non-void return, the method may return the expected `Task`, but it can alternatively return the value itself in the case of `Task<T>`(of type `T`), just like the `CountPrimesAsync` method does: it explicitly returns an `int`, although the method itself returns a `Task<int>`. This works because the compiler wraps that return value in a `Task<int>` - after all, there is an `await` in there somewhere, which means the method returns sooner than its actual end.

To clarify, CountPrimesAsync builds a Task<int> object and returns the total primes found from its task delegate. Then the actual return value is:

```
return await task;
```

Remember that await "strips" the Task and just uses the result (once it's available). This await actually returns immediately to its caller as a Task<int> that is awaited upon by the **Calculate** Click event handler as shown above. Note that we could make CountPrimesAsync a non-async method and simply return the created Task<int> without any awaits inside – the effect would be the same.

There's more...

The Task<int> is built using Task.Run which is a shortcut introduced in .NET 4.5 to create and start a Task and get the Task reference back in one stroke. It's also possible to use the Task.Factory.StartNew method to get the same effect (available from .NET 4), but Task.Run is shorter.

Cancellation uses the familiar CancellationToken, but to cancel a Task we can't simply return; if we did, that task would simply be considered as completed successfully. Cancellation with tasks is conveyed via an exception of type OperationCanceledException, which is the one thrown by the call to CancellationToken.ThrowifCancellationRequested. This is why the try/catch block is required in the calling code.

Reporting progress is done with the IProgress<T> interface defined in .NET 4.5. We can provide our own implementation, but we can also use the stock implementation provided by .NET 4.5 called Progress<T>, that accepts a delegate in the constructor that is invoked any time the code calls the IProgress<T>.Report method. In our case, that delegate simply hands off the provided value to the Value property of ProgressBar.

What about non-CPU bound operations?

This await/async stuff has a name; Task Asynchronous Pattern (TAP), similar to other asynchronous patterns that exist in .NET, Asynchronous Programming Model (APM) and Event Asynchronous Pattern (EAP).

Here's an example of a non-CPU operation: getting information from a network. Here's a simple synchronous code to get the job done (_result is a TextBox):

```
var wc = new WebClient();
_result.Text = "Please wait...";
try {
    _result.Text = wc.DownloadString("http://msdn.microsoft.com");
}
catch(WebException ex) {
    _result.Text = "Error: " + ex.Message;
}
```

Simple and to the point (although the "Please wait..." message will never show). Error handling is also simple with a normal `try/catch` block. However, the thread blocks while the call is out and this freezes the UI, assuming it started on a UI thread.

Fortunately, `WebClient` supports the EAP model for asynchronous calls like so:

```
var wc = new WebClient();
_result.Text = "Please wait...";
wc.DownloadStringCompleted += (s, args) => {
   if(args.Error != null)
      _result.Text = "Error: " + args.Error.Message;
   else
      _result.Text = args.Result;
};
wc.DownloadStringAsync(new Uri("http://msdn.microsoft.com"));
```

This looks very awkward; no straightforward exception handling. The event handler must come before the actual code that starts the operation with `WebClient.DownloadStringAsync`. We know the order is different, but it looks unnatural; and that's for just one operation. Also, we had some "luck" here: the completed event is raised on the same `SyhnchronizationContext` as the calling code; `WebClient` is "polite"; not every class is.

The C# 5.0 version looks like this:

```
async void OnGetDataAsync(object sender, RoutedEventArgs e) {
   var wc = new WebClient();
   _result.Text = "Please wait...";
   try {
      _result.Text = await wc.DownloadStringTaskAsync(
          "http://msdn.microsoft.com");
   }
   catch(WebException ex) {
      _result.Text = "Error: " + ex.Message;
   }
}
```

Notice the similarity with the synchronous code. Exception handling is as usual. The compiler breaks the method behind the scenes, but that doesn't concern us. `WebClient.DownloadStringTaskAsync` returns a `Task<string>`, which means it can be `await`ed upon ("`await`able"). The UI remains responsive during the I/O call.

More async

The async/await feature of C# 5.0 is a major one, and complete treatment of this is beyond the scope of this recipe. Here are a few more notes on this feature:

- Many new APIs in .NET 4.5 use this Task Asynchronous Pattern. WebClient is one such class. Another one is WebRequest that originally uses the APM (BeginGetResponse/EndGetResponse), but now also has a TAP version with GetResponseAsync that is awaitable.
- The System.IO.Stream class that uses the APM (for example, BeginRead/EndRead), now has a TAP version (ReadAsync, WriteAsync).
- The Task class has some helpers for TAP usage. Task.Delay for example, returns a Task that completes in the specified time. This can be used for timeouts without blocking.
- Awaiting can be combined with Task.WhenAll and Task.WhenAny that return Task objects that are naturally awaitable. For example, suppose we want to use WebClient to get some data, but will wait no more than 3 seconds for the result, otherwise it should be considered a timeout. Here's an elegant solution:

```
async void OnGetData(object sender, RoutedEventArgs e) {
   var wc = new WebClient();
   var t1 = wc.DownloadStringTaskAsync(
      "http://msdn.microsoft.com");
   var t2 = Task.Delay(3000);
   var tresult = await Task.WhenAny(t1, t2);
   if(tresult == t1)
      _result.Text = t1.Result;
   else
      _result.Text = "Timeout!";
}
```

Task.WhenAny returns a Task<Task> which sounds complicated, but when awaited upon, simply returns the Task that completed first.

Anything can be awaited provided it follows a predefined pattern. That pattern includes a GetAwaiter method that must be implemented on the awaited object (either on the actual type or as an extension method), and that returned "awaiter" must implement the INotifyCompletion interface (with one method named OnCompleted that accepts an Action delegate provided by the compiler, which is the compiler-generated continuation), an IsCompleted property, and a GetResult method. Anything that satisfies these demands can be awaited; the Task and Task<T> classes implement this pattern.

Index

C

D

E

F

G

H

I

K

P

R

S

T

U

V

W

Z

Thank you for buying
Windows Presentation Foundation 4.5 Cookbook

About Packt Publishing

Packt, pronounced 'packed', published its first book "*Mastering phpMyAdmin for Effective MySQL Management*" in April 2004 and subsequently continued to specialize in publishing highly focused books on specific technologies and solutions.

Our books and publications share the experiences of your fellow IT professionals in adapting and customizing today's systems, applications, and frameworks. Our solution-based books give you the knowledge and power to customize the software and technologies you're using to get the job done. Packt books are more specific and less general than the IT books you have seen in the past. Our unique business model allows us to bring you more focused information, giving you more of what you need to know, and less of what you don't.

Packt is a modern, yet unique publishing company, which focuses on producing quality, cutting-edge books for communities of developers, administrators, and newbies alike. For more information, please visit our website: `www.PacktPub.com`.

About Packt Enterprise

In 2010, Packt launched two new brands, Packt Enterprise and Packt Open Source, in order to continue its focus on specialization. This book is part of the Packt Enterprise brand, home to books published on enterprise software - software created by major vendors, including (but not limited to) IBM, Microsoft and Oracle, often for use in other corporations. Its titles will offer information relevant to a range of users of this software, including administrators, developers, architects, and end users.

Writing for Packt

We welcome all inquiries from people who are interested in authoring. Book proposals should be sent to `author@packtpub.com`. If your book idea is still at an early stage and you would like to discuss it first before writing a formal book proposal, contact us; one of our commissioning editors will get in touch with you.

We're not just looking for published authors; if you have strong technical skills but no writing experience, our experienced editors can help you develop a writing career, or simply get some additional reward for your expertise.

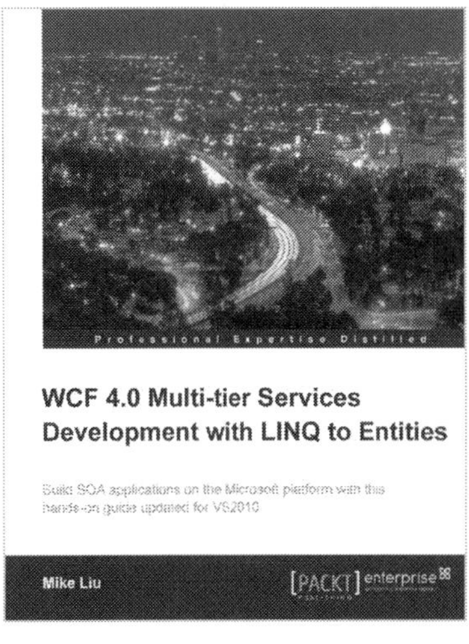

WCF 4.0 Multi-tier Services Development with LINQ to Entities

ISBN: 978-1-84968-114-8 Paperback: 348 pages

Build SOA applications on the Microsoft platform with this hands-on guide updated for VS2010

1. Master WCF and LINQ to Entities concepts by completing practical examples and applying them to your real-world assignments
2. The first and only book to combine WCF and LINQ to Entities in a multi-tier real-world WCF service
3. Ideal for beginners who want to build scalable, powerful, easy-to-maintain WCF services

---

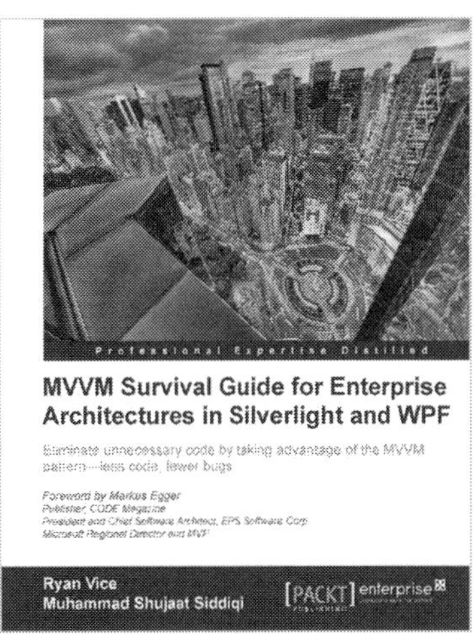

MVVM Survival Guide for Enterprise Architectures in Silverlight and WPF

ISBN: 978-1-84968-342-5 Paperback: 490 pages

Eliminate unnecessary code by taking advantage of the MVVM pattern—less code, fewer bugs

1. Build an enterprise application using Silverlight and WPF, taking advantage of the powerful MVVM pattern
2. Discover the evolution of presentation patterns—by example—and see the benefits of MVVM in the context of the larger picture of presentation patterns
3. Customize the MVVM pattern for your projects' needs by comparing the various implementation styles

Please check **www.PacktPub.com** for information on our titles

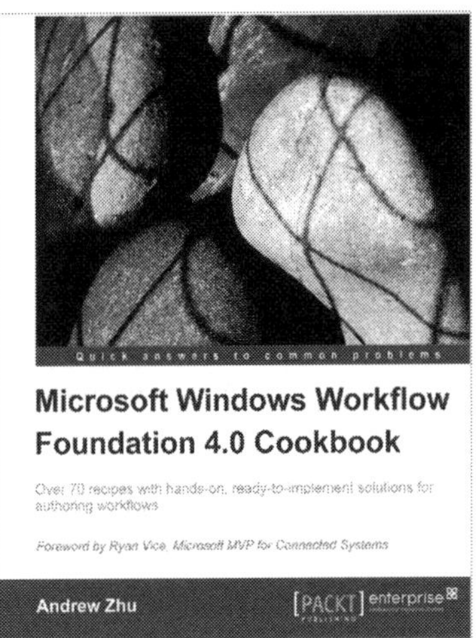

Microsoft Windows Workflow Foundation 4.0 Cookbook

ISBN: 978-1-84968-078-3 Paperback: 255 pages

Over 70 recipes with hands-on, ready-to-implement solutions for authoring workflows

1. Customize Windows Workflow 4.0 applications to suit your needs
2. A hands-on guide with real-world illustrations, screenshots, and step-by-step instructions
3. Explore various functions that you can perform using WF 4.0 with running code examples

---

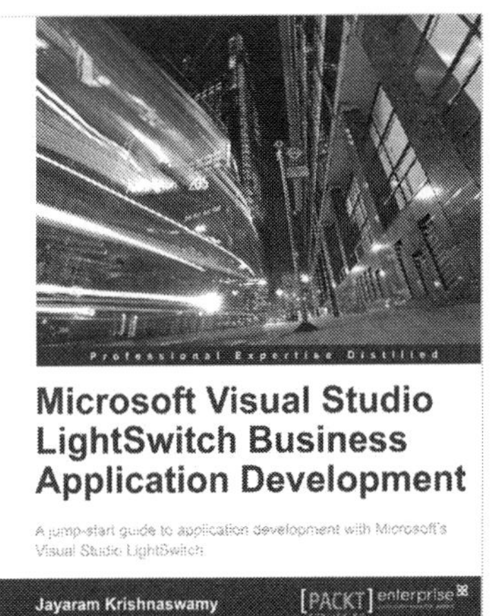

Microsoft Visual Studio LightSwitch Business Application Development

ISBN: 978-1-84968-286-2 Paperback: 384 pages

A jump-start guide to application development with Microsoft's Visual Studio LightSwitch

1. A hands-on guide, packed with screenshots and step-by-step instructions and relevant background information—making it easy to build your own application
2. Easily connect to various data sources with practical examples and easy-to-follow instructions
3. Create entities and screens both from scratch and using built-in templates

Please check **www.PacktPub.com** for information on our titles

24034441R00249

Made in the USA
Lexington, KY
04 July 2013